BERKSHIRE BEYOND BUFFETT

LAWRENCE A. CUNNINGHAM

BERKSHIRE BEYOND BUFFETT

The Enduring Value of Values

⇟ Columbia Business School
Publishing

Columbia University Press
Publishers Since 1893
New York   Chichester, West Sussex

Library of Congress Cataloging-in-Publication Data
Cunningham, Lawrence A., 1962-
Berkshire beyond Buffett : the enduring value of values / Lawrence Cunningham.
pages cm
Includes bibliographical references and index.
ISBN 978-0-231-17004-8 (cloth : alk. paper) — ISBN 978-0-231-53869-5 (ebook)
1. Berkshire Hathaway Inc. 2. Buffett, Warren. 3. Corporate culture
4. Investments—United States. 5. Mutual funds—United States. I. Title.
HG4930.C86 2014
338.8'60973—dc23
2014013371

Columbia University Press books are printed on permanent and durable
acid-free paper.
This book is printed on paper with recycled content.
Printed in the United States of America

c 10 9 8 7 6 5 4 3 2 1

Cover design: Noah Arlow
Cover image: Steven Noble

References to websites (URLs) were accurate at the time of writing.
Neither the author nor Columbia University Press is responsible for URLs that
may have expired or changed since the manuscript was prepared.

For my three beloved girls: Stephanie, Rebecca, and Sarah,
fountains of eternal value.

CONTENTS

PART II

PART III

FOREWORD

Author's Note: After Berkshire Hathaway's 2014 annual meeting, I asked Warren Buffett who should write the foreword to this book. He immediately suggested Tom Murphy, a legendary businessman whom Warren said he had tried to model himself after. Warren later added a further explanation: "Most of what I've learned about management, I learned from Murph. I kick myself, because I should have applied it much earlier." When I relayed that to Tom, he modestly ducked any notion of being Warren's role model, but agreed to write the foreword anyway, and I am honored that he did.

L.A.C.

It's hard to remember a time when Warren Buffett wasn't well known. But in 1986, when a small TV and newspaper company named Capital Cities bought the broadcasting giant ABC, few people recognized the name of the man who financed 18 percent of the deal. A small number of investors knew about his record, and Wall Street was learning. But the general public had yet to meet this low-profile Omaha analyst, a man who would become America's premier teacher of all things business and attract an international media following eager for his insights. Warren Buffett would one day help make business understandable to the average person, while earning the notice and respect of the country's most sophisticated financial minds.

But this was 1986, and no one could have predicted what lay ahead for Warren. In the decades that followed, he would build a $300 billion company, one acquisition at a time, a feat that would awe even those of us who have known him for so long. Larry Cunningham's book is a comprehensive look at many of the lessons to be gleaned from Warren's experience in putting together an organization structured to thrive long into the future.

I met Warren in 1969 through a Harvard Business School friend who invested with him. I knew instantly how fortunate I was: Warren was the smartest person I had ever met. It wasn't long before I flew to Omaha and asked him to join my board at Capital Cities Communications. It was a sale I didn't make. He told me my multiple was too high; I said it wasn't. He said he wouldn't be a director, but he offered, instead, to be a sounding board if I needed one. So I ended up with the best of two possible worlds: I had the most valuable director who wasn't a director. How lucky can one man get? And by the way, for the record, I was right about that multiple!

I remember what Warren told me just before the ABC deal was completed. He warned me that my happy life as a paddleball-playing, below-the-radar businessman was about to change. My new responsibilities would up the ante in ways large and small, but one thing was certain: because I was to be head of a television network, my anonymity would be a thing of the past. Was I ready for a change this big?

He might have asked himself that question as well. Capital Cities became ABC, Inc., and Warren finally joined our board. His more frequent presence in New York and Washington, where he had been on the Washington Post board, exposed him to the national press and generated media coverage. He continued to turn down interviews and speaking engagements; but the genie was out of the bottle, and this genie was colorful and played a ukulele. In hindsight, those of us who knew him well understood his uniqueness and appeal. His national standing and attendant level of journalistic interest was not surprising.

It has now been almost three decades since Capital Cities acquired ABC for $3 billion. That deal, the largest non-oil merger at the time, has been dwarfed by the size of today's transactions. Warren's business base during that period has grown even more exponentially. Berkshire's trajectory has been so consistent and seamless that Warren's own professional transition has gone almost unnoticed. The man who began his business life as a precocious "stock picker" and investor has morphed into chief executive of one of the largest collections of businesses in the world. Larry Cunningham's book astutely chronicles this development and, with Larry's years of experience writing about Warren and studying Berkshire's businesses, helps us understand how this happened.

The skills that set Warren apart were clear to all of us who knew him in those early years. He had invited me to call for advice, and I did. I soon had a bird's-eye view of Warren's breadth and nuanced understanding of a business's long-term prospects. I considered our conversations "Acquisitions 101"—a class Warren could teach with his eyes shut. In those days, I was focused 100 percent on growing Capital Cities. I had a great partner in the late Dan Burke, who ran the company's operations, and his help gave me time to dream. Warren reinforced those dreams. I focused on finding bigger and bigger TV and radio stations, plus newspapers and other properties that we could buy and improve. Warren has done this on a vast scale at Berkshire and with companies in a diverse range of businesses. He was always available if I needed another opinion. I learned a lot from him, and he generously claims to have learned from me. In my role as a member of the Berkshire Hathaway board, he continues to educate and surprise me.

Warren is a student of entrepreneurial success and a man who deeply appreciates how businesses are created and built, brick by brick, by those with a good idea, immeasurable drive, and strong character. We are both proponents of a decentralized management philosophy: of hiring key people carefully, of pushing decisions down the organization, and of setting overall principles and resisting temptation to be involved with details. In other words, don't hire a dog and try to do the barking.

Decentralization, though, is not a magic bullet. We used to remind ourselves that in the wrong environment, chaos and anarchy sit side by side with decentralization. One wrong hiring decision at a senior level can really hurt hiring decisions down the line. We have all been there. If we're lucky, such errors of judgment are few and discovered quickly. If not. . . I rest my case.

Decentralization worked well for Capital Cities because the company was a loose confederation of small, and in many cases far-flung, individual operating units. But given the distances involved, it was critical to let managers know exactly what we wanted them to do. We worked to make cost-consciousness a part of our company's DNA. We wanted operators to make their own decisions, and we promised to gauge performance over the long haul. We stressed a basic, operator-autonomous philosophy at all management meetings, to the point that managers could almost repeat the words with us. Every big meeting and annual report began with the following credo:

Decentralization is the cornerstone of our management philosophy. Our goal is to hire the best people we can find and give them the responsibility and authority they need to perform their jobs. Decisions are made at the local level, consistent with the basic responsibilities of corporate management. Budgets, which are set yearly and reviewed quarterly, originate with the operating units that are responsible for them. We expect a great deal from our managers. We expect them to be forever cost-conscious and to recognize and exploit sales potential. But above all, we expect them to manage their operations as good citizens and use their facilities to further the community welfare.

The principles worked in practice, and managers took pride in keeping down costs. Indeed, at budget meetings, you frequently found executives competing to be the most effective tightwad. Cost control was the baseline of our company culture, and we built from there. Two other components made all this all work. One was the sense of purpose and professional pride that drove our managers. They owned their bottom line, and they owned their property's success and reputation. They took it seriously, and they found the independence motivating. The other was that we rewarded our managers well, with a system that recognized performance and encouraged long-term commitment to the company.

Then came 1986 and completion of the merger with ABC. We had quadrupled the size of the company overnight. Now we assessed the best way to combine the two entities quickly, recognizing that we faced precipitous change in the economics of the business. We made management changes and began to adjust the size of our workforce. We started the process by bringing together, within days of our closing, the senior managers of both companies at an off-site meeting.

Warren joined us and reinforced our management philosophy in a question/answer session that would become an annual tradition. Some two hundred managers began to understand the skills and characteristics that distinguish Warren's way of thinking. He is a gifted teacher who makes complex issues seem simple. The executives were wowed by his brilliance, by his sense of fun, and by his ability to place issues and events in historic context. They saw that he is pragmatic and realistic, yet at heart an optimist. He also used humor very effectively.

In hiring, for example, he used to tell our executives this: "You should look for three qualities: integrity, intelligence, and energy." And the kicker: "If you don't have the first," he'd say, "then the other two will kill you."

Warren's message in that aphorism is that the character of your employees is key to building a company, and that was our view as well. He understood that key messages need to come from the top, so everyone knows what is expected. We were on the same page, and one of the ways we chose to communicate it was through the reading of our credo. What began with *"Decentralization is the cornerstone of our company…"* ended with this thought:

> You have heard a great deal about profits. You can miss your budget. You can make mistakes, but only honest mistakes. There is no second chance at Capital Cities/ABC if you discredit yourself and your company with unethical or dishonest actions or activities.
>
> If I were a young man or woman, this is the kind of company I would want to work for and grow with. I hope you feel the same way.

The values we tried to instill at Capital Cities and ABC are similar to those that tend to characterize Berkshire Hathaway and its subsidiaries. From afar, it may look like Berkshire's wide-ranging businesses are very different from one another. In fact, as Larry's book discusses, though they span industries, they are united by certain key values, like managerial autonomy, entrepreneurship, frugality, and integrity. That is not happenstance.

Warren wants to work with people he respects and admires. It is very important to him. He has, above all, scouted for companies whose managements share his values, and he has cemented those values across the Berkshire Hathaway organization.

That achievement, as this book shows, contributes significantly to the company's stable underpinnings and its durability.

Tom Murphy

PREFACE

I began researching this book after widespread praise for Warren Buffett became paradoxical: his goal has been to build Berkshire Hathaway into a lasting corporation, yet even great admirers say the company cannot survive without him.[1] The topic was a theme of Berkshire Hathaway's 2013 annual meeting. As a Berkshire shareholder for two decades and editor of *The Essays of Warren Buffett: Lessons for Corporate America*, first published in 1997, I knew enough to believe in Berkshire's future but was intrigued by those questioning it.

Although much has been written about Buffett as a person and as an investor, there has been scant treatment of Berkshire as an institution. My hypothesis was that Berkshire has distinct features and a strong corporate culture that will endure beyond Buffett. I understood that to identify and explain that culture would require looking beneath the familiar surface of Buffett's philosophy—acquiring great companies run by outstanding managers. I would need to start at the top but then look at each part, especially Berkshire's fifty significant direct subsidiaries.[2]

I also appreciated that I might not find what I was looking for. Perhaps there was no Berkshire culture and no common ground among the subsidiaries. Conglomerates do not necessarily have discernible corporate cultures, especially if each subsidiary operates independently or if the parent's rationale for acquisitions is as simple as buying a good business at a fair price.

Corporate culture can be a mystery at the simplest of companies; that of Berkshire can seem tantamount to explaining the rings of Saturn. At the outset of my work, I addressed the challenge by scrutinizing Berkshire's and Buffett's publications for artifacts of corporate culture. The materials I scoured included the company's annual reports and Buffett's letters to shareholders, particularly those addressing the subsidiaries and their histories and leaders. I also examined all of Berkshire's press releases, especially ones reporting on its acquisitions, and the statements, appearing in every Berkshire annual report for decades, of its creed (called "owner-related business principles") and acquisition criteria. These materials gave me preliminary outlines of Berkshire culture as seen from the parent level.

Then I turned to the subsidiaries. For former public companies, I reviewed filings with the Securities and Exchange Commission, paying particular attention to disclosure describing their sale to Berkshire. I read books profiling the subsidiaries, their founders, and senior managers. Among these were autobiographies, biographies, and in-house corporate histories. I studied scores of encyclopedic entries developed by independent archivists as well as profiles appearing in scattered chapters of a dozen leading books about Buffett. I supplemented all of this research—containing both laudatory and critical perspectives—with written surveys and interviews of dozens of current and former officers and directors of Berkshire subsidiaries and hundreds of shareholders.

The clues quickly added up as a pattern emerged: when profiling each subsidiary, the same traits began to appear repeatedly, nine altogether. Not every subsidiary had all nine, but many did, and most manifested at least five of the nine.[3] Moreover, the traits shared a common feature: all were intangible values that managers transformed into economic value. A portrait of Berkshire culture crystallized. It is distinctive, durable—and unique to Berkshire. What's more, it is this culture that I think will allow the company to endure upon Buffett's departure.

Here is a roadmap of the content of this book. The introduction paints a broad picture of Berkshire culture and describes what I call "the value of values"—the practice of transforming intangible values into economic value. Part I goes back to Berkshire's inauspicious origins, the first decade that laid the groundwork for the culture that would be formed. It then spotlights today's extraordinary diversity at Berkshire and reviews the notion of corporate culture that holds it together. En route, we encounter cultural profiles of a sampling of Berkshire subsidiaries.

In part II, each trait is distilled and illustrated, portraying the cultural histories of Berkshire's subsidiaries and showing how they fit into the larger Berkshire culture. Most of these chapters feature several subsidiaries and related stories of culture to exemplify a single theme. Yet common pervasive traits cannot be suppressed, so each chapter hints at themes made explicit in others. Stories illustrate challenges and setbacks alongside strengths and accomplishments owing to particular traits. Together, they demonstrate the distinctive economic value of Berkshire culture that would be foolish to squander.

The final chapters of part II present other iconic companies that have endured despite the passing of idolized founders. The penultimate chapter provides an analogy between Berkshire and its Marmon Group subsidiary, another conglomerate built by unique personalities (brothers Jay and Robert Pritzker), and one that many wrongly believed would see its demise along with its founders' passing. Part II's closing chapter looks at some of the public companies in which Berkshire owns a minority interest, less significant economically and culturally, but worth a glance to see what their cultures say about Berkshire culture. Many reflect how great institutions can transcend their defining personalities, whether Walmart after Samuel Walton or the Washington Post Company after Katherine Graham.

Part III stresses that even strong corporate cultures are rarely self-sustaining, so ongoing reinvestment in Berkshire culture will be necessary. Buffett built an institution that *can* survive him, if successors maintain it. Under a multi-part succession plan, Buffett's estate will continue for many years as Berkshire's controlling shareholder, gradually transferring shares to charitable organizations; together with a large bloc of like-minded Berkshire shareholders, this ownership will help sustain Berkshire by resisting pressures to focus on short-term results.

Investments and operations will be managed by leaders chosen from a group of current Berkshire executives, all accomplished and capable, though taking on jobs more daunting than that Buffett has faced, given his deep involvement in each step of building Berkshire. Part III draws lessons for Buffett's successors and offers takeaways from Berkshire's experience for those outside it, including businesses that would like to emulate the Berkshire model.

People question Berkshire's staying power for the wrong reasons. The strength of Berkshire's culture provides ample internal security for its indefinite continuation. The greater threat to keeping Berkshire as an outstanding public conglomerate is external, chiefly short-termism. Related pressures would exist whether Buffett retired yesterday or works forever. This book is principally a testament to the construction of an impressive corporate culture, topped off with new questions about outside forces that may put it in jeopardy.

New York, New York
October 2014

ACKNOWLEDGMENTS

Thanks to Warren E. Buffett for his support of this book project and for creating such a fascinating subject to write about. With characteristic generosity, he gave the green light to Berkshire Hathaway colleagues to help with my research, corrected errors in the manuscript, and granted permission to use the Berkshire corporate logos on the book jacket. I owe him continuing gratitude for letting me publish *The Essays of Warren Buffett: Lessons for Corporate America*, and for participating in the 1997 symposium showcasing that book, which features a selected arrangement of his letters to Berkshire shareholders.

At the 1997 symposium, he introduced me to other Berkshire insiders who provided encouragement on this book: Howard G. Buffett, his son, Berkshire director since 1993, and probable future Berkshire board chairman; Ajit Jain, a Berkshire insurance executive since 1985 and oft-mentioned potential successor as chief executive officer; Carol Loomis of *Fortune* magazine, who has edited Buffett's letters to Berkshire shareholders since 1973; and Charles T. Munger, Berkshire director and vice chairman since 1978, who urged me to stress the close connection between autonomy and permanence.

For extensive astute comments on the manuscript, vastly improving the book, thanks go to the following individuals: George J. Gillespie III, counsel and confidant to Buffett since 1973 when the two began serving as directors on corporate boards together; Donald E. Graham, Buffett colleague since 1974 when they both joined the board of the Washington Post Company, Graham's family business and long-time Berkshire investee; and Simon M. Lorne of Millennium Management, former long-time partner of Munger, Tolles & Olson, Berkshire's lead outside law firm. For writing the foreword, thanks to Thomas S. Murphy, a Buffett friend and associate since 1969, who has exerted a far greater influence on both Buffett and Berkshire than is generally appreciated.

I thank the following current and former Berkshire subsidiary officers and directors for help, whether through interviews that animate the book, completing my managerial surveys that speak to Berkshire culture, or providing other input: Paul E. Andrews Jr. (TTI); Ed Bridge (Ben Bridge Jewelers); William C. Child (RC Willey, retired); Doris Christopher (the Pampered Chef); Kevin T. Clayton (Clayton Homes); Tracy Britt Cool (several subsidiaries); James L. Hambrick (Lubrizol); Thomas J. Manenti (MiTek); Franklin ("Tad") Montross (Gen Re); John W. Mooty (former chairman and substantial shareholder, Dairy Queen); Robert H. Mundheim (former director, Benjamin Moore); Olza M. ("Tony") Nicely (GEICO); Mary K. Rhinehart (Johns Manville); Richard Roob (Benjamin Moore, retired); W. Grady Rosier (McLane); Richard T. Santulli (NetJets, retired); Michael Searles (Benjamin Moore); Kelly Smith (the Pampered Chef); Drew Van Pelt (Larson-Juhl); Jim Weber (Brooks); and Bruce N. Whitman (FlightSafety).

I am grateful to the hundreds of Berkshire owners who completed my shareholder surveys, including the following: Charles Akre; J. Jeffrey Auxier; Christopher M. Begg; Arthur D. Clarke; Robert W. Deaton; Jean-Marie Eveillard; Thomas S. Gayner; Timothy E. Hartch; Andrew Kilpatrick; Paul Lountzis; Blaine Lourd; Nell Minow; Mohnish Pabrai; Larry Sarbit; Guy Spier; Kenneth H. Shubin Stein; and Timothy P. Vick. For help administering some of the surveys, thanks to Buck Hartzell and The Motley Fool; Robert P. Miles, who hosted my book lecture at the University of Nebraska during the 2014 Berkshire Hathaway annual shareholders' meeting weekend; and John and Oliver Mihaljevic, who not only connected me with many Berkshire shareholders but reviewed the manuscript and let me post occasional blog pieces on some of the ideas in this book.

For insights, critiques, and extensive data, hats off to Steven Keating and Rodney Lake, who have taught George Washington University Business School's Applied Portfolio Management course for many years and hosted me to lecture about this book at the annual Ramsey Student Investment Fund conference. I appreciate the critiques and helpful suggestions on the manuscript contributed by Kelli A. Alces (Florida State University); Deborah A. DeMott (Duke University); Prem Jain (Georgetown University); John Leo (the Manhattan Institute); Jennifer Taub (Vermont Law School); Evan Vanderveer (Vanshap Capital); and David Zaring (University of Pennsylvania). For locating resources, verifying facts, and generating information, thanks to Nicholas Stark, research librarian at the George Washington University Library. For editing yet another of my books, thanks to Ira Breskin, my freelance editor since 2000. And for careful fact-checking of the manuscript, I am especially grateful to three of my exceptional students: Lillian Bond, Nathanial Castellano, and Christopher Lee.

Thanks to those friends and strangers alike who kindly helped me resolve some of the many questions of detail that arise in a work of this type: Scott A. Barshay (Cravath, Swaine & Moore); Jeff Hampton (author, *McLane*); Carla and Roderick Hills (cofounding partners, Munger, Tolles & Olson); Janet Lowe (author, "*Damn Right*"); Peter Rea (author, *Integrity Is a Growth Market*); Joel Silvey (historian of recreational vehicles); Bruce Smith (Pennsylvania Railroad Technical and Historical Society); Michael Sorkin (*St. Louis Post-Dispatch*); and Brent St. John (grandson-in-law of the founder of MiTek).

For help with innumerable queries, thanks to executive assistants at Berkshire and elsewhere, including Debbie Bosanek and Deb Ray (Buffett's office); Debby Hawkins and Griffin B. Weiler (Santulli's office); Patricia Matson (Murphy's office); Denise Copeland (Clayton Homes); Doerthe Obert (Munger's office); Julie Young (Lubrizol); Julie Ring (MiTek); and Linda A. Rucconich (FlightSafety). In my office at George Washington University, thanks to the excellent support staff, including Bonnie Sullivan, Sara Westfall, and Lillian White; in my New York office at Cardozo Law School, thanks to Matthew Diller and Edward Stein for facilitating it, and to the outstanding staff for supporting me there, especially Lillian Castanon, Val Myteberi, Sandra Pettit, and Josh Vigo.

My thanks go to the whole team at Columbia University Press, led by Myles C. Thompson, a publishing visionary whose books I have admired for two decades. The supporting cast included insightful developmental editor, Bridget Flannery-McCoy; efficient associate editor, Stephen Wesley; and the careful off-site production team at Cenveo, led by Ben Kolstad. Helpful comments during the writing of the book were provided by Columbia's editorial board and five anonymous outside peer reviewers.

Above all, for everything under the sun and the moon and beyond, thanks to Stephanie Cuba, my wife of infinite excellence. She is my editor in chief, best friend, love of my life, and secret sauce. Thanks to our two darling daughters, Rebecca and Sarah, fortunately cut from that same cloth. This family deserves my deepest gratitude for their extensive and unwavering support while I devoted countless hours to this project. You are my rock stars, and this book is for you.

BERKSHIRE BEYOND BUFFETT

Introduction

Berkshire Hathaway is an accident. No one planned it out. No strategic plan was ever devised. With many unusual features, from its governance to its philosophy, Berkshire is unique in corporate history. And from humble roots in 1965, Berkshire is now one of the largest corporations the world has ever seen.

The company and its iconic leader, Warren E. Buffett, became famous for savvy stock picking through the 1990s, acquiring lucrative minority stakes in public companies, including American Express, Coca-Cola, the Washington Post Company, and Wells Fargo. Today, Berkshire is a huge conglomerate with wholly owned businesses in every artery of commerce, finance, and manufacturing. For example, Berkshire owns the second most popular car insurer in the United States (GEICO), one of the major transcontinental railroads in North America (Burlington Northern Santa Fe), two of the biggest reinsurers in the world (Gen Re and National Indemnity), a global energy supplier (Berkshire Hathaway Energy, formerly known as MidAmerican Energy), and pacesetters in fields as different as diamonds and mobile homes.

If Berkshire were a country, and its revenues its gross domestic product, the company would be among the top fifty world economies, rivaling Ireland, Kuwait, and New Zealand. If it were a state, Berkshire would rank thirtieth, in the cohort of Iowa, Kansas, and Oklahoma. Its subsidiaries employ more than 300,000 people—about the population of Pittsburgh. Among American corporations, Berkshire Hathaway is outsized only by a handful of behemoths the scale of ExxonMobil and Walmart (in both of which Berkshire owns a minority interest). Berkshire's cash alone—$40 billion or more in recent years—exceeds the total assets of all but the largest one hundred American corporations.

Berkshire has outperformed the broader stock market for its shareholders 80 percent of the time, often by double digits. Through 2013, Berkshire's average annual gain was 19.7 percent, more than double that of the Standard & Poor's 500 index, a cross-section of public company stocks. With a market value of $300 billion, Berkshire has generated considerable wealth, direct and indirect, for employees, customers, suppliers, and other constituencies.

Thanks to Berkshire, Buffett is a mega-billionaire, and fellow shareholders are multi-millionaires and billionaires.[1] Berkshire subsidiaries are the progenitors of thousands of millionaires too, and not just the founders or senior executives.[2] Ordinary citizens have accumulated great wealth through the many business opportunities these enterprises feed: distributors of Benjamin Moore paints, sales center managers at Clayton Homes,[3] franchisees of Dairy Queen restaurants,[4] kitchen consultants for the Pampered Chef,[5] and direct sellers of products made by the Scott Fetzer Companies, whether Kirby vacuums, World Book encyclopedias, or Ginsu knives.

Despite Berkshire's substantial achievements, what has remained a mystery is how Berkshire functions so successfully given that it is made up of such a diverse group of subsidiaries. On the surface, there seems to be no common ground among them. Besides a portfolio of minority interests in scores of public companies, Berkshire wholly owns fifty significant direct subsidiaries, which, in turn, own another two hundred subsidiaries. The Berkshire corporate empire encompasses more than five hundred entities engaged in hundreds of different lines of business (a list appears in the appendix to this book).

Most are low-tech, such as Acme Brick, which makes and distributes bricks, whereas others are high-tech, like FlightSafety, which uses complex flight simulators to train airline pilots, and MiTek, which manufactures advanced engineering devices for the construction industry. Some, including Gen Re and National Indemnity, provide sophisticated financial services to multinational corporations like Ford Motor Company and PepsiCo, whereas others, like Clayton Homes, make simple loans to middle-class

Americans buying manufactured housing. Within Berkshire there are several nested conglomerates like the Marmon Group and Scott Fetzer—the former engaged in more than one hundred lines of business—and many small family firms, like Fechheimer Brothers, which makes police uniforms as well as a line of Berkshire Hathaway activewear.

Diverse as they are, a close look at Berkshire's subsidiaries and the company's goals in acquiring them reveals distinctive common traits. The most important filter Berkshire applies when evaluating a potential acquisition is whether a company has ways to protect its ability to earn profits. Management experts refer to these as "barriers to entry," making it difficult for competitors to take market share away. Professor Michael Porter coined the phrase "sustainable competitive advantage" to convey a similar idea about the durability of business value.[6] Buffett draws on medieval imagery, portraying a business as a "castle" and such barriers and advantages as "moats," the water-filled ditches dug around castles to defend against invaders. One prevailing common trait of Berkshire's subsidiaries is that all have a moat.

At Berkshire, barriers to entry are strong for companies such as Burlington Northern Santa Fe Railway and Berkshire Hathaway Energy, whose operations are so costly to replicate that they achieve "natural monopolies"—those in which society benefits if rendered by a single operator rather than multiple competitors because the required investment is so large in relation to the payoffs. Other Berkshire companies maintain competitive advantages through close customer relationships. For example, Lubrizol's chemists collaborate with equipment manufacturers and oil company customers on new products, while logistics mavens at McLane, a wholesale grocer and distributor, partner with retail customers on store operations. Brand loyalty is the moat for Brooks (running shoes), Fruit of the Loom (underwear), Justin (cowboy boots), NetJets (fractional aircraft ownership services), and See's (candies).

Every business needs a moat to endure and prosper. Berkshire has to have one in order to beat out rivals for acquisitions and investments. If each Berkshire subsidiary must have a moat, it invites asking: What is Berkshire's moat? A tempting answer is Warren Buffett; the argument that I will make in this book, however, is that there is much more to it. This stands to reason: mortality means no *person* can be a moat, because that would not be a durable advantage.

Some treat Buffett's identity as a negative for Berkshire's future. For instance, the credit rating agency Fitch has long highlighted as a risk for

Berkshire that Buffett is a "key man" and that Berkshire's "ability to identify and purchase attractive operating companies is intimately tied to Buffett."[7] When you cannot separate the identity of a company from its leader, the company's durability is doubtful.[8]

On the contrary—a company often proves its sustainability by prospering through a succession of senior leaders, even iconic ones. Burlington Northern Santa Fe (BNSF), an amalgamation that dates to 1849, illustrates this. Among its earliest leaders was nineteenth-century railroad magnate James J. Hill, who stressed that a company achieves "permanent value" only when "it no longer depends on the life or labor of any single individual."[9] Examples abound in the dozen multigeneration family businesses among Berkshire subsidiaries. These include subsidiaries in their fifth or fourth generations and many in their third or second. This is an impressive concentration of longevity since most family businesses fail; only 30 percent succeed to the second generation, 15 percent to the third, and just 4 percent to the fourth.[10]

Leadership transitions need not be smooth to vouch for corporate durability. Numerous Berkshire subsidiaries have had high turnover in the corner office, both before and after joining Berkshire. In the recent past, during Berkshire's ownership, there have been several abrupt chief executive switches within a few years at Benjamin Moore, Gen Re, and NetJets, among others. To quote a more recent BNSF executive, reflecting on the tribulations the company faced in its first century and a half: "It's a wonderful company, and the fact that it has survived so much and is still in the position it's in is a tribute to what a good company it really is and the people in the company."[11]

So, Berkshire's moat cannot be Warren Buffett. A tempting possibility, then, is the power and financial resources of Berkshire's insurance companies. They command considerable moats, GEICO by being the low-cost car insurer and Gen Re and National Indemnity by commanding reputations for prudent underwriting of risk and immense financial strength. All generate premium volume well in excess of claims. This produces investable funds at no cost—called "float" because the premiums are held by the insurer until claims are paid. On the other hand, no insurance company is immune from disaster, and both GEICO and Gen Re have experienced life-threatening difficulties in their histories. The insurance companies are impressive, however, and the float they generate provides ample capital for investment in sister subsidiaries and securities of other companies. But the insurance subsidiaries *contribute* to Berkshire's moat rather than define it.

Likewise, Berkshire's investment securities widen Berkshire's moat but do not constitute it because, even without them, Berkshire would be formidable. Berkshire's sizable long-term common stock holdings once represented a large portion of its financial picture, but today they are a fraction (one-fifth of assets, one-tenth of revenues).[12] Moreover, despite the permanency of many such holdings, Berkshire does not control its investees as it controls its subsidiaries. Berkshire still owns every subsidiary acquired since 1970; among the hundreds of securities reported in its portfolio over the years, however, some no longer exist (e.g., F. W. Woolworth), others were taken over (e.g., Beatrice Foods, General Foods), and many equity positions were sold (e.g., Freddie Mac, McDonald's, The Walt Disney Company). Investments strengthen Berkshire's fortress but, as with the insurers, they are only part of the story.

What, then, is Berkshire's moat? The answer: Berkshire's distinctive corporate culture. Berkshire spent the last five decades acquiring a group of wholly owned subsidiaries of bewildering variety but united by a set of distinctive core values. The result is a corporate culture unlike any other. And this is Berkshire's moat.

Berkshire's culture offers value in its business acquisitions, and this enhances Berkshire's competitive position versus rival buyers. To give one of many cases, in 1995, Berkshire acquired RC Willey, a family-owned furniture retailer, for a price 12.5 percent less than a rival bid; Berkshire paid $175 million, *besting* offers exceeding $200 million.[13] The owners chose Berkshire because of cultural values, including its reputation for integrity, how it gives its managers operational autonomy, and its commitment to holding the subsidiaries it acquires forever.[14]

The exchange of values is a two-way street. In 2011, Berkshire acquired Burlington Northern Santa Fe Railway, a widely held public company then in the S&P 500 (Berkshire replaced it after the acquisition). It paid $100 per share even though Buffett said it was worth closer to $95.[15] Many observers were confounded but the value of values explains the 5 percent gap. When buyers and sellers both value a specific set of intangibles, as Berkshire and its subsidiaries do, the upshot is a wider price band within which a deal can be done.[16]

It is common in corporate acquisitions to coax agreement on price by thoughtful understanding of each side's goals. If two sides cannot agree on price, for instance, a seller may offer to retain some contingent liabilities, or a buyer may propose to leave out some intellectual property assets (like patents). Given differing valuations of such elements—different appetites and risk profiles—such trading can induce agreement on price.[17]

Berkshire, by contrast, creates scenarios in which intangibles substitute for money. Benjamin Graham, Buffett's intellectual patriarch and author of renowned books on investing, taught Buffett to hunt for investments where price was significantly less than value, delivering a margin of safety.[18] Price is what you pay; value is what you get, usually measured by earnings or net assets.

With Berkshire, you have to increase the value side of the equation beyond earnings and net assets to include the intangible cultural traits. People value such things differently—just as buyers and sellers value contingent liabilities and patent technology differently.

Berkshire deserves credit for this achievement of value creation. It is as if Buffett found that applying Graham's price–value margin of safety left too small a pool of potential acquisitions. So he perfected a business model in which the element of value increased. This enables Berkshire to pay a lower price for any given value or to accept paying a premium, depending on relative appetites and profiles.

While Buffett perfected this model at Berkshire, the value of these values transcends any one person. Berkshire's subsidiaries likewise enjoy economic value as the result of their intangible values, as their stories in this book illustrate, and the shared values among them form a distinct and enduring corporate culture for Berkshire.

I

1
Origins

In 1956, a twenty-six-year-old Warren Buffett formed Buffett Partnership Ltd., an investment firm run from his native Omaha. His philosophy was to find companies priced below book value; such bargain opportunities were common then and yielded gains, though several failed eventually because they lacked durable competitive advantages. One of those companies, of which Buffett took control in 1965, was Berkshire Hathaway, Inc.

At the time of its acquisition, Berkshire Hathaway was a New England textile manufacturer. It was the product of a 1955 merger between two companies with late-nineteenth-century origins—Berkshire Fine Spinning Associates, a 1929 amalgamation of textile companies, including Berkshire Cotton Manufacturing Company, founded in 1889, and Hathaway Manufacturing, dating to 1888. Via the 1955 merger, control of Berkshire Hathaway was shared by two families, the Chaces and the Stantons, who had owned its constituents for generations.

These companies had once been distinguished textile manufacturers, but they battled competitive onslaughts, largely due to cheaper labor costs, first in the southern United States and later from abroad. Berkshire Hathaway survived by cutting costs, including closing facilities and laying off workers. The Stantons, especially brothers Otis and Seabury, bickered among themselves and feuded with the Chaces over strategy, such as how much to reinvest in an ailing business. Its thinly traded stock sold at one third to one half of book value; in 1965, book value was $19.24 per share, or $22 million for the whole company.

Buffett first heard of Berkshire a decade earlier while working for his mentor, Benjamin Graham, at the Graham-Newman investment firm. Buffett had acquired a personal stake in Berkshire Hathaway in 1962, and brokers alerted him of opportunities to buy larger blocks at prices below $8 per share. Berkshire periodically repurchased shares, and Buffett figured he could buy a block of these discounted shares and cash out at a higher price when Berkshire was repurchasing. At a time when the stock traded at less than $10, Seabury Stanton asked what Buffett would sell his block for; Buffett said $11.50. Seabury sought Buffett's promise to tender if the company made such an offer, and Buffett agreed. Thinking they had a deal, Buffett ceased acquiring shares. So when the company shortly thereafter offered $11.38, Buffett thought he was being chiseled.

In response, Buffett turned the tables, bought more shares, and persuaded Otis Stanton and eventually Seabury Stanton to sell to him as well. At that point, Buffett decided to become better acquainted with his investment. He visited Berkshire's mills, toured the plant, and interviewed managers—conventional exercises for business buyers, but something Buffett would rarely repeat in his career. Buffett learned about textile manufacturing and came to admire the talents of his tour guide, vice-president of manufacturing Kenneth V. Chace (whose last name is coincidental; he was not related to the family owners). Once the Buffett Partnership gained a controlling interest in Berkshire stock, the Stantons resigned from management. Buffett was elected a director, and the board named Ken Chace president.

The local press portrayed Buffett's acquisition of Berkshire Hathaway as a hostile bid, stoking rumors that he was a takeover artist prepared to hasten the liquidation of the struggling company. Buffett recoiled at having a reputation as a liquidator and took pains to avoid acting like one. Yet Berkshire's textile operations continued to decline for years as the forces of globalization hammered the industry. Rivals moved manufacturing abroad, where labor costs were low and export shipping cheap, thanks to increasingly versatile intermodal containers. Even with corporate belt tightening and tolerating losses for shareholders, Berkshire was forced to gradually curtail operations through the 1970s, with Buffett finally shuttering the mills for good in 1985.

Buffett's acquisition of Berkshire was a great learning experience for him—learning what not to do. From then on, he made it Berkshire policy never to engage in hostile takeovers and vowed never to liquidate an acquired subsidiary. As a rule, Berkshire would acquire only companies with top management in place, to avoid having to arrange managerial shuffles. Above all, Berkshire would seek businesses with long-term economic value and willingly pay a fair price for them. The anguish of closing the textile business forged Buffett's commitment to permanence. During the mid-1980s, Berkshire would divest a few other failing businesses the Buffett Partnership had initially acquired—such as the department store chains Diversified Retailing, Associated Retail Stores, and Hochshild Kohn—but thereafter foreswore doing so.

Buffett says he would have been far better off had he never heard of Berkshire Hathaway. But the lessons learned from that first acquisition put an indelible stamp on what the company would become.

While Berkshire Hathaway's textile operation continued to deteriorate after 1965, Buffett was simultaneously building what turned into a force in the insurance industry, a fortress in the investment field, and the most unusual conglomerate in history. In 1967, Berkshire acquired two Omaha-based insurance companies, National Indemnity Company (NICO) and National Fire & Marine Insurance Company, for a combined $8.5 million.

These insurance operations provided a source of capital, as customers pay premiums that the insurer holds until needed to cover claims. As an investor, Buffett relished this source of capital, referred to as float. Berkshire deployed float in three ways in the ensuing five decades: to reinvest in and grow the insurance operations, to buy minority stakes in larger companies, and to acquire wholly owned subsidiaries.

During the 1970s, Berkshire used much of the considerable float that NICO and its other insurers generated to expand insurance operations, including acquiring a minority position in Government Employees Insurance Company (GEICO). To strengthen capital resources and broaden policy reach, Berkshire formed or acquired numerous other insurance companies—all of which remain viable today.[1]

But insurance was not Buffett's only interest. Among Berkshire's first noninsurance acquisitions was Sun Newspapers of Omaha, Inc., a group of area weeklies acquired in 1969. Fellow Omaha denizen and Buffett family friend Stanford Lipsey ran the company. Although the company was never financially significant, it put a feather in Berkshire's cap.[2] In 1973, Sun won a Pulitzer Prize for a series of stories about Boys Town, the orphanage on the outskirts of Omaha immortalized by the 1938 movie of the same name starring Spencer Tracy as its visionary founder,

Father Edward J. Flanagan. The orphanage occupied a sizable boarding school campus, thanks to endless fundraising campaigns that pled both the school's noble mission and its persistent poverty. In 1972, therefore, many knew about its excellent program, but few had any inkling that the school's endowment exceeded $200 million.[3] The public discovered this truth—and the related mismanagement—as a result of the investigative reporting of Sun Newspapers.

The newspaper industry was also among the earliest Berkshire common stock investments. In 1973, Berkshire acquired a minority stake in the Washington Post Company, a holding company controlled by the Graham family and named after the metropolitan newspaper it owned. The family matriarch, Katherine ("Kay") Graham, had taken the company public in 1971 by selling Class B shares, held in large numbers by its employees.

Acquiring blocks of the shares on the open market, Buffett assured Graham that he respected the family's traditions and management and did not wish to interfere with either.[4] Over the ensuing decades, the two developed a relationship that could be seen as a model between an astute shareholder and an owner-oriented manager. Graham sought Buffett's counsel, and he backed her decisions.[5]

In stages during the early 1970s, Berkshire made another large and defining investment as it acquired a majority of the stock of Blue Chip Stamps. The company had something in common with both Berkshire's textile business and its insurance companies. Like the insurance companies, it generated float; like the textile business, it was dying.

Trading stamps were a marketing device popular in the 1950s and 1960s. Companies like Sperry & Hutchinson (S&H) Green Stamps and Blue Chip sold stamps to retailers, such as gas stations and grocery stores, who distributed them to customers in proportion to a sale. Customers redeemed accumulated stamps for a selection of consumer goods like coffee makers and toasters. The stamp companies got cash from retailers up front but did not incur prize costs until redemption, thus creating investable float.

A group of California retailers formed Blue Chip as an alternative to S&H and then monopolized the state's market. Rivals, including S&H, sued for damages, and the government required the company to sell much of its ownership to unrelated parties. That made Blue Chip an investment opportunity for many, including not only Buffett but the manager of a California investment partnership, Charles T. ("Charlie") Munger, a polymath who in 1962 also co-founded a Los Angeles–based law firm, today's prominent Munger, Tolles & Olsen.[6] Buffett, through Berkshire and other vehicles, became the largest shareholder of Blue Chip, Munger's partnership being Blue Chip's next largest shareholder.[7]

By virtue of their respective Blue Chip investments, Buffett and Munger became functional business partners and began a lifelong friendship. Munger, an Omaha native then living in Pasadena, California, contributed to Berkshire culture from the start. He encouraged Buffett to adopt a long-term view of business opportunities, rather than the approach of bargain hunting Buffett had practiced in his early career. Munger advised that it's better to buy a good business at a fair price than a fair business at a good price. In addition, Munger embraced a more qualitative approach to investment than Buffett had, factoring in not only statistical analysis of balance sheet quantities and earnings, but soft factors like entrepreneurship, integrity, and reputation.

Returns on investments in Blue Chip were reasonable in the early years, once it settled lawsuits, and the company continued to produce modest float.[8] But the business model faded as consumer tastes and the economic environment changed. People lost interest in stamp collecting and redemption,[9] while spiraling inflation and gasoline prices stimulated retailers to focus on lower prices rather than costly perks.[10] Eventually, Blue Chip's business wound down as retailers ceased buying stamps, though it remained open for decades to allow customers to redeem those outstanding. Berkshire folded Blue Chip into its corporate family by merger, and it became an artifact of American and Berkshire history. But while it lived, Blue Chip played a role in a trio of acquisitions that would lay the foundation of Berkshire culture: See's Candies, Wesco Financial, and the *Buffalo News*.

～

In 1971, an executive at Blue Chip Stamps, William Ramsey, called Buffett with a potential acquisition candidate: See's Candies.[11] Buffett told Ramsey to call Munger, who liked the prospect of acquiring a branded chocolate company with loyal customers up and down the state of California.

The third-generation family business dated to 1921, when Charles A. See moved from northern Canada to southern California seeking a better life.[12] Fire had destroyed his pharmacy business, and a stint as a chocolate salesman convinced him to make a go of it in the candy business. With his mother, Mary; his wife, Florence; and his two young children he resettled in Los Angeles and befriended a local businessman, James W. Reed. Together the group launched See's Candies, Inc. in 1922.

The shop, designed to resemble Mary See's home kitchen, made and sold boxed chocolates, many using Mary's secret recipes, with only fine and fresh ingredients. Mary's bespectacled, silver-haired, grandmotherly face became the face of the firm. The company's logo features Mary See's matronly smile at the center of a simple black-and-white design, conveying the sense of old-fashioned, homemade quality that Charles favored. Deliveries arrived in logo-emblazoned Harley-Davidson motorcycles with sidecars. Another marketing innovation offered bulk chocolate at great discounts to churches, clubs, and other groups, which resold the candy at a profit for fundraisers. Mary See died in 1939 at the age of eighty-five, but her spirit, the spirit of the company, endured.

By then the company had a dozen stores, held a production facility in Los Angeles, and had expanded to San Francisco, where it soon opened nine more shops and another plant. Charles's son Laurance joined the business during this period, and when Charles passed away in 1949, became president.

The 1950s were the era of suburbanization in the United States, and Laurance led the way as he opened See's Candies in the new shopping malls that were springing up across California. By 1960 the chain consisted of 124 stores. During the 1960s, See's moved into Arizona, Oregon, and Washington and grew to 150 shops. With solid profits, See's outperformed local competitors and rivaled Hershey, Russell Stover, and other national brands.

In 1969, Laurance died. His younger brother, Harry, a stockholder and director, was to succeed him, but Harry was torn over succession, as he also ran a vineyard elsewhere in the state. Reluctantly, the See family, which owned 67 percent of the stock, decided to sell. In a move that would later be considered quaint for Berkshire Hathaway acquisitions, Buffett and Munger toured the Los Angeles plant in 1969.[13]

The See family asked $30 million for their business (technically $40 million, but the company had cash on hand in excess of $10 million). However, Buffett noticed that pretax income was only $4 million and that the balance sheet showed net assets of only $7 million. He was not yet in the habit of paying a premium for intangible values.[14] But Munger convinced Buffett of the qualitative aspects of the business, and together they decided their best and highest offer would be $25 million. The See family accepted. Years later, Buffett acknowledged that this bid was very low, which he attributed to his ignorance of the value of franchises.[15]

But why did the See family, with three generations of experience living their franchise, accept this low bid? Autonomy is not a likely reason, as the

See family would no longer be in management. But Buffett and Munger hand-picked the company's new president, Charles N. Huggins, and everyone understood that Huggins, who had been with See's since 1951 (and who would continue until 2005), was to preserve See's traditions, not transform the company. And few changes ensued, as the company continued to operate the way it had for the previous fifty years: homemade chocolate produced and sold in an old-fashioned way. Permanence—it appears at least in hindsight—was part of the exchange. By the mid-1990s, See's sold more boxed chocolate in the world than any company except Russell Stover,[16] and today it earns $80 million annually.[17]

If the See's acquisition involved paying a price below value, the opposite occurred in the second acquisition of the trio that spawned Berkshire culture. During 1972 and 1973, Blue Chip acquired 8 percent of Wesco Financial Corporation, a company Munger's partnership had invested in. Based in Pasadena, Wesco was founded by the Casper family. Its principal business was a mutual savings and loan association, which catered to military veterans and thrived because of a commitment to low cost. In 1973, Wesco management proposed to merge it into Financial Corporation of Santa Barbara (FCSB), with Wesco stockholders receiving FCSB shares. Wesco stockholders disagreed over the adequacy of the FCSB shares they were to receive. Buffett and Munger believed that Wesco shares were undervalued and that FCSB's were overvalued. They therefore opposed the merger.

Munger proposed buying enough Wesco shares to block the deal, whereas Buffett thought they should simply accept their losses. Instead of doing either, Munger beseeched Wesco's chief executive, Louis R. Vincenti, to abort the merger. Munger indicated that Blue Chip would be interested in acquiring Wesco, but Vincenti advised that the question was for Wesco shareholders, not for him. So Buffett met with Elizabeth ("Betty") Casper Peters, a large shareholder and head of the family bloc. He explained the potential benefits of ownership by Blue Chip, including intangibles, especially a shared orientation as co-owners. Peters, who was eager to see the family business grow, backed the decision to pull the plug on the merger.

The merger did not go through, and Wesco's stock price dropped, as typically happens in such a scenario, from a high of $18 to $11. Blue Chip could then have begun acquiring shares at the low market price that Buffett and Munger's scuttling of the merger had engendered. Although they wished to acquire Wesco, they did not think it would be fair to pay the low market price after their interference with the merger caused it to drop. So they ordered their brokers to acquire the stock at prices as high as $17 and subsequently made a formal tender offer at $15. Blue Chip eventually acquired majority control of Wesco, and Munger persuaded Vincenti to stay on.

People following the acquisition were dumbfounded. Why had Blue Chip paid a higher price than needed? The Securities and Exchange Commission (SEC) opened an investigation[18] (apparently at the instigation of FCSB).[19] Authorities suspected that paying more than market value indicated that Blue Chip had unlawfully manipulated Wesco's stock price or violated laws regulating trading in stock by tender offer bidders. Investigators were perplexed, as they believed that rational businesspeople always paid the lowest price available and charged the highest price obtainable. Their curiosity was aroused in part by the ambiguous relationship between Buffett and Munger and the confusingly complex structure of the various businesses in which they had become involved.

It was hard for people to understand what Buffett and Munger spent a year explaining: they paid a higher price to show integrity. Moreover, such a premium had economic value, because integrity is a reputational advantage that others would weigh in subsequent dealings. Buffett and Munger stressed both the immediate value of winning Vincenti's respect and the longer-term value of Blue Chip's "general business reputation."[20] The authorities were finally persuaded.[21] Blue Chip acquired 80 percent of Wesco, and the company remains part of Berkshire, wholly owned since 2011.[22]

The third of Buffett and Munger's early defining acquisitions added the unconventional motif that would come to characterize Berkshire's approach to business: the *Buffalo Evening News*. Dating from 1881, the *News* helped build the tradition of newspapers shaping American civic debate. Credit went to Edward H. Butler Sr., who founded the paper.[23] A biography portrays Butler as "emblematic of the late-nineteenth-century new journalists who built the modern press by wrenching civic discourse from its narrow partisan roots and carving out vital new cultural, social, economic, and political roles for newspapers."[24] Following Butler's death in 1913, his son, Edward Jr., devoted his life to running the business according to his father's principles. After his death in 1956, his wife, Kate Butler, took up the mantel.[25]

Advisers had long encouraged Kate Butler to minimize the taxes that would be due upon her death by transferring assets during her lifetime.[26] They noted that failure to do so might necessitate a "fire sale" of the newspaper to make the payments. She died in August 1974 without having heeded the advice. As a result, her executors eventually put the paper up for sale. In December 1976, the estate offered the paper to the Washington Post Company, on whose board Buffett sat.[27] Buffett told Kay Graham that if the *Post* did not wish to buy the *News* that he might. After the *Post* declined the opportunity, Buffett and Munger pursued it.

Buffalo then had two newspapers, the *News* and the *Buffalo Courier-Express*. The *News* had more advertising revenue than the *Courier*, and its circulation in the weekday market was higher. However, it ceded the weekend to the *Courier* by not having published a Sunday paper since the 1920s. Instead, it put out on Saturday afternoon a "Week-End" edition, a lighter version of what papers nationwide included on Sunday—arts, comics, opinion, television guide. Buffett had noted in periodic analysis of the newspaper industry that second papers were disappearing in most cities and foresaw the trend continuing. He perceived an opportunity with the *News* and, without conducting any due diligence, agreed to acquire it from Butler's estate for a negotiated price of $35.5 million.[28]

Buffett and the paper's managing editor, Murray B. Light, quickly got to work on the competitive front. The *News* reconfigured its Week-End edition, moved its release to Sunday morning, and began a Saturday morning issue comparable to its weekday paper. Ahead of the switch, the paper ran a promotion. It offered customers five weeks of the new program at the old rate, effectively throwing in the new Sunday paper for free. With the free papers committed for five weeks of delivery, the company boosted ad revenue by guaranteeing advertisers the Sunday circulation for that period.

Two weeks before launch date, the *Courier*, realizing this venture was a competitive threat, sued the *News*, alleging an illegal attempt to monopolize the local newspaper market. It claimed that the *News*'s giveaway program showed a predatory intent to ruin the *Courier*. In publicity campaigns to win over locals, the *Courier* portrayed Buffett as a monopolist liquidator poised to destroy Buffalo as a two-paper town. In court, its lawyers lambasted him for never having visited the plant and never having engaged acquisition consultants to evaluate the transaction.

A federal trial judge, Charles Brieant, agreed with the *Courier*. He suggested that a maximum of two freebies would have been valid. He then caricatured the case and personalities involved, skewering Buffett as an outside invader and accusing him of using "anti-competitive tricks and devices."[29] Brieant buttressed his view of Buffett as a predatory monopolist by citing the fact that he had conducted no due diligence. An appellate court, led by Henry Friendly, repudiated Brieant's ruling as legally and factually flawed.[30]

But the suit took two years to resolve, entailed millions in legal fees, and delayed the *News*'s new Sunday paper.

To help deal with the crisis, Buffett persuaded Stan Lipsey, who had sold the Sun Newspapers to Berkshire, to oversee the *News*. Lipsey found that the paper was in excellent editorial shape but poor fiscal condition. He built on its strengths and, after suffering losses for several years, made the paper profitable by 1980. It eclipsed the *Courier*, which dissolved. Lipsey remained at the helm until 2012, anchoring the *Buffalo News* (as it came to be called) while Berkshire acquired scores of local newspapers that year and the next, notably the *Omaha World-Herald*.[31]

~

During the corporate control battles of the 1980s, many companies placed blocks of stock in friendly hands as a defensive measure. On several occasions Berkshire played the friend, dubbed a "white squire" or "white knight," depending on whether buying a minority or a controlling block. One of those companies was Salomon Brothers, Inc., the investment banking firm.

In 1987 Salomon's largest shareholder, Minorco, objected to recent expansion and perceived disagreement among the firm's senior directors about business strategy.[32] Dissatisfied with management's response, Minorco began discussing a sale of its 12 percent block to Ronald O. Perelman, a corporate raider who had seized control of Revlon, Inc., the cosmetics giant, in a hostile bid. Salomon executives, led by John Gutfreund, feared that their company would be Perelman's next target.

Among many defensive steps, including repurchasing the Minorco block, Gutfreund solicited Berkshire as a white squire. Buffett dictated favorable terms: a preferred stock that paid 9 percent, which either Berkshire could convert into common or Salomon would redeem in fifths annually from 1995 through 1999. In exchange, the preferred could not be sold as a bloc to any single party; moreover, before making any sale, Berkshire was required to offer it to Salomon for repurchase. Berkshire also agreed that it would not acquire more than 20 percent of Salomon's stock for at least seven years.[33]

The cultural significance of this investment for Berkshire crystallized four years later, when Salomon was embroiled in a scandal involving illegal attempts by some employees to corner the bond market. Regulators and prosecutors were prepared to indict Salomon, a grave step against any company, which would destroy the firm's standing. The stigma would stoke defections by rattled customers and employees, flight that could spell Salomon's demise. To avert that fate, the Salomon board cleaned house and asked Buffett to serve as interim chairman.

In a press interview in May 1991, Buffett announced off the cuff a directive to Salomon personnel that became embedded in Berkshire's DNA: do nothing that you would not be happy to have an unfriendly but intelligent reporter write about on the front page of a newspaper. He repeated that admonition in related congressional testimony and has reiterated it regularly to the chief executives of Berkshire's subsidiaries.[34]

Buffett consciously committed to changing Salomon's corporate culture. It had a reputation for operating just within the letter of the law, whereas Buffett promoted playing well within the boundaries of propriety. In addition to proselytizing, he established a new tone by appointing hand-picked senior officers, including Deryck Maughan, an esteemed banking executive; Robert E. Denham, a distinguished corporate lawyer then serving as managing partner of Munger, Tolles & Olson; and Robert H. Mundheim, an eminent business law professor and dean of the University of Pennsylvania Law School. The envisioned culture had a key trait found in today's Berkshire subsidiaries: an investment in reputation and integrity. For Salomon Brothers, Buffett offered an object lesson in the value of values, stressing the kinship of ethics and profits.

In their earliest acquisitions, Buffett and Munger began their lifelong relationship and forged principles that would contribute to defining Berkshire. Their deals demonstrated the difference between price, which is paid, and values, which are exchanged: they underpaid for See's, while compensating for that with permanence, and overpaid for Wesco in the name of integrity. The early deals showed a willingness to be unconventional despite costs: they were suspected of wrongdoing for overpaying in Wesco and for ignoring due diligence exercises at the *Buffalo News*. Buffett's role at Salomon Brothers further etched the importance of integrity into Berkshire culture.

The SEC's probe after Wesco taught the importance of simplification, as Buffett and Munger clarified their relationship and streamlined the corporate structure. They consolidated the subsidiaries into Berkshire, making it the primary corporate entity for their businesses, and named Buffett chairman and chief executive and Munger vice-chairman. Ultimately, Buffett came to personify Berkshire, leading on acquisitions and shaping culture, and Munger played the Delphic consigliore. Explaining roles in 1999, a few decades into their venture, Buffett said, "Charlie is broader in his interests than I am. He doesn't have the same intensity for Berkshire that I have. It's not his baby."[35] Munger agreed: "Warren's whole ego is poured into Berkshire."

2

Diversity

By 1986, Berkshire owned a range of companies, from candy to insurance, and with its next two acquisitions continued to diversify. Early that year, the management of the Scott Fetzer Company, led by Ralph E. Schey, had proposed a leveraged buyout. The plan drew attention from takeover artists, including the notorious raider, Ivan Boesky.[1] Buffett followed the high-profile battle in the newspapers and finally wrote Schey a letter. He stressed Berkshire's aversion to hostile bids, and told Schey to call if he wanted to discuss a friendly deal. The acquisition that resulted brought to Berkshire a new mix of businesses, including Ginsu knives, Kirby vacuums, and the World Book encyclopedia.

The company was established in 1914 when George Scott and Carl Fetzer founded a machine shop in Cleveland, where they manufactured flare pistols.[2] During the 1920s, they formed a joint venture with local inventor Jim Kirby, of the eponymous vacuum cleaner. The three went into business together, perfecting not only the product but a direct-sales method of distribution through independent dealers. Kirby vacuums became an American household staple, selling millions over ensuing decades. From the 1920s through the 1960s, Scott Fetzer did little else than sell that product.

But in the late 1960s, Scott Fetzer transformed itself into a diversified corporation, riding a wave of conglomerate building that occurred during that period. It soon operated through 31 different business divisions, with offerings from chain saws to trailer hitches, each managed autonomously by division heads. Schey, who became president in 1974, sold off some companies while adding new ones, including the crown jewel, World Book, in 1978.

By 1986, Scott Fetzer was a sizable publicly traded conglomerate bearing modest debt. The combination made it attractive for the era's raiders and leveraged buyout operators. They could finance a takeover with borrowings repaid by selling off the individual divisions and with additional credit assumed by the target. Yet Scott Fetzer was also professionally managed, with leading products in numerous fields and proven profitability. That combination was, unsurprisingly, attractive to Buffett, as Scott Fetzer was a miniature of what Berkshire would become on a massive scale. Berkshire paid $315 million—plus promises of managerial autonomy to Schey and his team and permanence for the company and its shareholders. Both promises contrasted sharply with what Boesky portended.[3]

Berkshire's other 1986 acquisition brought the company into yet another industry. On January 15, 1986, a long-time Berkshire shareholder, Robert W. Heldman of Cincinnati, sent Buffett a letter. Heldman introduced himself as the chairman of Fechheimer Brothers Company, a company Buffett had never heard of. When the two men later met in Omaha, Heldman explained that the firm had been making and distributing uniforms since 1842, catering to the public service industries: corrections, fire, military, police, postal, and transit. Customers include the United States Navy, police departments in Cincinnati and Los Angeles, and transit authorities in Boston, Chicago, and San Francisco.

Heldman's father, Warren Heldman, joined the firm in 1941. He would be followed by his sons, Robert and George, who would ultimately be followed by their sons, Gary, Roger, and Fred. Innovation had long been a hallmark of Fechheimer, with offerings including specialized pants developed in partnership with federal authorities for law enforcement personnel. Government contracts helped the textile manufacturer cope with the challenges presented by cheap foreign labor and international shipping thanks to a patchwork of laws that require government agencies to "buy American."[4]

In 1981, however, Fechheimer had been sold in a leveraged buyout to an outside investment group, though family management retained an equity interest. Despite a heavy debt load, the company's budget consciousness enabled it to meet obligations. By 1985, it had retired a large portion of its debt and boosted the value of its equity. It was time for the outside investors to go.

Heldman thought Berkshire would be a good buyer. The family, spanning several generations, enjoyed running their business and wished to continue doing so without interference from a new owner and the fear of being sold on a whim.

Buffett agreed. He liked Fechheimer's strong record of profitability and industry leadership and admired its committed family management. Berkshire acquired an 84-percent interest for $46 million, with the family retaining the rest. Notably, no one from Berkshire paid a field visit to Cincinnati, and no one from Fechheimer conducted any reciprocal due diligence. In fact, ever since the federal judge gratuitously excoriated him for not conducting due diligence in the *Buffalo News* acquisition, Buffett had made it a point of pride to skip such exercises, making his earlier visits to the Berkshire Hathaway textile mills and See's chocolate factory stand out as anachronisms.

Fechheimer and Scott Fetzer differ greatly. Fechheimer is a very old, multigeneration private family firm in a specialized line of business tailored to institutional customers. A small firm of which Buffett had been unaware, it was operated by owner-managers, who steered the company prosperously through the challenges of a leveraged buyout by the time it arrived at Berkshire. Scott Fetzer, on the other hand, assumed its conglomerate form in the late 1960s and engages in many lines of business, selling products retail through a network of independent distributors and dealers. A large publicly traded firm that Buffett followed in the news, it had been operated by a cadre of professional managers who steered the company to Berkshire as an alternative to leveraged buyout. Even the structure of the deals differed: full ownership of Scott Fetzer versus a 16-percent retained family interest in Fechheimer.

What both companies had in common that appealed to Buffett were good management, proven profitability, and industry leadership. The other common denominator was what each valued in Berkshire: autonomy and permanence. Scott Fetzer—both management and shareholders—rejected the hands-on control and piecemeal liquidation of the Boesky leveraged buyout in favor of the managerial autonomy and permanence of Buffett and Berkshire. The Heldman family, having seen a leveraged buyout through, turned to Buffett, who offered a permanent home at Berkshire and hands-off management.

Today, Berkshire's subsidiaries engage in a multitude of unrelated businesses, each contributing in its own way to Berkshire. In an effort to organize the diversity, four business sectors are outlined in Buffett's annual letter to Berkshire shareholders, and each sector is broken down into further subdivisions. The first sector, insurance, is Berkshire's oldest and the most important in terms of historical contributions to business value. The second, regulated or capital-intensive industries, is the newest sector and is becoming increasingly important in terms of revenues and earnings. The third sector is finance and financial products, the smallest of the four, though significant in absolute size. The final sector is a broad cluster of companies, encompassing various types of manufacturing, service, and retailing, including Fechheimer and Scott Fetzer.

Berkshire's insurance sector consists of large companies that underwrite personal car insurance (e.g., GEICO) as well as large business risks (e.g., Gen Re and NICO), along with a dozen smaller operations engaged in a wide variety of insurance, running the gamut from boats to workers' compensation. All in all, the sector insures just about everything you could think of—from your neighbor's car to urban skyscrapers, from the café down the block to the world's largest airlines.

Berkshire's second business sector, regulated or capital-intensive industries, involves two distinct business activities. One is energy and consists solely of Berkshire Hathaway Energy (formerly known as MidAmerican Energy), a global conglomerate invested in energy, including solar and wind, and interests in natural gas pipelines. The other is transportation, headlined by Burlington Northern Santa Fe, among the largest North American railroads. Berkshire's transportation interests also include two aviation specialists: FlightSafety, which provides pilot training, and NetJets, the pioneer in fractional aircraft ownership. Berkshire's transportation sector also includes Forest River, manufacturer of boats and recreational vehicles.

Berkshire's finance sector encompasses three companies, whose financing operations may be similar but whose products differ substantially: Clayton Homes, a builder, seller, and financier of manufactured housing; CORT, which leases furniture; and XTRA, a lessor of trucking equipment.

The final sector—the one Fechheimer and Scott Fetzer occupy—includes eight subdivisions. The subdivisions contain similar types of business activity yet broad variety. For example, both See's and Dairy Queen are part of the food sector, but the business models of these two companies differ markedly, See's being a chain of company-owned stores and Dairy Queen a system of franchises.

Berkshire's jewelry subdivision includes three retailers, Ben Bridge Jewelers, Borsheim, and Helzberg Diamonds, and also a manufacturer and wholesaler, Richline. The home furnishings subdivision parallels this, consisting of four kindred retailers, Jordan's Furniture, Nebraska Furniture Mart, RC Willey Home Furnishings, and Star Furniture, but also a manufacturer of picture frames, Larson-Juhl. Similarly, the media sector includes scores of local newspapers like the *Buffalo News*, the *Omaha World-Herald*, and the *Richmond Times-Dispatch*, along with an international press release service called Business Wire.

Berkshire's construction subdivision produces building materials (Johns Manville), bricks (Acme), paints (Benjamin Moore), and steel connectors (MiTek). The apparel sector subsidiaries, Brooks, Fruit of the Loom, Garan, H.H. Brown Shoe, and Justin Brands, together offer nearly every kind of footwear—cowboy boots, dress shoes, work boots, golf shoes, and running shoes—as well as athletic gear, children's clothing, intimate apparel, and the uniforms of Fechheimer.

The sales subdivision is a hodgepodge of companies distributing electronics (TexTronics Inc. or TTI), kitchen utensils (the Pampered Chef), and party favors (Oriental Trading). Finally, the industry subdivision includes an agricultural equipment manufacturer (Chore-Time Brock or CTB), a specialty chemical maker (Lubrizol), and a global metal cutting powerhouse (Israel Carbide/International Metalworking Companies or ISCAR/ IMC), along with conglomerates Scott Fetzer and the Marmon Group.

Berkshire's diversity by business line is matched by diversity in almost every measurable category—acquisition price, valuation, dollar contribution to Berkshire, firm size, employment base, and various financial characteristics. Having all these companies under one roof, so to speak, a degree of homogeneity might be expected, such as a uniformly low price-to-book ratio, following Buffett's original investment philosophy, or a maximum price-to-earnings ratio, applying conventional value-investing filters. This is not the case at all. Unifying traits and commonalities at Berkshire will not be found in such metrics, but rather in more intangible features.

∽

Berkshire's 1986 payments of $46 million for Fechheimer and $315 million for Scott Fetzer foretold of the wide-ranging acquisition prices it would pay over the ensuing decades. During the first ten years that followed, Berkshire's acquisition prices ranged from less than $100 million to

Table 2.1
Acquisition Prices

($ billion)		($ million)	
44	Burlington Northern Santa Fe (BNSF)	800–900s	Fruit of the Loom, Pampered Chef, TTI
22	Gen Re	600–700s	Dairy Queen, NetJets
10	Lubrizol	400–500s	Dexter, Justin, MiTek, Scott Fetzer, XTRA
5–9	ISCAR/IMC, Marmon Group, MidAmerican (Berkshire Hathaway) Energy	300s	Business Wire, CORT
2–4	GEICO, Shaw	200s	Applied Underwriters, Ben Bridge, Garan, Jordan's, Larson-Juhl
1.5–1.9	Clayton, FlightSafety, Johns Manville, McLane	100s	CTB, Helzberg, H.H. Brown, RC Willey, Star
1–1.4	Benjamin Moore, Forest River, Medical Protective	<100	Borsheim, *Buffalo News*, Central States Indemnity, Fechheimer, Kansas Bankers Surety, Nebraska Furniture Mart, NICO, Richline, See's, Wesco

Note: Aggregate amount for acquisitions made in stages.

$2.3 billion for the consolidation of GEICO. Over the next twenty years, the scale increased and the range widened, with many deals between $400 and $900 million, several more than $1 billion, and a handful more than $10 billion (see table 2.1).

Berkshire acquisition prices have implied different valuation benchmarks in terms of price-to-earnings ratios or price-to-book value. Berkshire's various subsidiaries were acquired at price-to-earnings ratios ranging from 8-to-1 to more than 30-to-1, and price-to-book ratios from less than 1-to-1 to more than 5-to-1 (see table 2.2). The range of multiples reflects subsidiary diversity as well as the wide array of valuation techniques that apply at different times to varying business types (e.g., insurance, utilities, finance, manufacturing, retailing, and services). For example, asset-intensive manufacturing operations may be valued at lower multiples of book value compared to service or retailing concerns.

Table 2.2
Price Ratios

Price-to-Earnings Ratios		Price-to-Book Value Ratios	
< 8	Fruit of the Loom	< 1.00	Fruit of the Loom
8–10	Garan	1.00–1.99	Clayton, CTB, Garan, Justin, XTRA
11–13	Johns Manville, Lubrizol, XTRA	2.00–2.99	Benjamin Moore, Dairy Queen, FlightSafety, Gen Re, Johns Manville
14–17	Benjamin Moore, Clayton, Dairy Queen	3.00–3.99	BNSF, See's, Shaw
18–22	FlightSafety, Gen Re, Justin, Shaw	4.00–4.99	Lubrizol
23–30	BNSF, CTB	> 5	MidAmerican (Berkshire Hathaway) Energy
> 30	MidAmerican (Berkshire Hathaway) Energy		

Note: Most of the data are sourced from Bloomberg. The ratios are the announced total value of the deal divided by the target's trailing twelve-month net income for price to earnings (PE) and book value for price to book (PB). For Fruit of the Loom, acquired in bankruptcy with negative earnings and book value, PE is based on trailing earnings before interest, taxes, depreciation, and amortization (EBITDA) and PB is based on enterprise value. Data for FlightSafety and See's are sourced from Berkshire Hathaway annual reports.

Berkshire's subsidiaries make varied contributions to corporate results. Berkshire's total 2013 revenues were $182 billion: $130 billion from non-insurance businesses, $37 billion from insurance operations, and $15 billion from investments and other sources.[5] Some subsidiaries generate less than $250 million of that, many up to $1 billion, others more than $10 billion, and one (McLane) nearly $46 billion. If Berkshire's subsidiaries were stand-alone corporations, eight would be in the Fortune 500, using the revenue cutoff of $5 billion for 2013 (see table 2.3). Berkshire subsidiaries employ different numbers of people, several fewer than one hundred and several with more than twenty, thirty, or forty thousand (see table 2.4).

Berkshire subsidiaries have unique financial characteristics. Profit margins (earnings divided by revenues) range from 1 to 25 percent, and returns on capital span a narrower but still wide range. Subsidiaries generally enjoy strong economics, measured by proxies like return on assets

Table 2.3
Revenue and Pre-tax Earnings of Berkshire's Subsidiaries

	Revenue ($ billions)		Pre-tax Earnings ($ millions)
McLane	45.9	BNSF	5,900
BNSF	22.0	Berkshire Hathaway Energy	1,800
GEICO	18.5	NICO	1,700
Berkshire Hathaway Energy	12.7	Marmon Group	1,200
NICO	12.0	Lubrizol	1,200
Marmon Group	7.0	GEICO	1,100
Lubrizol	6.1	McLane	500
Gen Re	5.9	Gen Re	300

Note: The amounts for Lubrizol are estimates. The amounts for NICO combine the operations of the Berkshire Hathaway Reinsurance Group and the Berkshire Hathaway Primary Group.

Source: Berkshire Hathaway Annual Report (2013), p. 64.

Table 2.4
Employment Numbers for Berkshire's Subsidiaries

Employees	
> 40,000	BNSF
> 30,000	Fruit of the Loom
> 25,000	GEICO
> 20,000	McLane, Shaw
> 15,000	Berkshire Hathaway Energy, Marmon Group
> 10,000	Clayton Homes, ISCAR/IMC
> 7,500	Forest River, Lubrizol
> 5,000	Johns Manville, NetJets, Scott Fetzer
> 2,500	BH Media, CTB, FlightSafety, Garan, Nebraska Furniture Mart, Richline, See's, TTI
> 1,000	NICO and a dozen non-insurance subsidiaries
< 1,000	A further dozen non-insurance subsidiaries; all other insurance subsidiaries

(after-tax earnings on unleveraged net tangible assets). For many Berkshire companies, this runs anywhere from 25 percent to more than 100 percent; for most subsidiaries, the range is a respectable 12 to 20 percent. But some fail to approach even the low end of this range, reflecting occasional mistakes in Berkshire's acquisition decisions.[6]

The costliest mistake was a replay of the original Berkshire Hathaway deal, this time involving a New England shoe company. Founded by Harold Alfond in 1956 in Dexter, Maine, with a stake of $10,000, Dexter Shoe became a dynamo, producing millions of shoes in local factories annually. It built a niche in the golf shoe market and won awards from department store customers for excellence among suppliers. Dexter maintained production in the United States, paying higher wages than rivals and seemed to outdo competing imports from low-wage countries in terms of quality and style.

In 1993, Berkshire acquired Dexter for $443 million, all in Berkshire stock. It had positive traits seen in other early Berkshire acquisitions—an entrepreneurial founding family akin to See's, a budget consciousness akin to Wesco—as well as solid branding, distribution, and customer relations. But Dexter also had one latent negative trait identical to that of Berkshire Hathaway's textile operations: manufacturing plants in the U.S. with costs ten times those in China. Eventually, rivals would produce shoes as good as Dexter's but at one-tenth the cost. By 2007, Buffett confessed that acquiring Dexter was the worst deal he ever made.[7]

At that point, Berkshire transferred Dexter's business to H.H. Brown Shoe Company, a prosperous footwear subsidiary acquired in 1990. Also of New England bloodlines, H.H. Brown dates to 1883, when Henry H. Brown founded the company in Natick, Massachusetts, then a center of the nation's shoemaking industry. In 1927, Brown sold the company for $10,000 to Ray Heffernan, a twenty-nine-year-old who ran it until he died at the age of ninety-two in 1990.[8]

Heffernan grew the business steadily over the years, making acquisitions and pioneering many product innovations, including the use of Gore-Tex in shoe linings. By 1990, the company ran four plants, all in North America, employed three thousand people, and grossed $25 million annually.[9] As Heffernan's health declined, leadership of H.H. Brown fell to his son-in-law, Frank Rooney, long-time CEO of a rival shoe company.[10] After Heffernan died, the family wished to sell. During a golf game, Rooney mentioned this desire to John Loomis, a friend of Buffett and a Berkshire shareholder, who told Rooney to call Buffett.[11] A deal was quickly made for Berkshire to acquire H.H. Brown for $161 million. Buffett persuaded Rooney to stay on, which was important to Berkshire, as it had given up recruiting subsidiary managers.

H.H. Brown was the leading U.S. maker of work shoes and boots and had a proven record of profitability. The company produces its premium brand shoes in the United States, charging higher prices to recoup costs, while making standard brands more cheaply overseas. Brown also sells military boots through the post exchanges on U.S. military bases, benefiting from federal "buy American" laws, and makes work boots for laborers required to wear them by the federal Occupational Safety and Health Administration. Brown thus managed to survive—and thrive—by a combination of tradition and adaptation that had eluded Dexter.

Aside from illustrating the diversity of Berkshire operations, even within a single line of business, what is remarkable about the Dexter and Brown story is the ending. Berkshire did not sell Dexter but repurposed it in H.H. Brown. Brown then closed Dexter's U.S. operations, relocated them abroad, enabling the Dexter brand to endure.

~

Berkshire acquired its subsidiaries over a span of fifty years (see table 2.5). Its smaller acquisitions—the *Buffalo News*, See's, Wesco, Fechheimer—tended to occur in the earlier decades, whereas the largest have occurred more recently. As its capital resources have grown, Berkshire has increasingly put a premium on identifying larger acquisitions. But large acquisitions remain scarce, and a larger number of smaller acquisitions can often be more profitable than holding cash or government securities for long periods.

It is commonly believed that Berkshire's acquisitions target privately held companies. While that is true, looking at the number of private companies acquired, the total dollars paid in public company deals (more than $100 billion) exceeds that paid in private-company deals. In half of the acquired public companies, however, a large percentage of the stock was owned by single families, and at least some family members served as directors or officers (see table 2.6).

Most Berkshire acquisitions start and end with Berkshire owning 100 percent of the selling company's shares. But in several cases, Berkshire's ownership position begins small and grows to 100 percent. Examples include Burlington Northern Santa Fe Railway, GEICO, and Blue Chip

Table 2.5
Acquisition Times

	Insurance	Non-Insurance
1960s	National Indemnity (NICO), National Fire & Marine	
1970s	BH Homestate	*Buffalo News*, See's, Wesco
1980s		Borsheim, Fechheimer, Nebraska Furniture Mart, Scott Fetzer
1990s	Central States, GEICO, Gen Re, Kansas Bankers Surety	Ben Bridge, H.H. Brown, Dairy Queen, FlightSafety, Helzberg Diamonds, Jordan's, Star, MidAmerican (Berkshire Hathaway) Energy, NetJets, RC Willey
2000–2005		Benjamin Moore, Clayton, CTB, CORT, Forest River, Fruit of the Loom, Garan, Johns Manville, Justin, McLane, MiTek, Pampered Chef, Shaw, XTRA
2006–2010	Applied Underwriters, BoatUS, Medical Protective, US Liability	Business Wire, ISCAR/IMC, Larson-Juhl, Marmon Group, Richline, TTI
2010s	Guard	BNSF, Lubrizol, Oriental Trading

Table 2.6
Ownership Types

Public (Dispersed Ownership)	Public (Sizable Family Ownership)
BNSF	Benjamin Moore
CORT	Clayton Homes
Fruit of the Loom	CTB
Gen Re	Dairy Queen
Johns Manville	FlightSafety
Lubrizol	Garan
MidAmerican (Berkshire Hathaway) Energy	Justin/Acme
XTRA	Shaw Industries
	Wesco

Table 2.7
Founding Times

	Insurance	Non-Insurance
19th century	Medical Protective	Benjamin Moore, BNSF, H.H. Brown, *Buffalo News*, Fechheimer, Fruit of the Loom, Johns Manville, Justin, McLane
20th century pre-World War II	GEICO, Gen Re, National Indemnity (NICO)	Acme, Ben Bridge, Borsheim, Dairy Queen, Helzberg Diamonds, Jordan's, Lubrizol, Nebraska Furniture Mart, Oriental Trading, See's, Star, RC Willey
20th century post-World War II	Applied Underwriters, BoatUS, Central States, Kansas Bankers Surety	Business Wire, Clayton, CORT, CTB, FlightSafety, Forest River, Garan, ISCAR/IMC, Larson-Juhl, Marmon Group, MidAmerican (Berkshire Hathaway) Energy, NetJets, Pampered Chef, Scott Fetzer, Shaw, TTI, XTRA
21st century		Richline

Stamps. In several cases, as with the Heldmans at Fechheimer, selling share-holders retained a portion on an indefinite or permanent basis.[12] In yet other deals, Berkshire's initial position was less than 100 percent, but plans were agreed for it to acquire the rest in due course.[13]

It is frequently said that Berkshire subsidiaries are very old, but this is also not the case. Rather, they are of different vintages. Ten date to the nineteenth century (Fechheimer being the oldest, dating to 1842); half were founded before World War II, and the other half since (see table 2.7). Among the youngest are Richline, a jewelry manufacturer established in 2007, and Forest River, the recreational vehicle manufacturer founded in 1996 out of the ashes of an older group of assets. Of contestable age, given corporate mergers, reorganizations, and consolidations, is Burlington Northern Santa Fe, which dates to 1849 but was formed in 1995, and Berkshire Hathaway Energy, formed in 1998 but the product of mergers and acquisitions by a company founded in 1971.

Berkshire also claims geographic diversity. Nearly half of the states in the United States are home to headquarters of one or more Berkshire

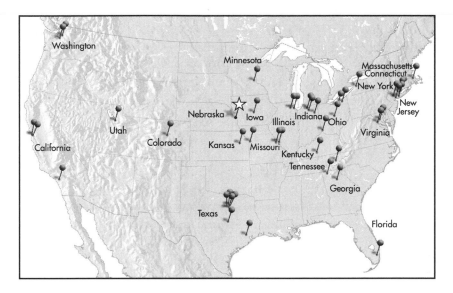

Figure 2.1
Map of Berkshire Hathaway companies.

subsidiaries, which dot the map across the country (see figure 2.1 and table 2.8). Omaha is home to Berkshire's headquarters, several insurance subsidiaries, and four other subsidiaries. Another fifteen Berkshire subsidiaries cross the Midwest, seven are located out west, eleven are in the south, and nine are in the east

The locations of Berkshire subsidiary headquarters reflect that Berkshire is principally an American company, though several subsidiaries—Gen Re, Lubrizol, and MiTek among them—have long maintained international operations. Even so, Berkshire has only acquired one significant non-U.S. subsidiary: ISCAR/IMC, a global leader in the manufacture of metal cutting tools.[14]

ISCAR/IMC was founded in 1952 by Stef Wertheimer, today an Israeli billionaire, who in 1937, at age nine, fled Germany with his parents to escape Hitler's Nazism. The family settled in Tel Aviv, where Wertheimer later joined the British Royal Air Force (RAF) as an equipment technician. Using the skills he acquired with the RAF, Wertheimer opened a small metal tool cutting factory in the backyard of his home, which he called ISCAR, short for Israel Carbide.

Wertheimer and his family, led by his son Eitan, transformed the tool company into the world's largest metalworking network. ISCAR is the

Table 2.8
States Hosting Berkshire's Subsidiaries

MIDWEST

Nebraska (all in Omaha)	Applied Underwriters, BH Homestate, BH Media, Borsheim, Central States, Nebraska Furniture Mart, NICO, Oriental Trading
Illinois	Marmon Group, Pampered Chef
Indiana	CTB, Forest River, Medical Protective
Iowa	Berkshire Hathaway Energy
Kansas	Kansas Bankers Surety
Minnesota	Dairy Queen
Missouri	Helzberg Diamonds, MiTek, XTRA
Ohio	Fechheimer, Lubrizol, NetJets, Scott Fetzer

WEST

California	Business Wire, See's, Wesco
Colorado	Johns Manville
Utah	RC Willey
Washington	Bridge, Brooks

SOUTH

Florida	Richline
Georgia	Larson-Juhl, Shaw
Kentucky	Fruit of the Loom
Tennessee	Clayton
Texas	Acme, BNSF, Justin, McLane, Star, TTI

EAST

Connecticut	Gen Re, H.H. Brown
D.C./Virginia	BoatUS, GEICO
Massachusetts	Jordan's
New Jersey	Benjamin Moore
New York	*Buffalo News*, FlightSafety, Garan
Israel/Holland	ISCAR/IMC

flagship member of a group of metalworking firms called International Metalworking Companies B.V. (IMC). The group consists of scores of subsidiaries founded by local entrepreneurs over the past century and now operates in a dozen countries. All manufacture specialty metal products, primarily for domestic aerospace and automotive industries. IMC's products are small, cheap tools used in the large expensive machinery of customers. The value added by these tools is substantial, as they make the machinery more efficient, thereby increasing customer profits.

By 2005, the Wertheimer family needed to address the challenges of generational transfer. Eitan Wertheimer wrote Buffett a short letter, introducing the company and its industry.[15] Buffett invited Wertheimer to Omaha and within a few hours believed a deal was possible. Berkshire soon bought 80 percent of ISCAR/IMC, with the Wertheimer family retaining the rest. In 2013, the Wertheimer family exercised their right to sell the remaining 20 percent to Berkshire, bringing Berkshire's total price to $5 billion.

Berkshire's concentration of acquisitions in the United States results principally from historical fortuity, as the company gelled ahead of globalization. It does not imply limits in the Berkshire model's effectiveness on a global stage. On the contrary, the ISCAR/IMC business model—itself a network of firms—may suggest the feasibility of expanding Berkshire globally.

$\approx$

Berkshire's scores of subsidiaries—including Fechheimer, Scott Fetzer, Dexter, H.H. Brown, and ISCAR/IMC, as well as See's, Wesco, and the *Buffalo News*—vary in nearly every way, from products sold to profit margins earned, and their particular road to Berkshire. Yet, as our encounter with these subsidiaries has demonstrated, there is a common thread running throughout. But given Berkshire's scale and the complexity of its corporate family, it will take a little more digging into the subsidiaries to synthesize Berkshire culture and to find out how they promote Berkshire's durability.

3

Culture

On corporate culture, Buffett is fond of quoting Winston Churchill: "You shape your houses and then they shape you."[1] Companies self-select for membership in the Berkshire family. Business owners do not sell to Berkshire (and Berkshire does not buy businesses) unless they concur with the norms and standards of the culture.

Corporate culture is complex at any organization but especially at a conglomerate of Berkshire's scale and diversity. Corporate culture is defined by a set of shared beliefs, practices, and outlooks that determine a corporation's expectations and influence the behavior of its personnel toward colleagues, customers, and owners alike.[2] The tone is set at the top and percolates throughout the organization through daily decisions, challenges, and crises. The values of a company are at the core of its culture, as they establish the standards to achieve its goals.[3]

At Berkshire, these values first began to take shape from the acquisition criteria Buffett established to identify potential subsidiaries. In 1986, Berkshire ran an advertisement in the *Wall Street Journal* indicating its interest in acquisitions and its criteria for making them. These same criteria have been published every year since in Berkshire's annual reports and have never changed, except in terms of minimum desired size, which rose from $5 million in annual earnings back then to $75 million today: proven profitability, good unleveraged returns on equity, management in place, basic businesses, and a fair price.

Another formal expression of Berkshire's tone that helped shape its values is a set of owner-related business principles that define how Berkshire and its subsidiaries relate to its shareholders and other constituents. Like the acquisition criteria, these principles are published in every annual report. It is an impressive list of fifteen principles that Berkshire's chief executive lives by. Examples include conceiving of the organization as a partnership despite using the corporate form, minimizing the use of borrowed money, assessing whether to reinvest earnings or pay dividends based on whether a dollar reinvested will increase shareholder value by at least as much, and holding subsidiaries forever. Most importantly, these principles reflect that Buffett has always been a shareholder first and manager second. His managerial convictions elevate shareholder interests. Buffett admires managers who run their businesses as if they owned them.[4] This mind-set instilled values of budget consciousness and investment savvy into Berkshire from the outset.

Berkshire's owner-related business principles, especially conceiving of Berkshire as a partnership, focus on shareholders. The company treats its shareholders not merely as temporary holders of its equity, but as business partners in an endless venture. Such a value is one of the most prevalent at Berkshire, as its subsidiaries—including many family businesses—are seeking a permanent home for their company, and Berkshire prides itself on holding its subsidiaries permanently. They are owners for whom Berkshire's managers, including Buffett and those of the subsidiaries, are stewards. The principles also stress that Berkshire's chief executive and controlling shareholders will treat fellow shareholders loyally as partners, rather than as mere sources of capital.

Berkshire's approach succeeds in attracting a shareholder group with unusual characteristics for corporate America: Berkshire boasts one-fifth the share turnover of other large firms, unusually high annual meeting attendance (drawing 35,000 in recent years), ownership dominated by individuals and families (not the financial institutions or mutual funds that own most stock of other large public companies), and a high degree of portfolio concentration among shareholders.[5] As a group, Berkshire shareholders accept the concept of Berkshire as a partnership in which they own not just a liquid stock but a permanent stake.[6]

Berkshire, though publicly traded and listed on the New York Stock Exchange since 1988, retains partnership characteristics carried over from

Buffett's early days running a private investment firm. The Berkshire board, for instance, has always been comprised of friends and family: Buffett's late wife Susan for many years and their son Howard since 1993; Buffett's best friend, Charlie Munger, since 1978; fellow Omaha businessman, Walter Scott Jr., since 1988; and, since 1997, Ronald L. Olson, named law partner in Munger, Tolles & Olson, which Berkshire uses extensively for acquisitions and other legal work.

Expansions of the board in 2003–2004 added long-time business associates Donald R. Keough, a veteran executive at Coca-Cola, in which Berkshire holds a substantial equity position, and Thomas S. Murphy, long-time chief executive of Capital Cities/ABC, another Berkshire investee. Others include old friends David S. ("Sandy") Gottesman, a New York investor and Buffett's friend since 1962, and William ("Bill") H. Gates III, founder of Microsoft Corporation and Buffett's friend since 1991.

Berkshire's directors act like owners: purchasing chunks of Berkshire stock, receiving nominal pay without stock options, and serving without the directors' liability insurance that other boards take for granted. While Buffett has owned the lion's share of Berkshire—as much as 40 percent—other directors, their families, and clients of institutions they run collectively own well more than 10 percent.[7] Otherwise, the board's most important contribution to Berkshire culture has been to affirm and reinforce the values that Buffett has continually injected into it.

Unlike many conglomerates, Berkshire headquarters employs no operating managers, only a small staff of officers focused on financial reporting. From 1981 to 1993, Michael Goldberg oversaw a group of Berkshire businesses and moved senior managers among them.[8] For example, he asked Brad Kintsler to run a series of insurance companies before assigning him the presidency of Fechheimer (and Buffett later asked Kintsler to run See's after Chuck Huggins retired).[9] From 1999 to 2011, David L. Sokol, brass-knuckled chief executive of MidAmerican Energy (now Berkshire Hathaway Energy), was a roving troubleshooter for sister subsidiaries and, since then, Tracy Britt Cool, a junior manager, has assisted subsidiaries in need. But beyond such limited resources, and the occasional replacement of chief executives, the subsidiaries are on their own for managerial talent. Their boards, if they have them, are small (often just three members) and meet rarely (perhaps once per year).

Berkshire's culture is the sum of the cultures it brings to the acquisition and ownership process and the operating cultures of all its subsidiaries. The stories of these subsidiaries, as told by founders themselves or other authorities, reflect the beliefs, practices, and outlooks that define their corporate cultures. The cultural histories include legends about the people who began a company, lore about the challenges faced, and the trials of transitions.[10]

Corporate culture matters because it translates into business performance. For example, a company whose management and shareholders embrace a long-term outlook can better weather financial volatility. Companies with reputations for thrift and conservatism are less likely to default and therefore enjoy higher credit ratings and lower borrowing costs, and the stock prices of such companies tend to be less volatile, attracting investors.[11] A business known for integrity—treating suppliers, employees, and customers as the business would like to be treated if the positions were reversed—will usually win more interest and cooperation among such groups than rivals who are chiselers. Such a reputation for excellence—in merchandising, manufacturing, services, or other business activities—can manifest in better terms of trade at the outset of relationships and more flexibility to cope with periodic adversity.[12]

One study of hundreds of large companies showed that companies that project strong positive corporate cultures enjoy outsized economic performance.[13] Others have explored how such cultures win respect within the business community.[14] Professor Raj Sisodia and Whole Foods cofounder John Mackey argue that long-term economic value is better achieved by companies that simultaneously pursue economic profits and intangible values.[15] Robert Mondavi, who earned a fortune while developing Napa Valley into an institution of winemaking, says that behind his success was a quest for an intangible notion of excellence.[16] Yet it is not always easy to measure or even identify the particular advantage or the process through which intangibles take on economic value. Part II will endeavor to illuminate such intangibles through numerous examples from the stories of Berkshire and its subsidiaries.

Corporate culture, a modern concept akin to vague notions like team spirit, is trickier to define than venerable tools of business analysis, such as return on investment. A soft and capacious variable, culture results from multiple inputs, which may conflict with one another. Whether called corporate culture or something else, the manifest recurrence of a discrete number of traits is significant to the identity, performance, and durability of Berkshire as an institution.

Identifying Berkshire culture by examining its subsidiaries does not mean that each subsidiary has every trait or that each trait applies to every

Table 3.1
Some Highlights of Part II

Trait	Essence	Primary Illustration(s)
Budget conscious	A penny saved is a nickel earned	GEICO (car insurance)
Earnest	The value in promise keeping	NICO (commercial and catastrophic risks) Gen Re (reinsurance)
Reputation	Results benefit from reputation	Clayton Homes (customers, investors) Jordan's Furniture (customers) Benjamin Moore (distributors) Johns Manville (people, environment)
Kinship	Wealth *can* last more than three generations when families value identity and legacy	Nebraska Furniture Mart (Blumkin family) RC Willey (Child family) Star Furniture (Wolff family) Helzberg Diamonds Ben Bridge Jeweler
Self-starters	To the entrepreneur go the spoils	FlightSafety (pilot training) NetJets (fractional aircraft ownership) Garan (Garanimals children's line) Justin/Acme (branded boots/bricks) Dairy Queen (business franchise)
Hands off	Delegate everything but reputation	The Pampered Chef (consultants) Scott Fetzer (dealers) Lubrizol (Berkshire saga)
Investor savvy	Price is paid, values are exchanged	McLane (geographic blanketing) MiTek (bolt-ons and tuck-ins) Lubrizol (turning point) Berkshire Hathaway Energy (capital pipeline)
Rudimentary	Impossible dreams are impossible, so stick to your knitting	BNSF (old economy, good economics) Shaw Industries (learning from mistakes) Fruit of the Loom (excess leverage)
Eternal	Berkshire as a permanent home, a Boys Town for the corporate homeless	Brooks (serial corporate owners) Forest River (post-LBO/bankruptcy) Oriental Trading (post-LBO/bankruptcy) CTB (post–private equity) CORT (after multiple LBOs) TTI (avoiding temporary owners)

subsidiary. It is more like the culture of a good basketball team. Competitive players tend to be fast, strong, and tall. But not every player must have all three traits. A team can succeed with some players who are short but fast and strong and others who are slow yet big and powerful. The player traits taken together add up to a team culture. More than the sum of its parts, team culture also includes norms instilled by coaches, such as sportsmanship and teamwork. Similarly, the Berkshire traits, though not necessarily pervasive in each subsidiary, together create Berkshire culture, with shaping provided from the tone at the top.

Business leaders build cultures by promoting or exemplifying given values. Values contribute to decision making, and motivate and attract people who share them; they repel those who don't.[17] Values are also sticky—they are hard to change and tend to endure. The simpler the values are to convey, the more durable they tend to be. The earlier a business leader taps the potential of shared values, the more resilient a corporate culture becomes, offering the leader an enduring legacy. Table 3.1 gives a thumbnail sketch of the cultural traits identified in the stories that follow in Part II. For mnemonic power, the teacher in me found a way to put all the values into an acrostic spelling out B ● E ● R ● K ● S ● H ● I ● R ● E.

4

Budget-conscious and Earnest

1936, San Antonio, Texas. Leo Goodwin, a fifty-year-old insurance manager, was working closely with U.S. military personnel at USAA, an insurer that catered to the military.[1] He was concerned that his customers were paying too much for car insurance and calculated that by putting the least risky drivers into an insurance pool and selling policies without agents, a company could discount prices by up to 20 percent and still turn a profit. This simple idea blossomed into GEICO, a car insurance company that is one of the cornerstones of Berkshire's business, epitomizing the first of the Berkshire values I'll explore—budget consciousness, in the strict sense of frugality and thrift.

GEICO's start came when Goodwin persuaded a local banker, Cleaves Rhea, to stake $75,000, which, along with his own $25,000, provided the seed capital to implement his idea.[2] For the pool, Goodwin targeted U.S. military officers as well as other federal government employees, perceiving them to be among the least risky drivers. Since such workers are concentrated in the nation's capital, Goodwin and his wife, Lillian, moved to Washington, D.C., to launch the new company, called the Government Employees Insurance Company—GEICO for short. Toiling twelve-hour days, six days per week, the Goodwins built GEICO with sheer grit. They marketed by direct mail, handled underwriting details, and managed claims. On weekends, Leo Goodwin drove to military bases and made his sales pitch door to door.

To complement the commitment to low-cost insurance, GEICO stressed customer service. For instance, in 1941, after a hailstorm damaged cars across town, Goodwin arranged with local shops to work overtime on repairs and got suppliers to expedite shipping of roof tops and window glass.[3] GEICO customers appreciated getting their cars back in service before neighbors insured with competitors.[4]

Goodwin's business model was simple: low-cost insurance, sold without agents, to targeted risk pools that were given quality customer service. First-year results were promising: 3,754 policies written, $103,700 in premiums, and a staff of twelve.[5] Underwriting results (the difference between premiums written and policy claims paid) were negative early on but soon swung to a small underwriting profit. Despite the adversity of the Great Depression and the displacement of World War II, the "thrifty" business model was vindicated as GEICO grew steadily in policies, premiums, and profits.

In 1948, Rhea's family sold its stake in GEICO to several private investors. Helping the Goodwins to locate these new investors was their friend, banker and GEICO senior officer Lorimer ("Davy") Davidson. Among others, Davidson placed a large block of stock with Graham-Newman, whose named partner, Benjamin Graham, became GEICO's chairman.

Graham-Newman's GEICO position represented a large portion of the firm's assets. The investment concentration departed from Graham's usual preference to diversify. But then, federal authorities ruled that an investment company such as Graham-Newman could not own such a large stake in an insurance company. So the firm distributed its GECIO shares to its partners to hold directly. At that point, the shares were held by so many people that federal law required them to be registered with the Securities and Exchange Commission, which made GEICO a public company.[6]

A few years later, Buffett was enrolled in Graham's investment class at Columbia Business School, located on the university's main campus in the Morningside Heights neighborhood of Manhattan. Graham's biography listed his position as chairman of GEICO, a company Buffett had never heard of in an industry he knew nothing about. Eager to learn more, Buffett decided to visit the company's Washington headquarters.

On a cold Saturday in January 1951, Buffett boarded the 6:30 A.M. "Morning Congressional" train of the Pennsylvania Railroad from New York.[7] Arriving in Washington four hours later, he found the GEICO building, then at 14th and L Streets Northwest, was closed.[8] But the young Buffett caught the attention of a custodian, who indicated there was someone working on the top floor. It was Davidson. Buffett told Davidson he was Graham's student, and Davidson went on to spend four hours explaining the company and the industry to Buffett.

Buffett's key takeaway: "GEICO's method of selling—direct marketing—gave it a wide cost advantage over competitors that sold through agents, a form of distribution so ingrained in the business of these insurers that it was impossible for them to give it up."[9] Inspired by his chat with Davidson, Buffett studied GEICO and the insurance industry carefully. He then wrote a report about GEICO for "The Security I Like Best" column in the *Commercial and Financial Chronicle*, a widely read trade publication.[10] Putting his money where his writing was, Buffett bought 350 shares of GEICO stock during 1951 at a cost of $10,282, representing half his net worth. (The next year, Buffett sold his GEICO shares for $15,259. That taught a lesson about buy-and-hold: by 1995, that stake was worth more than $1 million.)

Throughout the 1950s, Leo Goodwin continued to build GEICO, emphasizing its goal to keep costs at an absolute minimum. However, the goal of low costs was not merely to increase profits. In fact, Goodwin insisted on passing along most of the savings to customers in the form of lower premiums. That, in turn, attracted more customers. Greater total premium volume and, ultimately, profit, resulted, as did deepening customer loyalty across a widening base.

By the end of the decade, GEICO had more than seven hundred thousand policies and wrote $65 million in premiums.[11] Goodwin retired in 1958, handing the reins to Davidson, who sustained GEICO's unique business model, continuing its tradition of thrift, increasing volume by keeping premiums low. By 1965, insurance premiums tallied $150 million and earnings doubled to $13 million.[12]

In the 1970s, after Davidson retired and the Goodwins passed away, the GEICO story took a different turn. Growth in premium volume became more important than cost management or underwriting quality, and policies were written or renewed with little regard to relevant information such as policyholder accident histories.[13] In 1973, the company opened eligibility to all, regardless of employment, believing that technology and statistical modeling enabled screening more effectively than occupational groupings. Yet the company lacked the requisite computer systems to aggregate or analyze the data.[14] Policies and premium volume soared.

Also during this time, many states adopted no-fault insurance laws. Previously, insurers of culpable drivers paid claims. Since GEICO's good drivers were rarely at fault, GEICO rarely owed claims. No-fault switched the emphasis from who was at fault to how much damage occurred. GEICO's management failed to appreciate how such changes would affect the company. For several years, it underestimated losses and thus underpriced insurance, an error that drove the company to near-bankruptcy in the mid-1970s.[15]

In 1976, a GEICO director, Samuel C. Butler, senior partner of Cravath, Swaine & Moore, recruited John J. ("Jack") Byrne, a forty-three-year-old prodigy of the insurance industry, as chief executive. Byrne promptly improved the company's approach to estimating losses and restored the company's traditional underwriting discipline. He took other steps to control costs, including refusing to renew policies of high-risk drivers, and increased revenues by raising premiums. To relieve pressure and maintain public confidence, Butler and Byrne arranged for a consortium of insurers to assume a large book of GEICO's policies. To raise capital to meet claims, GEICO made a secondary offering of its stock. In that offering, Berkshire bought a 15 percent stake.

GEICO escaped a doomed fate, thanks to Byrne's leadership and Berkshire's capital infusion. It emerged a much smaller company, with a market share of less than 2 percent, where it would remain for more than a decade. Byrne, along with his colleague and successor, William B. Snyder, adhered to the business model Goodwin had established: being the low-cost seller in a large market in which competitors were wedded to the costly practice of marketing through agents.[16] In 1980, Berkshire more than doubled its stake in GEICO, soon owning half the stock.

Budget consciousness was, above all, GEICO's secret sauce. In 1986, GEICO's total underwriting expenses and loss adjustment expense accounted for just 23.5 percent of premiums.[17] Rivals' costs were fifteen percentage points above that. It sported a combined ratio—expenses plus claims as a percent of premiums—of 96 in a year (1983) when the industry's was 111. The difference was GEICO's moat that thus protected a business castle.[18] Buffett explained:

> GEICO's growth has generated an ever-larger amount of funds for investment that have an effective cost of considerably less than zero. Essentially, GEICO's policyholders, in aggregate, pay the company

interest on the float rather than the other way around. (But handsome is as handsome does: GEICO's unusual profitability results from its extraordinary operating efficiency and its careful classification of risks, a package that in turn allows rock-bottom prices for policyholders.)[19]

In 1995, Berkshire paid $2.3 billion for the other half of GEICO (princely, compared to the total of $46 million it laid out for its first half begun nineteen years earlier). Buffett noted the importance of attracting and keeping good customers and accurate reserving and pricing. But he stressed the vital key was the rock-bottom costs that permitted low premiums:

> The economies of scale we enjoy should allow us to maintain or even widen the protective moat surrounding our economic castle. We do best on costs in geographical areas in which we enjoy high market penetration. As our policy count grows, concurrently delivering gains in penetration, we expect to drive costs materially lower.[20]

Buffett attributes the prosperity GEICO enjoys today to Olza M. ("Tony") Nicely, who joined GEICO in 1961 at age eighteen and has been CEO since 1992—one of several Berkshire executives who have been with their company more than fifty years. Buffett stresses that Nicely inherited a company commanding merely 2 percent of the market without significant growth and turned it into a powerful industry force—while maintaining underwriting discipline and keeping costs low.[21] Under Nicely, GEICO clocked many productivity gains. As one example, during a three-year period in the early 2000s, policy volume rose by 42 percent (from 5.7 million to 8.1 million), whereas the employee base fell by 3.5 percent, contributing to a productivity growth (in policies per employee) of 47 percent.[22]

While Nicely exemplifies managerial quality at Berkshire subsidiaries, his colleague Louis ("Lou") Simpson, GEICO's chief investment officer for decades, earned a place in the hall of fame. Berkshire distinguishes between the operating and investment activities of its insurance subsidiaries. From 1980 to 2010, Simpson managed what became a $4 billion portfolio of common stock investments at GEICO, applying principles akin to those Ben Graham established and that Buffett expanded upon.[23] The impressive results, an average annual return beating the S&P 500 by half, added to GEICO's financial strength.[24]

GEICO's business model is more than merely being the low-cost producer in a commodity market. Its budget consciousness influences incentives for employees and treatment of customers. All employees receive generous incentive-based profit sharing. Payouts are based on two equally weighted factors: growth in policies in force and profits on seasoned policies (excluding first-year policies, which are not profitable in a direct-sales business given marketing and initiation costs).[25] The payouts can be large, having added from 17 to 32 percent of base salary.[26] So a salaried employee earning a base of $75,000 can readily yield herself a six-figure income.

GEICO's budget consciousness is a commitment to its customers' budgets. For example, GEICO caps its underwriting profit at 4 percent.[27] If premiums exceed expenses and claims by a greater magnitude, GEICO does not pocket the profits but reduces premiums. This is not altruism. The strategy attracts more customers, which increases aggregate profits, even when the underwriting profit percentage is capped.

GEICO's tagline—"save 15 percent or more off car insurance"—highlights its thrift-based business model. Under Nicely's leadership, GEICO has been aggressive in getting the word out. Its advertising budget, a discretionary commitment, grew from $33 million in 1995 to $800 million in 2009. This may sound extravagant, but consider what it buys: during that period, GEICO's market share grew from a stagnant 2.5 percent in 1995 to 10 percent today.[28] The payoff in market share translated into more premiums, float, and profit, all of which tripled during that period. The increase in advertising budget also catapulted GEICO's mascot, the gecko, to fame. The gecko debuted in company ads in 2000 and has even toured in a national gecko exhibit at several zoos to promote wildlife conservation.

GEICO has been like rocket fuel propelling Berkshire's prosperity. During Berkshire's ownership, GEICO has moved from a minor player in the national auto insurance market to second by market share—with substantial room for growth ahead. Preserving GEICO should be essential to whoever owns or runs Berkshire Hathaway. The permanence GEICO has with Berkshire is why in 2010, at age ninety-five, Lorimar Davidson made a video recording saying how happy he was that his beloved GEICO would forever reside with Berkshire.[29]

GEICO's commitment to handling customer claims is unwavering. It prides itself on receiving the fewest customer complaints filed with insurance regulators.[30] GEICO intends to keep the promises it makes—earnestness is a characteristic of any top insurance company and a sacred vow at Berkshire's. The importance of being earnest in the insurance field is most salient, however, not in short-term/low-stakes settings such as car insurance, but in the long-term/large-stakes settings handled by GEICO's sister insurance companies, National Indemnity and Gen Re, which have increasingly added strength to Berkshire's financial fortress.

~

Berkshire's earnestness is captured in the business-minded creed at National Indemnity Company (NICO), founded in 1940 by Jack Ringwalt and his brother Arthur.[31] As insurance agents, they were surprised when two Omaha cab companies could not obtain insurance. So they went into the insurance business to provide it. The Ringwalts—whose father and uncle were also Omaha insurance agents—built NICO on one bedrock principle: "There is no such thing as a bad risk; there are only bad rates."[32] Translation: we can make any promise, so long as we are paid enough in premiums to be able to cover it if called upon to do so. The company still follows this principle today.[33]

The Ringwalts' creed led them to underwrite risks other insurers would not. Jack Ringwalt explained in his witty memoirs that this was the best way to make money, particularly in his case, because his competitors "had more friends, more education, more determination, and more personality than I."[34] Starting with unusual auto risks, National Indemnity expanded to write insurance for hole-in-one contests, lion tamers, and radio station treasure hunts.[35] The Ringwalts carefully calculated the odds and took risks only if they could get the right rate.

In 1967, Jack Ringwalt wanted to sell NICO but continue to run the business. Through a mutual friend, Buffett learned of this interest and Ringwalt's likely asking price. When the two met, Buffett agreed without hesitation on the price Ringwalt named. Ringwalt made his reasons for selling clear: "If I don't sell the company, my executor will, and I'd rather pick the home for it."[36]

NICO stresses that an insurance policy is merely a promise, and that while promises vary in quality, its promises are the highest quality. In an insurer, earnestness requires achieving financial strength sufficient to meet its promises. True, insurers make promises in contracts whose breach prompts lawsuits and regulatory scrutiny. But neither guarantees performance, some insurers get reputations for "slow pay" or "bounced claims,"[37] and the risk of overpromising into insolvency is real.[38]

By the early 1980s, NICO's convictions and superior capital strength enabled it to expand its business into some basic reinsurance transactions in what soon came to be called the Berkshire Hathaway Reinsurance Group. These began with backstopping structured settlements, procedures for settling claims with payment installments over long periods of time. For example, an accident victim, paralyzed with limited mobility, is granted an insured $5,000 monthly for life. For such a settlement to be made, there can be no question about the insurer's creditworthiness. Backstopping those insurers, NICO carved a niche by offering matchless security and always making good on its promise to pay.

Through what is now called the Berkshire Hathaway Primary Group, NICO added a specialty risk division in 1985. It is devoted to underwriting large and unusual risks for proportional premiums—professional athletes against permanent disability, rock stars against laryngitis, and international sporting events from the Olympics to the World Cup against disruption. NICO launched the division by advertising in a weekly insurance trade journal that it was looking for risks where the premium would be at least $1 million (in today's dollars, more than twice that).[39] The ad yielded six hundred replies, yielding $50 million in premiums—a marketing success that within five years proved to be an equal underwriting success.

NICO writes policies others won't or can't, whether multi-billion-dollar satellites or multi-million-dollar reward contests for Grab.com, Pepsi Co., and other corporate customers.[40] In 2014, it insured an offer by Quicken Loans to pay a $1 billion dollar prize to anyone picking the exact 2014 men's NCAA basketball tournament bracket of sixty-four teams—the odds of which being one in 128 billion.[41] In the months after the terrorist attacks of September 11, 2001, NICO wrote large terrorism policies, a $1 billion policy for several international airlines, a $500 million policy for an overseas oil platform, and a large portion of the coverage for the Sears Tower in Chicago.

NICO's growing financial strength—backed by investments in high-quality marketable securities—enabled it to become the market leader in writing catastrophic loss policies. Called "CAT covers" ("CAT" for "catastrophic") in industry jargon, these are reinsurance contracts that primary insurers (and some reinsurers) buy to protect against a single catastrophe— say a hurricanes or a tornado—that triggers crippling payouts on a large number of policies simultaneously.

NICO has more capacity than other insurers to sell CAT covers. This is partly due to its vast balance-sheet strength and also because Berkshire's long-term outlook makes it—and its subsidiaries—indifferent to year-to-year swings in results. Competitors, in contrast, care a great deal about steady year-to-year earnings. With such strengths, NICO is able to write policies for amounts that competitors are unable to consider; and NICO remains extremely choosy, rejecting more than 98 percent of business offered to it.[42]

Berkshire's CAT cover business was begun from scratch by Ajit Jain,[43] who for years also ran all of the Berkshire Hathaway Reinsurance Group. Buffett extols Jain's virtues repeatedly and emphatically in Berkshire annual reports:

> In Ajit, we have an underwriter equipped with the intelligence to properly rate most risks, the realism to forget about those he can't evaluate, the courage to write huge policies when the premium is appropriate, and the discipline to reject even the smallest risk when the premium is inadequate. It is rare to find a person possessing any one of these talents. For one person to have them all is remarkable.[44]

National Indemnity has driven Berkshire Hathaway's growth for several decades. Four decades after acquiring National Indemnity from Ringwalt, Buffett wrote that, but for NICO, Berkshire would have been worth half its value.[45] National Indemnity's promises are sacrosanct. Its financial fortress enables it to sustain its historical commitment to backstop any risk at the right price. Customers willingly pay for such earnestness.

∼

Gen Re's principal business is reinsurance, backstopping other insurers for portions of policies they write. Buffett noted when discussing the industry in 2008, a year that battered insurers amid a roiling financial crisis: "Reinsurance is a business of long-term promises, sometimes extending for fifty years or more. This past year has retaught clients a crucial principle: A promise is no better than the person or institution making it."[46]

Earnestness, in other words, is a vital quality for a reinsurer, an ironclad intention to meet promises made. The essence of earnestness is sincerity, the traditional decree to mean what you say and say what you mean. Gen Re, like NICO, insures large and unusual risks, with policies spanning decades, making promises whose size or duration renders the company's word a precious asset (a source of business moat). A track record of covering claims increases the value of their promises, translating the intangible trait of earnestness into quantifiable economic gain.

Gen Re, which Berkshire acquired in 1998, traces its roots to the 1921 merger of two Norwegian companies that plied the reinsurance field at a time when many Americans disdained it as akin to gambling. Gen Re pioneered the concept in the U.S. It brought legitimacy to the business by adopting a conservatism that became its trademark: only accepting reinsurance business when policies satisfied rigorous standards for quantifiable risk that could be properly priced in the premium, only investing in assets of high quality and low risk, and building large reserves greater than required to assure ability to cover multiple catastrophes.

By the 1970s, that success drew competitors and induced large companies to form captive insurance arms to self-insure against property and casualty damage. Gen Re's business volume and profits fell. Departing from its traditional fortitude, it tried to offset the decline by acquiring a primary insurer. It soon learned the perils of insurance companies chasing new business and abandoned the effort. A contemporary executive explained that insurance is "no place for fast-moving profit hounds and that survival [is] the real measure of success in a business that, in a sense, depends on disaster."[47]

In the 1990s, globalization and financial industry growth again pressured Gen Re's traditional model. In response, Gen Re, among the world's largest reinsurers, expanded into financial products and asset management. In 1994, it acquired 75 percent of Germany's Cologne Re,[48] the world's fifth largest reinsurer—also the oldest, dating to 1846. On the domestic side, in 1996, Gen Re acquired National Reinsurance Corporation (National Re), a top-twenty reinsurer that shared the company's strong conservative values while catering to smaller companies.[49]

In December 1998, Berkshire paid $22 billion of Berkshire stock to acquire Gen Re, whose ownership of Cologne Re had inched up to 82 percent. Berkshire's acquisition of Gen Re was a watershed event, for both Berkshire and the insurance industry. The takeover was seen as the deal of the decade for the industry, making Berkshire a major player in reinsurance. The acquisition resulted in 18 percent of Berkshire being owned by new owners (though many sold their shares), and Gen Re's CEO, Ronald E. Ferguson, was invited to join the Berkshire board (though he declined).[50] Berkshire was attracted to Gen Re because of its reputation for conservatism, integrity, and earnestness.

Disclaiming any ability to improve how Gen Re or Cologne Re ran their reinsurance businesses, Berkshire's ownership would give Gen Re's management maximum freedom to exploit its strengths. Standing alone, Gen Re's freedom was constrained by pressure to avoid earnings volatility.[51] It would sometimes decline good business opportunities out of a fear that occasional large losses would produce wide swings in results, which customers, shareholders, and analysts disfavor. Berkshire's capital strength and long-term horizon immunize Gen Re from such concerns, enabling it to make business decisions on the merits of the proposition rather than under the pressure of short-term second-guessing.

Buffett had known Ferguson, Gen Re's chief executive, for many years. Berkshire and Gen Re had done significant business with each other, and Gen Re had helped with GEICO's 1976 resuscitation from near-death.[52] What neither Buffett nor Ferguson knew, however, was that Gen Re's reserving practices and underwriting discipline had slipped. It had under-reserved for the risks it covered. Underwriters used those low reserve figures to set prices on new policies. Ensuing losses exceeded premium revenues. Underwriters also pursued business they should have rejected, often through excessive concentration in particular risks. Earnestness had been compromised.

From 1999 to 2001, Gen Re incurred underwriting losses adding to $6.1 billion.[53] That meant related float cost Berkshire money. It took a couple of years for the festering problems to become evident to Buffett, as it takes time for insurance policies to run their course. Fallout from the terrorist attacks of September 11, 2001, revealed Gen Re's cultural problems. For example, the company had covered an intolerable concentration of nuclear, chemical, and biological risks. Losses ran so high and problems so deep that, but for Berkshire's ownership of Gen Re, the costs of covering the destruction of September 11 might have put it out of business.[54]

Shortly before September 11, 2001, Buffett replaced Ferguson with Joseph P. Brandon, a bright forty-three-year-old Gen Re executive, and promoted forty-five-year-old Franklin ("Tad") Montross, a long-time Gen Re underwriting manager, to president. Buffett gave this duo increased authority to rapidly correct past errors and return Gen Re to its traditional conservatism.[55] Corrective measures began with installing incentive compensation plans tied to float growth and the cost of float. Today, these are the metrics that matter most at Gen Re.

Throughout those trying years, Gen Re retained financial strength, maintaining its AAA rating (in 2003, only two reinsurers had AAA ratings: Gen Re and NICO). Gen Re became Berkshire's largest source of float at $24 billion in 2007, confirming the restoration of underwriting discipline, conservative reserving, and careful business/client selection.[56] Earnestness—which the Gen Re story shows must be jealously guarded— was back.

But Gen Re's culture soon faced another test—of legacy, leadership, and resilience—amid a national investigation into dubious industry practices. Insurers had created arcane policies (called "finite covers") for one another to achieve various accounting and operational objectives, including assuring adequate loss reserves. As early as 2003, Virginia state insurance regulators questioned practices at a Gen Re counterparty, the now-defunct Reciprocal of America. Gen Re cooperated by supplying information to the Virginia regulators as well as opening its books to authorities in other states and the federal Securities and Exchange Commission.

Scouring those books, authorities seized upon notes from a phone call of October 31, 2000, between Ferguson and Maurice R. ("Hank") Greenberg, chairman of American International Group (AIG), a big Gen Re client. Greenberg explained that an AIG subsidiary had recently paid large losses on catastrophic policies and that, as a result, AIG wanted to refresh its reserves. He proposed for AIG and Gen Re to exchange some policy risks in a transaction that would allow AIG to increase reserves.

Ferguson assigned the transaction to two senior Gen Re underwriters, who negotiated the deal along with several colleagues. In doing so, however, it became intertwined with other AIG–Gen Re transactions such that, to an outside observer, it could have seemed as if no risk had been transferred, meaning AIG was not entitled to increase its reserves. If so, the transaction would appear to be an artifice. Prosecutors began a criminal case against Ferguson, several Gen Re managers, and another AIG employee. (Greenberg was not charged in the criminal case though for a decade he battled a civil case begun by New York attorney general Eliot Spitzer.)[57]

Two Gen Re managers soon entered plea bargains, agreeing to admit to concocting a fraud and testifying against others involved in exchange for leniency in their sentencing. The case against Ferguson and the others crawled along for six years, with a jury trial in 2007–08, followed by an appeal. The jury returned convictions in February 2008, but the appellate court threw them out in June 2012. At that point, the government settled, with each employee paying fines ranging from $100,000 to $250,000.[58]

Following standard practice in such cases, authorities had cast a drag-net, and in 2005, the SEC informed Brandon that it was investigating his role in the incident as well. He reported to Ferguson and one other target reported to him. Brandon cooperated without seeking immunity. In February 2008, buoyed by the short-lived jury verdict, government authorities felt as if they had a strong hand to play. As a result, during March and early April, they encouraged Buffett to fire Brandon.[59]

The pressure proved overwhelming—and may have been unfair.[60] Prosecutors have strong leverage in a weapon called "corporate criminal liability." It enables the authorities to hold corporations criminally liable for the crimes of employees. All it takes are credible allegations of one employee committing one crime while on the job. Harkening back to the case of Salomon Brothers, for corporations whose businesses depend on reputations, especially Gen Re (and Berkshire), a corporate indictment can be disastrous.

Prosecutors are supposed to avoid heavy-handed use of this power; specifically, they aren't meant to pressure corporations to oust employees without traditional due process. For example, it is a violation of an employee's constitutional rights for prosecutors to pressure a company into terminating promised funding for an employee's legal defense.[61] In practice, however, prosecutors are not always restrained.

Market reaction to Brandon's dismissal was mild. Some thought the move was inevitable given the environment: the trial put a pall over Gen Re, and there are few better ways of clearing corporate air than firing a CEO.[62] Observers agreed that Brandon was a great manager who had returned Gen Re to its conservative heritage with stringent standards and controls; they also knew that his replacement, Tad Montross, who had led the effort alongside Brandon, reflected Gen Re's deep bench.[63]

Today, Montross stresses underwriting profit and believes underwriting discipline is ingrained in Gen Re's DNA, as he put it in correspondence for this book. When he reviews quarterly results with Gen Re's associates, he reminds them that Gen Re has a "no exit strategy"—that, like Berkshire, its time horizon is forever. Today's Gen Re is like the Gen Re of the early twentieth century, taking commitments very seriously and planning to be around to make good on them.

∾

The business models of Gen Re/NICO and GEICO could scarcely be more different: GEICO's durable competitive advantage (its "moat") is being the low-cost producer, allowing it to pass on virtually all savings to customers;

Gen Re's and NICO's moats are being high-margin producers and charging for premium offerings. However, budget consciousness and earnestness are traits at all three companies—and at Berkshire's dozens of smaller insurance operations as well.

Buffett summed up both when describing Berkshire's 2005 acquisition of Medical Protective Corporation, a medical malpractice insurer. He said the company adopted "the attitudinal advantage that all Berkshire insurers share, wherein underwriting discipline trumps all other goals."[64] Medical Protective made a commitment to promise keeping intended to "assur[e] doctors that long-to-settle claims will not end up back on their doorstep because their insurer failed," Buffett wrote.

Budget consciousness is not unique to Berkshire's insurance subsidiaries but widely practiced across Berkshire. Other Berkshire subsidiaries that make thrift part of their moat include Nebraska Furniture Mart, RC Willey, and other furniture store chains, as well as makers of carpets, underwear, and tools—Shaw Industries, Fruit of the Loom, and ISCAR/IMC, three of Berkshire's ten largest subsidiaries. Nor is earnestness unique to Berkshire's insurers; it is pervasive among Berkshire's businesses, as the next chapter on reputation will demonstrate.

5

Reputation

Among the culprits of the 2008 financial crisis was one corner of the real estate industry that peddled irresponsible mortgages to unsuspecting and impecunious homeowners. When revealed, the dubious practices put many banks and finance companies out of business and sent millions of homes into foreclosure. Within the sector hit hardest, manufactured housing, a single exception stood out in the industry: a Berkshire subsidiary called Clayton Homes, Inc. Clayton Homes is a stellar example of a business that has benefited financially from its reputation.

Its founder, James L. Clayton, was born in 1934 on a Tennessee share-cropper's farm in a log cabin with no electricity or plumbing.[1] As a child laborer, he earned twenty-five cents a day driving farm mules that pulled logs to make rows in the cotton fields. He saved his money, and by age twelve, he owned a small cotton patch.

After high school, Clayton headed for Memphis. There he sold vacuum cleaners between college classes by day and played guitar in honky-tonks by night.[2] Later he transferred to the University of Tennessee in Knoxville, where he studied engineering while running his own used-car lot with his brother Joe. By starring on a local radio show and rubbing elbows with the likes of country music star Dolly Parton, Clayton became a mini-celebrity in Knoxville.

The Clayton brothers acquired a Volvo franchise in 1958 and an American Motors dealership in 1960. Both businesses struggled, however, and eventually went bankrupt. Jim Clayton headed for law school, earning a degree from UT Knoxville in 1964. Upon graduating, he helped classmates sell the mobile homes they had been living in, which gave the entrepreneur another business idea: a retail outlet in modular homes. With a $25,000 loan, Jim launched that business in 1966.

The market was vibrant, and the business succeeded, averaging sales of two homes a day in the early years. The success motivated Clayton to expand into manufacturing the homes. He kept costs low and inventory turnover high, improving profit margins. In addition to both making and selling manufactured homes, in 1974 Clayton started to finance them, using a separate subsidiary he named Vanderbilt Mortgage & Finance, Inc. That arm of the business would prove lucrative and catapult Clayton to among the nation's largest lenders to lower-income families.

In 1983, Jim Clayton sold 20 percent of Clayton Homes, Inc. in an initial public offering of its shares and listed them on the New York Stock Exchange.[3] Proceeds of the offering were $10.5 million, valuing the company at $52.5 million. The price soon skyrocketed to value the whole business at $120 million, making Jim Clayton's personal stake worth $95 million. Just two years earlier, an appraiser had put the value of such a stake at $7.5 million. "Now you know," Jim later noted, "why so many entrepreneurs dream about taking their companies public."[4]

To weather the economic adversity of the period, which beset top competitors like Oakwood Homes and Fleetwood Enterprises, Clayton concentrated on his customers' circumstances. He figured that his typical customer—blue-collar workers and retirees—could afford to pay at most $200 per month. Clayton worked backward to build and finance homes priced for that budget.[5]

In 1987, taking vertical integration to the ultimate level, Clayton opened its first manufactured-home community, in Texas, and soon added sites in Michigan, Missouri, North Carolina, and Tennessee. In every year from 1989 through 1992, *Forbes* named Clayton Homes one of the best small companies in America. It boasted ten manufacturing plants, 125 company-owned dealerships, and 325 independent dealerships operating in half the states.

Prosperity continued through the 1990s as the company grew in all ways, adding manufacturing plants and dealerships and increasing sales and financing revenue. In 1996, Clayton achieved its sixteenth consecutive year of record earnings. Revenues passed the $1 billion mark the following year. Growth was supplemented by acquiring existing mobile home communities in new territories. By 1998, Clayton owned seventy communities that were home to 18,900 families.

In 1999, when *Forbes* named Clayton one of America's top 400 large companies, Jim Clayton passed the CEO reins to his son, Kevin. The next year, as the economy sagged, the manufactured housing industry went into a tailspin, which worsened as the decade progressed. While competitors downsized aggressively and closed plants extensively, Clayton was able to minimize its need for both. Thanks to the successful vertical integration of the business that generated multiple revenue streams, the company even managed to maintain profitability throughout the decade.[6]

The company is always scrupulous in dealing with home buyers and the financiers who invest in the pools of mortgages it underwrites. Jim Clayton criticized unsavory peer practices that made it too easy for customers to borrow, such as manipulating the terms of down payments or allowances, contrasting the culture at Clayton Homes:

> At Clayton Homes, we can't ever compromise our credibility by participating in such schemes. Unethical behavior is not and will not be tolerated. We now sell over a billion dollars of mortgages every year, and investors who buy those mortgages never meet the customers, or see the collateral. The trust and faith enjoyed by our company from so many shareholders, investors and suppliers, and our 8,000 team members is so very important. We must always take our credibility and integrity seriously.[7]

The opportunity to acquire Clayton came to Berkshire's attention fortuitously in 2003.[8] Albert L. Auxier, who taught finance at the University of Tennessee, made an annual trip to Omaha with his students to meet Buffett—one of several dozen student groups Buffett hosts annually. Auxier's students always brought a present, which, in 2003, was Jim Clayton's new autobiography, *First a Dream*. Buffett knew of the man and the company. Berkshire had made disappointing investments in the bonds of Oakwood Homes, a competitor whose questionable consumer lending practices were uncovered only after it went bankrupt.

Berkshire offered to buy Clayton Homes in April 2003 for a price 7 percent above its average market price over previous months. Many institutional shareholders of Clayton objected. Some challenged the deal in court,[9] whereas another, Cerberus Capital Management, told Clayton management it wanted the chance to make a competing bid. The result was a six-month delay in getting the Clayton shareholder vote, which finally approved the Berkshire deal. That same year, seizing an opportunistic expansion, Clayton acquired many of Oakwood's assets out of bankruptcy.

In the early 2000s, promoters of manufactured homes spurred business by siphoning funds to buyers who should not have purchased homes with loans lenders should not have made. What distinguished Clayton Homes was that its financing division, unlike that of competitors, did not engage in predatory lending or exploit its customers' naivety. Jim Clayton attributed the difference to his company's maintenance of a "sacred wall" between sales and credit that competitors failed to maintain.[10]

The industry's problems crystallized during the 2008 financial crisis, and Clayton took advantage of them. Before 2008, it grew its own business by applying prudent lending criteria that resulted in a well-performing portfolio of loans. After 2008, it prospered while its chief rivals, such as Champion, faltered. Clayton and its customers compared actual mortgage payments with actual income, and loans were made only when the relation proved affordable. Competitors, on the other hand, assessed long-term affordability using teaser rates that applied in early years but increased later.

Amid the crisis, Clayton was an exception: no purchaser of the loans it originated or had repackaged for sale ever lost a dime of principal or interest.[11] The results were astounding for the industry—as well as for Clayton and Berkshire. In 1999, the three largest manufacturers were Champion, Fleetwood, and Oakwood, which together commanded nearly half the output. Clayton was fourth. By 2009, the top three had all disintegrated, and Clayton Homes, which had acquired much of Fleetwood and Oakwood as well as several other rivals, was number one.[12] Those who invested in pools of manufactured housing mortgages lost large sums of money. Clayton Homes, an industry leader, shows that integrity is not only a moral virtue but a business value.

~

Jordan's Furniture, Inc. sells $950 per square foot of furniture annually, six times the industry average, and turns its inventory thirteen times a year, an even greater multiple of the furniture retailer norm.[13] The secret is a reputation for unique customer service, an intangible value that the company handily translates into economic value.

The business dates to the 1920s, when Samuel Tatelman sold furniture in the Boston area from the back of his truck. Within a few years, he opened a store in Waltham, a middle-class Boston suburb. He was soon joined in the business by his son Edward.[14] The business was run in modest fashion, concentrating on local traffic and advertising in the Waltham town newspaper. During Edward's tenure, the store never employed more than a dozen people.

In 1973, however, Edward passed business leadership to his sons, Barry and Eliot, who aggressively widened their customer base by advertising on the radio and later on television. The brothers were their own spokesmen in these commercials, putting a personal touch on the pitch and giving instore customers a sense of celebrity sighting.

In 1983, with business booming at the Waltham store, Jordan's added a new store in Nashua, New Hampshire, just over the Massachusetts border. In 1987, they opened today's flagship Avon, Massachusetts, location, drawing so many customers to the grand opening that, legend has it, nearby Route 24 suffered its worst traffic jam ever. The brothers reportedly went on local radio begging off the traffic, which, of course, only drew more customers to the store.

Jordan's takes an innovative approach to customer service, going beyond a wide selection at good prices and prompt delivery with offerings of what Jordan's calls "shoppertainment." At the Avon store, for instance, customers are welcome to take a seat in its forty-eight-seat movie theater to watch a flight-simulator movie on a forty-foot screen. Jordan's Natick, Massachusetts, store carries a New Orleans theme, where customers can stroll along a model of Bourbon Street, tour a Riverboat, and take in a multimedia celebration of Mardi Gras. The concept entertains and attracts people of all ages, but has a special advantage for its largest demographic, families with children.[15] It can be difficult for young families to handle bored kids when shopping for furniture. The entertainment at Jordan's engages them, enabling parents to relax while shopping, thus increasing their satisfaction and Jordan's sales.

The company also cultivates a reputation for commitment to its community. This business philosophy entails generous support to civic and charitable organizations, such as Massachusetts Adoption Resource Exchange, which helps place foster children in permanent homes, and Project Bread, which helps feed poor families. One device used to consolidate that community impulse: the store requests donations from customers who enjoy its flight-simulator movie and turns these over to charity.

Buffett learned of Jordan's Furniture by industry word of mouth. Over the years, whenever Buffett would ask the managers of Berkshire's other furniture stores for the best names in the business, they would invariably name the Tatelman brothers.[16] When agreeing to buy the company in 1999, Buffett stressed the reputation that Eliot and Barry had earned from their employees, customers, and community, which he called "unparalleled."[17]

As part of the sale to Berkshire, the Tatelman brothers distributed a portion of the proceeds to Jordan's employees. Every worker got a bonus of at least fifty cents per hour they had worked at the company. The total pool amounted to $9 million. Long-term employees became very wealthy that day.

Jordan's continues to expand and deepen its promotional approach. It opened a large store in Reading, Massachusetts—and closed the original Waltham store, which the company had long outgrown—sporting not only a giant showroom, but a 3D IMAX movie theater. Eliot Tatelman still appears in the company's commercials, looking like an aging rocker, his long white hair in a ponytail. He is a local celebrity, whom customers like to meet. Jordan's reputation for unmatched customer service has paid off.

∼

The business value of integrity compounds over years but can vanish in days, as constituents of Benjamin Moore & Co. have learned.

The company was founded in 1883 in Brooklyn by twenty-seven-year-old Benjamin Moore, along with his forty-three-year-old brother Robert. Moore articulated several business principles to guide his company:

1. A fair deal for everyone.
2. The giving of value received without any graft or chicanery.
3. Recognition of the value of truth in the representation of our products and an effort at all times to keep the standard of our goods up to the highest mark.
4. The practice of strict economy without the spirit of parsimony, and the exercise of intelligent industry in the spirit of integrity.[18]

Moore's motto was "quality, start to finish." It charged a premium price for it, even when that sacrificed market share. To reinforce its investment in quality, the Moore brothers began the practice of selling paint through independent distributors. Other paint makers might sell in hardware stores, or as private-label products of customer retailers, or in their own retail stores. Benjamin Moore & Co. adhered to the model of distributing exclusively through certified dealers. Those distributors, in turn, invested considerable effort in building their businesses to keep their end of the bargain.

Benjamin Moore won a reputation for leadership in safety and environmental matters. Some of the company's growth in the 1940s was based on research and development of more durable and environmentally friendly paints, including latex-based paints. In 1968, Benjamin Moore removed lead from its paint formulations—ahead of the curve of regulation and litigation that has embroiled competitors over ensuing decades.[19] In the 1970s, after passage of the Occupational Safety and Health Act (OSHA), the company developed color-coded coatings to meet the new standards.

Benjamin Moore made environmental consciousness good for business. For example, in the 1980s, federal agencies implemented rules limiting release of harmful volatile organic compounds (VOCs). The company produced paints tailored to the various ways the regulations were implemented by different agencies nationwide. In 1992, it opened a paint farm to test products for environmental soundness and a corporate-wide training center to promote environmental efficiency. Throughout the 1990s, the company led the industry in its commitment to the highest environmental, health, and safety standards. For instance, its Pristine Eco-Spec line of acrylic latex interior paints, introduced in 1999, released no harmful VOCs. Customer demand for such responsible products is high, and people are willing to pay a premium for them.

The company's tradition of integrity is demonstrated in endless efforts to improve the positions of its distributors and draw new entrepreneurs into the business. In the 1960s, the company advanced the funds required to begin a distributorship, then about $200,000, to minority entrepreneurs. In the 1980s, the company offered distributors financing to support their purchases of its computerized color systems.[20] After the 1992 Los Angeles riots, Benjamin Moore won praise for these longstanding programs, which focused on neighborhood investment.[21] The company stressed that all such programs were not products of altruism, but were simply good business practices.

In 2000, Benjamin Moore's directors, facing consolidation, considered strategic alternatives, such as acquisitions, a merger, or a sale. One director, Robert H. Mundheim, whom Buffett had appointed as general counsel of Salomon Brothers after its bond-trading scandal, volunteered to call Buffett.[22] Benjamin Moore was Berkshire's kind of company, and Buffett proposed that Berkshire acquire it for $1 billion in cash; the Benjamin Moore board asked Mundheim about countering, but he explained that doing so would be futile.[23] As part of its acquisition, however, Berkshire promised to maintain the company's historic policy, dating to the nineteenth century, of relying solely on its thousands of independent dealers, a valuable asset to the business comprised of people who had invested their livelihoods in the dealerships.[24]

In July 2007, Buffett promoted Denis Abrams, long-time vice-president of Benjamin Moore's operations, to serve as president. When asked that summer how different Benjamin Moore was before and after Berkshire's acquisition seven years earlier, Abrams said: "very little," as the company stuck to its "history and tradition," thanks to how "Berkshire does not dictate to the operating companies how they should operate."[25] Asked what happens when executives of Berkshire's subsidiaries "screw up," Abrams said he would have no idea because he wasn't aware of any such case.[26]

But within a year, things did begin to change, and within five, Abrams learned first-hand of Buffett's reaction to a Berkshire executive screwup. The precipitating factor was the economic recession that began in early 2008. Benjamin Moore struggled, facing shrinking sales as people curtailed their home improvement activities. The company coped through layoffs, including termination of several senior sales executives, salary freezes, reduced commissions on sales, and a reduced ad budget. Dips in market share—and employee morale—resulted.[27]

Some blamed Berkshire for the company's woes, because Benjamin Moore's top executives were well paid and earned bonuses by meeting profit goals on the backs of workers. A common complaint held that Berkshire withdrew $150 million annually from Benjamin Moore, despite the company having no quarterly sales growth from 2008 through mid-2012.[28] Yet Benjamin Moore was profitable during the decade, revenue remained consistent, and such a dividend is within a parent corporation's discretion, especially given duties its managers have to their shareholders.[29]

Abrams focused on distribution channels. He told the sales force to persuade distributors to become exclusive dealers in Benjamin Moore paints. Abrams allegedly condoned strong-arm tactics, such as threatening to encroach on territory by opening company-owned stores nearby.[30] Some distributors complained about more expensive terms for inventory financing or being charged for advertising that was never provided.[31]

As out of sync with Benjamin Moore tradition as such tactics were, Abrams's downfall was negotiating deals with large chains. When these deals came to Buffett's attention in June 2012, some completed and others pending, Buffett informed Abrams they were unacceptable.[32] They violated Berkshire's commitment of exclusivity to Benjamin Moore's distributors. Abrams, who was in discussions with Lowe's, a large retail chain, replied that such sales arrangements were essential to restore growth and regain market share.[33] Buffett replaced Abrams with Robert Merritt, who quickly assured the troops of doing a better job.[34]

Merritt began to settle the company back into its traditions. Observers credited his efforts to rekindle the company's special historical relationships with dealers.[35] But he, too, soon was dismissed amid a flurry of rumors about gender bias and locker room humor among senior managers at the company. Underscoring the central issue facing Benjamin Moore, Buffett heralded the appointment of Merritt's successor, Michael Searles, saying that he "understands the importance of the independent retailer" and "is committed to the strategy we have set forth and the commitment we have outlined to the dealer network."[36]

Undoing 130 years of tradition is not easy, but the Benjamin Moore saga shows the fragility of intangibles like corporate culture. Keeping corporate culture strong, on the other hand, are the many distributors who continue to believe in the company. According to one such distributor, Kim Freeman:

> I have been a Benjamin Moore dealer for the past 10 years in Canada. I sincerely hope Berkshire Hathaway and Mr. Buffett return the company to its original principles. We, as the frontline sales force to a cultivated niche market, need to be treated as business partners, not errant children to be controlled or dismissed in the quest for greater market share. Opportunity for more market exists further afield of the large centers. We can make the company grow, contribute to our communities, and realize a good [return on investment] when we are considered important to Benjamin Moore's success. We have lost some great Ben Moore staff and dealers lately, and although it's understandable there will always be evolution, I sincerely hope we can get back on track.[37]

Benjamin Moore's history and its contemporary problems reveal some ways that values can collide, in this case between fidelity to distributors and profitable growth. But Freeman rightly observes that companies can harmonize contending values, as Benjamin Moore has done for more than a century. And Searles agrees. In a business environment where others saw adversity, Searles sees opportunity. As he put it in an interview for this book: "While rivals like Porter and Sherwin Williams shift to other distribution channels, Benjamin Moore gains a huge strategic marketing advantage: the only major brand committed solely to the success of the independent dealer network."[38]

~

Johns Manville Corporation, a manufacturer and marketer of premium-quality building products, has explicitly adopted a commitment to forging a corporate culture of integrity. It strives to be a reputable business by stressing four core values: people, passion, performance, and protection. These values differ from those the company showed historically. For decades, corporate officials ignored or misunderstood the truth about its products, which had seriously injured thousands of people and caused significant environmental damage.

Johns Manville was formed in 1901 by the merger of H. W. Johns Manufacturing Co. and Manville Covering Co. It manufactured textile products and construction materials using asbestos. Manville was founded in Wisconsin in 1886 by Charles B. Manville. Johns was formed in New York in 1858 by twenty-one-year-old Henry Ward Johns, who died in 1898, an early death thought to have been caused, ominously, by asbestosis.[39]

The resulting company, Johns Manville, developed and marketed thousands of applications for asbestos, a natural mineral useful principally because of its fire-retardant properties. The company, which went public in 1927, was a highly centralized, hierarchical, and bureaucratic organization—not a Berkshire kind of company.[40] It might have operated in relative public obscurity but for the fact that asbestos, despite positive uses, is a deadly carcinogen.

From as early as the 1930s to as late as the 1970s, Johns Manville's management denied responsibility. Its efforts to warn employees, customers, or other users were belated. Its general counsel in the 1930s gained infamy for having attempted to squelch, downplay, or dodge the serious medical risks asbestos posed, hazards all scientists then understood and most lay people today are aware of.[41]

Despite the problems asbestos caused, Johns Manville ran a profitable business. It boomed during World War II when the government used asbestos in building warships and fighter jets—while fully informed of the risks and providing warnings to personnel.[42] Johns Manville's prosperity

continued after the war and through 1970, though it faced challenges including bouts with sluggish growth. In response, it expanded into additional
businesses, including many unrelated to asbestos.

During the 1950s and 1960s, employees filed workers' compensation
claims based on illnesses tied directly to asbestos exposure.[43] In the 1960s,
the mainstream press popularized scientific research demonstrating the
dangers of asbestos. The bad publicity prompted the company to add product warnings but did not stimulate any further action.

A blow struck in 1973 when a federal appellate court, affirming a jury
finding of negligence and awarding large damages, excoriated the company
for its callous indifference to the devastation its products caused.[44] This
result attracted more lawsuits, most of which settled, which begat more
lawsuits, ad infinitum. By 1977, Johns Manville had exhausted its insurance
coverage, and no insurer would write a new policy. The company was on
its own.

Asbestos began to consume the company, as a 1979 *Fortune* magazine story noted that managing litigation had become "almost a separate
business."[45] Meanwhile, Johns Manville's operations continued, growing
revenues, adding products, and acquiring companies. But the legal problems mounted, with thousands of cases pending and average settlement
amounts rising. Actuaries predicted total exposure of $2 billion over ensu-
ing decades, twice the company's assets.[46]

To manage these staggering realities, the company filed for bankruptcy
in August 1982, then the largest in U.S. history. An elaborate restructuring
plan resulted. As an operating company, Johns Manville exited the asbestos
business and would be shielded from further claims; concurrently, to pay
asbestos-related liabilities, independent trusts were formed, whose principal assets would be a controlling interest in the operating company's equity.

The plan offered a fresh start. But Johns Manville's public image was
destroyed, the company having lost the trust of employees and customers.
To regain favor, management implored employees to focus on operating
the company conscientiously and oversaw the management of the trusts
to assure scrupulously fair administration of claims. Both efforts continued during the protracted period of the bankruptcy process, which
lasted until 1988.

A totally new Johns Manville emerged from the ruins. It reversed the
cultural backwash that drowned it in asbestos liability. The company sought
input from employees and provided them with more generous medical
monitoring and protection. During a decade of corporate rehabilitation,

the company gradually turned a corner to become the Johns Manville of today that embraces corporate integrity and reputation.

Those managing the trusts, meanwhile, wished to diversify their concentration in the stock of Johns Manville. In June 2000, they agreed to sell the company to a leveraged buyout operator for $2.4 billion. But on a Friday in December, the deal was aborted after financing fell through. The following Monday, Buffett called the trust's chairman, Robert A. Falise, and made an all-cash offer of $1.9 billion with no financing contingency.[47] The trustees accepted the next day, and both sides signed a contract a week later.

Johns Manville's "incredible and multifaceted odyssey," as Buffett characterized it,[48] did not end with its takeover by Berkshire. Under incumbent CEO, Charles L. ("Jerry") Henry, through his retirement in 2004, and his successor Steven B. Hochhauser, Johns Manville achieved record profits of $334 million in 2005 and $345 million in 2006.[49] That string was interrupted in 2007, however, when David L. Sokol, then Berkshire's roving troubleshooter, joined its board and replaced Hochhauser with a MidAmerican Energy colleague, Todd M. Raba, who navigated the company through the construction downturn and ensuing recession.[50] Succeeding Raba in 2012 was Mary Rhinehart, a 34-year veteran of Johns Manville, eager to prove the compatibility of profits and integrity.

Despite continuing challenges, Johns Manville's contemporary corporate culture is committed to integrity, an about-face from the culture of obfuscation that plagued the business for so long. Johns Manville overcame adversity and healed self-inflicted wounds, showing it is never too late to learn. Berkshire could not have acquired the old Johns Manville, but the new one fits the Berkshire model, and Berkshire's culture helps to reinforce its commitment—now decades old—to being a reputable business.

The Johns Manville story spotlights the value of values. The company's harrowing corporate history taught it the value of commitments to employee and customer health and safety. Until bankruptcy in 1982, it overemphasized immediate profit seeking, but today appreciates that economic prosperity is sustained by commitment to broader, longer-term concerns. The Johns Manville story provides a business case for driving shareholder returns while taking responsibility for health and environmental safety.[51]

∼

At Clayton Homes, Jordan's Furniture, Benjamin Moore, and Johns Manville, investing in the value of reputation has clearly paid off. But such integrity is not easy to maintain. While people generally say they want the kinds of things today's Johns Manville promises—a clean environment and safe workplaces—they are not always willing to pay for them.[52] If they did, all businesses would readily choose the moral high ground and pass the costs on to customers. But reality poses challenges for businesses to simultaneously protect consumers, secure employees, control habitats, and deliver shareholder returns. Reputation is vital to the family firm, where intangibles such as legacy and identity prove to have great economic pay-offs, as the stories of several prominent Berkshire family companies in the next chapter will attest.

6

Kinship

Until the year before Rose Blumkin died in 1998 at age 104, she was gain-fully occupied in the job she had held most of her adult life: chairman of the Nebraska Furniture Mart, Inc., her family business.[1] A decade earlier, she engaged in a family feud over her retirement—insisting on working despite the urging of her grandchildren, by then in their sixties, to step down. Berkshire stayed out of the dispute, respecting the principle of autonomy, but in the end played a unique mediating role to help resolve the family quarrel.

The Nebraska Furniture Mart story represents a good introduction to the advantages and challenges of working with family companies. They often have an ingrained sense of permanence that makes them attractive to Berkshire and fit the Berkshire culture, but they can also bring prickly problems that cannot be solved as easily as replacing one CEO with another. Despite these difficulties, the values that many family companies carry with them—like mutual support and loyalty—have made them worth the effort for Berkshire.

Rose was born on December 3, 1893, near Minsk, Belarus, into a family of eight children. Her father, Solomon Gorelick, was a rabbi; her mother, Chasia, ran a grocery store where Rose worked from the age of six. Rose, who stood at less than five feet tall, became a grocery clerk at thirteen and store manager at sixteen, supervising six men. At twenty, she married Isadore Blumkin, a shoe salesman.[2]

In 1916, before the Russian Revolution, the Blumkin family was destitute and fled to America. This required traveling separately. Two of Rose's siblings and her husband departed before her, and her parents and other siblings followed.[3] Rose managed her escape by sweet-talking a Russian border guard—demonstrating a skill in salesmanship that would prove of great value in her future.

When she arrived in the U.S., Rose lacked education (she had not even attended elementary school) and spoke no English. By 1922, the entire family reunited in Nebraska, where Rose and Isadore settled down and had four children. Rose learned English in her first few years in the country, sharpening her knowledge with tutorials from her eldest daughter based on what she had learned in school each day.

In Omaha, Isadore and Rose ran a secondhand clothing shop. Their business model was simple: cut prices, expand product offerings, and market heavily. After toiling in this business for years, Rose adopted a new vision in 1937. On a visit to Chicago, center of the country's wholesale furniture trade, she had seen the vast American Furniture Mart. Inspired, she decided to open a rival facility in Omaha, the Nebraska Furniture Mart, which would sell appliances, carpets, and home furniture.

The business was intensely competitive, with many area furniture sellers commanding abundant resources, ideal locations, and brand name recognition. Undeterred, Rose found ways to buy furniture cheaply and sell it at prices that beat the competition. She operated her business out of the family home, storing furniture and appliances in spare rooms and assuring enough sales to meet inventory bills on time. Such thrift and customer service produced favorable word of mouth around town. People interested in good deals on furniture were told to see Mrs. B., as she came to be known. Her credo also became famous: "Sell cheap, tell the truth, don't cheat nobody."

That motto, of course, could apply equally to other Berkshire subsidiaries. For example, Nebraska Furniture Mart's business model echoes that of GEICO's: both seek to be the low-cost seller and thereby generate enough volume to drive top-line sales for superior bottom-line results. Budget consciousness is a conservative description of the mindset at Nebraska Furniture Mart.

In response to Mrs. B.'s low-cost strategy, Nebraska Furniture Mart's competitors cried foul, as rivals often do when facing such a business model.

They alleged that Mrs. B. was using illegal tactics to outsell them with such low prices. Local businesses urged manufacturers to boycott Mrs. B., and at least one supplier complained that its suggested retail prices were being ignored.[4] Mrs. B. responded aggressively, finding other suppliers in neighboring cities at even lower cost that enabled her to cut prices yet again, gaining market share.

Nonplussed, adversaries sued Mrs. B., alleging violation of various contracts and fair trade laws. Mrs. B. turned that to her advantage by garnering positive publicity over the suits. She also got the cases thrown out by proving that she fairly, legally, and profitably sold carpeting at steep market discounts. According to legend, after making her case in court, she sold the judge $1,400 worth of carpeting.

Mrs. B.'s children joined her in operating the business. Her son, Louis ("Louie"), became president. Like his mother, he had a knack for buying wholesale appliances and furniture at low prices. Buffett wrote: "Louie says he had the best teacher, and Mrs. B. says she had the best student. They're both right."[5]

Mrs. B. and son Louie were joined in the family business by Louie's sons, all of whom devoted their working lives to it, just as their grandmother and father had. The entire family made it a point to gather each July 4 for a celebration where everyone sang "God Bless America"—exuberantly led by Mrs. B. in tribute to her immigrant past.

By 1983, Nebraska Furniture Mart operated out of a huge store—two hundred thousand square feet—and generated annual sales exceeding $100 million. A peerless operation nationally, the store did more volume than all of its Omaha-based competitors together.

Buffett, an Omaha native, was awestruck by the Blumkins' story and had always been interested in acquiring the business, but Mrs. B. consistently demurred. In 1983, the time was ripe, however, as Mrs. B. was nearing ninety and wanted to make a permanent home for her family's business, while continuing to manage it. Buffett impressed on Blumkin that Berkshire offered not only cash but autonomy and permanence. Berkshire bought 90 percent of Nebraska Furniture Mart, and family members kept the rest. The cash price was $60 million. Shortly after closing, as part of Berkshire's annual audit, its outside accountants appraised the company's value, based on an up-to-date inventory, at $85 million.[6]

By the late 1980s, the Blumkin grandchildren had climbed up the ranks, and Mrs. B. had become alienated. They encouraged Mrs. B. to retire in 1989 at age ninety-six, but she felt insulted. In response, she opened a rival store across the street—Mrs. B.'s Clearance and Factory Outlet—that gave the Nebraska Furniture Mart a run for its money. The family beseeched her to come back. In 1992, Berkshire helped smooth over the family dispute by buying Mrs. B.'s Clearance and Factory Outlet and merging it with Nebraska Furniture Mart. The family proceeded to open additional stores—in Kansas, Iowa, and Texas—using the business principles Mrs. B. had laid down decades earlier. The Blumkins still run the company today.

Mrs. B.'s skills—including drive and tenacity—were good for business. But not all such skills are good for the *families* of businesspeople. Such a mismatch between professional and personal traits can occur in anyone, but it is a common problem among family business operators. It is particularly difficult when a founder's persistence prevents him or her from retiring on terms that provide a satisfactory transition to succeeding generations. This was the Blumkin family's problem, and it was not easy to resolve.

With a reservoir of mutual support the family had developed since immigrating and with Berkshire's influence, the Blumkins were able to work out their problems. Berkshire's principle of operational autonomy played an important role in this. Both sides in the family feud saw Berkshire as unbiased, and both welcomed Berkshire's acquisition of Mrs. B.'s second business and its merger with Nebraska Furniture Mart. Berkshire benefits from the family values that bless the Blumkins; reciprocally, the Blumkins benefit from the supportive and resourceful Berkshire culture.

∿

As the Blumkin story indicates, one downside of the family business is difficulty in deciding how to move forward at turning points, when a founder refuses to retire, a business reaches a certain scale, senior family members face concerns about estate tax obligations, or younger family members develop new career interests. Berkshire's culture, along with its capital resources, offers solutions to the recurring challenges that vex family businesses, from succession struggles to coping with the emotional conflict that occurs when selling.

Selling the family business poses difficult decisions about managing the resulting wealth and handling the future. Family members can disagree, and individuals can be torn between staying involved to preserve a legacy versus the desire for liberation from heavy responsibilities. Berkshire's culture of permanence offers an attractive outcome. For families who wish to continue to be involved in managing the family business,

Berkshire likewise provides a solution. So valuable is Berkshire's culture—especially the values of permanence and autonomy—that business sellers undeniably treat it as a valuable part of what they receive on the sale. It is its culture that enables Berkshire to acquire companies at lower prices than rival bidders.

Take RC Willey Home Furnishings, a furniture store chain based in the western United States that the Blumkin family brought to Berkshire's attention. Berkshire acquired RC Willey in 1995 for $175 million, a price the selling family accepted despite receiving several competing offers greater than $200 million, attributing the difference to Berkshire culture.[7] For those eager to compute exchange rates between cultural traits and economic values, this case gives you a quantitative value for Berkshire's culture: in this case, it was worth $25 million to a family that owned a $200-million business—or one-eighth of the total in the exchange. The family received the funds plus the value of Berkshire culture; Berkshire gained a company that fits into its culture and helps to reinforce it.

RC Willey is a characteristically Berkshire company, beginning with its entrepreneurial founding in 1932 during the Great Depression. Like Samuel Tatelman, who sold furniture from his truck in Boston before opening Jordan's Furniture, Rufus Call Willey sold home appliances door to door in rural Syracuse, Utah, out of the back of his red pickup truck.[8] An electric company employee, Willey's moonlighting involved marketing Hotpoint brand ranges and refrigerators to people not yet accustomed to the electricity newly supplied to the area.[9] His employer encouraged this side business, as appliance usage stoked demand for electricity.

To entice sales, Willey let customers try the novelties for a week before committing; to close the deal, he would arrange three-year installment plans with seasonal payments due at harvest time. During World War II, when sales fell, Willey expanded his side business to include refurbishing used appliances he recovered from salvage yards. After the war, when sales rebounded, Willey established a small store adjacent to his home.

Pancreatic cancer cut Willey's life short in 1954, and people wondered whether the business could survive without RC. As a company history notes, "To his customers, RC Willey *was* the company."[10] His business would in fact continue under the leadership of his son-in-law, William H. ("Bill") Child, and Bill's brother Sheldon. Many family members joined them as employees over the years: their father; Bill's eight children and two sons-in-law; and Sheldon's two sons and one son-in-law.[11]

Child adhered to the values Willey had applied in building his business, especially his religious and work ethics and creative customer service. One thing changed, however. Willey had been a big spender and a naïve creditor, lending to customers with poor repayment histories. The result, when Child assumed control, was a company with more debt and weaker assets than expected. It took Child several years to stabilize the company's financial condition.[12] That harrowing experience taught Child indelible lessons in frugality. He rebuilt RC Willey without borrowing funds and by running credit checks on all customers.

After securing the company's finances, the Childs expanded the appliance business to include furniture and steadily enlarged the footprint of their store, growing it over the years from a mere six hundred square feet to one hundred thousand square feet. They opened a second store in 1969 and gradually added stores throughout the 1980s and 1990s, and also opened a large distribution center in Salt Lake City. To acquire the second store, rather than load the company with debt, Child used personal funds to buy land and construct the building and then leased the premises to the company until it could afford to own the land and store outright.[13]

Customer service ran the gamut from small courtesies to extraordinary acts. At the stores, the Childs offered free hot dogs to all its shoppers and small complimentary gifts like tape measures and yardsticks.[14] Deliveries were punctual, and the stores stocked as wide a range of lines as possible at the lowest possible cost. As for extraordinary service, in the early 1970s, the company RC Willey used to finance its customer warranties went bankrupt. Although RC Willey had no obligation to do so, it accepted responsibility and covered all the warranties.[15] The cost: $1.5 million; the gain: priceless customer affection.[16]

In 1975, RC Willey led the furniture industry in offering customer financing by issuing store credit cards. Doing so eliminated third-party lenders, enabling the company to charge a lower interest rate while earning additional profits. The innovation had an added tax advantage. Taxes on cash sales were due when made, whereas taxes on credit sales were deferred until the full amount due was received. By the early 1990s, RC Willey's profits from credit card operations exceeded $18 million annually, plus millions more from the tax advantage.[17]

Bill Child knew the Blumkin family from their roles in the furniture business. Irv Blumkin admired Bill Child and RC Willey and often mentioned this to Buffett.[18] In early 1995, Child told Blumkin that estate planning had led the family to consider selling. Child wanted to be sure the company would continue for decades.[19] Child sent Buffett the company's financial statements. Buffett was impressed by a steady 17-percent annual growth rate in sales and profits and the fact that the company was debt free.[20] Buffett promptly wrote back with a valuation summary. He and Child agreed on a deal and closed in short order. When Berkshire acquired RC Willey in 1995, it owned six stores and generated $257 million in annual sales.

Later, when Bill Child proposed opening a store outside of Utah, Buffett opposed the idea, as Child's Mormon religious beliefs prevent him from operating company stores on Sundays. Such practice is common in Utah, home to a large Mormon population, but Buffett was skeptical about whether a retailer could prosper elsewhere without the benefit of Sunday sales. Buffett explains what ensued:[21]

> Bill then insisted on a truly extraordinary proposition: He would personally buy the land and build the store—for about $9 million as it turned out—and would sell it to us at his cost if it proved to be successful. On the other hand, if sales fell short of his expectations [$30 million in first-year sales],[22] we could exit the business without paying Bill a cent. This outcome, of course, would leave him with a huge investment in an empty building. I told him that I appreciated his offer but felt that if Berkshire was going to get the upside, it should also take the downside. Bill said nothing doing: If there was to be failure because of his religious beliefs, he wanted to take the blow personally.

RC Willey's Idaho store opened in 1999 and was an instant success, ringing up sales of $85 million during 2000. Child transferred the property to Berkshire, and Berkshire wrote him a check. As Buffett noted, highlighting the uniqueness of Berkshire's corporate culture that this represents: "If a manager has behaved similarly at some other public corporation, I haven't heard about it."[23]

RC Willey continued to grow, opening additional stores in California, Idaho, and Nevada. In 2001, after forty-six years at the helm, Bill Child stepped down as CEO and president. But to this day it remains a family business: Child's nephew, Jeffrey S. Child, is now president; his nephew-in-law, Scott L. Hymas, is CEO; and another nephew, Curtis Child, is CFO.[24]

~

Experts on family business routinely advise members to plan for succession, engage professional managerial assistance, and use a paid board of advisers. Despite such routine advice, families often hesitate to bring in outsiders. As a result, when the family business faces a crossroads, it may be unprepared.

Such were the woes of Houston-based Star Furniture Company when, once again, Berkshire rescued an excellent family business from fortune's fate.[25] As in other deals, the financial price Berkshire paid was only part of the exchange. The rest of the remuneration was in the value of Berkshire culture, especially autonomy and permanence.

Star Furniture was a multiple-family business founded in 1912, owned by and supporting seven different families. The son of one, Melvyn Wolff, joined the company reluctantly, as his partners did not embrace his entrepreneurial vision. The company struggled: there were too many owners; it had too little capital and too much debt. It tended to make meager profits, and in some years, lost money.

Wolff began to force changes in 1962. Until then, he aimed to outperform his company's chief rival, a massive furniture store twenty-five times its size. He finally figured out that such an effort was doomed. He learned in a marketing seminar not to "attack a superior force along a broad front."[26] This meant not trying to emulate the larger store, which offered a selection for every taste, but to carve out a niche. Doing research, Wolff identified what niche his rival was weakest in and riveted on it: the high end of the middle market.

To seize this niche required expansion and therefore capital, which the beleaguered company lacked. After striking out with all local banks in Houston, a friend connected Wolff with a banker in New York, who agreed to make a big loan with one condition: he required an audited financial statement. Wolff protested, arguing that was expensive and unnecessary. The banker explained its importance: "For all I know, your accountant could be your brother-in-law." Wolff then laughed out loud. His accountant was, in fact, his brother-in-law.

Wolff's partners opposed the loan and the expansion plan. So he made a buyout offer, funded by selling the store the company owned and closing two it rented—leaving it with three to nurture. At that point, Wolff enlisted his sister, Shirley Toomin, to join the business. Over the next two decades, the siblings focused solely on the high-end middle market. Brother and sister drove impressive growth, gradually moving operations toward the freeways that crisscross Houston and honing the company's image to its target market. By 1996, Star was among the larger furniture store chains in the United States.

Wolff and Toomin had virtually their entire net worth in the stores, and they wanted to diversify. They were concerned that, on their deaths, their estates would be saddled with large tax bills that could be met only by selling stores. The scenario was anathema because it would displace the scores of loyal employees who had spent their careers helping build the business.

The siblings had to start this project from scratch, which was not easy. In retaining advisers, they considered all the alternatives: an employee stock ownership program to vest ownership in the employees, an initial public offering (IPO), a merger with a comparable furniture store chain, or sale to a number of larger chains or financial buyers. At first, they opted for the IPO, as pursuing it enabled the preservation of other options in case the IPO did not succeed. Preparing for the IPO took work—meeting minimum volume levels and numbers of stores in additional cities and hiring professional management. In the end, however, they realized that neither the IPO nor the other solutions provided the liquidity, autonomy, and permanence they sought.

That's when it occurred to Wolff to connect with Berkshire. He had heard about it often over the years from the Blumkins and the Childs. A few days before Berkshire's 1997 annual meeting, Wolff asked bankers at Salomon Brothers to help him reach Buffett; Wolff soon heard from Robert Denham, a fellow Texan and counsel to Berkshire, whom Buffett had enlisted to help rehabilitate Salomon after its bond trading scandal in the 1990s. At Buffett's invitation, Wolff attended the Berkshire meeting and was impressed with the culture he detected.

A few days later, Buffett and Wolff met in New York. Buffett offered a price and said, in line with Berkshire practice, that it was non-negotiable. Wolff tried to negotiate anyway but to no avail. In the end, the deal made sense, not only in its strict financial terms but in giving Wolff the intangibles he sought for his company and his family, notably autonomy and permanence.

∾

All the planning in the world cannot solve every unique family business problem. Few problems are more acute than those facing senior family members torn between a desire to protect the family and to be free of the business. But it is this kind of dilemma that Berkshire culture can fix.

One such case concerned Helzberg Diamond Shops, Inc., a third-generation jewelry chain Berkshire acquired in 1995—the same year it acquired RC Willey. Helzberg was founded in 1915 by Russian immigrant Morris Helzberg.[27] All Morris's children worked in the store, and the youngest, Barnett, at age fourteen, took leadership when Morris suffered a disabling stroke and the older brothers were off at college or fighting in World War I. Barnett expanded the business from a single Kansas City store to a chain of dozens before handing it over to his son Barnett Jr. in 1963.

Barnett Jr., who had worked at the company since 1956, faced a shifting demographic: most Helzberg stores were in downtowns where traffic was declining as shopping malls emerged in the suburbs. To address the shift, Barnett Jr. first began closing the downtown stores, shrinking the chain's size to fifteen, before rebounding with an aggressive expansion program during the 1970s. Barnett Jr. launched a marketing campaign that became a pop sensation: "I Am Loved." The company put this slogan on lapel pins and buttons it gave away in the stores. Evoking the era's love-in spirit was the tag line: "If you can't give your love a diamond, at least speak your feelings with an *I Am Loved* button." The slogan—still strong today—soon appeared on drinking glasses, golf balls, and souvenir items. They were handed out to millions of potential customers.

By 1989, Helzberg had grown to eighty-one stores, and Barnett Jr. was beginning to tire of his job. He realized he was overworked the day his seven-year-old son wrote "sleep" on a school assignment asking what his father did best.[28] Barnett Jr. opted to curtail his role and turn the presidency over to Jeffrey Comment, who had been an executive at John Wanamaker & Co., a Philadelphia-based department store. Comment was the first person outside the Helzberg family to hold an executive position at the company. He drove rapid growth by opening more and larger stores, including "superstores" opened in strip malls.

In 1994, Barnett Jr., mulling the future of the family business, considered strategic options. At the time, the company was the nation's third largest jewelry store chain, with 143 stores and annual sales nearing $300 million. Barnett Jr. consulted financial firms in New York but, averse to layoffs and divestitures, dismissed typical options such as an IPO or selling to a competitor.[29]

Barnett Jr. had mixed feelings common to heads of family businesses. He acknowledged that although Comment had helped relieve the managerial burden, he still felt a great responsibility. He sought a way to remove this weight while preserving the business. His dream, having been a Berkshire shareholder since 1989 and having attended its annual meetings, was selling to Berkshire.[30] The dream came true by chance.

In New York meeting with Morgan Stanley in May 1994, a week after that year's Berkshire annual meeting, as Barnett Jr. strolled on Fifth Avenue, he happened to see Buffett near a crosswalk at 58th Street.[31] Barnett Jr. introduced himself and gave Buffett a short "elevator" pitch about Helzberg Diamonds.[32] Buffett invited Barnett to send him the details. Helzberg's financial picture was impressive, and Buffett loved the story of a single shop becoming a large chain. Sales growth was strong: $10 million in 1974; $53 million in 1984; $282 million in 1994. The stores were large, on average ringing up $2 million in annual sales, a far greater per-store productivity than its competitors.

When the two later met, Buffett asked Barnett Jr. to name a price, customary in Berkshire acquisitions, but then the two haggled over it, unusual for Berkshire acquisitions.[33] Barnett Jr. had consulted with an accountant from Deloitte to identify what they considered a comparable Berkshire acquisition.[34] On that basis, Barnett Jr. lobbed what he knew was a high asking price, $334 million payable in Berkshire stock.[35] As a rule of thumb, jewelry retailers are worth about half their annual gross sales plus inventory, putting Helzberg's fair market value at $141 million plus inventory. Buffett countered at less than half Barnett Jr.'s asking price. The two finally settled on $167 million.

Barnett Jr. received much higher offers for the company.[36] But the Berkshire deal was worth more than its face value because it also assured keeping the business intact, maintaining headquarters in Kansas City, and retaining personnel—all important to the Helzberg family.[37]

∾

If you can imagine the relief Barnett Helzberg Jr. felt after landing his third-generation jewelry chain a permanent home with Berkshire, consider the mindset of fourth-generation family members dealing with the legacy of their business, as was the case with Ben Bridge Jeweler, Inc. Samuel Silverman began the business in 1912 in downtown Seattle. In 1922, he invited his son-in-law, Ben Bridge, to join the operation as a partner. In 1927, when Silverman retired, he sold his interest in the business to Bridge, who renamed it eponymously.

Bridge adopted two defining traits that have been handed down through the family company. The first is a policy, strictly followed and applied to both family and non-family members, of only promoting from within the firm.[38] Such an esteemed practice provided a discernible benefit to the company: low employee turnover.

The second is a policy of conservatism in expansion, never overextending the company's financial resources. The company always maintained a slow rate of growth in numbers of stores. Mr. Bridge instilled such budget consciousness as the result of personal lessons learned during the Great Depression. He was nearly forced to declare bankruptcy, an embarrassing agony he swore his company would not face a second time. As his grandson Ed Bridge remarked years later: "He never wanted to owe anybody again."[39]

Ben's sons, Herb and Robert ("Bob"), carried on these traditions of integrity and budget consciousness as they slowly nurtured the business beyond its Seattle origins. Bob managed the second shop, in Bremerton, Washington. During the 1950s, it struggled, however, and never had the exciting feel of the Seattle flagship, which his brother and father ran. Herb, meanwhile, quarreled with his father about how to run the Seattle shop, leading him to threaten to take a job in Denver at Zales, a competitor. Ben Bridge called a family meeting.[40]

"Boys," the old man told his sons, as he laid his store keys on the table, "I'm out."[41] In the interest of keeping the family business together, Ben Bridge explained to Herb and Bob, he was leaving it. "He wanted the family business to be a unity venture," his grandson Ed reflected long afterward.[42] Such aspirations are common in family businesses, but it is rarely easy for the patriarch to surrender the reins, making this gesture a tribute to Ben Bridge.

The Bridge brothers got the message and united to run the family business. Faithful to their father's teachings, they pursued expansion cautiously. One early opportunity they took was running the jewelry departments for all J. C. Penney stores in the Seattle area. After developing skills in chain-store management in a shopping mall environment, the brothers gained confidence about their ability to expand Ben Bridge. By 1978, they had made Ben Bridge into a six-store chain.

It was then that their children, cousins Ed and Jon, stepped up to leadership positions. They had spent their youths working in the stores, sweeping floors and polishing silver. In 1978, after college, Ed went on the sales floor. Within a few months, however, the company's long-time chief financial officer (CFO) announced his retirement. Ed was tapped to replace him at just twenty-two years of age. Ed was promoted again three years later to become head merchandiser, while cousin Jon, fresh out of the military after his own stint on the sales floor, became CFO.

Thus began the careers of Ed and Jon, who would continue to carefully shepherd the slow growth of the family business. They opened stores in Portland, Oregon, in 1980, and in San Mateo, California, in 1982. By 1990 Ben Bridge Jeweler had thirty-nine stores, twenty of them in California, a much more rapid rate of growth than their elders had logged, though still slow by industry standards.

In 1990, Ed and Jon formally assumed managerial leadership of the fourth-generation family business and carried on the company's traditions faithfully—and prosperously. Store sales volumes grew, profits rose, and expansion followed more easily than the company's patriarchs could have imagined. By the end of the 1990s, Ben Bridge Jeweler had sixty-two stores in eleven states.[43]

At this time, the Bridge cousins faced a nagging concern of many family businesses: the company's long-term future. That concern entailed numerous sub-issues, including succession to assure managerial continuity and resources to enable the payment of estate taxes. As with their predecessors—Silverman, Ben, Herb, and Bob—cousins Ed and Jon looked to guarantee their family company's continued existence for future generations. They considered the familiar range of options, including going public, but such routes risked jeopardizing the company's virtues and culture.

Instead, in December 1999, Ed called Buffett. Barnett Helzberg Jr. had told the Bridges that Berkshire would be a great fit and a wonderful home.[44] Helzberg assured them that the family could run its business as it had in the past. At Berkshire, Ben Bridge would join a collection of companies that shared the aspiration for family continuity along with other cultural traits, including budget consciousness and a reputation for integrity.

Ed explained the business to Buffett and supplied the most recent financial figures. Buffett savored the company's annual sales growth at its stores: 9 percent, 11 percent, 13 percent, 10 percent, 12 percent, 21 percent, and 7 percent over the previous seven years. He appreciated the company's prudent approach to expansion. And, Buffett also liked that the company was managed by the fourth generation of the family and knew from Barnett Jr. that the company and the family enjoyed extraordinary reputations.

Ed said that it was vital to the Bridge family that the company be allowed to operate as it had always operated. The family did not want directives from a larger owner when they and their kin had a century of successful experience. Buffett promised Ed that he and Jon would be in charge. They knew they could trust this assurance.

Buffett named an offering price, half cash and half stock, and the Bridge family accepted. The company prospers today, expanding into new stores cautiously while sustaining impressive levels of growth in same-store sales. Ben Bridge Jeweler is more than a century old and is now in its fifth generation of family management.[45]

~

Many families selling to Berkshire, like the Tatelman brothers of Jordan's Furniture, and the Bridge family, shared sales proceeds with their employees. When Wolff and Toomin did so for Star's employees, Buffett wrote: "[We] love it when we become partners with people who behave like that."[46] After Barnett Helzberg Jr. did so, Buffett noted: "When someone behaves that generously, you know you are going to be treated right as a buyer."[47]

Intangibles like these—partnership, generosity, fairness—glue family businesses together. Along with valuing soft factors, such as family identity and legacy, these traits help family firms prosper indefinitely, as founders go, second-generation siblings join, and third-generation cousins come to be co-managers. Berkshire seeks out family businesses whose members prize such qualities and offers them autonomy and permanence. The mutual payoff is a durable, multi-generational family business.

Having reached its fifth generation, Ben Bridge holds the endurance record among Berkshire subsidiaries, rivaled by such fourth-generation dynasties as Benjamin Moore and Fechheimer Brothers, and many third-generation firms. Sustenance is rarely easy for a family business, but the more members embrace these intangible values, the greater their economic payoff. Berkshire culture attracts and sustains such businesses.

7

Self-starters

Among Berkshire's entrepreneurs are several recipients of the Horatio Alger Award, given annually by the society of that name to businesspeople who epitomize the dream of moving from poverty to prosperity in a single generation.[1] In addition to Jim Clayton, winners include Albert Lee Ueltschi, a Kentucky-born entrepreneur who founded FlightSafety International Inc. While many associate entrepreneurship with a habit of incubating businesses and moving on to the next one, Berkshire's entrepreneurs are more inclined to focus on innovation within a business and to toil assiduously in that one domain.

In the case of Ueltschi (pronounced *yool*-chee), it was all about aviation. At age sixteen, the Kentucky native opened a hamburger stand called Little Hawk and used the profits to take flying lessons. His passion for flight led him to teach other aviators using a plane he acquired with a loan secured by Little Hawk.[2] In 1939, Ueltschi was training a federal aviation inspector to conduct snap rolls in an open cockpit plane. On one maneuver, as the plane rolled, Ueltschi's seat unhinged and his parachute failed. Ueltschi survived but was convinced that there had to be a safer way of teaching aviators to fly. Ueltschi would eventually create the world's premier pilot training school, using flight simulators to teach routine patterns and emergency drills.

In 1942, Ueltschi began working with Pan American World Airways (Pan Am), the unofficial U.S. flag carrier, whose pilots were known as "Masters of Ocean Flying Boats."[3] In 1946, he became the personal pilot for Pan Am founder and legendary businessman, Juan Trippe, a job Ueltschi would hold until he stopped piloting planes at age fifty-one in 1968. From this vantage point, Ueltschi perceived another need: formal training for a growing civilian pilot corps.

After World War II, the dominant segment of airline traffic was private corporate fleets carrying company managers. Corporations would buy retired military aircraft and refurbish them for their executives' use. But many pilots lacked training to fly these planes. To provide it, in 1951, Ueltschi started FlightSafety, which he operated out of the Marine Air Terminal at LaGuardia Airport in New York, where the company's headquarters remain today.

At first, Ueltschi hired experienced commercial pilots from the major airlines to conduct training. Practice involved using both the client's aircraft and instrument trainers Ueltschi rented from commercial airlines. Early clients included Burlington Industries, Eastman Kodak, and National Distillers. As his company succeeded and private business aviation proliferated, Ueltschi made a big bet on the future of flight training: he mortgaged his house to raise funds to expand FlightSafety.[4] He also plowed all of FlightSafety's profits back into the business, relying on his Pan Am salary for personal and family expenses. In another innovative financing device, he got several corporate customers, including Alcoa, Coca-Cola, and Eastman Kodak, to prepay for services five years in advance.[5]

These funds brought Ueltschi closer to his vision, when in 1961, he acquired several flight trainers of his own. They were used to teach pilots to "fly blind," meaning to rely on instrument panels rather than eyesight. After Pan Am created a business jet division to market Falcon Jets for a French manufacturer, Ueltschi persuaded Trippe to include pilot and technician training as part of the purchase price.[6]

In 1961, Ueltschi recruited Bruce N. Whitman, a young entrepreneur equally passionate about flight, then working for the National Business Aviation Association. Whitman became FlightSafety's number two—a role he played until finally succeeding Ueltschi when the latter retired in 2003 at age eighty-six.[7] Ueltschi and Whitman grew FlightSafety steadily through the late 1960s, taking the company public in 1968, with Ueltschi retaining a 34-percent interest.

By the early 1970s, FlightSafety's principal competition in the business aviation market was from aircraft manufacturers, which provided pilot training as part of the purchase price of new aircraft. Ueltschi and Whitman realized that FlightSafety's success depended on persuading manufacturers to outsource this function. They explained to manufacturers that investing in FlightSafety training would improve their aircraft's safety record, a valuable reputation for which customers are willing to pay.[8]

During the 1970s, most manufacturers signed up with FlightSafety. They realized they would do better focusing on design and production while putting training in the hands of specialists. Learjet, for instance, opted to delegate pilot training for its aircraft to FlightSafety, which built a training center at a Learjet plant. FlightSafety soon struck similar deals with other manufacturers, solidifying its business position by 1980. Before long, FlightSafety provided training for the planes built by most business aircraft manufacturers, including Beechcraft, Bombardier, Cessna, Dassault Falcon, Embraer, and Gulfstream.

Further growth in the 1980s came from expansion into military pilot training, with FlightSafety winning a 1984 Air Force contract at Fort Rucker in Alabama. In a budget-conscious move, it was the lowest bidder by virtue of having acquired a facility near the base and installing a simulator there.

In addition, this entrepreneurial culture spurred the creation of a new profit center, manufacturing and selling simulators, which still prospers today. The culture also prompted the development of training programs for ship captains operating oil tankers at customers like Texaco, commanders of military vessels for the U.S. Navy, and operators of nuclear power plants. But these ventures eventually closed as FlightSafety opted to stick with what it does best, Whitman explained in an interview for this book.

In the 1980s, FlightSafety courted regional commercial airlines. In a replay of its efforts in the 1970s, it persuaded these potential customers to outsource pilot training. These airlines agreed that letting specialists provide this expertise would enable them to concentrate on scheduling, routing, marketing, and customer service. Although the major U.S. commercial carriers did not generally outsource training, FlightSafety occasionally landed their business, as it did with TWA in the 1980s.

FlightSafety's success was fortified when insurance companies began crediting customers whose pilots had taken refresher training courses that FlightSafety offered. One insurer, USAIG, developed a program called "Safety Bucks," offering a discount from their premiums if the customer used it to pay for FlightSafety training.[9] Next to come around were labor unions, initially opposed to outsourcing but finally grasping its value, too. Overseas frontiers followed, as the company won contracts to train young pilots for international carriers such as Air France, All Nippon Airways, Japan Airlines, Korea Air, Lufthansa, and Swissair. FlightSafety opened training facilities across the globe near aircraft manufacturing plants, commercial airline headquarters, or airports.

In the mid-1990s, Ueltschi turned to succession. He had always promised Whitman that he would succeed him as chief executive, but Ueltschi was concerned about takeover risk upon exiting with his block of stock.[10] Then, serendipitously, in late 1996, a shareholder of both FlightSafety and Berkshire who knew of Ueltschi's dilemma wrote to Robert Denham, the long-time Berkshire lawyer and Buffett confidant who had helped orchestrate Berkshire's acquisition of Star Furniture.[11] Buffett called Ueltschi to discuss FlightSafety's future. When they met for a hamburger lunch in New York, they instantly connected and signed a deal within a month. Berkshire offered FlightSafety shareholders either cash or stock.

At the time of Berkshire's acquisition, FlightSafety had operations around the world using 175 simulators for a wide range of planes. A capital-intensive business, simulators cost as much as $19 million apiece. In the next eight years, FlightSafety added more than one hundred, making its aggregate cost of simulators $3 billion.[12] Given that pilots are trained one at a time, Buffett estimated that the company required $3.50 of capital investment to produce $1 in revenue. High operating margins are thus vital to yield reasonable returns on capital. Whitman—among the handful of Berkshire CEOs who have spent more than fifty years with their company—has led FlightSafety to generate those returns.

Today, FlightSafety operates 320 simulators and has manufactured more than eight hundred.[13] In any given year, FlightSafety conducts as many as 1.2 million hours of instruction, training 100,000 pilots, technicians, and other aviation professionals for airlines and more than 3,800 corporate flight departments.[14] Whitman has diversified FlightSafety into helicopter training—on models including AgustaWestland, Airbus, Bell, and Sikorsky—and has grown its U.S. military training component. FlightSafety teammates, as Whitman calls the company's workforce, are sustained by entrepreneurial passion, adding markets by demonstrating the value of outsourcing training to a trusted expert.

~

FlightSafety's largest customer is fellow Berkshire subsidiary NetJets, a company created by Richard T. Santulli, who resides with Ueltschi and Whitman in the pantheon of Berkshire's great entrepreneurs. The company's roots date to 1964, when several retired Air Force generals formed Executive Jet Aviation, Inc.[15] The company chartered business jets for private use and earned a reputation for excellence in customer service and safety, although temporary ownership by the Penn Central Railroad from the late 1960s through the railroad's scandal-ridden bankruptcy gave it a bad name for a few years.

In 1984, Santulli, a Brooklyn-born mathematics whiz with two degrees from Polytechnic University of New York, bought the business. He had spent the 1970s writing computer programs for Goldman Sachs, eventually running the firm's leasing unit. In 1980, he embarked on his own.

At Executive Jet, Santulli's math background proved valuable.[16] Over the previous two decades, his predecessors kept detailed records on the company's charter aircraft concerning destinations, layovers, seasonality, flight duration, and equipment maintenance. His mathematician's mind perceived intriguing relationships; his entrepreneurial instincts sensed lucrative business opportunities.

Harvesting the data, Santulli gradually came to envision a new approach to the business. Instead of chartering planes one at a time, he would sell fractional interests in given planes to multiple owners. His company would then operate the fleet in exchange for customer service fees. The time-share concept had worked in the real estate world; why not aviation?

The math/business problem Santulli solved was this: if he sold a certain number of shares, how many additional planes would be necessary to enable guaranteeing customers' use of their plane? The answer varied by scale: with all of the shares in one hundred planes fully sold, for example, the company would need to own another twenty-six (called its "core fleet") to guarantee availability for all customers; with eight hundred planes sold, a core fleet of eighty would do, still a capital-intensive venture but driving higher returns.[17]

With skill and daring over the next decade, Santulli turned this vision into a billion-dollar business. In 1986, Santulli bought eight Cessna Citation S/IIs and recruited a top-flight crew to pilot the fleet.[18] Even then, there existed a large clientele who hated the hassles of scheduled commercial airline travel. But only a few could afford private jets, and the chartering option brought its own headaches. Santulli's model of fractional ownership offered something new and in between: the ease and freedom of private aviation at a fraction of the cost.

Still, target customers were affluent, and services priced at a premium. Fractional ownership entails paying a share of the plane's cost in exchange for a part of its use. Depending on a plane's size and model, the purchase price runs one-sixteenth to one-half of the total, in exchange for fifty to four hundred hours of annual flying time. A monthly maintenance fee is added, along with an hourly charge for flight time used.

As with traditional private planes, advantages of fractional aviation include flexibility. Instead of finding flights commercial airlines offer, customers name departure and arrival times and locations, often using smaller, more convenient airports, shorter flight routes, and swifter travel times. Another key advantage: skirting the cumbersome security checks at commercial airports.

Like the real estate time-share business it mimicked, NetJets, as the company came to be called, drew controversy from its earliest days. Crews at established corporate flight departments sniffed that it was predatory, charter aviation firms portrayed its economic features as a legalized Ponzi scheme, and owners of private aircraft frowned on the potential adverse effect on how jets are valued.[19]

Despite controversy, the company quickly attracted several hundred customers, generating considerable revenue. But costs, especially the costs of owning the company's core fleet, were high, which kept margins low. The company narrowly escaped bankruptcy in the early 1990s, when Santulli personally guaranteed bank loans of $125 million.[20] Competitors also entered the field, making it difficult to raise prices, particularly if NetJets was to maintain the leadership advantages of having been the industry's first mover.[21]

To stay in first place required acquiring more planes in inventory to sell, which also meant enlarging the core fleet. To obtain capital, Santulli turned to his friends at Goldman Sachs, which acquired a 25-percent stake in the company.[22] Santulli, along with his brother Vincent, also an entrepreneur, got the customer base up to nearly seven hundred, attracting numerous large corporate customers like General Electric.[23] Other clients included wealthy individuals who used the NetJets service for personal use: Arnold Schwarzenegger, David Letterman, Pete Sampras, Tiger Woods . . . and Warren Buffett.

By the late 1990s, Santulli had cemented the company's leadership, generating more than $1 billion in revenue.[24] At that point, Goldman Sachs thought it time to exit, favoring an IPO. Santulli demurred. The entrepreneur planned to launch NetJets in Europe, extending his franchise.[25] But profits do not come quickly in this business. Start-up costs for a four-plane core fleet were $100 million. The short-term outlook of public markets is inhospitable to such a venture, which needs patient capital. So in May 1998, Santulli called Buffett, who as a customer had extolled NetJets as friendly, efficient, and safe.

Buffett saw huge potential at NetJets in both North America and Europe. At the time, NetJets served more than 1,000 customers, employed 650 pilots, and managed 163 jets (including twenty-three in its core fleet).[26] Its balance sheet was lean, with debt of only $102 million. The safety record was impeccable, and all NetJets pilots trained at FlightSafety. With Berkshire's capital and credit to guarantee NetJets's debt, Buffett and Santulli shared a vision of vast growth and quickly cut a deal.

Goldman Sachs was disappointed in the price it received in the sale to Berkshire of its 25-percent stake.[27] It preferred an IPO, as proceeds would have been far greater. In an interview for this book, Santulli explained that he favored the sale to Berkshire because, along with the money, he valued the Berkshire culture of autonomy and permanence.[28] Buffett told Santulli that NetJets was Santullli's tapestry, Berkshire supplying paint and brushes but otherwise staying out of the way.[29]

During Berkshire's first decade of ownership, NetJets grew rapidly. It financed expansion of the core fleet and inventory for sale, increasing both assets and liabilities; it delivered profits most years, reaching $206 million in 2007 and $220 million in 2008. Buffett regularly cheered about NetJets's industry domination, with the largest fleet value of any rival by far.[30] Santulli was widely seen as among the few Berkshire subsidiary chiefs who might one day succeed Buffett at Berkshire's helm.

Beginning in 2009, however, the economic recession reduced the value of all asset classes.[31] For NetJets's vast airplane fleet, that meant a $700 million write-down, erasing several years of profits and tallying a large net loss that year.[32] The debt, of course, remained, by then $1.9 billion. With expenses also running high, Buffett began to see problems at NetJets, arising from its sizable debt and capital needs, reduced asset valuations, and the cost of its young European division. In doing so, Buffett said he had "failed" Berkshire shareholders in his stewardship of NetJets.[33] While continuing to applaud Santulli's record for customer safety and satisfaction, Buffett in late 2009 sent in a new chief executive to prune costs and pare debt.

The new chief, David Sokol, who had intervened at Johns Manville in 2007, was also on the short list to succeed Buffett. Sokol cut costs aggressively, as he had when building MidAmerican Energy, but doing so at NetJets was a high-wire act, given that it offers a premium brand, not a low-cost commodity product. Sokol's process was painful, summarily firing employees, selling assets, and provoking resentment within the company for failing to respect the NetJets corporate culture, including its entrepreneurial roots and high-end services.[34] Also controversial: in late 2010, NetJets acquired Marquis Jet Partners, a firm that sells thinner slices of NetJets offerings, down to 1/32 of an interest.

In early 2011, however, Sokol resigned from Berkshire under a cloud for buying stock in the Lubrizol Corporation a week before pitching the company as a Berkshire acquisition, a story that will be recounted in the next chapter. Sokol's successor at NetJets, Jordan Hansell, an Iowa lawyer Sokol had named as chief counsel for NetJets, now steers the entrepreneurial firm between the premium brand it is and the budget consciousness of Berkshire culture. Santulli, for his part, launched a new helicopter-leasing business, Milestone Aviation, whose pilots, naturally, train at FlightSafety. His company prospers today; Buffett and Santulli remain good friends.

⁓

Moats include becoming the low-cost producer in a commodity business—as with Berkshire's furniture stores—or being the only or a leading producer of a desired service—as with FlightSafety and NetJets. Clayton Homes developed a moat through an unrivaled commitment to customer affordability; Benjamin Moore carved out a niche in the high end of the paint business. Other business models at Berkshire include honing a unique distribution channel (e.g., the direct-sales marketing of Scott Fetzer's Kirby vacuums) or providing commercial items that save business customers money (ISCAR/IMC).

Product branding is among conspicuous and commonly cited sources of business moats. Many people seem to believe that Buffett's investment tenets limit him to companies with brand-name recognition, like American Express or Coke. Such branding is valuable to help a company generate and maintain market leadership and profitability, but this view of Buffett misses more than half the picture at Berkshire. Of the entrepreneurial routes to creating a moat, branding is one of the more difficult. It takes a combination of appeal, skill, and luck—a desirable product creatively pitched that clicks for often-inscrutable reasons.

The combination worked for Garanimals, a line of children's products launched in 1972 by Garan Inc., a company whose entrepreneurial spirit not only helped to propel that brand but to overcome adversity facing

American textile manufacturers. The company was formed in New York City's garment district in 1957, when seven competitors merged, choosing the name Garan as an abbreviation of guarantee (which is how the company's name is pronounced).[35] Sports shirts were its biggest seller, made in factories in Kentucky and Mississippi and mostly sold under private labels through mid-market department stores like R. H. Macy's, Sears, and F. W. Woolworth's.

In 1961, Garan went public, raising funds to finance its own receivables without having to rely on "factors," third parties who manage and collect merchandisers' receivables for a percentage of the balance, a standard but costly industry practice. A majority of shares were acquired by senior managers, including the president, Samuel Dorsky, and his number two and successor, Seymour Lichtenstein—another Berkshire chief who has spent a fifty-year career with his company.

Sales and profits rose as Garan diversified product lines and leased or built more manufacturing facilities in numerous locations across the South. After a rough patch in the late 1960s and early 1970s due to the pervasive problem of rivals using cheap foreign labor and international shipping, Garan regained its footing by imposing cost controls, decentralizing, and increasing productivity.

In 1972, it introduced the Garanimals label, a children's clothing line that soon became a best-seller for the company and remains so today. The Garanimals line offers a unique way to mix and match outfits using color and style coding that is easy for children to master. The concept reflects the connection between how children are dressed and self-esteem. Self-confidence arises from an accomplished sense of creativity and independence. Garan retained the noted psychologist Dr. Joyce Brothers as a consultant, who attested that the Garanimals brand "helps the preschooler to handle his or her own wardrobe. That sense of 'I can' fosters the child's growing sense of independence."[36] Parents valued this concept, which boosted Garan's market share and resulting business value.

During the 1980s, Garan joined other textile manufacturers in moving production abroad to sustain growth and expansion, though continued some domestic manufacturing. When Walmart emerged as a force in retailing, it became one of Garan's largest customers. Garan also obtained licensing deals to decorate its garments with collegiate logos and Disney characters. The early 1990s were prosperous, but rising costs, intense competition, and continued domestic manufacturing impaired performance in the latter part of the decade. Increasing reliance on Walmart proved a mixed blessing; it was a valuable account to have but stoked worries in the financial community about dependence on Walmart's fortunes.

Lichenstein and his colleagues coped by operating on strict budgets, broadening the Garanimals line, and increasing its manufacturing abroad. Garan used little debt and had paid a dividend every year since 1962. Although publicly held, 40 percent of Garan's stock was concentrated: 12 percent owned by Lichenstein, 12 percent by Dorsky's heirs, and a further 16 percent by other managers. In 2002, recognizing a need for additional capital to sustain its position, but without compromising its continuation, management contacted Buffett. A deal was soon made, and another team of entrepreneurial managers joined Berkshire.

~

Justin cowboy boots are as well known as kindred western brands Colt 45 guns, Levi's jeans, and Stetson hats.[37] H. J. Justin founded a boot repair service in 1879; following his death in 1908, H. J.'s three sons took over and began making cowboy boots. In the 1930s and 1940s, as the cowboy lifestyle faded with the storied Wild West, the brothers worried about the future of the cowboy boot business. So they redirected toward a more general boot and shoe clientele.

The founder's grandson, John Justin Jr., born in 1917, was a hard-driving entrepreneur from a young age. Justin Jr. sought control of the family business and eventually won it. He did not like how his elders had run the business by committee and wanted to be the sole leader. Once in control, he demanded dedication from employees. For example, he required nightly reports from his sales force to assure himself that they worked as hard as they could and met every possible account each day.[38]

Justin Jr. had a passion for his product, its Texas heritage, and his family's name. He had great respect for the cowboys whose boots his family had made for so long. Even as he sought to expand the target market beyond cowboys, for the longest time he did not even own a pair of cowboy boots. Only after his wife chided him, at age thirty-six, did he start wearing his products. Thanks to her, the man became a walking advertisement for the brand.[39]

Another oddity: Justin Jr. had never ridden a horse until 1954, at age thirty-seven. He took a crash course in Cheyenne, Wyoming, that year when visiting an annual rodeo event. Justin explained the reason he rode: "I knew it would be good for business."[40] He grew to love riding and ended up participating in rodeo events for the next thirty-five years. The Wyoming trip inspired another tradition that would last decades: the Justins hosted an annual supper party in honor of the Fort Worth stock rodeo show.[41] The tradition fostered deep relationships with rodeo stars and their fans, a valuable customer base.

In 1954, much in the way that Jim Clayton built affordable mobile homes and Richard Santulli offered fractional interests in aircraft at NetJets, Justin Jr. identified a need in the marketplace that would prove lucrative: the rodeo.[42] Rodeo riders sought a boot more suitable to calf-roping, which requires a flatter heel than typical cowboy boots. Justin experimented but kept meeting difficulties combining the traditional upper of a cowboy boot with a shoe-like heel. The designs didn't look or feel right. Inspiration struck when Justin Jr. recalled a military boot used by the ROTC at Texas A&M University. He adapted the military design for rodeo use and named it the Roper. It took a great deal of trial and error, but the Justin team finally got it right. The Roper was a hit with the rodeo set and beyond, becoming one of the company's best sellers.

Justin Jr. was a fan of Texas Christian University football.[43] In the mid-1950s, he tailored a special pair of boots to wear to their games. Inlaid on the front was a horned frog, the team's mascot and nickname. Justin Jr. had once again invented a product tailored to his customer base—other fans clamored for them and Justin produced them in large numbers. Press coverage prompted interest from fans of other schools, so the company turned the whimsical innovation into a line, making boots for all of Texas Christian's rivals. Long before such university apparel branding proliferated, Justin forged a productive marketing program selling to big schools, such as Baylor University, Texas Tech University, University of Kansas, and University of Texas.

Beginning in the late 1950s, Justin targeted a broader market with a style based on the spirit of the old Wild West that was sweeping the nation. The ad campaign featured cowboys wearing traditional western garb in cattle country. To complement the outreach to a general audience, Justin Jr. emphasized service to retail dealers, saying "they were king."[44] The coordinated effort succeeded. The company tapped new markets and minted the Justin brand in the minds of American consumers. During Justin Jr.'s tenure, annual sales rose from $1 million to $450 million.[45]

In 1968, Justin Jr. had a medical scare—appendicitis.[46] He became concerned about the future of his family and the company without him. Everything he had was tied up in the company, and he worried over the liquidity, valuations, and taxes. At his attorney's suggestion, he agreed to merge the company with Forth Worth Corporation, a larger enterprise that included Acme Brick Company, then preparing to list on the New York Stock Exchange. By selling Justin to Fort Worth, he would obtain liquid assets, get a public listing to provide a valuation, and address the payment of estate taxes.

The deal closed, but Justin Jr. quickly grew disillusioned.[47] The Fort Worth managers seemed more interested in the quick buck than long-term value. They were willing to juice the books rather than be conservative, and were less open with their business partners than Justin Jr. preferred. After airing his objections and threatening legal action to rescind the merger, the Fort Worth team offered to surrender managerial authority to Justin Jr. He accepted and took control of the entire operation—bricks as well as boots, though he knew nothing about the brick business.

Justin Jr. enjoyed manufacturing and found that he could add value at Acme, which was struggling in the late 1960s. In 1970, Acme's business ground to a standstill as orders declined amid a housing downturn. Rather than curtail production, however, Justin Jr. built up inventory. He figured closing the plant would cost more than running it at low capacity. In addition, company records dating to 1917 indicated that the brick business was cyclical. The economy soon recovered, bringing with it a rising demand for bricks that Justin was able to meet readily and profitably.

By the 1980s, Acme Brick's brand dominated the market—a feat for what many would say is a commodity. The company hired Dallas Cowboys football star Troy Aikman as its spokesman. Acme stamps its residential bricks with its logo and gives a one-hundred-year guarantee. Surveys show that consumers recognize and prefer the Acme brand. Growth continued by an organic expansion of the brick business, and through diversifying acquisitions in construction materials (e.g., American Tile Supply in 1994 and Innovative Building Products in 1997). Justin Jr. had branded a commodity product, proven by the 10-percent premium Acme charges.[48]

In 1985, Justin Industries, as the company had been renamed, became the target of a hostile takeover. With its stock price far below intrinsic value, bidders proposed to "unlock" that value, perhaps by breaking up the company. Justin's board said no. The company acquired a competitor, Tony Lama Company, an acquisition it had long sought but the timing for which had never been right. Justin, usually averse to debt, assumed all of Lama's liabilities, making his company less attractive to bidders. In addition, Justin loyalists purchased large blocks of stock. Feeling secure, Justin Jr. spent the rest of the century focused on his business—but even with the takeover threat behind him, it wasn't all smooth sailing.

In 1998, the company planned a computer system overhaul to integrate all divisions and functions. By linking everything from sourcing to sales and from bookkeeping to personnel, efficiency would rise and costs would fall. They launched the new system just before the Christmas shopping season, but rather than increasing efficiency, the whole computer system failed. Justin Jr. looked to his hand-picked successor, Randy Watson, who dove in, reassured jittery colleagues, and directed improvisation. But the failure took eighteen months to rectify, and the company was not back at full speed until the fall of 2000. During this period, competitors gained market share and Justin nearly went out of business. To survive, Watson closed two boot factories, laying off five hundred employees—an action that likely saved the business but which has haunted Watson ever since.[49]

In late 2000, Justin Jr. developed serious health problems and sought prompt action to secure his company's legacy. An investor group asked Buffett if Berkshire might join them in acquiring the company.[50] Buffett explained that Berkshire rarely invests with others but said he would be happy to meet Justin Jr. and flew to Forth Worth to do so. Shortly after making a deal, in February 2001, Justin Jr. passed away. Upon acquisition, Berkshire split Acme and Justin into separate operations, each a standalone subsidiary. Justin Jr.'s legacy includes an entrepreneurial culture within both companies, though it manifests differently in each.

Watson heads the boot company, called Justin Brands, and observers say Watson's entrepreneurial and managerial likeness to John Justin Jr. is eerie. Perhaps this is because, in running the company, Watson remembers the kinds of questions Justin Jr. would ask him, such as, "Are all of the salesmen working as hard as they can?"[51] When facing difficult decisions, Watson still asks, "What would Justin Jr. do?"[52] A diligent salesman and merchandiser with a big personality, Watson maintains the close ties with the rodeo set that his mentor had established; in 2013, Ernst & Young named Watson one of its regional Entrepreneurs of the Year.[53] Results are strong: sales growth exceeded 10 percent in every year from 2008 to 2012.[54]

Acme Brick is run by Dennis Knautz, an accountant by training and temperament who joined the company in 1982.[55] Given the physical weight of brick, Acme is decentralized, regional in both manufacturing and distribution. Accordingly, Knautz treats each sales location as an independent business operation. Operators become entrepreneurial, producing a culture akin to franchises such as Dairy Queen, whose story of branding products and spawning thousands of entrepreneurs rounds out this chapter.

∾

International Dairy Queen, Inc.'s roots date to the 1927 founding of Homemade Ice Cream Company in Davenport, Iowa, by John F. ("Grandpa") McCullough and his son Alex. They were innovative ice cream makers, experimenting in Grandpa's basement with temperature and texture, and soon moved operations across the state line to Green River, Illinois.[56] The McCulloughs eventually pioneered semi-frozen and soft ice creams, which Dairy Queen would famously mint into an iconic brand.

In 1938, Grandpa McCullough persuaded one of his customers, Sherb Noble, to host an all-you-can-eat sale of soft ice cream to test consumer interest. The sale was a hit, and repeat events at other stores confirmed Grandpa's hunch that people would have a taste for soft ice cream. He had discovered a secret of the trade: ice cream was frozen solid for the convenience of ice cream makers and sellers, not for the enjoyment of consumers.[57]

At first, the McCulloughs could not interest any manufacturer in designing or building the necessary freezers and dispensers to serve soft ice cream. Luckily, however, Grandpa happened to see a newspaper ad in the *Chicago Tribune* describing a newly patented continuous freezer that could dispense the product. Grandpa contacted the inventor, Harry M. Oltz, and the two made a deal in the summer of 1939 to share rights to the equipment and royalties from ice cream sales.

In 1940, the McCulloughs invested with Noble to launch the first Dairy Queen store. It prospered, inspiring the group to open seven regional stores within a few years. After World War II, the chain hit its stride. Crowds at one store in Moline, Illinois, caught the attention of Harry Axene. An entrepreneurial farm equipment salesman, Axene wanted to invest in the business. He contacted the McCulloughs and acquired rights to sell the ice cream in designated states. Within those, Axene resold ice cream sales territories for an initial fixed fee plus ongoing royalties on ice cream sales. He opened many stores that way in the Midwest and by 1947 had established one hundred Dairy Queen outlets nationwide.

While the stores succeeded, the business arrangements resembled a one-time sale of intellectual property rights rather than ongoing franchise relationships. Neither Axene nor the McCulloughs provided centralized coordination. Since store operators were entrepreneurs who invested their life savings in their businesses, they ran them as they pleased. Little uniformity existed as the stores spread rapidly across the United States and Canada—1,400 by the early 1950s and 3,000 by 1960. As one Dairy Queen veteran joked: "Dairy Queen started by growing arms and legs all over the place, but it was a body without a head."[58]

The organizational slack became apparent in 1954 when Oltz's patent for the continuous freezer expired, prompting some store operators to stop paying royalties.[59] The McCulloughs sued, arguing that royalties were not limited to the patent but encompassed payments for the Dairy Queen trade name. The stakes rose when some operators claimed they had acquired their rights not from the McCulloughs but from Axene. The litigation became protracted, costly, and diverting. Anxieties caught up with the parties in 1962, and the McCulloughs settled.

The McCulloughs relinquished all claims and sold their interests to an investor group comprised of several operators of a great number of stores in large territories—Gilbert Stein, with 173 stores in Illinois and Missouri; James C. Cruikshank, who owned sixty-four stores in Georgia; and Burt and Miller Myers, a father-and-son team with hundreds of stores across Minnesota, Wisconsin, and eastern Canada. The group paid the McCulloughs $1.5 million and then borrowed to acquire other territories. A second stage of entrepreneurship had begun.

Hungry for central coordination, the group created a new company called International Dairy Queen to organize the system. Based in Minnesota, they formally adopted the franchise business model that was gaining popularity. The model, incubated as early as 1924 by Allen and White's A&W Root Beer and 1939 by Howard Johnson, proliferated after World War II.[60] Before then, franchising tended to be used only in product distribution settings, especially gas stations and car dealerships. After the war, the format was comprehensive, including a business plan, marketing strategy, operating manual, and quality control standards.[61]

The birth of the Dairy Queen franchise organization was unique in that the franchisees of Dairy Queen—Stein, Cruikshank, the Myerses— created the franchisor. Usually a company organizes the business and then recruits and trains franchisees, as is the case with Midas Muffler, Radio Shack, and Ramada Inns.[62] At Dairy Queen, the franchisees organized the franchisor and, in effect, trained it. In addition to acquiring territories, they integrated purchasing, advertising, new store development, employee training, product research, and overseas opportunities. They updated franchise agreements, requiring franchisees to pay not merely royalties on branded products, as the McCulloughs and Axene had, but a percentage of all sales.

While these efforts were meaningful steps toward unifying the system, there were shortcomings. One factor was reconciling the different strategic views of the franchisees, all successfully running their chains as they saw fit. Even once they agreed on strategy, problems lingered due to the loose approach taken since the beginning by the McCullough family and Axene. By the late 1960s, the new franchisor had lost its focus on the franchisees, and Dairy Queen executives proposed an IPO. Preparing for it, advisors urged adding more stores to the program to establish growth potential.[63] Dairy Queen followed the advice, but in its zeal to meet quantity targets, it compromised on quality. Many of the new stores were in bad locations, poorly managed, and inadequately financed.[64]

Exacerbating headquarters' loss of focus on franchisees, the franchisor followed the conglomerate fashion of the period by acquiring businesses in unrelated fields, including a ski-rental company and a chain of campgrounds.[65] In 1970, Dairy Queen proposed to acquire the National Car Rental System, a franchise business recently turned around by a group of fellow Minnesota businessmen led by Kenneth C. Glaser, William B. McKinstry, Rudy Luther, and John W. Mooty.[66] While nothing came of this overture, and National Car was sold to Household Finance International, Inc., Dairy Queen soon contacted the Minnesota businessmen again, this time asking if they would be interested in acquiring Dairy Queen.

McKinstry and Mooty conducted extensive due diligence. While the franchisor had acute financial problems, on balance, the franchises were in good shape. It seemed possible to correct the problems of the franchisor and turn Dairy Queen into a marquee business. This meant firmly establishing a comprehensive organization—something that had never been developed during the McCullough—Axene period and had only begun to be created by the franchisees. Dairy Queen stores operated prosperously across North America, but due to the company's haphazard origins, many stores, including those in Texas, had little or no affiliation with the franchisor.

The Minnesota group acquired Dairy Queen and immediately went back to basics, with a focus on organizing the franchisees. The investors paid $3 million in cash and committed $2 million in working capital in exchange for a large majority of Dairy Queen's stock. They promptly injected another $5 million, cut overhead, and adopted policy based on what was in the best interests of the franchisees.

The new owner-managers, under McKinstry's chairmanship for a short period and then under Mooty's direction, spent the next decade integrating the system. They staked millions more dollars in acquiring all territories in North America—starting with California and Pennsylvania and ultimately including western Canada and Texas (the latter alone cost $14 million). They closed nonperforming stores, promoted uniform standards, and established an efficient distribution system and a successful advertising program. Dairy Queen expanded its menus well beyond ice cream to include a full range of hamburgers, hot dogs, and other staples of American fast food.

In 1980, revenues surpassed $1 billion, making Dairy Queen the fifth largest U.S. fast-food concern after Burger King, Kentucky Fried Chicken (KFC), McDonald's, and Wendy's. Dairy Queen had more stores—4,800 and counting—than all other fast food chains except for KFC and McDonald's. In 1985, Dairy Queen launched a hit, the Blizzard, soft ice cream blended with candy, cookies, or fruit. During the next two years, stressing its roots on the operations side, it acquired rival franchise restaurant chains: Wyoming-born Karmelkorn in 1986 and California-based Orange Julius in 1987.

The group broadcast its commitment to continuity in management and ownership and permanence, values vital to the franchisees.[67] Dairy Queen stores are hometown operations. Virtually all are franchises, not company owned. They are run by entrepreneurs, often as family businesses. Many acquire additional stores as the business prospers or family grows. The investment group encouraged this expansion, preferring the security of working with long-time franchisees.

Dairy Queen is a hyper-decentralized organization with the franchisees having ample autonomy. Some franchisees own territories that they subdivide, and some such subdivisions are further divided among multiple franchisees. Many subgroups of franchisees develop associations among themselves, often along regional lines to enable coordination to meet local needs. Most substantial is the Texas Dairy Queen Operators' Council, which coordinates marketing and operations for stores in Texas, a nod to the history of the Texas stores being outside of the original Dairy Queen organization.

Franchisees of Dairy Queen are often active in local communities, sponsoring Little League baseball teams, leading church activities, and serving on school boards. The stores host community and social gatherings and serve as hangouts congenial to families. Dairy Queen has assumed a distinctive place in American culture, reflected in popular books such as

Larry McMurtry's *Walter Benjamin at the Dairy Queen: Reflections at Sixty and Beyond*; Bob Greene's *Chevrolet Summers, Dairy Queen Nights*; and Robert Inman's *Dairy Queen Days*.

In 1996, Rudy Luther, who held 15 percent of Dairy Queen's stock as a member of the Minnesota investment group, died. His family asked Buffett if he would be interested in buying the stake. Buffett was not, though he had previously indicated interest in Berkshire buying the whole company and reiterated this. The family and management, led by Mooty, decided it was time to sell, and a deal was made for Berkshire to buy Dairy Queen.[68] At the time of Berkshire's acquisition, Dairy Queen hosted 5,792 stores in 23 countries, as well as 409 Orange Julius and 43 Karmelkorn operations. To make the deal tax-free to the shareholders of Dairy Queen, the selling group insisted that Berkshire offer to pay either in cash or in stock.

Had it not been for Berkshire, Mooty is convinced that he and his investment group would still own Dairy Queen. In an interview for this book, Mooty explained that the deal closed, possibly at a price below financial value, because Berkshire offered something prized by each of Dairy Queen's three constituents—shareholders, employees, and franchisees.[69]

For shareholders, all members of the investment group opted to take Berkshire stock, representing a large percentage of each member's net worth. They believed that Berkshire was an unusually well-run company, with valuable stock to own permanently. Management and other employees appreciated Berkshire's commitments to autonomy. Berkshire had a proven track record of keeping existing management in place, a promise whose credibility was enhanced by the absence of managerial layers at Berkshire's corporate headquarters. Finally, Berkshire's commitment to permanence reassured the franchisees that, knowing Buffett, they would be in good company for decades to come.

John Mooty's son, Charles W. Mooty, served as Dairy Queen's chief executive officer from 2001 through 2007, succeeded by John Gainor, whom the Mootys and senior managers named with Buffett's approval.[70] Today, there are 6,300 Dairy Queen restaurants.[71] Among larger franchisees is the Frauenshuh Hospitality Group, a family business headed by Matthew Frauenshuh (pronounced *frown-shoo*). Long-time owner of sixty-one outlets across the Midwest, in 2011 it acquired another fifty-eight in Kentucky and Indiana, financed in part with $26.5 million staked by GE Capital.[72] Dairy Queen franchisees continue to gather regularly at annual or biannual meetings to exchange business ideas and socialize.

A Dairy Queen insider explained its history this way:

I have always thought of Dairy Queen as the [company] that succeeded in spite of itself. Although most of our problems are the result
of early mistakes made in setting up our franchise system, that same
system has also made us successful. Look at the typical store managers, a mom and pop who invest their life savings and work day and
night to succeed. Then multiply that experience thousands of times.
That entrepreneurial spirit has always been, and still is, the lifeblood
of the Dairy Queen system.[73]

An entrepreneurial spirit pervades Berkshire culture. Berkshire managers
tend to be self-starters by nature, propagating cultures of experimentation,
innovation, and tenacity. Like the protagonists of Horatio Alger novels,
they offer many tales of rags to riches, of transforming mom-and-pop operations into multi-million-dollar businesses. Buffett set the example, as a
quintessential entrepreneur in the field of acquisitions, where his persistent
opportunistic agility transformed a dying textile business into a galactic
conglomerate. Entrepreneurship feeds on another Berkshire trait inherent
in business models such as Acme Brick's distribution centers and Dairy
Queen's franchisees: the philosophy of hands-off management that gives
people autonomy, where the next chapter will pick up.

8

Hands Off

At corporate headquarters in Omaha, Berkshire employs two dozen people; worldwide, Berkshire subsidiaries employ more than 300,000. The practice at the top is hands-off, stressing decentralization and individual autonomy—values that define Berkshire culture. In contrast, most business organizations are hierarchies with a bureaucratic chain of command. They act through committees and meetings, with multiple layers of reporting and review.

Berkshire's hands-off management approach was made by choice but became necessary by default—with such a large number of subsidiaries in such a broad range of businesses, strict hands-on control would not be feasible. The choice to operate in a decentralized manner from the beginning reflected a belief in the value of autonomy and a conviction that people properly entrusted with authority will generally exercise it faithfully.[1] Business value results from letting responsible people make decisions, whether about manufacturing, distribution, customer service, acquisitions, or any other aspect of running a business.

And just as Berkshire Hathaway takes a decentralized approach, so do many of its subsidiaries; throughout the Berkshire universe are scores of companies in which individuals are supported by a larger corporate structure but empowered to drive their own success.

∽

The Pampered Chef, founded by Doris Christopher, provides a vivid illustration of some advantages—and pitfalls—of organizations that grant broad autonomy. Although a hands-on manager, Christopher's business model is based principally on empowering others.

During the late 1960s, Christopher taught home economics in a special program at the University of Illinois.[2] In 1980, at age thirty-five and with her children in school, she faced the challenge of finding a work—family balance that would allow her to enjoy a rewarding career and joyous parenting.[3] In resolving this challenge, Christopher earned both a Horatio Alger Award and an Ernst & Young Entrepreneur of the Year designation.

At her husband's suggestion, Christopher seized upon a modern version of the old-fashioned Tupperware business model: direct marketing of sophisticated cooking tools sold at gatherings in people's homes. In 1980, she borrowed $3,000 under a life insurance policy—the only debt the company would ever incur. Christopher bought an inventory of gadgetry wholesale and began her business. She hosted "kitchen shows" (not *Tupperware parties*) and would dub her sales team "kitchen consultants" (not *Avon ladies*). At the shows, consultants demonstrate wares by cooking dishes, and all guests then enjoy a feast.

The business, initially operated from Christopher's basement, grew slowly at first. Year-one (1981) sales totaled $67,000, with twelve kitchen consultants on board. In 1984, sales reached $400,000, outgrowing the basement. By 1989, two hundred kitchen consultants generated revenues of $3.5 million.

As the number of kitchen consultants steadily rose, revenue grew in tandem: 1991, $10 million; 1993, $65.3 million; 1995, $200 million; 1997, $420 million.[4] By this time, the Pampered Chef had grown to twenty-five thousand kitchen consultants—a figure that would double and then triple before long.

Christopher chose products carefully, with an eye toward making the cooking experience enjoyable for professionals and novices alike.[5] She experimented with all tools before marketing them and even developed recipes and menus to demonstrate their use.

The key to the company's success, however, was its team of kitchen consultants. An exquisite example of decentralization and autonomy, consultants make a modest initial payment for a starter demonstration set to use in their shows. The company adds new items a few times a year that consultants must buy and market. It supplies consultants with guidance for demonstrations, including recipes and care instructions.

Adding consultants increases revenue and profits—without increasing expenses. Consultants earn a starting commission of 20 percent on gross sales plus an additional 2 percent for gross sales above a target level. Consultants work as little or much as they wish, so long as sales reach a relatively low monthly minimum. Additional sales incentives include bonuses in the form of all-expenses-paid family vacations.

Christopher hails the consultants as the company's "crown jewel," stating they are "by far our most valuable asset" and the "heart and soul of our business."[6] She stresses that they are independent, not employees of the Pampered Chef, "an army of self-employed businesspeople."[7] They have no fixed hours or sales territories. Most direct-sales organizations conduct weekly sales meetings, but at the Pampered Chef, monthly meetings suffice. The monthlies are low-key pep rallies rather than the pressure cookers found at many corporate sales meetings. They are social as well as professional, which helps morale and offers the opportunity to exchange useful ideas.[8]

The Pampered Chef also uses the multi-level marketing model. Consultants can recruit other consultants and earn commissions on their sales, too (called "overrides"). The opportunity to generate overrides encourages people to build a sales team. The Pampered Chef ensures that these arrangements ultimately drive sales to consumers, and are not, as some have alleged about other multi-level marketers, merely used by larger distributors to extract sales from smaller and smaller ones down a daisy chain, amounting to no more than a pyramid scheme. In multi-level marketing programs, the trade-off between autonomy and authority is stark. Give distributors business power, and most will embrace it responsibly and profitably; restrain the sales force by strong internal control, and many will not perform as well.

Christopher is by nature a hands-on manager and built the Pampered Chef by working around the clock, immersing herself in operational details. The business model, however, required giving consultants autonomy, and scale eventually required delegation to colleagues at the corporate level. Christopher believes in the principle of "responsibility with authority."[9] She explains: "People don't like being dictated to. . . . Give [employees] the freedom to run with the ball."[10]

The Pampered Chef's greater problem had been managing revenue growth.[11] In the late 1980s, for example, recruiting multiplied so quickly that sales volume outpaced capacity for inventory management, order fulfillment, collections, and payment processing. The company faced a dilemma familiar to many successful entrepreneurs: sustain growth at some cost in service quality or cede growth and maintain standards. In direct sales, a recruiting freeze is often a death knell—a bad signal to consumers and a morale downer to the troops. But in 1990, the Pampered Chef opted for quality over quantity and imposed a temporary freeze on new recruits. This controversial and gutsy move meant putting fundamental values ahead of short-term profit, but it ultimately translated into economic gain. As Christopher reflected years later:

> Looking back, the recruiting freeze augmented our reputation with our sales force, customers, and vendors. People saw us as an honest company that was trying to do the right thing and not overestimate its capabilities. We are very conservative in our business practices by nature, and our people knew that. When we told them something, they knew it was the truth.[12]

By 2002, annual sales exceeded $700 million, thanks to sixty-seven thousand kitchen consultants.[13] Christopher cemented her plans for the company's future by contacting Berkshire and arranging a meeting with Buffett in Omaha. Eying her squarely, Buffett explained that selling to Berkshire would not increase her net worth and could decrease it.[14] The transaction involved trading an asset she owned outright for cash that she would invest in diverse assets. In the future, he advised, the company would likely be worth more than the asset portfolio. So, he wondered, why would she sell?

Christopher explained her decision in terms of the value of values: she wanted to sell to Berkshire in order to protect her sales force and employees and to maintain the culture they had built together. Christopher had considered a public offering, which can yield rich paydays for accomplished entrepreneurs. (Remember Jim Clayton noting how the millions he netted going public explains why so many entrepreneurs consider an IPO.) But Christopher valued Berkshire because it did not interfere with operations and promised permanence.[15] Buffett, who has an uncanny ability to measure character in brief meetings, liked Christopher instantly. The two made a deal within three weeks. As in many other Berkshire deals, employees received a thank-you bonus of $1,000 for each year they had worked for the company.

An example of the support and consideration for these consultants was the way Berkshire addressed a political controversy that led to the termination of Berkshire's shareholder charitable contribution program in 2003. At most corporations, boards choose which charities receive corporate beneficence, but that goes against Berkshire culture. Conceived by Munger in 1981, Berkshire's program let shareholders name the organizations, with the aggregate amount set by the board.[16] The program was popular with Berkshire shareholders, not only because it allowed for effortless philanthropy, but also because this type of giving was modestly more tax efficient than direct philanthropic contributions. Shareholders designated a wide range of recipients, from Catholic Social Services to Planned Parenthood.

The program's size and reach drew attention from social activists on hot topics like abortion, who in the early 2000s orchestrated boycotts of Berkshire subsidiaries or their products. Among the targets was the Pampered Chef. Consultants reported to Christopher that they were receiving threats from activists to boycott their business if Berkshire continued to fund charitable organizations with positions they opposed. The boycotts impaired the potential earnings of the Pampered Chef consultants, an unintended side effect. The campaign became so intrusive that Christopher took the matter to Buffett.

Consequently, Berkshire discontinued its shareholder charitable contribution program. This decision reflected something unexpected about hands-off management coupled with individual autonomy: it does not leave people on their own but provides support. To make autonomy work in an intensely decentralized organization, this commitment must extend to all who exercise the autonomy on the organization's behalf. For the Pampered Chef, this includes its kitchen consultants. The cost to Berkshire of cancelling its shareholder charitable contribution plan was worth paying in the name of the more fundamental Berkshire values of autonomy and integrity.

Buffett put it this way:

> [The boycotts] meant that people who trusted us—but who were neither employees of ours nor had a voice in Berkshire decision making—suffered serious losses of income. For our shareholders, there was some modest tax efficiency in Berkshire doing the giving rather than their making their gifts directly. But these advantages paled when they were measured against damage done to loyal associates [of the Pampered Chef] who had with great personal effort built businesses of their own. Indeed, Charlie and I see nothing charitable in harming decent, hard-working people just so we and other shareholders can gain some minor tax efficiencies.

The true value at the Pampered Chef is in the fleet of kitchen consultants, as Marla Gottschalk, who became the company's chief executive in 2006, quickly realized. Gottschalk came to the Pampered Chef after a fourteen-year career as a senior executive at Kraft Food Groups Inc. and immediately noticed glaring cultural differences. Where Kraft favors a controlling managerial philosophy, Berkshire is hands-off; where Kraft has thick levels of managerial oversight, the Pampered Chef has a thin management layer.[17] Gottschalk's primary focus was on how to maintain the appeal of being a kitchen consultant and how to help consultants succeed. Every morning, Gottschalk studied two daily figures, sales volume and consultant numbers.[18] Of the two, she stressed, the number of consultants is by far the more important, as the consultants remain the company's most valuable asset.

In December 2013, having enjoyed a successful tenure, yet facing lackluster growth, Gottschalk stepped down as chief executive of the Pampered Chef. Christopher, returning to the helm from retirement, found the company's culture of autonomy and entrepreneurship intact. But the business model confronted challenges from Internet—based merchandising and other demographic changes. In an interview for this book, Christopher said she is happy serving her encore role as chief executive while looking for the right visionary to shape the next generation of the Pampered Chef.[19]

The Pampered Chef's direct-sales method has counterparts in the divisions of Scott Fetzer, which is best known for pioneering door-to-door sales of Kirby vacuum cleaners and World Book encyclopedias and the direct-response television marketing of Ginsu knives. The Kirby vacuum, for instance, has always been marketed with the Kirby Marketing System.[20]

Distributors pay Kirby a wholesale price and then resell through dealers who make door-to-door sales to consumers. Kirby requires all its salespeople to use the same printed materials, including owner's manuals and warranties. Beyond that, distributors and dealers run their businesses as they see fit. Self-starters thrive with such incentives. By empowering the sales force, the company increases sales without adding expenses, thus boosting profits and margins.[21]

A chief concern of any decentralized business model is policing personnel, such as when distributors mistreat dealers[22] or when dealers use illegal high-pressured sales tactics. At Scott Fetzer, distributors of Kirby vacuums are autonomous businesses. But they also represent the brand and company. Occasionally, they violate company policy on proper marketing and employment practices or even break consumer protection and fair labor laws.[23] Private lawsuits and state enforcement actions result.[24]

Avoiding the costs of legal entanglements and liability would require withdrawing distributor autonomy and revising the business model to subject all employees to comprehensive training, supervision, and remediation. Such an approach imposes direct administrative costs, as well as unobservable costs to entrepreneurship and the spirit of ownership that autonomy showers on self-starters. Managers at Scott Fetzer have concluded, based on decades of experience, that the distributorship system's autonomy value outweighs such costs.

∾

Berkshire corporate policy strikes a balance between autonomy and authority. Buffett issues written instructions every two years that reflect this balance. The missive states the mandates Berkshire places on subsidiary CEOs: (1) guard Berkshire's reputation; (2) report bad news early; (3) confer about post-retirement benefit changes and large capital expenditures (including acquisitions, which are encouraged); (4) adopt a fifty-year time horizon; (5) refer any opportunities for a Berkshire acquisition to Omaha; and (6) submit written successor recommendations.[25] Otherwise, Berkshire stresses that managers are chosen because of their excellence and are urged to act on that excellence.

Berkshire defers as much as possible to subsidiary chief executives on operational matters with scarcely any central supervision. All quotidian decisions would qualify: GEICO's advertising budget and underwriting standards; loan terms at Clayton Homes and environmental quality of Benjamin Moore paints; the product mix and pricing at Johns Manville, the furniture stores, and the jewelry shops. The same applies to decisions about hiring, merchandising, inventory, and receivables management, whether at Acme Brick, Garan, or the Pampered Chef. Berkshire's deference extends to subsidiary decisions on succession to senior positions, including CEO, as seen in such cases as Dairy Queen and Justin Brands.

Munger has said Berkshire's oversight is just short of abdication. In a wild example, Lou Vincenti, the chief executive at Berkshire's Wesco Financial subsidiary since its acquisition in 1973, ran the company for several years while suffering from Alzheimer's disease—without Buffett or Munger being aware of his condition. "We loved him so much," Munger said, "that even after we found out, we kept him in his job until the week that he went off to the Alzheimer's home. He liked coming in, and he wasn't doing us any harm."[26] The two lightened a grim situation, quipping that they wished to have more subsidiaries so earnest and reputable that they could be managed by people with such debilitating medical conditions.

There are obvious exceptions to Berkshire's tenet of autonomy. Large capital expenditures—or the chance of such—lead reinsurance executives to run outsized policies and risks by headquarters. Berkshire intervenes in extraordinary circumstances, for example, the costly deterioration in underwriting standards at Gen Re and the threatened repudiation of a Berkshire commitment to distributors at Benjamin Moore. Mandatory or not, Berkshire was involved in RC Willey's expansion outside of Utah and rightly asserts itself in costly capital allocation decisions, like those concerning purchasing aviation simulators at FlightSafety or increasing the size of the core fleet at NetJets.

Ironically, gains from Berkshire's hands-off management are highlighted by an occasion when Buffett made an exception. Buffett persuaded GEICO managers to launch a credit card business for its policyholders.[27] Buffett hatched the idea after puzzling for years over an additional product to offer its millions of loyal car insurance customers. GEICO's management warned Buffett against the move, expressing concern that the likely result would be a high volume of business from its least creditworthy customers and little from its most reliable ones. By 2009, GEICO had lost more than $6 million in the credit card business and took another $44 million hit when it sold the portfolio of receivables at a discount to face value. The costly venture would not have been pursued had Berkshire stuck to its principle of autonomy.

The more important—and more difficult—question is the price of autonomy. Buffett has explained Berkshire's preference for autonomy and assessment of the related costs:

> We tend to let our many subsidiaries operate on their own, without our supervising and monitoring them to any degree. That means we are sometimes late in spotting management problems and that [disagreeable] operating and capital decisions are occasionally made.... Most of our managers, however, use the independence we grant them magnificently, rewarding our confidence by maintaining an owner-oriented

attitude that is invaluable and too seldom found in huge organizations. We would rather suffer the visible costs of a few bad decisions than incur the many invisible costs that come from decisions made too slowly—or not at all—because of a stifling bureaucracy.[28]

Berkshire's approach is so unusual that the occasional crises that result provoke public debate about which is better in corporate culture: Berkshire's model of autonomy and trust or the more common approach of command and control. Few episodes have been more wrenching and instructive for Berkshire culture than when David L. Sokol, an esteemed senior executive with his hand in many Berkshire subsidiaries, was suspected of insider trading in an acquisition candidate's stock.

In 2010, Buffett asked Sokol, then running both MidAmerican Energy and NetJets after Richard T. Santulli left,[29] to scout acquisition opportunities. All Berkshire subsidiary chiefs are encouraged to seek acquisitions, but this assignment might have been a proving ground for Sokol, by then widely seen as the leading candidate to succeed Buffett.

Sokol began in a most un-Berkshire-like way, however, by hiring bankers to help with the search. Sokol instructed the team, from Citi, to focus on the chemicals industry. They identified eighteen potential targets, and Sokol was attracted to one, The Lubrizol Corporation, maker of specialty chemicals, including additives for the automotive and petroleum industries. On December 13, 2010, Sokol told the bankers to ask Lubrizol's chief executive, James L. Hambrick, if the company might be interested in speaking with Buffett about a Berkshire acquisition. Hambrick said he would raise the proposition with Lubrizol's board, and on December 17, Citi reported this to Sokol.

Sokol regarded Lubrizol as an outstanding company and an excellent investment. As a result, during the first week of January 2011, Sokol, with an annual income of $24 million,[30] bought $10 million worth of Lubrizol stock. (He had also bought, then quickly sold, a smaller amount of the stock in mid-December.) The next week, on January 14, Hambrick called Sokol to express interest and set a meeting with Buffett. Sokol then reported the acquisition opportunity to Buffett.

Buffett responded, "I don't know anything about Lubrizol."
Sokol said, "Well, take a look at it. It might fit Berkshire."
Buffett asked, "How come?"
Sokol replied, "I've owned it and it's a good company. It's a Berkshire-type company."[31]

Buffett studied Lubrizol's annual reports. He did not comprehend all of the chemical science, except to appreciate that petroleum additives are indispensable to running engines. However, understanding a business' arcane details is far less important than grasping the economic characteristics of its industry and the company's position, Buffett says.[32] After speaking with Sokol and lunching with Hambrick on February 8, Buffett had a sense of Lubrizol's culture and found the company's prospects favorable.

By March 14, Berkshire agreed to acquire Lubrizol for a 30-percent premium over Lubrizol's stock market price.[33] After the announcement, John Freund, a Citi banker and Buffett's stockbroker,[34] called Buffett to congratulate him, expressing pride in Citi's role in facilitating the deal. Surprised to hear of this role, Buffett had Berkshire's CFO, Marc Hamburg, call Sokol for information about Citi's participation in the deal and Sokol's ownership of Lubrizol stock. During the following week, Sokol would provide more details, as Berkshire's attorneys from Munger, Tolles & Olson grilled him while assisting Lubrizol's lawyers in drafting disclosure documents about the transaction. Buffett was in Asia that week, and when he returned, Sokol tendered his resignation. Sokol had tried to retire from Berkshire on two previous occasions, but Buffett and the other Berkshire directors had persuaded him to stay. This time he would go.

On March 29, Buffett drafted a press release reporting Sokol's resignation. He sent the draft to Sokol for review. The draft attributed Sokol's resignation to how recent events had dashed Sokol's hopes of succeeding Buffett at Berkshire. Sokol objected to this explanation. Not only did Sokol disclaim pretensions of succeeding Buffett, he said he was resigning for personal reasons and did not believe he had done anything wrong.[35]

So before issuing the press release the next day, Buffett replaced the original wording with an excerpt from Sokol's resignation letter. The release attributed Sokol's resignation to his desire to manage his family's resources. Buffett then lauded Sokol's "extraordinary contributions" to Berkshire, referencing MidAmerican Energy, NetJets, and Johns Manville. The release then summarized Sokol's Lubrizol stock purchases, concluding that they were lawful and reiterating Sokol's claim that they had nothing to do with his resignation.

The March 30 press release sparked criticism. People could not reconcile Berkshire's and Buffett's usual rectitude with mild commentary on what appeared to outsiders a case of insider trading. It "suggested a degree of [Buffett's] closeness to Sokol and perhaps a degree of reciprocity and a willingness to let him slide because he had done good things for Berkshire in the past."[36] Shareholders demanded to know why Buffett was not furious.

Buffett accepted the criticism, noting that had Berkshire's lawyers written the release, it would have been worded more carefully.[37] Munger acknowledged that the press release was flawed, though cautioned against letting anger figure in such exercises.[38] Corporate lawyers have honed the sober craft of drafting press releases, and CEOs usually entrust the task to them. Much as with Buffett's idea to move GEICO into the credit card business, his mistake of writing his own press release underscored the value of delegation. In the Sokol case, this was rather ironic, considering how critics soon attacked Berkshire culture as being too hands-off.

Berkshire's audit committee had lawyers from Munger, Tolles & Olson evaluate the case. On April 26, the committee concluded that Sokol's purchase of Lubrizol stock violated Berkshire policies. These policies restrict managers from buying stock in companies Berkshire is considering acquiring and bar putting confidential corporate information to personal use. Above all, Sokol violated rule one of Buffett's biannual letter to Berkshire CEOs mandating that they safeguard Berkshire's reputation. The audit committee's stinging rebuke overruled the slap on the wrist conveyed by Buffett's March 30 press release.

With the rebuke coming on the heels of the press release, critics objected to the absence of an impartial investigation. The audit committee is an arm of the board, and the Lubrizol episode raised the question of board oversight. Moreover, the committee might have retained any number of firms to conduct a review, yet used Munger, Tolles & Olson, which has deep Berkshire ties.

Nevertheless, the audit committee's repudiation of Buffett's initial judgment caused Buffett to change his mind. On April 30, at Berkshire's annual meeting, Buffett dedicated the opening segment to the topic. He showed a clip from his press interview at Salomon Brothers twenty years earlier in which he told employees to avoid behavior they would not wish reported on the front page of a newspaper. Then Buffett went on to denounce Sokol's conduct as "inexcusable and inexplicable"—a phrase Buffett had also used when addressing the perpetrators of the Salomon scandal.[39] Discussion turned to broader criticism then circulating about Berkshire's culture of hands-off management.

Critics contended that the very fact that Sokol (or any executive) would violate company policy raised doubts about the effectiveness of a company's internal control systems.[40] Modern corporate control systems rely heavily on formal commands, consisting of mandatory procedures, reporting, approvals, and redundant oversight. Berkshire, in contrast, puts its trust in people rather than in processes.[41] Critics suspected Berkshire's culture of autonomy and trust was a culprit in the Sokol affair.[42]

It would be an overstatement to suggest that any given violation is an indictment of a corporation's controls or culture. No system prevents all violations, not even the most effective command and control. Rather, the Sokol episode represented the kind of thing every company hopes that culture and controls will deter.[43] The episode did expose limits of the autonomy-and-trust model.[44]

Munger expanded on this theme at Berkshire's 2011 annual meeting on April 30:

> The greatest institutions . . . select very trustworthy people, and they trust them a lot . . . There's so much self-respect you get from [being] trusted and [being] worthy of the trust that [the] best compliance cultures are the ones which have this attitude of trust. [Some corporate cultures] with the biggest compliance departments, like Wall Street, have the most scandals. So it's not so simple that you can make your behavior better automatically just by making the compliance department bigger. This general culture of trust is what works. Berkshire hasn't had that many scandals of consequence, and I don't think we're going to get huge numbers either.[45]

In any corporate culture, it is important how officials respond to transgressions. In congressional testimony concerning the Salomon Brothers bond trading scandal, Buffett formalized his admonition to company personnel in words that reverberated through the arena of the 2011 Berkshire shareholders' meeting: "Lose money for the firm, and I will be understanding; lose a shred of reputation for the firm, and I will be ruthless."[46]

Amid the Sokol affair, other Berkshire subsidiaries found an opportunity to offer a lesson. Todd Raba, chief executive of Johns Manville, where Sokol had intervened as chairman, gave Buffett a copy of a note issued to his company's employees the day the audit committee report was published. It said:

> The audit committee clearly found that Mr. Sokol compromised the integrity-related values both Berkshire and JM have worked so hard to ingrain in the fabric of both companies. This should serve as a tragic lesson learned for every employee in JM. There are no gray areas when it comes to integrity. . . . [47]

In Sokol's case, Berkshire turned over all information to the Securities and Exchange Commission. The SEC looked into the matter, but ultimately dropped the case in January 2013. The SEC did not offer any explanation, but a victory was uncertain. For one, Sokol had no authority over whether Berkshire would acquire Lubrizol. That meant the "information" he had when he bought Lubrizol stock was neither ripe nor reliable. So the SEC might have had difficulty proving the legal requirement of "materiality." Plus, since Sokol was not a Lubrizol employee, he did not commit classic insider trading when buying its stock, so the SEC would need to show that he "misappropriated" Berkshire property, which was not obvious.[48]

The SEC's decision not to pursue a case against Sokol contrasts with the audit committee's judgment condemning him for violating Berkshire policy. Differences between business judgments and legal conclusions are common in corporate practice because ethics codes are often stricter than legal mandates. Law sets minimum requirements, leaving companies free to refine standards upward. In fact, many command-and-control structures are efforts to comply with the letter of the law; Berkshire's trust-and-auton-omy culture aspires to a higher bar.[49]

Consistent with the SEC's conclusion, Sokol's mistake was less in buying Lubrizol stock than in failing to disclose his recent purchase to Buffett. The audit committee's reaction underscored Berkshire's sensitiv-ity to public perceptions, whereas Sokol heralded the SEC's decision as his vindication. His attorney even argued that what he had done was expressly permitted by his employment agreement with Berkshire.[50] Sokol's infraction was small in relation to the price he paid, illustrating what ruthlessness means.

~

Bill Child, the entrepreneur who built family-operated RC Willey into a regional furniture and appliance powerhouse, relates the story of a rival who taught him lessons about autonomy.[51] The competitor had begun business, just as Willey had, from a building next to his house, with no overhead, low prices, and one-on-one service. The business grew, and he built a store in a commercial zone. He hired employees, and the business grew even more.

But the owner never empowered any of his employees. Instead, he tried to perform every aspect of the business himself, as he had always done. The result: customer service and employee morale both suffered.

Finally, the man could not sustain enough sales to cover the rising cost of overhead, and he lost his business. Child draws two lessons from the story:

> First, delegation is vital to growing a small business. Second, true delegation only exists when the leader trusts his people enough to allow them to perform their responsibilities without constant interference.[52]

Berkshire CEOs, in correspondence and interviews for this book, stress the value they assign to Berkshire's autonomy, which is useful for large corporations as well as small. At Clayton Homes, the large vertically integrated manufactured housing company, for example, Kevin Clayton explained that the company treats its business groups autonomously. Each group—manufacturing, retail, finance, insurance, trailer park—stands on its own. This, he explains, creates long-term economic value.[53] The company also embraces the 90/10 rule: junior managers should make 90 percent of the decisions, while senior managers collaborate on the other 10 percent, which involve unusual risk, require special skills, or go beyond the junior manager's expertise.[54]

In another interview for this book, Jim Weber, CEO of Brooks, Berkshire's running shoe subsidiary, said that he has never had so much autonomy in his business career and never felt so accountable and responsible. The lesson: reposing trust and confidence in business managers can be the most effective way to promote desired results.

Lubrizol's James Hambrick concurs about the value of autonomy at Berkshire and offers insight into making it work. He writes a quarterly report to Buffett.[55] Unless there is something notable in it, Hambrick does not hear back. The report covers both the operations of Lubrizol and the activities of Hambrick, who is constantly on the road connecting with the global company's 7,500 employees and innumerable stakeholders. Supplying the quarterly report means that when Hambrick sees an opportunity needing approval, he can summarize it and get Buffett's approval within minutes without needing to review the background. This approach is especially valuable to those Berkshire subsidiaries which, like Lubrizol, seek acquisition opportunities, as the next chapter will illuminate.

9

Investor Savvy

McLane Co. Inc., a grocery wholesaler and distributor, generates more revenue than most countries' gross domestic product: $46 billion in 2013.[1] The company's mammoth size resulted from steady accretive expansion during the late twentieth century, spreading across the U.S. one region at a time. Since its humble nineteenth-century founding, however, the company has done what Berkshire does: reinvest earnings in its most profitable opportunities.

Robert McLane began this practice in 1894, when running a grocery store in the small central Texas farming town of Cameron, and spent the next two decades nurturing the business into a regional player.[2] Efficient distribution systems were the central driver of expansion from those early days. A milestone occurred when McLane switched from using horse-drawn carriages to motorized trucks.

Robert and his son Drayton, who joined in 1921, steered the company through difficult periods. They survived adverse weather patterns during the 1920s that battered Texas farmers, who were their suppliers, and then they survived the Great Depression in the 1930s, which battered Texas merchants, who were their customers. Persistence paid off after World War II, as sales crossed the $1 million mark in 1946. The subsequent development of national highways reduced transport costs, stoking growth both within and outside of Texas.

Drayton's son, Drayton McLane Jr., entered the business in 1959 and spent the next forty years building it through an energetic combination of vertical integration and expansion into new geographic territories. He transformed the company from a simple grocery wholesaler into a logistics master for retail store customers, handling inventory control, ordering, food processing and warehousing, shipping, and data management.

Drayton started this transformation from the moment he entered the business. He established an innovative marketing program that offered independent retail grocers a way to compete more effectively with grocery store chains: pooling resources to buy larger quantities of private-label (generic) brands that McLane sold. McLane also assisted the group with advertising, merchandising, and store operations. Scores of customers enrolled, generating considerable gains for both parties. The effort drove McLane's revenues, which in 1964 reached $4 million.[3]

McLane also became the wholesaler for 7-Eleven convenience stores throughout central Texas. Drayton cultivated his company's relationship with 7-Eleven as the convenience store chain grew in the late 1960s and early 1970s. This experience positioned McLane to provide increasingly reliable distribution services for the emerging convenience store industry. This became one driver of the success of both 7-Eleven and the broader "c-store" sector, fostering such regional players as Pay Less, Wawa, and Zippo's. Convenience stores became the engine of McLane's growth, as 1975 revenues reached $66 million.[4]

McLane's first large-scale expansion outside of Texas occurred in 1976 when a joint venture partner enticed the company to build a distribution center in Colorado. From there, it established a customer base in a contiguous region—pushing northwest toward Oregon and Washington—and serviced it by sending trucks greater distances from the distribution center. McLane's growth beyond Texas was incremental, steady, and consistently followed the same strategy. Once business volume in an expanding area reached a critical peak, McLane built a new distribution center in the heart of the region. In addition to serving existing clientele, it again used the distribution center as a base to expand trucking routes into new territories beyond it—for example, extending from Oregon down to California and from there on to Arizona. McLane repeated this accretive practice a dozen times until it covered the country with a dozen regional distribution centers.

Each distribution center is autonomously managed as if it were a separate company.[5] Corporate headquarters appoints division presidents who make all divisional operating decisions. This is important because the customer base in each region differs—from the mix of store types to the variety of food products. McLane managers from existing divisions were involved in launching each new division. The model succeeded, as 1984 revenues demonstrated, surging to $1 billion.[6]

McLane supplemented this expansion strategy with a series of major acquisitions during the late 1980s and early 1990s, including a wholesale food supply company and the distribution centers of its valued customer, the Southland Corporation, owner of the 7-Eleven chain. These new companies strengthened McLane's core business. Other acquisitions enhanced McLane's vertical integration as a logistics manager, as it acquired two food-processing businesses (one from Southland), as well as a technology company that provided automation and financial services to the convenience store industry.

In 1990, with sales nearing $3 billion, McLane's national leadership in the wholesale distribution business was cemented when Drayton McLane got a call from the head of one of its customers, Samuel Moore Walton of Walmart, the nation's largest retailer. Walton told Drayton that Walmart was interested in buying his company. Drayton had gotten many opportunities to sell the company over the years and had declined them all. The business treasured its autonomy and family heritage too greatly. At this point, however, Drayton's father and sisters pointed out that the family was wrestling with estate planning matters—both how to distribute wealth among members and how to pay for looming estate taxes. So Drayton and Walton soon made a deal. One hitch: Walmart then owned a number of convenience stores, and McLane had always assured its customers it would never compete with them in the retail business. Walmart agreed to sell these stores.

Under Walmart's ownership, McLane's impressive historical record of revenue growth skyrocketed. Sales in 1993 exceeded $6 billion, marking an average annual growth rate in sales since 1964 of 30 percent.[7] In 2003, when McLane's revenue exceeded $20 billion, Walmart decided McLane was outside its core competencies and contacted Berkshire to offer it for sale. McLane was a perfect fit for Berkshire, given their shared values, and came with a valuable investment proposition: Walmart's ownership of McLane hurt McLane because Walmart's rivals would not buy from McLane on competitive grounds. This presented built-in growth for McLane under Berkshire's ownership, and Berkshire agreed to acquire the company.

After Drayton retired from McLane to buy the Houston Astros base-ball team in 1992, he was succeeded first by Joe Hardin, who presided for a decade, and then by W. Grady Rosier, who has run McLane since. Both successions were effective as McLane sustained its peerless growth trajec-tory, which the company continued through acquisitions.

Building on McLane's traditional food distribution business, Rosier oversaw its acquisition of Meadowbrook Meat Company, Inc. (MBM), a North Carolina–based food distributor to national restaurant chains, includ-ing Arby's, Burger King, Chick-fil-A, and Darden Restaurants (Capital Grille and Olive Garden). Founded in 1947 by J. R. Wordsworth, the second-generation family business generates annual revenues of $6 billion through a network of thirty-five distribution centers across the United States. After McLane's acquisition, nothing at MBM changed except for the larger scale that the association provided.

Rosier is also leading McLane's expansion into new products, princi-pally through acquisitions. In 2010, for example, it acquired Empire Dis-tributors, a wine and spirits distributor operating in Georgia and North Carolina. In turn, Empire promptly acquired Horizon Wine & Spirits, a wine and spirits distributor in neighboring Tennessee. In 2013, McLane made a joint investment in Missouri Beverage Company, adding another contiguous state to this expanding market.[8] In coming decades, expect to see McLane distributing wine and spirits across the United States.[9]

∿

Managerial savvy in capital allocation—whether for internal growth or external acquisitions—is important because mistakes are costly to share-holders. Mistakes are especially costly when managers overpay to acquire a new business. The risk of overpayment in acquisitions arises from a com-bination of managerial hubris and easy access to excess cash, newly issued stock, or borrowings. Managers overestimate what a new acquisition will do for a company, which then leads to value destruction.

Curbing managerial hubris and controlling the source of funds are among the ways to minimize the risk of overpayment. Berkshire's culture offers advantages along both lines. For example, acquisition markets tend to run in cycles, with bursts of activity followed by lulls. A common mis-take is to get in the wave and buy as the cycle shifts from being a buyer's market to a seller's market. Experts refer to this problem as the fallacy of "social proof," the belief that if everyone is doing something, it must be desirable.[10] Berkshire's elongated time horizon diminishes the temptation to follow the crowd.

Concerning funding—debt, stock, or excess cash—Berkshire's culture and structure limits access to all three, a check against improvidence. Rivals often finance acquisitions with borrowed money, frequently at costs higher than gains. Berkshire's culture of budget consciousness makes subsidiaries averse to debt for any purpose, including acquisitions. Other rivals pay in stock, but stock often feels like play money to managers, leading them to spend more freely. The psychology is akin to foreign currency when traveling abroad or gambling chips in a casino. At Berkshire, the problem of "funny money" is avoided because subsidiary acquisitions are never paid for in stock. (In fact, Berkshire has used its stock in only seven parent-level acquisitions, when sellers highly value that form of currency, as in the cases of Dairy Queen and Helzberg Diamonds.[11])

Not all subsidiaries can reinvest resources at high rates of return. Within Berkshire's structure, these subsidiaries distribute excess cash to Berkshire, which redeploys it to sister subsidiaries that can reinvest it at high rates of return. For example, both Scott Fetzer and See's Candies generated hundreds of millions of dollars of excess cash in their lifetimes with Berkshire. But See's only requires fractions of that to sustain itself,[12] and Scott Fetzer rarely finds the value-enhancing alternatives available to sister subsidiaries.[13] So Berkshire allocates the excess cash from one group of subsidiaries to another. The economic value to Berkshire of such cash cows is greater than the cash alone, as it produces advantages that result from commanding large capital pools, including the ability to act opportunistically and the chance to acquire large positions quickly.

At given subsidiaries, another strategy to mitigate the risk of overpayment in acquisitions is to use the same value-of-values approach to subsidiary acquisitions that Berkshire uses in its acquisitions. MiTek Inc., a St. Louis–based firm Berkshire acquired in 2001, has done so when acquiring some of the companies that led to revolutionary change in building construction in recent decades.

Comparing homes built through the 1960s with those since the 1990s, it is easy to notice great differences in the rooflines. Mid-century roofs were simple, short, and uniform within neighborhoods, as roof-making assemblies were cumbersome and costly to change from one home to the next. Roof trusses—the structural framework in the space between the rooms and roof of a building—were often pre-fabricated to save costs. But thanks to MiTek, the machinery has become so advanced that it is cheaper and easier to tailor the shape and style of roofs. Trusses now have elaborate cuts, peaks, valleys, and hips; they have longer spans and steeper pitches. Homes today are not only more varied at the roofline, but stronger and taller.

MiTek and its subsidiaries manufacture the machinery and components—saws, presses, and structural connectors—that builders need to turn architectural and engineering visions into reality. MiTek—now an amalgam of top companies across the multifaceted building components industry—develops automated machinery and equipment that reduces the risk of error and the need for manpower: a six-blade saw with digital readouts of blade angles; software that performs engineering analysis and provides production specifications; and lasers that project a roof truss onto the assembly table.

MiTek was built through merger by Paul Cornelsen, a Kansas farm boy whose business career began after service in World War II, when he cleaned locker rooms at a feed mill in Wichita.[14] From there, he spent thirty-five years working his way up the ladder at Ralston Purina, finally running its international division and serving as chief operating officer. In 1981, when a rival won the top job running the pet food company, Cornelsen left Ralston and took charge at Moehlenpah Industries (which he renamed MiTek).

An international maker of hydraulic equipment and roof assembly products founded by Walter Moehlenpah, the company had a good reputation in a competitive field for engineering, design, and production skills, especially its Hydro-Air Engineering unit. The business struggled, however, and Cornelsen set to straighten it out. In addition to selling the company's airplane and boat—unaffordable luxuries—and attracting new outside investors, he decentralized decision making and adopted a stock incentive program, through which Cornelsen came to share ownership with seven colleagues.[15]

After growing MiTek steadily through 1987, Cornelsen devised a creative merger. MiTek acquired Gang-Nail Systems, Inc., a larger archrival, and simultaneously sold half the resulting company to a British conglomerate called Bowater, later renamed Rexam plc, with MiTek's owner-managers keeping the other half subject to a Rexam option to buy them out. Cornelsen began to lean heavily on a team of executives to drive MiTek's acquisitions and prosperity: Eugene ("Gene") Toombs, recruited as his number two in 1989 from an Idaho packaging company; Thomas ("Tom") J. Manenti, who ran Gang-Nails; and Michael D. Conforti, who ran Hydro-Air Engineering.

When Cornelsen retired in 1993, Rexam exercised its right to acquire 100 percent of MiTek. A few years later, however, the conglomerate refocused on its core business of making aluminum cans.[16] This decision put

MiTek in limbo: it was up for sale but so profitable that Rexam held out for a high price; yet Rexam would not reinvest in the acquisitions Toombs and his team sought.[17]

So in 2001, Toombs, with Rexam's approval, proposed a sale to Berkshire.[18] He prepared an overnight package for Buffett. In it he put one of the company's products along with a letter explaining the business. On receipt, Buffett did not know what he had in front of him. He called it "an unprepossessing chunk of metal whose function I could not imagine."[19] It was a three-by-five-inch connector plate, MiTek's flagship product used to fabricate roof trusses. Once Buffett saw the importance and necessity of pieces like this to the roofing industry, Berkshire bought 90 percent of MiTek for $379 million; in a revival of the owner-manager structure Cornelsen had devised, the other 10 percent was acquired by a group of fifty-five MiTek managers, including Toombs and Manenti (Conforti had passed away in 2000).[20]

Since Berkshire's acquisition, MiTek has been increasingly acquisitive—closing more than forty deals.[21] Most of MiTek's acquisitions build on strengths, as when acquiring direct competitors or complementary product lines. Called "bolt-on" acquisitions, a good example is United Steel Products (USP). This company, founded in 1954, makes structural framing and connectors. MiTek had a longstanding exclusive distribution agreement with USP through which the two successfully collaborated on numerous projects. In 1998, when USP was acquired by Gibraltar Steel Corporation, USP's relationship with MiTek was one of Gibraltar's motivations.[22] That relationship also led to MiTek's acquisition of USP in 2011. The combination enabled bringing all aspects of the arrangement under MiTek's control.

In contrast to bolt-on acquisitions are those dubbed "tuck-in" acquisitions: the transaction brings a related but new business, not bolting on to anything, but not pure diversification either. For example, Benson Industries, which MiTek acquired in 2013, is the global leader in curtain wall systems for high-end buildings worldwide. An expensive alternative to conventional reinforced concrete, curtains are used in buildings intended to last for centuries. Examples of Benson projects include New York's Freedom Tower (One World Trade Center) and United Nations building and Singapore's Marina Bay Sands.

Berkshire encourages subsidiaries to make further bolt-on acquisitions, and most subsidiaries do so, MiTek with alacrity. In 2008, for instance, MiTek acquired Hohmann & Barnard (H&B), a New York–based family business founded in 1933, whose products focus on anchoring systems that support marble and granite facades on buildings of all sizes. Beyond bolting on to MiTek's existing construction materials businesses, H&B then made further bolt-ons. It acquired Blok-Lok, maker of wire reinforcement ties for masonry; Sandell, maker of a complementary line of products used in waterproofing a building as it is constructed; Dur-O-Wal, a direct competitor and pioneer in innovative masonry reinforcements; and RKL Building Specialties Co., another local rival.

Berkshire subsidiaries adopt their own acquisition philosophies, which may follow or vary from Berkshire's. For example, when making tuck-in acquisitions, many Berkshire subsidiaries promise both continuity and autonomy to newly acquired firms and managers. When making bolt-on acquisitions of direct competitors, in contrast, there may be no way to make either promise. Transaction value often lies in eliminating redundancies. When H&B acquired archrival Dur-O-Wal, for example, the two each continued to sell their respective patented innovations but eliminated duplicative operations.[23]

What unites Berkshire subsidiaries in the acquisition arena is that they share an investor's astuteness, including replicating Berkshire's approach of compensating sellers not only with economic value but with intangible forms of exchange, too. They look for cultures that fit their own. Most of Berkshire's more acquisitive subsidiaries had become acquisitive long before being acquired by Berkshire. Both before and after Berkshire's ownership, their cultures were a valued part of the deal.

Preliminarily, this means screening potential targets to ensure cultural fit. Such compatibility is important when joining any two businesses because a similar culture promotes a more productive union. Equally as important, congenial cultures enable the buyer to offer intangible values in the exchange. Following this practice in many of Berkshire's direct acquisitions, subsidiaries are able to acquire targets at prices lower than the seller would demand of a buyer lacking the cultural attraction.

In 2009, for example, MiTek acquired Heat Pipe Technology, a pioneer in providing sophisticated energy and humidity control piping for heating, ventilation, and air conditioning (HVAC) systems. The company was founded and owned by Khanh Dinh, who escaped from Vietnam before the war in the 1960s and established himself in Florida. Dinh is an inventor, engineer, and visionary who built his business from scratch. In evaluating a sale, it was vital to him that the buyer understood his business, appreciated his products, and collaborated on product development. MiTek met his requirements, lowering its bill in the acquisition.

MiTek's acquisitions are an inherent part of its business model. In turn, granting subsidiaries operational autonomy is a key feature of its strategy—USP, Benson, H&B, and Heat Pipe are autonomously operated. At headquarters, MiTek boasts a central mergers-and-acquisitions (M&A) function, with one executive responsible for finding and vetting opportunities. MiTek also has a liaison at headquarters to coordinate subsidiary back office needs—the accounting, human resources, and legal departments. The organization is decentralized, with a coterie of group presidents who report to the CEO overseeing the autonomous subsidiaries operating within their group.

MiTek's high comfort level with this kind of decentralization is reinforced by the autonomy Berkshire grants. MiTek's senior managers are not necessarily required to clear acquisitions ahead of time. As a matter of practice, MiTek's CEO keeps Berkshire's CEO informed by sending written notes monthly and calling when pending opportunities are sizable or further afield than typical bolt-ons. In addition, Berkshire's subsidiary chief executives are responsible for recommending their successors. When Toombs was about to retire, he called Manenti, who had retired a few years earlier, and asked him to return. Manenti had declined numerous business opportunities during his retirement, but this one he accepted because he knew that he would have the autonomy to run the business as he deemed appropriate. Manenti explained in an interview for this book: "Berkshire and Buffett give me total autonomy. Being treated that way makes it easy for me to treat our managers the same way."[24]

～

The Lubrizol Corporation's story narrates the reawakening of a noble but sleepy company, which turned into a huge profit center for Berkshire. Beginning with one large and transformative acquisition, followed by a series of bolt-ons, chief executive James L. Hambrick stimulated Lubrizol's workforce to leverage their knowledge of surface technology across multiple platforms.

Lubrizol was created in 1928 by a group of former Dow Chemical Co. employees, including three sons of Albert W. Smith, a chemistry professor who had cofounded Dow in 1897.[25] They formed the Graphite Oil Products Company, a chemical concern providing solutions for the emerging automotive and petroleum industries. For instance, they created a product—involving the arcane feat of suspending graphite in oil—to prevent squeaks and creaks in car suspension springs. In the 1930s, they conquered a problem that often deterred people from buying cars entirely, overheating engines, by creating a chlorine-containing additive to cool running engines. This lubricant additive explains the company's name today: Lubri-zol. In 1935, General Motors and other automakers endorsed Lubrizol (the hyphen was dropped in 1943) for use in their engines.

The founders perfected Lubrizol's business model and moat. The marketing team works closely with customers, manufacturers, and regulators to identify problems. This team explains any problems to Lubrizol's scientists, who research solutions. In additives, for example, Lubrizol works with manufacturers—makers of vehicles, marine diesel engines, power plant generators—who want lubricants like motor oil or transmission fluid to enhance operation and longevity. Lubrizol buys base oil and other petrochemicals and develops additives to create products that will do so, which it sells to lubricant makers. These customers, in turn, want their products approved for use in manufacturers' equipment, and Lubrizol provides the performance-tested certifications. As the intellectual and research link in the value chain, Lubrizol charges a premium for its expertise and validation, branding what would otherwise be commodity products.

By the late 1980s, Lubrizol was a global leader in producing petroleum additives. Yet the industry was now mature, with limited growth prospects. For example, in 1987, Lubrizol's annual revenues crossed the $1 billion mark, producing income of $81 million; in 2003, sixteen years later, net income was $91 million.[26] At this time, however, a young veteran chemical engineer who had joined Lubrizol in the 1970s at the age of eighteen rose to become president in 2002 and CEO in 2004.[27]

This employee, James Hambrick, had been a keen observer of Lubrizol's corporate development activities for a long time. Hambrick stressed that the nominal growth in revenues and tiny growth in income meant that Lubrizol was shrinking. It had survived on its additive business but was not prospering. Hambrick wanted to send a message to employees and customers that the only businesses that warrant reinvestment are those that earn high rates of return on capital and expertise.

Hambrick thought it would be disingenuous to ask Lubrizol's research scientists to invent Lubrizol into prosperity.[28] Instead, he proposed to translate core competencies into new product lines. Lubrizol's core competencies involved putting specialty chemicals on the most difficult surfaces, such as internal combustion engines running at high speeds for long periods. The strategic vision was to expand outward, putting specialty chemicals on every surface imaginable, from items as diverse as hair and paint to money.

In April 2003, Hambrick asked Lubrizol's board to authorize management to seek a big acquisition to expand beyond its traditional business. It took a year, but in early 2004, Lubrizol acquired Noveon International, Inc., a specialty chemical firm once part of The B. F. Goodrich Company, owned since 2001 by private equity firms. The businesses were complementary: Lubrizol led in fluid technologies for the transportation industry, whereas Noveon created personal consumer products and specialty coatings, polyvinyl, polyurethane, and liquid polymers. In technical terms, Noveon excelled in polymer chemistry, a complement to the traditional monomer chemistry underlying Lubrizol's additives businesses.

Paying $1.84 billion ($920 million in cash plus assuming $920 million in debt), Noveon had revenues of $1.2 billion, and Lubrizol had revenues of $2 billion. Buying a scientific business from private equity owners was a shrewd move. For one, such firms sometimes skimp on research and development vital to the prosperity of companies like Lubrizol and Noveon, revealing to a chemical engineer like Hambrick value propositions less visible to private equity investors.[29] In addition, private equity firms run short-lived funds that can result in pressure to sell, giving buyers an edge in price negotiations.

Lubrizol's acquisition of Noveon has proven pivotal. In personal care, Lubrizol became involved in making coatings for skin and hair products made by companies like Avon, Estee Lauder, and Procter & Gamble, against competitors like Dow Chemical's Rohm & Haas. Surface technologies encompass a range of industrial coatings, where customers might be Benjamin Moore, Sherwin-Williams, or Valspar, and competitors include BASF.[30] Lubrizol is poised to exploit specific niche applications of the future, including, for example, coatings for currency, as monetary authorities shift from using paper for money to various plastics.[31] Looking back on the Noveon deal, Hambrick explained:

> Noveon allowed me to demonstrate that I was serious in saying that if we cannot figure out how to grow additives, it [was] not worth reinvesting in. It was a signal to the outside world, including our customers, and it [was] going to send a huge signal to my organization. And if there [was] any way to ever jar the inertia of the organization, that

was it. The team would probably rather not admit it to me, but I am telling you, Noveon was an "Oh my gosh" moment at the company.[32]

In the decade following the addition of Noveon, Lubrizol made many smaller acquisitions, ranging in price from $100 to $500 million. All focus on surface-related chemicals, and all bring talented scientists and business managers that fit with Lubrizol's ethical and research-driven culture.[33] Lubrizol's acquisitions increase the research and development capability to exploit the company's deepest desires: "to use science where art had prevailed."[34]

Such new technologies widen Lubrizol's moat through patents and trade secrets. Recent examples, which add up to more than $500 million of investment, include acquisitions in the field of specialty thermoplastic polyurethanes (TPUs) as well as the acquisition of Active Organics, Inc., a Texas-based maker of botanical extracts useful in hair care products. In all events, Lubrizol is careful to avoid overpaying, as two examples will attest.

In the summer of 2010, Cognis, maker of specialty chemicals for the nutrition, mining, and personal care industries, was put up for sale by its private equity owners, Goldman Sachs and Permira, which had acquired it in 2001 from Henkel AG & Co. BASF Corporation, Dow Chemical, and Lubrizol all were interested, and the sellers invited preemptive bids. Lubrizol's was the highest, at nearly $4 billion, edging out BASF's, but Goldman and Permira signaled an inclination to go with BASF.[35] This meant that in order to have a chance at acquiring Cognis, Lubrizol needed to counter with a meaningfully higher bid. Hambrick reckoned that by putting another $250 million into the deal, Lubrizol might be able to wrestle Cognis away from BASF. But he declined the opportunity. Hambrick advises that, in acquisitions, you must "be disciplined, and there is a fine line beyond which you're being foolish."[36]

Concerning a later potential deal, on the Friday afternoon of Labor Day weekend 2012, Hambrick typed an email to Buffett.[37] Hambrick had concluded that it would be unwise to continue the pursuit. Hambrick felt the price was too high. So he hit "send" and hoped Buffett would concur. Not having heard back that night as would have been typical for Buffett, Hambrick called Buffett the next morning. "Warren Buffett here," Hambrick heard, on the first ring. Before Hambrick could state his last name, Buffett said, "Yes, James, got your email, good decision, no problem."

Lubrizol is a story of growth from acquisitions that amplified internal capability. By 2011, net income reached $1 billion.[38] Lubrizol joined what Buffett called the Berkshire "fabulous five," its five largest non-insurance companies. Lubrizol's scale and global reach enables it to make smaller acquisitions that add outstanding scientists, technology, and inventions, whose value it multiplies, a practice it calls "buying small and building large."[39]

And more is on the way. In 2014, Berkshire reinvested $1.4 billion in Lubrizol through an acquisition of Phillips Specialty Products Inc., a unit of Phillips 66 engaged in developing flow improvers for industrial pipelines. Berkshire paid for the acquisition by swapping a large portion of common stock of Phillips it owned.

~

In coming years, a large outlet for Berkshire's capital will be in the energy sector, chiefly through massive acquisitions by Berkshire Hathaway Energy (as MidAmerican Energy Holdings Co. was renamed in 2014). The energy company's roots date to the 1970s when the global oil shortages foretold an energy crisis. This inspired Charles Condy of San Francisco to form California Energy Co. (Cal Energy or CE) and develop geothermal power. In 1978, the ensuing crisis prompted Congress to pass laws promoting renewable energy, a boon for CE, which went public in 1987. Condy, who later became famous for founding one of San Francisco's best restaurants, Aqua, gained a reputation for being a free spender, and CE struggled.[40]

Energy was also on the mind of Walter Scott Jr., the second most prominent businessman in Omaha, with an office one floor below Buffett's, and a Berkshire director since 1988. He ran Peter Kiewit Sons Inc., a prosperous construction firm involved in building bridges, dams, highways, and power plants. As Kiewit diversified in the 1980s, it developed an interest in the emerging field of converting waste into energy.[41] Kiewit worked on a dozen projects with a division of Ogden Corporation, run by one David L. Sokol, whom Scott got to know well. In October 1990, after Sokol left Ogden, Scott encouraged him to scout for energy projects the two might pursue together.[42]

Sokol identified CE as a potential takeover target. In 1991, Kiewit invested $80 million to acquire 34 percent of CE's stock.[43] Scott soon joined CE's board, along with two other Kiewit executives. The CE board named Sokol chief executive; Condy left. Sokol cut costs, slashing $12 million of annual overhead within his first three months.[44] He relocated CE's headquarters from San Francisco to Omaha, to be closer to Kiewit, firing more than half the staff.[45]

CE grew dramatically, mainly through acquisitions that Sokol engineered along with his number two and successor, Gregory E. Abel. Kiewit provided acquisition financing, often taking large minority interests in CE plants.[46] As of 1992, CE operated five geothermal plants in California; within a few years, it also operated five in each of Indonesia and the Philippines.

In late 1994 and early 1995, CE waged a successful hostile tender offer to obtain control of Magma Power Co., a San Diego based competitor—in his pre-Berkshire days, Sokol was not averse to making hostile takeovers.[47] The $1 billion acquisition cemented CE's position as a leading energy company in California. In 1996, after the United Kingdom deregulated its utility sector, Sokol targeted Northern Electric, a large electric utility in northern England (today called Northern Powergrid Holdings Co.). Paying $1.7 billion, CE took a 70 percent interest alongside Kiewit's 30 percent stake. This made CE a global player in the energy business, which was brimming with new investment opportunities as regulators worldwide eliminated historical restrictions that limited ownership of utilities to local firms.[48]

In 1997, CE attempted a takeover of New York State Electric & Gas Corporation. Its board resisted the $1.9 billion overture, however, and CE quickly abandoned the effort.[49] By this time, CE's growth meant it no longer needed Kiewit's financial backing, and Kiewit was eager to cash out from the energy field. So CE spent $1.16 billion to repurchase all of Kiewit's stock and interests in other properties.[50] Scott and another Kiewit executive remained on the board, though a third Kiewit nominee resigned.

In 1998, CE acquired MidAmerican Energy in a $4 billion deal. MidAmerican Energy was a creature of the new era of energy deregulation, too, a product of mergers in 1990 and 1995 among regional utilities serving customers in Illinois, Iowa, Nebraska, and South Dakota. After this acquisition, CE reorganized, changed its name to MidAmerican Energy Holdings Co., and relocated headquarters to Des Moines, Iowa.

By 1999, after eight years as chief executive, Sokol wearied of running a public energy company.[51] He didn't like the analysts' pressure. They wanted short-term results, whereas he preferred to focus on the long term. They wanted more deal velocity. He wanted to make acquisitions selectively. Some energy stocks had become market darlings with high stock prices, such as Dynegy Inc. and Enron Corporation; MidAmerican Energy did not experience such frothiness.

In late 1999, Sokol asked MidAmerican's board about going private. They considered a management leveraged buyout (LBO) but didn't like this idea because it would entail breakups and layoffs. On a Friday afternoon, Sokol called Scott to discuss alternatives. Scott was with Buffett in

California that weekend. Scott asked Buffett if he might be interested in making an investment in MidAmerican Energy. After reviewing the company and meeting with Scott and Sokol during the week, Buffett agreed. For a total of $2 billion, Berkshire bought 76 percent, and Scott took the rest (along with small stakes owned by Abel and Sokol). The buyers also assumed MidAmerican's $7 billion in debt.

Sokol opined that the market had not yet appreciated the increased values that lay ahead as the result of ongoing deregulation in the energy sector.[52] There were 150 U.S. companies delivering power to the same customers that a dozen telecom companies served; Sokol forecasted industry consolidation that would shrink the number of energy suppliers to below twenty. Stressing that Berkshire intended to "pour a lot of capital into this sector,"[53] when asked how many of those 150 Berkshire hoped to buy, Sokol said, "As many as we can."[54]

Berkshire and MidAmerican's ensuing—and continuing—acquisitions vindicate Sokol's hope, as they have invested significant capital in the sector. For instance, in 2002 MidAmerican Energy paid nearly $3 billion to acquire two strategically located interstate natural gas pipelines: the Kern River Gas Transmission Company (running from Wyoming to Southern California) and Northern Natural Gas Company (running from Texas to the upper Midwest).[55]

In 2005, MidAmerican Energy and Berkshire together invested $5.1 billion to acquire PacificCorp., an energy generator in six large western states (California, Idaho, Oregon, Utah, Washington, and Wyoming). In the joint stake, MidAmerican Energy covered $1.7 billion, and Berkshire provided the greater share of $3.4 billion. Berkshire's direct investment reflects that MidAmerican Energy acquisitions, by far the largest that Berkshire subsidiaries make, are an important investment pipeline for Berkshire's excess cash. MidAmerican's contributions to the deals are often funded with borrowed money, unusual for Berkshire subsidiaries. But given that the company's operations in the utility field remain regulated, its borrowing costs are low and easily covered by its cash flows.

The newly competitive energy environment can lead to surprising payoffs. In late 2008, for example, MidAmerican Energy bid $4.7 billion to acquire Constellation Energy, a Baltimore-based power company then teetering on bankruptcy. The sweetheart price was quickly topped by a French competitor, leaving MidAmerican Energy at the altar. But the merger agreement's breakup fee kicked in. Combined with profit on the shares it had acquired, Berkshire netted more than $1 billion.[56] This transaction is just one example of how Berkshire avoids participating in auction processes with multiple buyers bidding for the same company. An auction often induces bidding based on the emotional desire to win rather than cold business analysis, a result behavioral economists call the "winner's curse."[57]

From 2008 to 2013, MidAmerican Energy and Berkshire staked billions more acquiring a potpourri of assets concentrated in alternative energy sources, especially wind and solar, including Alta Wind, Bishop Hill Wind, Juniper Wind, and Topaz Solar Farms. When current projects are completed, MidAmerican's investments in renewable energy will add up to $15 billion.[58]

From an investment viewpoint, regulated public utilities may not promise outsized payoffs, but they are secure investments with reasonable returns. In addition, MidAmerican's other energy investments promise sizable returns, particularly as industry consolidation accelerates.[59]

In 2013, the two struck again with a replay of the 2005 PacificCorp deal, jointly investing $5.6 billion to acquire NV Energy, whose principal businesses are Nevada Power Company and Sierra Pacific Power Company. MidAmerican Energy, now led by Abel, continues to hunt for such opportunities to invest its capital as well as Berkshire's. As it does, Berkshire's largest investment pipeline will expand to funnel massive amounts of capital into projects as far afield as hydro power, erecting a deep and wide moat around MidAmerican. In 2014, the two invested $2.9 billion to acquire AltaLink, a Canadian power transmission company, and the same week announced the new name of the old MidAmerican: Berkshire Hathaway Energy.

∽

For Berkshire, the economic value of subsidiary acquisitions has compounded as their number and size have increased. They are vehicles for allocating large amounts of capital. In each of 2012 and 2013, for example, Berkshire's subsidiaries made more than two dozen acquisitions. Transaction values ranged from less than $2 million to more than $1 billion. Total deal value was $2.3 billion in 2012 and $3.1 billion in 2013.[60] The opportunity to deploy large amounts of capital through a single subsidiary in individual transactions is vivid in the case of MidAmerican (now Berkshire Hathaway Energy). The intangible value of such opportunities assumed even greater significance in Berkshire's acquisition of Burlington Northern Santa Fe Railway, the lead story in the next chapter.

Table 9.1
Highlights of Recent Berkshire Subsidiary Acquisitions

Berkshire Subsidiary	Acquired Business	Year	$ (millions)*
Acme Brick	Jenkins Brick	2010	50
BH Media	Being built by acquisition of scores of local newspapers		
Clayton Homes	Cavalier Homes	2009	22
	Southern Energy Homes	2006	95
	Fleetwood	2005	64
	Karsten	2005	
	Oakwood Homes	2004	328
CTB	Meyn Food Processing	2012	
	Ironwood Plastics	2010	
	Shore Sales of Illinois	2010	
	Uniqfill International B.V.	2008	
	B. Mannebeck Landtechnik GmbH	2008	
	Laake GmbH	2007	
	Porcon Beheer B.V.	2007	
Forest River	Dynamax	2011	
	Shasta	2010	
	Coachmen	2008	
	Rance Aluminum	2007	
Fruit of the Loom	Vanity Fair Brands	2007	350
	Russell Corporation	2006	1,120
HomeServices	Being built by acquisition of scores of local real estate brokers		
ISCAR/IMC	Sangdong Mining (minority interest)	2012	35
	Tungaloy	2008	
Justin Brands	Highland Shoe Co.	2013	
Lubrizol	Phillips Specialty Products Inc.	2014	1,400
	Chemtool	2013	70
	Lipotec	2012	
	Active Organics	2011	
	Nalco's Personal Care Business	2011	
	Merquinsa	2011	
	Dow's TPU Business	2008	60
Marmon Group	Beverage Dispenser Division of IMI (including 3Wire Group, Display Technologies, and IMI Cornelius)	2013	1,100
	Tarco Steel Inc. (by Bushwick Metals)	2012	

(*continued*)

Table 9.1
(*Continued*)

Berkshire Subsidiary	Acquired Business	Year	$ (millions)*
McLane	Missouri Beverage Co. (joint venture)	2013	
	Meadowbrook Meat Co.	2012	
	Empire Distributors	2010	
	Horizon Wine & Spirits (by Empire)	2010	
Berkshire	AltaLink	2014	2,900
Hathaway	Nevada Power & Light	2013	5,600
Energy	Bishop Hill Wind	2012	
	Alta Wind	2012	
	Topaz Solar Farms	2011	
	American Electric Power	2009	
	Juniper Wind	2008	
	PacifiCorp	2005	5,100
	Kern River Gas Transmission	2002	950
	Northern Natural Gas	2000	1,900
MiTek	Truss Industry Production Systems (Wizard)	2014	
	Benson Industries	2013	
	Cubic Designs	2013	
	Kova Solutions	2013	
	RKL Building Specialties (by Hohmann & Barnard)	2013	
	Sandell (by Hohmann & Barnard)	2011	
	United Steel Products	2011	
	Dur-O-Wal (by Hohmann & Barnard)	2010	
	Gang-Nail, Ltd. (reacquisition)	2010	
	Heat Pipe Technology	2009	
	SidePlate Systems Inc.	2009	
	Hohmann & Barnard	2008	
	Robbins Engineering	2006	
NetJets	Marquis Jet Partners	2010	
NICO	Hartford Life International (by Columbia Insurance)	2013	285
Oriental Trading	MindWare Holdings, Inc.	2013	
Richline	HONORA Inc.	2013	
Scott Fetzer	Rozinn Electronics (by Scott Care division)	2007	
Shaw	Stuart Flooring	2010	
TTI	Ray-Q Interconnect Ltd.	2013	
	Sager Electronics	2012	

*Dollar amounts provided when publicly available.

Source note: The author compiled the information in this table from public sources; in addition, the figures concerning Clayton Homes were supplied by the company.

10

Rudimentary

National Indemnity's website awkwardly avows that it "might be one of the largest insurance companies you've never heard of." Many Berkshire companies can make a similar claim. Unless you are a Berkshire devotee or have some connection to given companies, before reading this book you were unlikely to be familiar with many Berkshire subsidiaries, including FlightSafety, ISCAR/IMC, Lubrizol, or MiTek. On the other hand, many Berkshire subsidiaries have instant brand name recognition: Dairy Queen, Fruit of the Loom, GEICO, and Justin. But what unites all of these Berkshire subsidiaries is a sense of modesty and simplicity.

Berkshire companies engage in businesses (energy, shelter, transportation, chemicals) or other pursuits that stick to basic principles and aptitudes (insurance, clothing, furniture, jewelry, vacuums, tools, and metalworking). Pilot training and fractional airplane ownership are as glamorous as Berkshire gets. Berkshire businesses favor simplicity to flash.

What are the appeals of such a business? What is there about rudimentary businesses as a class that make such a trait part of Berkshire's culture?

One popular answer is that Buffett is a technophobe. He jokes publicly and often about coming late to the advent of the cell phone, laptop, and social media. Anyone reading this book or scanning a list of the businesses of Berkshire subsidiaries (a list appears in the appendix to this book) might intuit such an aversion.

Berkshire's acquisition criteria state a preference for businesses that are easy to understand, noting that those with a high degree of technology are harder to grasp. But there is much more to this "rudimentary" feature of Berkshire culture than mere personal idiosyncrasies. Institutional permanence once again plays a role. Basic industries are defined as those that have been around for hundreds of years and are likely to be around for as many more: agriculture, energy, fishing, forestry, and mining, closely followed by chemicals, metal lurgy, and transport.

In this conception, old economy is good economy, and new economy is riskier. During recent periods of rapid technological advancement, people have obsessed over change and technology. Such an obsession increases the chance of wasting resources when trying to keep up with the fast pace; a focus on the rudimentary reduces the potential for such waste. Rudimentary businesses are also more insulated from technological onslaughts than are technology-driven businesses.

In rudimentary businesses, it is easier to embrace the adage, "if it's not broke, don't fix it." In cutting-edge businesses, it is difficult to be confident about resource allocation to sustain business direction. The payoffs can be big, and the allure is strong, which explains why so many take this route. But at Berkshire, it is more important to avoid losing money than to make it. Berkshire's acquisition criteria on this point are less about technology per se—many rudimentary businesses invest heavily in technology—and more about the importance of understanding any given business.

∼

Burlington Northern Santa Fe (BNSF)—an amalgamation of nearly four hundred different railroads dating to 1849 and among the four dominant companies today—hauls freight long distances across North America by rail. The business has been necessary and lucrative for a century and a half and will likely be at least as important and probably more profitable in the next century and a half. As independent railroad analyst Anthony B. Hatch put it, the industry has been experiencing a "rail renaissance."[1]

BNSF's culture, hatched in two stages, is almost tailor-made for Berkshire, fostering entrepreneurship and looking ahead as far as fifty years. The first stage, forged in the 1980s after the deregulation of railroads, represented a break with the industry's ancient traditions; the second, dating to the 1995 merger of two titans, marked the embrace of America's modern corporate practices.

From the 1850s through the end of the nineteenth century, railroads expanded capacity greatly, each reigning over specific territories. Their power and importance prompted federal regulation. In 1906, the Hepburn Act gave the Interstate Commerce Commission authority to set the prices railroads could charge customers—regulations that remained in place until 1980. The effect of such price control, which barges and trucking escaped, riveted the industry on cutting costs and crimped the railroad's incentives to promote customer service.[2]

Beginning in the 1930s, the industry idled as expanding alternatives—aviation, barges, trucking, and pipelines—diminished demand. From the 1950s on, with the proliferation of automobiles and the growth of suburbia, demand for passenger rail service eroded in many parts of the country. The industry had more assets than its business could support. In response to this excess, railroads merged with one another, whittling their number down from hundreds to scores.[3]

The initials in the name *BNSF* offer a flavor of that process. *Burlington* dates to 1849, with the founding in Illinois of the Aurora Branch Railroad, which grew into the Chicago, Burlington, and Quincy Railroad. *Northern* components include nineteenth-century industry forces: the Great Northern Railway and the Northern Pacific Railway. These two consolidated in 1970 to form Burlington Northern (called the BN).[4] The *Santa Fe* dates to 1859's formation of the Atchison, Topeka, and Santa Fe Railway, among the first to complete a transcontinental railroad.

By the 1970s, the railroad industry was in crisis. Rail continued losing ground to other modes of transportation, the passenger rail business all but died, and profits shrank, all while the costs of rail maintenance remained high. Milestones of the period underscoring the troubles included the federal government's creation of the National Railroad Passenger Corporation ("Amtrak") to provide passenger service and the bankruptcy of the Penn Central. A consensus emerged that regulation was part of the problem, leading to industry deregulation in the Railroad Revitalization and Regulatory Reform Act of 1976 and the Staggers Act of 1980.

Deregulation created a radically different business environment. The new world was competitive and demanded change in corporate operations. BN moved more aggressively than its rivals for one reason: its board appointed executives who came from outside the industry, a group with no allegiances to existing culture.[5]

At BN in the 1980s, policy changed to stress return on investment rather than scale of operations and a longer-term outlook than predecessors had held.[6] The railroad industry had not historically been characterized as entre-preneurial; employees thought of their jobs as running trains rather than serving customers.[7] Deregulation changed all that. The managerial mission shifted from being railroad operators to asset managers.[8] BN, for instance, began research and development to find cheaper, cleaner, and more local fuels to power locomotives.[9] By the early 2000s, senior executives spoke only in terms of return on invested capital rather than the industry's tradi-tional talk of market share.[10]

Historically, autonomy was not an industry hallmark either. Although company cultures varied, all had rigid command-and-control management systems. Some (such as Santa Fe) used a top-down militaristic style, oth-ers showed managerial arrogance, and a few (including Great Northern) were more caring for employees though still hierarchical.[11] At BN after deregulation, the historical practice of command-and-control changed, too. Management found that rigid adherence to rules and blind respect for hierarchies proved ineffective in business.[12]

Employee safety provides a vivid example of the cultural changes that occurred. For more than a century through the 1970s, all railroads had poor safety records. Old-fashioned railroad culture ensured it—macho men wore rings easily caught in machinery, sported beards that interfered with dust masks, and swung on and off moving equipment. Command-and-control cultures reinforced ignorance about danger and complacency about protec-tion. Management and workers, led by hostile unions, each held the other side responsible for injuries and accepted the status quo.

At BN, the depth of these attitudes led to the worst safety record in the industry.[13] But during the early 1990s, a group of senior managers created a revolution in railroad safety. They sold the agenda to colleagues by stressing the high costs of unsafe conditions: liability claims and settlements, along with disrupted operations. They banned climbing on moving equipment, wearing rings, and growing beards. The company began training programs to shift its culture from the bravado of traditional railroad lore to the pru-dence of contemporary attitudes.

BN's safety record improved greatly. Billions of dollars were saved, along with untold eyes, fingers, limbs, and lungs.[14] The company reinforced its successes with a merit system called the 2.5 Club, a reference to the industry's lowest injury rate (2.5 injuries per 200,000 man-hours). Every employee in the group received five shares of BN stock. So radical was this change—merit systems were unheard of in punitive-oriented command-and-control traditions—that proponents within management not only lobbied fellow executives but worked with union representatives to increase labor's support among the rank and file. The culture changed industry wide. For example, the Santa Fe developed improved safety measures, too, including giving employees one free pair of steel-toed boots every year.

When BN and Santa Fe merged in 1995, a second wave of cultural change came with it. The initial motivation was due to differences in culture between the two merging firms. BNSF's first CEO, Robert D. Krebs, explained: "I wasn't much on cultures until I got here and I realized how different the two were between BN and Santa Fe. I don't think you can overestimate the differences."[15] The cultures seemed incompatible:

> The Santa Fe had a reputation of being a cohesive unit of tough, single-minded executives. The BN, on the other hand, was considered "softer," less disciplined. The BN people would hold meetings and seemingly reach agreement, but they would begin questioning everything as soon as the meeting ended.[16]

Krebs and his executive team, including COO, Carl R. Ice, helped meld the cultures together, which was not easy. Contrasting background assumptions drove these alternative cultures and their corresponding managerial approaches:

> The guys from Santa Fe believed that people were inherently bad and [they behaved based on] rewards and punishments. [The BN guys] believed that people are inherently good and only do bad things when they are threatened.[17]

Krebs and Ice retained consultants to help BNSF managers develop a new culture. The effect was a practical compromise between extreme positions. Pragmatism would guide most issues, and resolution would differ with circumstances. For example, when asked whether the organization should be centralized or decentralized, the answer was *both*, depending on the context. Decentralization may be best for crew training programs, and centralization better suited for capital allocation decisions.

In 2000, Krebs was succeeded by forty-year-old Matthew K. Rose, whose background was in the trucking industry. The move echoed that of the BN board appointing railroad industry outsiders to lead the company after deregulation. Rose's appointment came after a pivotal period in the industry. The newly forged culture had come about through the most radical and rapid change in railroad history. Command-and-control was out. As railroad historian Lawrence Kaufman wrote in his history of BNSF:

> Today's rail workers are not as willing as their fathers were to accept either the harsh discipline or the demanding nature of their jobs. Change comes slowly in the railroad industry, but the more progressive leaders like Rose are trying to foster a more cooperative and even collegial culture.[18]

BNSF promoted another cultural change in the railroad industry: customer service, especially in the intermodal sector. This refers to the high-speed transport of trailers and containers that can be moved easily among trains, trucks, and vessels. Such shipments begin on trucks, so customers need reasons to put cargo on rail. Railroads win business by providing cheaper, safer, more reliable delivery. BNSF, which leads the industry in intermodal transport, began to offer service guarantees to customers. Customers pay a premium, boosting revenue, improving service, and attracting more business—a virtuous circle.

Premium services include cross-border container service with customs clearance, track upgrades to handle heavier cars and freight, better routes to speed travel, temperature controls, and guaranteed on-time service. A marketing slogan backs this promise: "It's on time or it's on us." BNSF led the industry in offering full money-back guarantees. It also was the first to offer an equipment guarantee program. The program lets customers secure specific car types, whether flatcar, boxcar, gondola, bulkhead, or refrigerated car. BNSF's services enable its marketing and sales team to differentiate BNSF from competitors—including the trucking industry.

Krebs had put BNSF at the forefront of this shift to a customer service orientation, and the combination of Rose's experience in the trucking industry and Ice's operational commitment to promoting a coherent culture reinforces this BNSF strength. Service innovation has supplanted cost cutting as the industry's strategic driver. BNSF moved from being the low-cost transporter to being a service provider that keeps its promises.

Today's customer-focused BNSF moves enormous volumes of coal, grain, oil, freight, and containers across the continent, especially over the western two-thirds of the United States. One particularly valuable line, created in the 1970s by BN, hauls coal from Wyoming's Powder River Basin. BNSF carries the coal north and south then in many directions via BNSF's other lines to coal-burning power plants nationwide. Another franchise serves thousands of grain elevators across the Midwest, transporting grain to the Pacific Northwest for local use or export to Asia and south to Texas for local use or export from the Gulf of Mexico. BNSF runs rapid intermodal transport between Chicago and Los Angeles, carrying truck trailers and sea containers.

Employing 43,500 people, BNSF has assets worth some $60 billion, produces annual revenues exceeding $22 billion, and adds $5 billion to Berkshire's yearly bottom line.[19] Assets include three transcontinental routes using high-speed links. The company hosts commuter trains in several locales, including southern California, New Mexico, and Puget Sound, plus numerous Amtrak passenger train services across America. BNSF maintains transfer facilities throughout the western United States to coordinate freight traffic movement. These include an extensive facility near the port of Los Angeles that directly links rail with overland and sea transport. BNSF owns thousands of locomotives and tens of thousands of freight cars in all shapes and sizes to meet customer needs.

BNSF—and its industry—compete with the trucking industry and have gained advantages in recent years. In the early 2000s, as railroad executives began to speak about return on invested capital, many long-term supply agreements made years earlier at deep discounts—up to 40 percent below market—expired. The companies renewed these agreements at market rates to drive up returns on invested capital.[20]

As fuel costs rose, BNSF began to make them a pass-through item of transport contracts. Rising fuel costs became a double benefit to rail: the companies did not have to absorb all costs, and customers found rail more fuel efficient than trucking, thus making rail a cheaper choice.[21] Increased U.S. trade with Asia and Mexico drove growth, too, especially at BNSF and Union Pacific, the nation's western railways. The railways mirror the country in many ways, with the overall reduction in demand for coal lately being a drag on profits, whereas the overall uptick in fracking, industrial activity, and automobile production has boosted revenues.

Berkshire acquired BNSF gradually, beginning with a series of open-market purchases of its common stock at prices up to $75 per share. In 2010, when it owned 22.5 percent, it acquired the rest in a negotiated acquisition. It paid $100 per share, in a mix of cash and Berkshire stock. It was the only price Berkshire offered, with no negotiation. Twice BNSF's board pressed its negotiating team to seek more than $100, and both times it was rebuffed.

Buffett explained to the team that his analysis of BNSF indicated that its value was about $95 per share. He was prepared to have Berkshire offer $100 in order to guarantee fairness to BNSF shareholders. He was also willing to offer Berkshire stock as part of the deal—not unprecedented in Berkshire acquisitions but done reluctantly—and to give assurances that the number of shares delivered would meet a minimum dollar amount. But he was unwilling to budge on price. BNSF did not seek out any competing bids, as advisers doubted that any superior proposal would be forthcoming.[22]

Some question whether $100 per share for BNSF meant Berkshire overpaid. The price was more than twenty times BNSF's earnings, high by many standards. The ratio was even higher after accounting for how BNSF's capital outlays exceed its depreciation allowance—which would reduce earnings. Critics also wonder about how valuable some BNSF assets are, especially rights of way, which are not useful in other applications and cannot readily be sold.

Take Buffett at his word and say BNSF was worth closer to $95 per share. Why pay $100? BNSF boasts many more intangible values, especially its logical cultural fit for Berkshire and its large size. There is also growth potential. Experts and industry insiders—Matthew K. Rose among them—expect a final round of railroad industry consolidation. They foresee two gigantic systems blanketing North America competing head to head in all regions.[23] BNSF will be one of them.

In addition to exemplifying engagement in rudimentary business—transporting energy, food, and freight across the continent—BNSF is budget conscious and earnest, invested deeply in its reputation, and promotes entrepreneurship in a much flatter organization compared to traditional railroad culture. It is imminently focused on the very long term, routinely acquiring or building assets expected to last up to fifty years. With returns on equity exceeding 20 percent annually in recent years, BNSF is worth every penny of what it cost to acquire.[24]

∽

It isn't just the fact of modest engagement in rudimentary businesses that distinguishes Berkshire subsidiaries; many also share events in their corporate histories in which they learned the hard way the value of sticking to the basics. In a number of cases, a company made a strategic shift, only to realize its mistake and return to fundamentals. Think of FlightSafety's short-lived entry into training ship captains and operators of nuclear reactors or Dairy Queen's flirtation with conglomerate status when acquiring a ski-rental company and a campground chain.

Adventure followed by course correction is an even more dramatic chapter in the corporate history of another mainstay of the Berkshire ship, Shaw Industries Group, Inc. Berkshire's largest non-insurance business when acquired in 2000 and still among the top dozen, Shaw Industries is the world's dominant carpet manufacturer. Its diversions into branding and retailing, however, induced it to refocus entirely and permanently on the rudimentary, basic, and modest task of being the world's low-cost producer in its industry.

Shaw Industries was founded in 1971 by two brothers, Robert E. ("Bob") Shaw and J. C. ("Bud") Shaw.[25] Their father, Julius ("Clarence") Shaw, had run a small fabric dyeing business in their hometown of Dalton, Georgia, a carpet manufacturing mecca. Other family members would play various roles, including cousin Elbert (employee training), brother-in-law Julian McCamy (director), and Bud's son Julius (from trainee to senior manager).

The business the brothers built differed entirely from the business their father had run. The latter's firm was small and focused on a narrow slice of the carpet business; what the sons created was a vast vertically integrated carpet manufacturer. Unlike their father, who was an autocrat with a provincial business sense, the Shaw brothers led an entrepreneurial operation with a flatter organizational structure. The seismic shift in their business venture came in the late 1960s when Bud proposed that he and Bob acquire Philadelphia Carpet Company, a manufacturer founded in the nineteenth century.

The brothers acquired Philadelphia using borrowed funds that were secured in part by the company's assets and in part with personal guarantees. (The deal was a prototype of the leveraged buyout that would soon become fashionable; the brothers' personal guarantees were in the entrepreneurial tradition followed by such Berkshire builders as Ueltschi of FlightSafety and Santulli of NetJets.) Shortly after acquiring Philadelphia, Shaw Industries went public. It used proceeds to retire debt, a sign of thriftiness that would continue to characterize the business.

The Shaw brothers wanted to grow their business into something that would endure. This attitude of permanence contrasted with sentiments at peer companies in the carpet industry. Many sold for quick cash payoffs to conglomerates that expanded during the late 1960s and early 1970s. As one Shaw Industries executive explained: "It was our philosophy from very early on that we were going to build an institution that would survive us all. . . . From the very beginning ours was to build something that would last."[26]

Businesses offering commodity-type products in highly competitive markets, like Shaw Industries, require an entrepreneurial approach that typical conglomerates cannot offer. Shaw's nimbleness positioned it to capitalize on business shifts. For instance, in 1972, population growth in California along with high transportation costs prompted Shaw Industries to construct a new finishing plant there. It established a nationwide distribution system. Throughout the 1970s, Shaw Industries continued to expand its role as a service provider across the industry. For example, it began to process yarn increasingly used in making the shag rugs so popular during the period. In 1973, it entered the field of continuous dyeing by acquiring a company specializing in that process.

As Shaw Industries grew, its divisions were operated autonomously, using a decentralized management structure. Bob Shaw came to see this as a net cost, however. For example, by the late 1970s, Shaw Industries had two broad lines of business, one overseen by Bob, the other by Bud. In Bob's carpet finishing line, the company helped carpet makers; in Bud's carpet making line, they competed with those very customers. To solve these problems, Bob reorganized. He assumed full managerial responsibilities across all segments and streamlined reporting chains vertically; Bud became chairman. Although there was a sacrifice in autonomy among division heads, the vertical integration of the units reduced overall costs.

Cost reduction became the company's mantra, reflecting the realities of the carpet industry. There was no consumer franchise and no brand loyalty. But a competitive advantage—a moat—could be established by becoming the low-cost producer of carpets. In a bold example, in 1982 Shaw Industries formed a trucking subsidiary. Until then, all carpet makers used the same carriers for distribution. Every company's delivery was the same. No company could compete on delivery service because no one controlled it. Shaw Industries created a strategic advantage over its competitors by establishing its own transportation system.

Shaw's delivery service got better—and that of its competitors worse. Why? Because Shaw's relatively larger size meant that it was the "filler" for the industry on the common carriers. When Shaw's orders were removed from those of others in its region, trucks had to make more stops to fill each load, which consumed both time and money. The payoff amplified: the trucking subsidiary was so efficient that Shaw's distribution centers could maintain lower inventory levels while still delivering product, which saved considerable costs. When Shaw Industries persuaded its retail customers that they could reduce inventory while still providing full customer services, they saved as well.

Shaw Industries complemented its cost-driven internal growth of the early 1980s with growth through acquisitions thereafter. It seized a major opportunity in 1988 when a well-known leveraged buyout operator of the period, William F. Farley, targeted Shaw Industries rival West Point-Pepperell. Its diversified businesses included a carpet manufacturer. As a defensive response to the hostile bid, West Point-Pepperell sold the carpet business to Shaw Industries for $140 million. The deal boosted Shaw's annual revenues above $1 billion. The next year it acquired the carpet business of Armstrong World. In integrating both companies, Shaw Industries revamped their cultures to align with its mantra of being the low-cost producer.

Despite emphasizing the competitive advantage of budget consciousness, in the mid-1990s, Shaw Industries made two mistakes. It tried to brand its carpeting and to enter the retail end of the business. Although both efforts failed, neither was illogical when Shaw Industries opted for them. The branding effort was made in the spirit—naïve but well intentioned—of educating consumers about the appeal of a product the company felt pride in. The retail strategy pursued vertical integration as a way to avoid reliance on other parties for business prosperity.

But the branding effort misread consumer appetite for information. Shaw's branding program, called Trustmark, "sank in a sea of technical details," providing yarn face weights and twist levels.[27] The branding effort confused customers and posed high internal costs due to labeling, sampling, and shipping. Julius Shaw called the branding flirtation a "fiasco."[28]

The retailing gambit did more severe damage. Hitting its industry like a sledgehammer, the strategy was almost impossible: keeping Shaw's distribution prowess while going into competition with its customers. To launch the effort, Shaw Industries acquired four hundred stores, from both smaller retailers and two large chains; it then divested one hundred of these as unprofitable. The costs of acquisition and divestiture wiped out any profit that the retained stores might have made.

Trade publications expressed consternation, and customers were furious. As a business rule, wholesalers do not go into competition with their retail customers. (That is why McLane, the wholesale grocer and distributor, promised its convenience store customers not to compete with them, and why, when Walmart acquired McLane, it divested a group of convenience stores.) Shaw's retail customers, the company's lifeblood, felt threatened. Many, including large accounts like Home Depot, simply stopped buying Shaw's products. Shaw Industries lost significant market share. Investors dumped its stock, sending Shaw's market price tumbling.

Beyond that external onslaught, Shaw Industries could not manage its stores. When run by small independent retailers, the owner-managers were entrepreneurial workhorses. But after selling to Shaw Industries for a small fortune, these individuals (whom the company asked to continue as managers) preferred more leisure time. Shaw Industries had difficulty monitoring and motivating them. In short, the company was good at being a low-cost producer of carpets but had no knowledge of running the retail end of the business and faint hope of branding such a commodity product.

By 1998, Shaw Industries abandoned the branding effort and withdrew from running retail stores. It made up with as many of its retailer customers as it could. Bob Shaw announced a return to basics—to doing what had made Shaw Industries great, which was being the low-cost wholesaler of quality carpets. In that vein, Shaw Industries also made an important acquisition, adding Queen Carpet, a longtime peer and friendly cross-town rival, then controlled by the Saul family of Dalton. Queen cultivated a similar corporate culture: a budget-conscious entrepreneurial family business with a sense of permanence. In addition, Queen had gained much of the business Shaw Industries had lost to the exodus of its customers.

Shaw Industries is unlikely to repeat the kinds of mistakes it made when attempting to brand carpets and go retail. But these errors do not impair its entrepreneurial spirit of nimbleness that is so important to business prosperity. On the contrary, as American tastes in recent years have shifted from carpets to other floor coverings, Shaw Industries has expanded its product lines to include hardwood flooring. It still uses its own trucking and distribution facilities—among the competitive advantages contributing to its business moat.

In June 2000, Shaw Industries saw another acquisition opportunity. The prospective partner, however, faced potential asbestos liabilities from past actions, and Shaw Industries wanted to eliminate the risk with an insurance policy.[29] Bob Shaw and Julian Saul made an appointment to discuss the insurance with Buffett. Although Berkshire agreed to write a policy of the size required, Buffett said it would not do so without a cap on its exposure. Shaw Industries opted to skip the merger.

The meeting with Buffett planted the seeds of mutual interest in an acquisition of Shaw Industries by Berkshire. Later that summer, the two made a deal. Berkshire acquired 80 percent of the company, with the Shaw and Saul families retaining the rest for several years—which Berkshire eventually acquired as well. At the time of Berkshire's acquisition, Shaw

Industries, with annual sales of $4 billion, was among Berkshire's largest non-insurance businesses.[30] It remains a stalwart, focusing on what it has always done best.[31]

~

If Shaw's detour into branding and retailing taught lessons about sticking to one's knitting, a final lesson concerns being modest in one's capital structure. This lesson in corporate finance comes from Fruit of the Loom, Inc.

Two old textile companies are the roots of today's Fruit of the Loom: Knight Brothers and the Union Underwear Company.[32] Knight Brothers was a New England family business dating to the mid-nineteenth century. In that era, clothing was typically sewn by hand at home using fabric bought from textile manufacturers. In 1851, Knight Brothers gave their fabric a homespun name, Fruit of the Loom, an innovation in branding decades before such marketing strategies became commonplace. (Some speculate that Fruit of the Loom was a play on the biblical phrase "fruit of the womb," meaning children.[33]) In 1871, when the U.S. Patent and Trademark Office opened, the Knight Brothers were among the first of millions to register a trademark, Fruit of the Loom's logo featuring an apple at the center of a fruit cluster.

By the early 1900s, competitors began manufacturing ready-made garments for homemakers eager to outfit families "off the rack" rather than continue to fashion homemade clothes. Knight Brothers shifted Fruit of the Loom's market focus from homemakers to wholesale apparel manufacturers. In 1928, in another innovation, the company licensed the Fruit of the Loom brand to garment makers. Among these was the young Jacob ("Jack") Goldfarb, who focused on the most popular style of low-priced men's underwear of the period, called the "unionsuit."[34] Goldfarb bought a twenty-five-year license from Knight Brothers to use the Fruit of the Loom label.

Although only a licensee of the brand, Goldfarb took the unusual step of investing his own funds in consumer advertising for Fruit of the Loom.[35] By the mid-1950s, Union Underwear was Fruit of the Loom's largest licensee by far. Thanks to Goldfarb's efforts, consumers associated Fruit of the Loom almost entirely and instantly with underwear rather than fabric, though Fruit of the Loom continued to be a leading fabric seller. In a twist, therefore, the licensee had become bigger than the licensor.

In 1955, the Philadelphia & Reading Coal and Iron Co., which ran an ailing business looking to diversify, acquired Union Underwear. In 1961, Philadelphia & Reading also acquired Fruit of the Loom Licensing Company, bringing licensor and licensee together under the same corporate roof. Goldberg retired in 1968, when Northwest Industries, a Chicago-based conglomerate, acquired Philadelphia & Reading. Despite such ownership changes, both Philadelphia & Reading and then Northwest let the company maintain the entrepreneurial spirit Goldfarb had infused.

Union Underwear continued Goldfarb's practice of branding through innovative advertising. To boost the Fruit of the Loom brand, it hired celebrities such as sportscaster Howard Cosell to feature in television commercials. An ad campaign of 1975 became a pop-culture sensation: three men dressed as elements of the brand, an apple, a leaf, and a grape bunch. The company bought the BVD trademark, an upscale brand, and expanded its own product lines to include blank T-shirts for customers to customize with silk-screen selections—a craze in the period.

By the 1980s, Northwest Industries had become a diversified conglomerate engaged not only in the underwear business but in such fields as car batteries, chemicals, liquors, railroads, steel turbines, and wines. The array drew the attention of leveraged buyout operators of the period—just as Scott Fetzer had attracted interest in 1986 from the likes of Ivan Boesky before Berkshire rescued it from his clutches.

In the 1980s, leveraged buyouts spread across corporate America. To acquire companies, operators borrowed funds secured by the target's assets and repaid by steadily selling off many of those assets. In 1985, Northwest Industries was the subject of such an LBO, organized by one of the most famous leveraged buyout operators ever, William F. Farley—the fellow whose targeting of West Point-Pepperell delivered its carpet business into the hands of Shaw Industries.

The Northwest Industries LBO followed the playbook: large borrowings repaid by sales of the target company's assets—except for Union Underwear, which Farley renamed Fruit of the Loom in recognition of the brand's value. Farley made a fortune in the process and then, in 1987, took Fruit of the Loom public. That move added to Farley's payoff while hobbling Fruit of the Loom with considerable unpaid LBO debt.

During his ownership, Farley served as chairman, but longtime Fruit of the Loom executive John Holland continued to influence operations. Thanks to Holland, the company extended the Fruit of the Loom brand into the broader apparel market. He added women's wear in 1984 and sportswear in 1987 and continued to drive activewear sales.

Despite Holland's business successes, Fruit of the Loom's leveraged capital structure drove the company to several years of losses in the late 1980s.[36] At the same time, competition intensified due to cheaper imports and an "underwear" battle with the company's archrival, Hanes.[37] In the 1990s, a national recession exacerbated these negative forces. Succumbing to mounting pressure, the company closed most domestic manufacturing plants, laying off 10,800 employees, and moved to Mexico, Morocco, and elsewhere abroad, and the business reincorporated in the Cayman Islands to reduce taxes.[38] In 1996, Holland retired, leaving Farley in charge.

Downsizing measures proved inadequate. Leverage and enduring external strains were too great as the company racked up losses. It also erred by making additional borrowings to fund acquisitions that turned out to be disappointing. In mid-1999, Farley resigned due to shareholder agitation, and by year end the company filed for bankruptcy. The administrators promptly recruited Holland out of retirement to revive the company's fortunes.

Soon after the bankruptcy filing, Berkshire signaled interest in buying Fruit of the Loom's apparel business. For Buffett, it was difficult to resist such a great story of American entrepreneurship, one dating to 1851 and interrupted by a short period of excessive leverage and poor stewardship. And he also had a personal connection.

When Philadelphia & Reading (P&R) bought Union Underwear back in 1955, it was controlled by Graham-Newman, where Buffett worked, and Buffett was also a shareholder of P&R. At the time, Buffett was delighted by P&R's acquisition of Union Underwear from Jack Goldfarb, as it was structured on mutually advantageous terms.[39] Forty-five years later, Fruit of the Loom's bankruptcy administrators named Berkshire the winning bidder, so Buffett's company bought Fruit of the Loom—again.[40]

Buffett requested that Holland, who had helped Fruit of the Loom navigate the adversity of the leveraged buyout, stay on to run the business. Holland returned the company's capital structure to basics—little debt and modest expenses for funding operations. Within a few years, Fruit of the Loom was revived, today being among Berkshire's largest subsidiaries by number of employees. In a sign of its prosperity, in 2006 Fruit of the Loom paid $1.12 billion to acquire Russell Corporation, owner of powerful brands, including Brooks running shoes.

~

At Berkshire, economic value arises from combining modesty about one's ability to understand any business with a preference for businesses that are relatively easy to understand. Zeroing in on rudimentary industries, basic businesses focused on what they do best, and simple capital structures, poses less risk than dabbling in exotic industries, adventuresome businesses, and heavy debt.

11

Eternal

During the period between Christmas and New Year's Eve of 2011, Jim Weber regularly checked his email, but not his voice mail. Back in the office on January 2, he retrieved his phone messages. One had been left five days earlier: "Jim, this is Warren Buffett. I have an idea I want to run by you. Please give me a call." Weber was mortified that he had not returned a message from Warren Buffett after almost a week had elapsed.[1]

When Weber made the call, Buffett said "Tell me about Fruit of the Loom and Brooks. To what degree are you integrated? Are you sharing many services or systems?" Buffett was referring to Brooks Sports, Inc., a company Fruit of the Loom had acquired as part of its acquisition of Russell Corporation several years earlier. Weber had run Brooks for a decade, and Buffett wanted to assess whether it should be spun off as a standalone subsidiary of Berkshire rather than remain tucked in two corporate levels below.

Brooks, founded in 1914 by Morris Goldenberg in Philadelphia, was, through the 1960s, a modest maker of athletic shoes, cleats, and ice skates.[2] In the 1970s, it rode the national jogging wave by making running shoes that were among the most sophisticated of the period. Growing too fast, however, Brooks soon ran into cash flow and product quality problems that impaired its independence and sustenance. It was passed around to a series of corporate owners—five in two decades—which left the company a corporate orphan.

In 1982, Wolverine World Wide Inc., maker of Hush Puppies, acquired Brooks out of receivership. Through the 1980s, Wolverine participated across the athletic footwear spectrum—basketball, fitness, tennis, training, and walking shoes—against industry giants such as Adidas and Nike. Wolverine transformed Brooks from a niche player to a generalist, moving from "class to mass" in hopes of prospering. It did not.

So, in 1993, Wolverine sold Brooks for $21 million to the Rokke Group, a Norwegian private equity firm. Losses continued for a year before the Rokke Group cleaned out senior management ranks.[3] As CEO, it hired Helen Rockey, a hard-charging executive who tried to refocus the brand as an outstanding choice for running aficionados—reverting from "mass to class."[4] The company also expanded into apparel for those same customers.

Yet serial ownership continued. In 1998, the Rokke Group (by then Aker RGI), sold a majority interest in Brooks for $40 million to J. H. Whitney & Co., a Connecticut private equity firm.[5] Weber joined Brooks as chief executive in 2001, the fourth person to hold that post in two years. Although Brooks's profitability improved under Rockey's leadership with annual sales of $65 million, the company slipped backward into losses under a bloated debt structure.[6] Whitney held Brooks only until 2004, when Russell acquired the running shoe company for $115 million. Finally, in 2006, Fruit of the Loom acquired Russell, whose brands also include Russell Athletic, Jerzees, and Spalding, for $1.12 billion.

Weber, through the zigzagging of different owners, always believed that Brooks would succeed best by committing to a niche strategy, manufacturing and marketing running shoes as a piece of equipment for the serious runner. He focused on the high end, shoes selling for $80 to $160 a pair, and exited from the cheaper lines. This move initially slashed revenue to $20 million, but the focus enabled rebuilding. Within a few years, revenue reached $69 million. The pace and ability improved during Berkshire's ownership, as sales grew steadily along with market share in Weber's target market.

So that 2011 holiday season, Buffett wondered whether Brooks would benefit from being an independent subsidiary within Berkshire and Weber running his own show.[7] Weber agreed that Brooks differed from the rest of Fruit of the Loom, now that it had successfully recommitted to the "class" rather than "mass" approach. He seized the opportunity Buffett offered and continued that momentum. At the Boston Marathon in 2013, for example, more runners wore Brooks shoes than any other brand except Asics.[8] Brooks has continued to enjoy exceptional results, with sales of $409 million in 2012, nearly $500 million in 2013, and on target to reach $1 billion by 2020. As a rule of thumb, shoe companies are worth twice sales, making Brooks as valuable today as what Berkshire paid for all of Russell less than a decade ago.

In an interview for this book, Weber attributed acceleration of the company's prosperous turn to the permanent home that Berkshire offers, in contrast to the corporate homelessness Brooks endured over the previous two decades.[9] Management can concentrate without interference and invest in the brand, assuming a fifty-year time horizon rather than focusing on meeting the short-term needs of fickle foster parents. Another reason for the company's success is Weber himself, an entrepreneur cast in the Berkshire mold, and another winner of Ernst & Young's Entrepreneur of the Year Award.

Berkshire is not often thought of as an orphanage for the corporate homeless, but it has given permanent homes to many, a Boys Town for business. At least seven subsidiaries found refuge in Berkshire after suffering from serial ownership by successive parents, leveraged buyout operators, private equity firms, or bankruptcy trustees—all working under short-term time frames.

∾

Running the gamut of such overseers is Forest River, Inc., Berkshire's recreational vehicle manufacturer.[10] Its roots trace back to Rockwood, a famous brand name in the field of recreational vehicles, founded in 1972 by Arthur E. Chapman. A few years after founding Rockwood, Chapman sold it to Bangor Punta Corp., a conglomerate that made airplanes, sailboats, and guns. In 1984, Lear Siegler, an even larger conglomerate, acquired Bangor Punta, putting Rockwood into yet a new corporate parent's hands. These hands changed again in 1986, when Forstmann Little & Co., a leveraged buyout operator, acquired Lear Siegler.

In accordance with the LBO playbook, Forstmann borrowed heavily to acquire Lear and sold off Lear's assets to repay the debt. Rockwood was sold to Van American, Inc., a company co-owned by Peter J. Liegl.[11] He and his partners grew Van American considerably. In 1993, to raise capital for expansion, they sold it to still another LBO operator while remaining in managerial roles. It thereafter went public as Cobra Industries. The company ranked among the industry's top five, selling travel trailers and motor homes under the Cobra and Rockwood brand names.

The LBO debt, however, made financial life difficult for Cobra. The LBO operators tried to dictate business strategy to Liegl and his colleagues. Disagreements finally resulted in the operators firing Liegl, leaving a vacuum. To fill it, the operators retained consultants who evaluated Cobra top to bottom. Despite such exercises, without competent managers in place, the company floated toward insolvency and filed for bankruptcy in 1995.

In 1996, the bankruptcy court administered the sale of many assets to repay the debt. Buying many of these assets (without the liabilities), including the Rockwood brand name, were Liegl and his new company, Forest River.

With the assets from Cobra Industries, Forest River began manufacturing pop-up campers and travel trailers. During its first three years, Forest River developed three new divisions: cargo, mobile offices, and marine. In the next few years, Forest River acquired three companies while creating another new division internally: Rockport Commercial Vehicles.

By 2005, Forest River generated $1.6 billion in sales.[12] Liegel's ambition was to broaden the company's manufacturing scope to include every class and type of recreational vehicle. For this, he would need capital. But his harrowing experiences had taught him to be wary of serial conglomerates, LBO operators, and even IPOs.

So in 2005, Liegl sent a two-page fax to Buffett explaining, point by point, why Forest River met Berkshire's acquisition criteria.[13] Buffett had not heard of the company or the man, but the story appealed and the figures added up. He made an offer the next day, and the two had a deal within a week.[14]

With a permanent home and autonomy, Liegl unleashed his energies to pursue his bold vision for Forest River. It acquired Rance Aluminum Fabrication (2007), Coachmen (2008), Shasta (2010), and Dynamax (2011). Through a combination of such acquisitions and continued internal growth, Forest River now makes every kind of recreational vehicle and several types of related equipment: travel trailers, fifth wheels, pop-up campers, park model trailers, destination trailers, cargo trailers, restroom trailers, mobile offices, and pontoons.

Forest River steadily gained market share.[15] It grew from sixty plants in 2005[16] to eighty-two plants in 2010,[17] and from 5,400 employees in 2005[18] to 7,653 employees in 2012[19] and 8,770 in 2013.[20] The scale pays off in ways traditional manufacturers of recreational vehicles have not exploited: Forest River's vast production capacity enables it to fulfill customer orders quickly while maintaining rigorous construction and inspection standards.

Results have been impressive: 2010 sales neared $2 billion with record earnings, and 2013 sales surged to $3.3 billion, up 24 percent on the year.[21]

When announcing Berkshire's acquisition, Liegl was quoted in an industry trade journal:

> [We are] guaranteeing as much as is humanly possible the continued existence of Forest River. Specifically, Berkshire Hathaway buys companies and keeps companies. They have the horsepower to do it, and by the same token, it's not a high wire act like it might have been if we had sold to an investment group. Forest River had no debt before this, and Forest River has no debt after this.[22]

Coping with the crushing debt burden of leveraged buyout operators was also the route to Berkshire taken by Oriental Trading Company. Begun in 1932 by Harry Watanabe, a Japanese immigrant living in Omaha, Oriental Trading was a retail shop selling novelties, like Kewpie dolls, imported from his home country. The store prospered, and Watanabe soon operated a dozen similar stores in the Midwest. World War II's restrictions on Japanese imports, however, spelled closure for all stores outside Omaha. Thereafter, Watanabe added ceramics to the product line and pursued carnival operators as customers, a prosperous niche through the early 1970s.

In 1977, Harry's son, Terrance ("Terry") Watanabe, expanded on his father's business model. Terry added toys and party goods to the product line and began a direct-sales marketing campaign targeting organizations hosting fundraising events, such as churches, clubs, and schools. Terry amplified the direct-sales business by marketing through a widely distributed product catalogue and an extensive door-to-door sales network. He added toll-free telephone ordering in the 1980s and leveraged the Internet in the 1990s.

By 2000, Oriental Trading offered 40,000 products to a customer list numbering in the tens of millions while employing nearly 2,000 workers. At that time, Terry tapped capital from private equity firm Brentwood Associates. The plan was for Brentwood to supply funds and Terry and his team to continue to manage. That arrangement changed, however, and Terry wound up selling his entire interest to Brentwood and resigning from his positions.

By 2006, Brentwood sought an exit strategy.[23] It partially succeeded when it arranged for the Carlyle Group to acquire a majority stake (68 percent) in Oriental Trading in a leveraged buyout. Despite a huge mailing list and annual sales of $485 million on assets of $463 million, the high cost of debt led the company to file for bankruptcy in 2010 when liabilities reached $757 million.[24] During bankruptcy, yet another LBO firm, Kohlberg Kravis Roberts, bought a large portion of the company's debt, which it hoped to sell at a profit or convert into equity.

After emerging from such tumult, in 2012, Oriental Trading turned to Berkshire to see if it would be interested in buying the company. The goal was to give the old family business a permanent home—not necessarily to maximize the price of the sale.

Buffett liked what he saw, stressing that the succession of ownership changes, which had been a cost, could now come to an end.[25] The company survived this difficult period because it had long ago established itself as an industry leader that offered outstanding customer service. The recent track record was strong, as Oriental Trading increased revenue in 2010, 2011, and 2012 and resumed earning profits. With a permanent home, good times were back, aptly, for a company whose business—novelties, toys, and party supplies—is about helping people have fun.

By design, LBOs and private equity stakes are short-term arrangements. Even "successful" ones can leave a business manager hungry for a permanent home. Take CTB International Corp., a business originally called Chore-Time founded in 1952 by Howard Brembeck. Brembeck was a Midwestern entrepreneur who operated from the basement of his home. The company designed and built equipment for poultry and livestock farmers, eventually expanding into bins for feed and grain storage.[26] Brembeck and his partners revolutionized the industry with such innovations as mechanized feeding and watering equipment for poultry.[27]

In 1996, the Brembeck family believed that the Indiana-based CTB was positioned for growth to transition from a family business while preserving Brembeck's legacy. But they lacked capital and so sought outside partners. Led by Brembeck's grandson, Joseph Christopher ("Chris") Chocola, one-time Republican U.S. Congressman from Indiana, the family engaged American Securities Capital Partners, a New York private equity firm. The firm advised CTB on ten acquisitions and an initial public offering in 1997.

Five years later, however, American Securities wanted out. Growth opportunities remained, but the company was a small-cap stock, not widely followed and little known outside its industry. The Brembeck family embraced Berkshire to provide the needed capital as well as a "permanent home."

Buffett called CTB "a strong company with great American values. It has an excellent franchise, strong market share in a basic industry and top-flight management."[28] CTB had shown that it was the kind of company that would be at home in Berkshire: budget conscious, earnest, reputable, family owned, entrepreneurial, and basic—farm equipment, as non-glamorous as they come. Since then, CTB has prospered, generating excess capital, which it has reinvested in a series of acquisitions.

$\sim$

A final example is CORT Business Services Corporation, a furniture leasing company long run by Paul Arnold, employed by the company since its 1972 formation. In 1988, it was a subsidiary of Mohasco Corporation, a carpet maker that had diversified into furniture making and leasing.[29] Mohasco defended against an unwanted takeover bid (by Nortek, Inc.) with a management-led leveraged buyout, arranged by Citicorp Venture Capital (CVC).

Heavy debt led the firm, within a year, to divest CORT, again to management groups that CVC also financed. Oddly, this put CVC on both sides of the transaction, backing both the seller and the buyer of the companies, not a promising negotiating structure. For CORT, the oddity proved ominous, as the company struggled under high leverage to maintain liquidity.

Arnold persevered through the struggle, however, meeting the debt burden as well as his payroll. In 1993, he persuaded CVC to restructure the debt on favorable terms and attract additional equity investment. He focused on his business, generating stable growth through many careful acquisitions and steady expansion into new markets.

In 1999, as CORT's financiers worked on yet another LBO, Arnold and his company reached a turning point. On November 23, Buffett got a fax from an acquaintance attaching a *Washington Post* article about the latest deal in the works for CORT. The company's financials impressed Buffett, as did Arnold when they met a week later. They soon made a deal for Berkshire to acquire CORT.[30] Buffett was attracted to CORT as a "fine though unglamorous business," which Arnold ran well.[31]

Arnold relished the permanent home Berkshire offered, which he enjoyed personally until his retirement in 2012 after four decades at the helm. His legacy at CORT was its transformation from a small business to the market leader, in part through closing more than fifty acquisitions.[32]

Arnold handed the baton to Jeff Pederson, a CORT executive since 2004, who continues to guide the company, which generated earnings in 2013 of $40 million.[33]

$$\sim$$

It is said that smart people learn from their mistakes and wise people learn from the mistakes of others. If true, wisdom is a trait of Paul E. Andrews Jr., founder and chief executive of TTI, Inc., a Texas-based electronics distributor originally called Tex-Tronics, Inc. Andrews arranged to sell his company to Berkshire after seeing others deal with struggles akin to those chronicled in this chapter.

Andrews founded TTI in 1971 in a spare bedroom of his small apartment after being laid off as a buyer for General Dynamics, where he had seen the difficulties manufacturers faced sourcing electronic components.[34] Sales that year were $112,000; by 2006, they tallied $1.3 billion.[35] That's huge volume for a company with numerous products—resistors, capacitors, and connectors—selling for less than $1 apiece.[36] In 2006, John Roach, chairman of Justin Industries when Berkshire acquired it in 2000, contacted Buffett about TTI and Andrews.[37] Roach had earlier helped John Justin Jr. find an eternal home for his beloved boot and brick business. Now Roach called to say that Andrews was seeking a permanent home for TTI. Andrews, sixty-four at the time, had an inspired and touching motivation. As Buffett explained:[38]

> Not long ago he happened to witness how disruptive the death of a founder can be, both to a private company's employees and the owner's family. What starts out as disruptive, furthermore, often evolves into destructive. About a year ago, therefore, Paul began to think about selling TTI. His goal was to put his business in the hands of an owner he had carefully chosen, rather than allowing a trust officer or lawyer to conduct an auction after his death.
>
> Paul rejected the idea of a "strategic" buyer, knowing that in the pursuit of "synergies," an owner of this type would be apt to dismantle what he had so carefully built, a move that would uproot hundreds of his associates (and perhaps wound TTI's business in the process). He also ruled out a private equity firm, which would very likely load the company with debt and then flip it as soon as possible. This left Berkshire.

It took Andrews and Buffett little time to agree on terms: they met in the morning and had a deal before lunch.[39] In reaching an agreement on valuation, Berkshire culture's promise of permanence was important. TTI achieved record sales and earnings in 2008 and again in 2010, although it operates in a competitive industry that kept margins tight in 2012 and 2013.[40] Internal growth is complemented by acquisitions, including Sager Electronics in 2012 and Ray-Q Interconnect Ltd. in 2013.

Berkshire does not go out of its way to hunt for companies that have proven their business models durable by brushes with serial owners, daring financiers, or bankruptcy trustees. But companies that survive such ordeals—including Fruit of the Loom and Johns Manville—prove their resilience. Owners or managers vie for the value of a permanent home that every Berkshire subsidiary cherishes.

Nor does Berkshire acquire companies in need of a business turnaround, a tough task often compounded by the need to effect changes in corporate culture. As Buffett noted when explaining how GEICO, despite its near insolvency in 1976, was not a turnaround: "When a management with a reputation for excellence tries to tackle a business with a reputation for bad economics, it is usually the reputation of the business that stays intact."[41] That's not to say that turnarounds should be forsaken. Some have made great successes of them. Exemplars are Jay and Robert Pritzker of The Marmon Group, the Berkshire subsidiary featured in the next chapter.

12

All One

Suppose you are an analyst asked to evaluate a diverse conglomerate comprised of hundreds of different companies in numerous sectors, including financial services, transportation, energy, construction, manufacturing, and so on. The businesses are low-tech and unglamorous. They are also leaders in their industries. The companies were acquired at different times without any master plan.

The conglomerate's aging chairman and vice-chairman have guided the company during the four decades since its inception. The two billionaires make essentially all important corporate decisions, with scant oversight from the board of directors. Adhering to a hands-off management policy emphasizing individual autonomy, all other decisions are made by managers of the various subsidiaries. If pressed to predict the conglomerate's fate after the passing of its chairman and vice-chairman, what would you say?

This scenario describes the task that analysts faced in the mid-1990s when evaluating what would happen to the Marmon Group after Jay and Robert Pritzker passed away, and of course, it also describes the task an analyst would be faced with today in considering the future of Berkshire Hathaway. Many analysts thought that the Marmon Group was too unwieldy for any but the Pritzkers to run and predicted it would perish soon after they left.

The analysts were wrong. In 2008, the Marmon Group became a subsidiary of Berkshire Hathaway, and it continues to operate pretty much as it had for decades.[1] This is why the story of the Marmon Group is so poignant. A conglomerate that might be called a mini-Berkshire, it possesses the same cultural traits as Berkshire and its sister subsidiaries. These common traits explain why Marmon, one of Berkshire's largest and most profitable subsidiaries, fit right in at Berkshire.

There are further similarities between Berkshire and the Marmon Group at the parent level—capital strength, growth by acquisition, multiple rivers of cash flows. These common features offer grounds to predict that the fate of Berkshire, as with Marmon, can be secure despite a founding genius passing from the scene. If the Marmon Group survived the Pritzkers, a testimony to them, then Berkshire can survive Buffett, a testimony to him.

～

In the late 1800s, Nicholas Pritzker and his family immigrated to the United States from Ukraine.[2] They settled in Chicago, where in 1902, Pritzker founded the law firm Pritzker & Pritzker. The firm prospered through the late 1920s, earning a strong local reputation specializing in real property law. It gradually shifted to investing in real estate under the leadership of the founder's son, Abram Nicholas ("A. N."), whose investments provided the foundation of the Pritzker family empire. By 1940, the interests were so substantial that Pritzker & Pritzker ceased being a law firm and became solely a family investment firm.

The family business would succeed explosively under the stewardship of A. N.'s sons, Jay and Robert ("Bob") Pritzker, who put their complementary talents together to amplify results. Jay was trained as a lawyer, earning a law degree from Northwestern University, and gained business and deal-making experience serving after World War II in the U.S. agency that administered German-owned companies. Among his gifts is one Buffett shares: the ability to envision the details of a business operation from reading its financial statements. He was also a master of negotiations and deal making.

Jay's brother Bob had the eye for business operations and organization. Bob Pritzker studied advanced industrial engineering at the Illinois Institute of Technology. He developed expertise in industrial processes and manufacturing. These skills enabled him to diagnose operating deficiencies at troubled companies and prescribe remedies.

The combination of Bob's operational insight and Jay's deal-making acumen proved of incalculable value as the brothers built one of the largest private businesses in the world. A favorite arrangement: Jay negotiated to buy a troubled company at a discount from book value, and then Bob worked with management to reengineer the company to render it worth multiples of that.[3]

The first example, a prototype, was the Colson Company, a small, unprofitable, Ohio-based maker of bicycles, casters, rockets, and wheelchairs. Jay's analysis suggested that the company was worth more liquidated than as a going concern. He acquired it for a price far less than liquidation value. Joining the existing management team, Bob immediately sold the bicycle-related assets, aggressively cut costs in the rocket-making operation before terminating it as well, and then left the company's managers to focus all their capital and energy on the profitable production of casters and wheelchairs.

If Jay were lather and Bob rinse, the Pritzker formula became lather, rinse, repeat. Bob's techniques included finding economies of scale between existing and acquired businesses. Jay added further value through advantageous corporate structures that reduced tax expenses and achieved financing benefits. That said, Bob Pritzker did not refer to such strategies as "synergy." The Pritzkers were skeptical of the concept of "synergy" in business acquisitions, which can create rosy projections about payoffs and lead to unnecessary dismantling of acquired firms.

The Marmon Group made commitments to keep the companies it acquired and invested generous financial and human capital in their success. The Pritzker brothers invariably retained existing management and followed a hands-off policy that gave managers autonomy in making operating decisions. Although the Pritzkers preferred to buy and hold companies they acquired, given their model of acquiring ailing companies, they were prepared to discontinue losing operations and reinvest in those with potential. For instance, in 1963 Colson acquired Marmon-Herrington Company, successor to the Marmon Motor Car Company. Management strengthened the company by divesting makers of heavy-duty tractors, transit vehicles, and bus chassis and reinvesting proceeds in the core business.

However, willingness to divest should not be confused with a desire to do so. Some get the wrong impression of the Pritzker strategy. Their turnaround approach is very different from the buy-and-flip takeover artist prepared to sell companies as if they were merchandise. On the contrary, Bob and Jay were long-term investors who embraced an eternal view of ownership. Given that the Marmon Group made more than one hundred acquisitions, the number of divestitures was surprisingly small.[4]

By 1971, the Marmon Group, wholly owned by the Pritzker family after a short time as a public company, had steadily acquired a number of small and medium-sized companies in a variety of rudimentary manufacturing businesses. All were basic and modest, as their names might suggest: Amarillo Gear, Keystone Pipe, Penn Aluminum, Sterling Crane, and Triangle Suspension Systems.

In the mid-1970s, the Marmon Group made a big acquisition: Cerro Corporation, a conglomerate engaged in mining, manufacturing, trucking, and real estate, with $800 million in annual revenue. The corporation's profile conformed to the Pritzkers' substantive acquisition criteria: assets were worth more on the block than in operation. But it was unusual in other ways, being a hostile takeover of a publicly traded corporation.[5] Bob Pritzker completed the arduous task of reshaping the company's culture, which was overly structured and tense, inculcating instead an entrepreneurial spirit.[6]

More typical acquisitions promptly followed. In 1977, the Marmon Group bought Hammond Corporation, the organ maker that also owned a glove manufacturer, Wells Lamont. The organ business was a disappointment, but the glove business became the leader in the field.[7] In 1978, the Marmon Group bought American Safety Equipment Corporation, maker of seatbelts.

By the end of the 1970s, the Marmon Group was a prosperous, valuable, and highly diversified conglomerate. Member companies engaged in manufacturing agricultural equipment, apparel accessories, automotive products, cable and wire, piping and tubing, musical instruments, and retailing equipment, as well as services involving mining and metals trading.

In 1981, the Marmon Group made its second big acquisition: the $688 million takeover of Trans Union Corp., a conglomerate that was once part of the empire of John D. Rockefeller Sr.[8] Chief businesses were making and leasing rail tanks for transporting oil and other cargo and a consumer credit service. Aside from size, this deal epitomized the Pritzker model: Jay found value in its successive years of losses that produced investment tax credits to reduce the Marmon Group's tax expense; Bob discerned valuable operating gems hidden throughout.[9] (The deal also heightened director attention in American boardrooms after an influential court held Trans Union's directors personally liable for failing to become informed about the background of the transaction.[10])

Through the 1980s and 1990s, the Marmon Group continued acquisitions regularly in an array of basic businesses. The acquisition rate was intense, although many deals were of modest size: thirty acquisitions in 1998, thirty-five in 1999, and twenty in 2000.[11] Assimilation was not a problem, as the company operated in a decentralized manner. Most succeeded, and only a handful had to be shut down. None was sold, although in 2001, Marmon divested two longer-standing companies, Jamesway, a farm equipment company, and Long-Airdox, a maker of coal-mining equipment.[12] From the early 1990s, Marmon's subsidiaries increasingly made bolt-on acquisitions to add growth.

As early as the late 1980s, critics questioned whether the Marmon Group's vast size, frenetic growth, and extreme diversification could be maintained within its corporate structure.[13] Who but Jay and Bob Pritzker could administer such a sprawling behemoth, they wondered? In 1999, Jay died; in 2002, Bob retired (he died in 2011).

When Bob retired from the Marmon Group, he carved out the businesses that made up Colson to run for himself, and Trans Union's consumer credit division was moved elsewhere in the Pritzker family empire; both were later sold.[14] But little else changed at the Marmon Group, and under the stewardship of two successive chief executives, John D. Nichols (2002–2006) and Frank S. Ptak (since 2006), the Marmon Group has continued to prosper.

Both Nichols and Ptak spent most of their careers in senior positions at Illinois Tool Works Inc. (ITW). A third-generation Chicago-based manufacturer formed by Byron L. Smith in 1912, ITW has much in common culturally with the Marmon Group, and the two grew in tandem during the latter part of the twentieth century.[15] ITW, however, is massive: in 2005, ITW operated 625 businesses in forty-four countries, built through a combination of internal growth and opportunistic acquisition.[16]

To manage such an enormous conglomerate, Nichols, Ptak, and other ITW executives applied a management principle called 80/20. The 80/20 principle refers to a thought process based on a common statistical distribution: 80 percent of given outcomes are contributed by 20 percent of the inputs. At ITW in the 1980s, Nichols and Ptak discovered its utility when studying why profit margins were eroding.

Repeatedly across the company, they found that 80 percent of sales came from 20 percent of the product mix, and 80 percent of profits were due to 20 percent of customers. Armed with the 80/20 insight, they zeroed in on what specific parts of the business contributed most and least to overall performance. With laser focus, they allocated time and resources to the divisions, products, and customers that drove the greatest profits. The effect was to increase decentralization, which made ITW's vast size an advantage.

Nichols, ITW's CEO from 1980 to 1996 when he retired, came out of retirement in 2002 to succeed Bob Pritzker at the Marmon Group. Applying 80/20 thinking, Nichols made one significant organizational change at Marmon after the Pritzkers left: dividing the company into ten business sectors, each with a president reporting to him.[17] This enabled him to oversee the sprawling organization while facilitating growth and acquisitions at divisional and product levels.

In 2006, Ptak took over as Marmon's chief executive officer, and Nichols became vice-chairman. Ptak had been a Marmon director since 2003 and a colleague of Nichols at ITW for decades. A certified public accountant, Ptak is also a director of Morningstar, Inc., the provider of independent investment research.

In 2008, Berkshire bought control of Marmon from the Pritzker family under an agreement to buy the rest in a series of purchases that were completed in 2014. The $8 billion deal was sealed quickly, with neither haggling nor due diligence.[18] Buffett, who met Jay Pritzker in a business transaction in 1954 and followed his career avidly, said that simplicity was just as Jay would have wanted it.[19]

Ptak continued to run the Marmon Group as before, relentlessly applying the 80/20 principle. In 2012, this led him to a further adjustment. The divisions (eleven by then) were organized into three new autonomous companies, each led by a senior Marmon veteran. In accordance with the Marmon Group's history, under Ptak it prospers, with shareholders' equity rising from less than $5 billion in 2006 to nearly $7 billion in 2012. Critics, convinced that the Marmon Group would collapse without the Pritzkers, had been proven wrong.

~

What secrets explain the Marmon Group's success? The Berkshire traits: an entrepreneurial family operation of autonomously run divisions engaged in rudimentary businesses with permanent time horizons, known for budget consciousness, earnestness, and integrity. In the years before and after

Berkshire's acquisition of the Marmon Group, Nichols and Ptak have sustained these values:

> *Budget conscious.* The Marmon Group is budget conscious. Neither Jay
> nor Bob believed in conducting extensive studies, holding lengthy
> meetings, or engaging in protracted deliberations about business
> matters. Corporate headquarters employs few people. Ptak boasts
> that the Marmon Group's overhead, 22.5 percent in 2012, is among
> the lowest in manufacturing.[20]
>
> *Earnest.* The Marmon Group keeps its promises.[21] Managers joining the
> company knew they could count on whatever the Pritzkers said
> upon acquisition. They were the kind of people, in turn, who treated
> someone's word as their bond. In their markets, they were known as
> people to be trusted. The Marmon Group won such a reputation for
> earnestness as well—and Nichols and Ptak had done for themselves
> and their colleagues at ITW.
>
> *Reputation.* The Pritzkers exuded integrity—they believed that making
> money was far less important as a measure of success than demonstrating integrity. Jay Pritzker appreciated that there is often a
> tension between what is best for a business long term and what
> might seem good for shareholders short term.[22] Their buy-and-
> hold strategy was part of this investment in reputation. The Pritzk-
> ers acquired companies to keep and run them, not to divest assets
> and lay off workers. People wanted to do business with Jay and
> Bob Pritzker—and the Marmon Group continues to attract such
> interest.
>
> *Kinship.* The Marmon Group is a family business, run by brothers Jay and
> Bob Pritzker, who had an exceptional ability to work well together.[23]
> This ability was handed down to them by their father. Indeed, they
> emulated the business model he had established, including the
> turnaround approach. For example, the elder Pritzker bought Cory
> Corp., an appliance maker, in 1941 for $50,000 and sold it in 1967 to
> Hershey for $23 million.[24] The brothers passed the gene onto their
> children as well, some of whom joined the family business.
>
> The Pritzker family also ultimately exhibited some of the down-
> side of family businesses. Feuding erupted among children and
> grandchildren after Jay died and Bob retired. Squabbles addressed
> what to do with Marmon. Eleven heirs seemed poised to split it up
> and sell it off. As is its wont, Berkshire came to the rescue.

Self-starters. The Marmon Group is the epitome of an entrepreneurial culture. Bob and Jay Pritzker were quintessential self-starters. So were other family members. Another brother built from scratch the Hyatt Hotel chain, which Jay's son, Thomas J. Pritzker, later ran.[25] The Marmon Group business model remains oriented this way: turnarounds call for innovation, risk taking, creativity, and tenacity.

Hands off. When the Pritzkers passed from the scene, Marmon's managers—hundreds of them—continued to operate their businesses without a hiccup. The Marmon Group always followed a hands-off management policy giving managers wide autonomy. The Pritzkers never let headquarters call operational shots; in fact, headquarters employed no marketing, sales, engineering, or operations personnel. The Marmon Group managers focus on their businesses. They are not moved around to groom for upward corporate mobility. Those eager for more responsibility simply grow their businesses.

At the Marmon Group, the Pritzkers often divided companies into smaller units when finding that efficient. Using the 80/20 principle, Ptak continues to focus everyone in the organization on determining what inputs drive the most desired outputs and allocating time and resources accordingly. This promotes a hands-off approach, as the Marmon Group becomes ever more decentralized.

Investor savvy. The Pritzkers set the standard for investment savvy and incubated a corporate culture that follows suit. From 1980 to 1989, revenue doubled from $2 billion to $4 billion; earnings more than doubled from $84 million to a record $205 million; return on equity grew from 19.1 percent (five points above the Fortune 500 median) to 26.3 percent (ten above that). There were some rough years, however, with earnings in 1990 down 40 percent to $125 million despite nearly $4 billion in revenue.[26]

By 2005, revenue was $5.6 billion and income $556 million, for a profit margin of 9.9 percent; in 2008, the year Berkshire acquired a majority stake, revenue was $6.9 billion with a 14.1% profit margin. In the 2009 recession, revenues slid to $5 billion and the margin rose to 14.8%. Since then, progress has been steadily upward, with rising net worth. (See Table 12.1.)

The Marmon Group reinvests for internal growth and to sustain the tradition of acquisitiveness that the Pritzker brothers established. In 2013, for example, Ptak led the $1.1 billion acquisition of IMI, manufacturer of beverage dispenser machines for the retail industry.

Table 12.1
The Marmon Group: Selected Financial Information

	2005	2006	2007	2008	2009	2010	2011	2012	2013
Revenue	5,605	6,933	6,904	6,919	5,062	5,963	6,913	7,163	6,979
Income	556	884	951	977	751	855	1,018	1,163	1,176
Margin	9.9%	12.8%	13.8%	14.1%	14.8%	14.3%	14.7%	16.2%	16.5%
Equity	4,495	4,486	5,037	4,311	4,840	5,393	6,065	6,854	n/a
Return on Equity	n/a	19.7%	21.2%	19.4%	17.4%	17.7%	18.9%	19.2%	17.2%

Sources: The Marmon Group 2012 Annual Brochure; Berkshire Hathaway Annual Report 2013.

Rudimentary. The Marmon Group, a conglomerate, concentrates on rudimentary manufacturing companies in the least glamorous, most basic,
yet vital businesses. The companies have no flash or even very much
popular brand name recognition. Moreover, Marmon, despite its scale
and capital strength, has always been modest. As a private company
owned by a publicity-shy family, the company has kept a low profile.

Eternal. The Marmon Group distinguished itself from competitors in
the acquisition field by its "buy-fix-hold" philosophy. Rivals were
the takeover artists, leveraged buyout operators, and private equity
firms who often preferred to acquire and flip for a profit. Marmon's
bias toward the permanent was reflected in its preference to retain
incumbent management, give it autonomy, and stake substantial
capital at its disposal.[27]

The overlapping traits of Marmon and Berkshire are reasons the Marmon
Group is a perfect fit as a Berkshire subsidiary. Combined with additional
similarities at the holding company level, they speak to corporate durability—
what the Marmon Group's surviving the Pritzkers says about the prospects
for Berkshire surviving Buffett.

Marmon and Berkshire have both been built by acquisitions. Acquisitions are made in accordance with stated criteria applied with discipline.
The acquisition criteria of the two companies are similar, particularly in
terms of insisting on good companies at fair prices and avoiding those
posing a bad fit. At the same time, neither company believes in strategic
plans. As a senior executive of the Marmon Group put it in a description

that applies equally to his company as to Berkshire: "We're not planners, we're opportunists."[28]

Both have grown to generate multiple earnings streams adding up to oceans of cash flow. Both regularly, if not always, outperform the S&P 500. Both companies command enormous capital resources. As a result, their respective subsidiaries benefit from the affiliation. Their corporate backers enable investments that peer stand-alone companies can not make. Accompanying the essentially unlimited capital comes a mandate of stewardship.

Historically, both the Marmon Group and Berkshire cultivated a reputation as buyers of choice. Both were able to do this in part because of their ownership structures. When the Marmon Group made a promise, it was the promise of Bob and Jay Pritzker, whose family owned the company; when Berkshire made a promise, it was the promise of Warren Buffett, the controlling shareholder. With the passage of time and the addition of large numbers of subsidiaries exuding the same values, however, the Marmon Group and Berkshire—and their respective subsidiaries—acquired reputations independent of these individuals.

Finally both the Marmon Group and Berkshire were founded and developed by powerful leaders who left indelible marks on their companies. Notably, all of them—Bob and Jay Pritzker and Warren Buffett, along with Charlie Munger—possessed similar personal qualities relevant to such leadership:

- Know what you don't know and admit it: Bob knew manufacturing and did not venture far from it; Jay excelled at deal making, finance, law, and tax—and left operations to Bob; Buffett and Munger say operations and technology are not within their circle of competence and shy away from them.
- Have broad vision: Bob viewed potential deals from multiple angles simultaneously; Buffett and Munger view them against multiple alternative opportunities.
- Be patient: Appreciate long-term values, but be swift and agile in decision making, especially about acquisitions.
- Know that capital assets require reinvestment to maintain: Depreciation expense is a cost of operations, not a mere accounting convention that can be ignored in favor of cash flow analysis.
- Maintain cool rationality: Use common sense and think logically.

Each of these men deployed these skills in the early years with the mission of building a company; they used these skills in their later years with a view to sustaining it.

On a whimsical note, Berkshire and the Marmon Group share a pedi-gree of nomenclature. The words Berkshire and Marmon are historical anachronisms: Berkshire Hathaway is a long-defunct textile company and Marmon a long-defunct automaker. In 1964, when Colson acquired Marmon-Herrington, it adopted "the Marmon Group" as its corporate name. The choice was an inspired bit of Americana. At the first Indianapo-lis 500 auto race in 1911, the winning car was made by Marmon Motor Car Company, a producer of high-end automobiles.

~

Every company is unique, of course, and there are important differences between Berkshire and Marmon. Concerning acquisitions, for example, the Pritzkers used the Marmon Group to engage in hostile takeovers. Berkshire forswears them, as we know from examples like Berkshire riding in as a white knight to save Scott Fetzer from a raid by Ivan Boesky and, during the heyday of hostile takeovers in the 1980s, acquiring white squire positions in several companies to provide a takeover defense.

The Marmon Group engaged in bidding auctions for target companies, a practice Berkshire also generally avoids. For example, in 1995, the Marmon Group topped a competing bid for Atlas Steel, a specialty steel maker in Asia. In doing so, however, Bob Pritzker stressed a Marmon/Berkshire com-monality: "We're in it usually for the long run. We don't just buy and sell companies."[29] Similarly, the Pritzkers sought turnaround situations, which Berkshire does not. Bob had the industrial engineering skills to make such an approach sensible from an operations standpoint, and Jay had the financial astuteness to assure related profitability. Berkshire has avoided turnaround situations because they are outside Buffett's circle of competence—and he stresses that few have the skill. The Pritzkers were in this rare group.

Concerning investors, the Marmon Group was privately owned—entirely by the Pritzkers—whereas Berkshire is a public company. Were Berkshire also privately held, the precedent of the Marmon Group sur-viving its founders would be a definitive basis for predicting the same for Berkshire after Buffett. While the precedent does not make such a definitive case, the Marmon Group's cultural features have contributed to its longev-ity, even as its ownership structure has changed from being privately held to being the subsidiary of a public company.

Even so, the post-Pritzker Marmon Group provides one potential model for the post-Buffett Berkshire Hathaway. The incremental changes that Nichols and Ptak made in the post-Pritzker years, with a few autono-mous companies housing eleven divisions today, made the Marmon Group more manageable for newcomers and helped focus acquisitions and other growth strategies. While Berkshire has not imposed such order, it has the blueprint for such an organizational structure in the way that Buffett pres-ents the subsidiaries in Berkshire's annual report: insurance; regulated/capital-intensive businesses; finance; and manufacturing, retail, and services. The Marmon Group also offers an in-house professional services firm to group members wishing to delegate back-office tasks; it handles accounting, budgeting, human resources, finance, and legal tasks. Berkshire delegates these functions to each subsidiary, although there is a centralized account-ing and auditing system that could be replicated to provide other functions.

Finally, the Marmon Group's acquisitions were made with retained earnings from its industrial companies and reinvested in other industrial companies. In contrast, Berkshire generates large amounts of capital from insurance operations and invests the results not only in wholly owned subsidiaries but in minority stakes of other public corporations and some private ones. While not defining Berkshire culture as wholly owned subsid-iaries do, some portfolio investments shed light on the concept of corporate culture and help us understand Berkshire culture. The next chapter will look at some of the more illuminating investments in Berkshire's portfolio.

13

Berkshire's Portfolio

When Berkshire was negotiating to acquire Burlington Northern Santa Fe Railway, Roger Nober, the railroad's general counsel, observed that Berkshire's other rail investments could pose regulatory concerns.[1] Buffett readily agreed to divest any stock investments as necessary, and Berkshire soon sold its 1 percent stake in Norfolk Southern Corporation and 2 percent position in Union Pacific Railroad Co.[2] He would not have agreed to sell a subsidiary to satisfy the same regulatory concerns. Similarly, if Berkshire faced insurance claims exceeding cash reserves, the stocks would be liquidated first, before any subsidiary. For Berkshire culture, relative permanence is just one of many differences between its controlled subsidiaries and the minority stock positions held in its portfolio.

As a minority shareholder, Berkshire could influence but not dictate the affairs of companies such as Norfolk Southern or Union Pacific—or even those of which Berkshire owns 9 to 14 percent, such as American Express, Coca-Cola, or Wells Fargo. In these companies, Berkshire cannot appoint or control all directors or officers or set anyone's pay. In contrast, owning all the stock of Benjamin Moore, Gen Re, NetJets, and other subsidiaries gives Berkshire total authority over them, including the power to hire and fire and discretion regarding how to allocate profits and determine salaries. Berkshire's subsidiaries identify with Berkshire in ways investees do not, most visibly defining themselves in their logos—"A Berkshire Hathaway Company" follows their names.

Investees—companies in which Berkshire has a minority interest—may fail, be acquired, reorganize, or become marketable securities that Berkshire sells or trades. Among Berkshire's former investees that no longer exist due to merger or other corporate mortality are Beatrice Foods, Capital Cities/ABC, F. W. Woolworth, General Foods, and Knight Ridder. Among those Berkshire has sold are Freddie Mac, Johnson & Johnson, Kraft Foods, McDonald's, Petro China, Travelers, and the Walt Disney Company. Berkshire traded shares in Phillips 66 to pay for Lubrizol's acquisition of Phillips Specialty Products; traded shares in Graham Holdings, successor to the *Washington Post*, to acquire a television station; and traded shares in White Mountain Insurance Group, a company founded by Jack Byrne, who rescued GEICO from oblivion in 1976, for selected insurance assets.

The scale of Berkshire's subsidiaries dwarfs that of its stock portfolio. For example, at the end of 2013, the total cost of Berkshire's portfolio of investees was $56 billion, one-third the cost of Berkshire subsidiaries, and not much more than Berkshire invested in either BNSF or Berkshire Hathaway Energy alone.[3] These investments had a market value of $115 billion, less than a fifth of Berkshire's total assets.[4] Today, 80 percent of Berkshire consists of subsidiaries and only 20 percent investees, a reversal from the early 1980s when Berkshire consisted of 80 percent investees and 20 percent subsidiaries.[5]

With some companies, such as BNSF Railway and GEICO, Berkshire initially took a minority position and subsequently acquired the rest, making them into wholly owned subsidiaries. From an investment standpoint, evaluations of minority interests and whole companies are kindred, as both include assessing a business's economic characteristics and relating price to value. To qualify as an investment for Berkshire, whether investee or subsidiary, a business must have a moat, something to protect sustained profitability. In Berkshire's subsidiary acquisitions, however, non-economic values play a role that minority purchases on the open market ignore.

When Berkshire purchases a minority position in a privately negotiated setting, such values do play a role. Examples include buying convertible securities or warrants, as with Gillette and Salomon Brothers in the late 1980s; Goldman Sachs, USG Corporation, and others amid the financial crisis of 2008; and taking a stake in a private company, such as Mars, Inc. or Wm. Wrigley Jr. Co. in 2008.[6] In such deals, Berkshire can offer not only economic payments but valuable intangible promises, including autonomy and permanence. But in most common stock purchases, Berkshire buys anonymously at market without such an opportunity.

These differences mean that Berkshire subsidiaries constitute Berkshire culture in ways that investees do not. Controlled subsidiaries like Ben Bridge Jewelers, Clayton Homes, Dairy Queen, Lubrizol, and See's Candies give Berkshire its identity, while investees of the past—and even larger current holdings like an $11.7 billion purchase of 6 percent of IBM in 2011 or a $3 billion purchase of 1.8 percent of Walmart in 2006 and 2009—at best contribute obliquely to this identity. (For a contrast, compare Berkshire's subsidiaries with table 13.1's list of leading current investees.)

Berkshire's investee portfolio is like a business unit within Berkshire equivalent to a large subsidiary. While investees do not define Berkshire culture, their purchase and sale reflect Berkshire's values, and many boast strong cultures, big personalities, and fascinating histories. Of particular significance are two of the oldest (*Washington Post* and Gillette, now Procter & Gamble), two of the largest (CocaCola and Walmart), and two of the most opportunistic (Goldman Sachs and, especially, USG, which is also a prime candidate for full acquisition). For a glimpse into the future, finally, we'll look at another candidate for full acquisition—Heinz—and the novel partnership Berkshire made with a private equity firm to acquire half of it. At 50 percent, Heinz is neither an investee nor a subsidiary, and the transaction defines a new model for the next generation of Berkshire deals.

∽

Berkshire's 1973 investment in the Washington Post Company became legendary due to Buffett's role on the company's board of directors from 1974 to 2011 and his close relationship with successive chief executives, Katherine ("Kay") Graham and her son, Donald E. ("Don") Graham. The Graham family sold the flagship newspaper in 2013, renaming the company Graham Holdings, which today owns a mix of other media-related assets. Shortly thereafter, in 2014, Berkshire traded its stock in Graham Holdings for one of those business units—a Miami television station.[7]

The *Washington Post* traces its roots back to 1877 and publisher Stilson Hutchins, who wanted to focus attention on national affairs from the viewpoint of the Democratic Party.[8] In 1905, the paper was acquired by John R. McLean, a publisher in the mold of newspaper magnate William Randolph Hearst, who expanded coverage to include features and sports. On his death in 1916, McLean was succeed by his son Edward, who in the

Table 13.1
Selected Leading Berkshire Investees

Investee	Market Value ($ million)	Percentage Owned by Berkshire (%)
American Express	13,681,349	14.27
Bank of America	*	*
Bank of New York Mellon	828,828	2.15
Chicago Bridge & Iron	733,115	8.90
Coca-Cola	16,184,000	9.06
ConocoPhillips	957,466	1.10
Costco	528,930	0.99
Deere	339,468	1.04
DIRECTV	2,426,036	6.95
DaVita HealthCare	2,047,671	16.52
ExxonMobil	3,834,548	0.92
General Electric	304,122	0.11
General Motors	1,606,800	2.88
Goldman Sachs	2,184,196	2.88
IBM	12,522,183	6.54
Johnson & Johnson	30,891	0.01
Kraft Foods	10,317	0.03
Lee Enterprises	302	0.17
Liberty Media	837,897	4.97
Mastercard	307,180	0.34
Moody's	1,842,247	11.59
Mondelez	20,282	0.03
Media General	92,227	5.25
M&T Bank	615,167	4.13
Munich Re	4,415,000	11.20
National-Oilwell Varco	724,519	2.07
Precision Castparts	502,895	1.36
Procter & Gamble	4,462,070	1.94
Sanofi	1,747,000	1.70
Starz	160,461	4.97
Suncor Energy	434,980	0.87
Tesco	1,666,000	3.70
Torchmark	325,226	4.68

(*continued*)

Table 13.1
(*Continued*)

Investee	Market Value ($ million)	Percentage Owned by Berkshire (%)
U.S. Bancorp	3,137,800	4.33
USG	1,208,246	25.10
Visa	314,000	0.24
Viacom	625,311	1.69
Verisk Analytics	105,266	0.93
Verisign	626,998	8.00
WABCO	368,051	6.51
Walmart	4,470,000	1.52
Wells Fargo	21,370,054	8.81

Note: Shaded entries indicate portfolio concentration, highlighting stocks that aggregate nearly 70% of the total.

The share data in table 13.1 are sourced primarily from CNBC, which collated them from Berkshire Hathaway's 13-F filings with the Securities and Exchange Commission (February 14, 2014 and February 26, 2014), most at year-end 2013. Also included are year-end 2013 market prices. Supplemental information, such as concerning non-U.S. stocks and portion of investments represented in Berkshire's portfolio, comes from Berkshire Hathaway annual reports.

*Through 2021, Berkshire has the option to acquire for $5 billion 700 million shares of Bank of America stock, whose current market value is $11 billion. Exercise of this option, which Berkshire likely will do on the eve of its expiration, would make Bank of America among Berkshire's largest holdings.

1920s became ensnared in the disgrace du jour of the nation's capital, the Teapot Dome scandal, a fateful distraction from the business, precipitating its financial failure.

Out of bankruptcy in 1933, the *Post's* assets were acquired by Eugene Meyer, Kay Graham's father. A Republican banker from New York, Meyer believed—as Buffett would later—that a newspaper could offer both civic virtue and private profits. The paper succeeded under Meyer, until his appointment by President Harry S. Truman to be the first president of the World Bank. He then transferred control of the paper to Kay and her husband, Philip L. Graham. As her father had envisioned, under Phillip's leadership through 1963 and Kay's thereafter, the Washington Post Company prospered as a business and also provided a public service.

Kay Graham published the Pentagon Papers in 1971 against the advice of lawyers who explained that publishing the top secret government history of the Vietnam conflict could expose the company to criminal liability. To her, the paper's reputation for integrity was worth more; the Supreme Court soon upheld the *Post*'s right to publish, vindicating Kay's stance.[9] Graham also presided over publishing the paper's series by the young dynamic duo of Bob Woodward and Carl Bernstein on the Watergate affair that toppled President Richard M. Nixon. Graham believed in the autonomy of these journalists and the paper's top editor, Ben Bradlee. Such events demonstrated Graham's and the *Post*'s earnestness and made both heroic figures in contemporary American culture.

On the financial end, Meyer funded the company's profit-sharing plan and compensated employees with stock, making it necessary for the private company to maintain a market for its own shares. To eliminate this burden, in 1971, Graham arranged for the company to make a public offering of its Class B shares—she retained a majority of the Class A shares and her children the rest of the Class A, securing the Graham family control of the company.[10] In 1973, Berkshire acquired more than a 10-percent stake. Buffett assured Graham, however, of his respect for the family tradition of ownership and control. Graham appreciated this and, in 1974, nominated Buffett to join the corporate board. Buffett was the board's lead outside director, according to her son Don, who joined the board at about the same time.[11]

The Graham–Buffett relationship served as a model for how managers and shareholders can help one another. Graham credited Buffett with teaching her the fundamentals of business and finance;[12] he appreciated her judgment, convictions, and owner orientation. Buffett counseled the Grahams on matters of corporate affairs, managerial strategy, and acquisitions, including buying radio and television media around the country. Buffett suggested moving the company's pension fund from a large bank to small firms, a step that reduced costs and increased gains. He also advised using excess cash to buy back stock (leading, ultimately, to an increase in Berkshire's stake to nearly 25 percent).

Don Graham succeeded his mother, sustaining the core newspaper business for many years while diversifying into television broadcasting, cable, the Kaplan education service, *Slate* online magazine, and *Trove* personalized news service. In 2013, the Graham family sold the flagship newspaper for $250 million to Jeff Bezos, founder of online retailer Amazon.com, amid challenging times for print media. After the sale, Berkshire's interest in the resulting company, Graham Holdings, had a market value of about $1 billion. In 2014, Berkshire traded this stock for a television station, formally ending a four-decade relationship on the friendliest of terms. The station's call letters? WPLG, for Philip L. Graham.

~

Berkshire bought Gillette preferred stock in 1988 for a combination of cash and the value of its reputation for opposing hostile takeovers. When the Procter & Gamble Company (P&G) acquired Gillette in 2005, Berkshire's Gillette shares were exchanged for shares in P&G. They remain an impressive investment in Berkshire's portfolio: acquired at a cost of $336 million, they are worth $4.5 billion and represent 2 percent of P&G's ownership. But Berkshire has sold many P&G shares over the years, reducing its old Gillette stake by half.

Gillette was founded in 1901 by King C. Gillette, a traveling salesman whose frustration with the dangers and dulling edges of his straight razor blades inspired him to make a razor that required less skill to use safely. Teaming up with scientist William Nickerson, he raised capital to launch a company and patent an invention. Originally called American Safety Razor Co., renamed Gillette Safety Razor Co. in 1903, these men and their successors built the business into a global brand. The company diversified from the 1960s through the 1980s, adding Cricket lighters, Right Guard and Soft-and-Dri deodorants, Paper Mate pens, as well as Braun and Oral-B.

Gillette's excess cash attracted takeover bids during the 1980s, including one from Ronald O. Pereleman, which the board beat back. Defending against such battles led the company to sell convertible preferred to Berkshire, putting a sizable block in a known opponent of hostile bids supportive of Gillette's management. Buffett joined the Gillette board. Gillette continued to concentrate on razors while also diversifying, highlighted by the acquisition of Duracell International Inc., the battery maker. By 2004, the year before merging into P&G, Gillette's sales surpassed $9 billion.

P&G, with 2013 sales of $84 billion, is one of the oldest companies in the United States, dating to the 1837 candle-and-soap partnership of William Procter and James Gamble.[13] Pioneers in branding, their moon-and-stars logo launched in 1850, and their product history is of ancient vintage: Ivory Soap dates to 1879. The business (which became a corporation in 1890) staked its culture on branding with the creation in 1931 of a formal brand management system. Some say that the field of marketing was born at P&G.[14] Internal growth led to the development of Tide detergent in 1946 and Crest toothpaste in 1955, whereas acquisitions brought Charmin toilet paper in 1957 and Folgers coffee in 1963.

Larger acquisitions followed, including the Richardson-Vicks Company in 1985 (owner of the Vicks, NyQuil, and Oil of Olay brands), Noxell Corporation in 1989 (Noxema products and Cover Girl cosmetics), and Revlon's Max Factor cosmetic and fragrance lines in 1991. The vast scale of the businesses led to periodic restructurings, including one begun in 1998 that reorganized the company along product rather than geographic lines. Growth through brand management, product development, and acquisitions continued.

P&G's culture is sticky—based on core brands and the steady establishment and entrenchment of new ones—and it is stronger than any given chief executive. For example, while P&G prides itself on having had twelve CEOs in twelve decades since incorporation, one of those terms, that of Durk Jager, lasted only seventeen months, during 1999 and half of 2000. P&G's earnings fell during early 2000, and its stock price dove. Having risen during 1999 from $88 to $109, P&G's stock price sank in 2000 from $114 in January to $53 in March, before recovering by year end and rising steadily from there.[15] Analysts attributed Jager's short and troubled tenure to overlooking how "reinventing corporate culture is not a neat, straight-line process."[16]

P&G and Gillette hailed their merger as a great cultural match. This proved only partly true, however, as operational practices clashed: Gillette was a decentralized and entrepreneurial place where people preferred to make decisions quickly and to coordinate by exchanging memos.[17] At P&G, decisions are reached only after considerable deliberation requiring several face-to-face meetings. The companies melded operations by embracing P&G's traditions and nudging Gillette's old culture aside.[18] It was once easy to imagine Berkshire owning Gillette outright, as Buffett used to laud the old razor-and-battery maker, but it seems unlikely that Berkshire will acquire the rest of P&G.

∾

With sales in 2013 reaching $50 billion, the Coca-Cola Company is about as powerful a brand and company as can be, at home in Atlanta and around the world. Its success is due ultimately to a single product, originally a mixture created in 1886 by pharmacist John Styth Pemberton of sugar, water, caffeine, and cocaine (extracts of the coca leaf and the kola nut). In 1891, fellow pharmacist Asa G. Candler gained control of the product and initiated steps to launch the business. Among early moves was the first bottling franchise in 1899, an investment in local partnerships that became the scaffolding to build the brand: the company makes concentrate for sale to bottlers that mix it into liquid form and package it for sale to retailers. Other early milestones include the 1905 removal of cocaine from the mix and the 1916 creation of the unique contour-shaped bottles.

In 1919, Candler sold the company to Ernest Woodruff and an investor group which promptly took it public. In 1923, Ernest's son, Robert Winship Woodruff, became president, a position he held through 1954, followed by serving as a director into the 1980s. Coke went global in the 1940s, establishing bottling plants near the fronts in World War II. With the stewardship of CEO William Robinson, in 1960, Coke acquired Minute Maid Corporation and in 1961, launched Sprite, the first of many brand expansions it would continue as it developed a product line of five hundred different drinks.

Under Paul Austin during the 1970s, despite reasonable sales, the company stumbled from one problem to another. Bottlers felt misunderstood, migrant workers in the Minute Maid groves were mistreated, environmentalists complained about its containers, and federal authorities challenged the legality of its franchise bottling system.[19] Although Austin launched Coca-Cola into China and was responsible for other international achievements,[20] critics say he neglected the flagship brand by diversifying into water, wine, and shrimp. With investors punishing the stock, the board finally ousted Austin in 1980, replacing him with Roberto C. Goizueta, Coca-Cola's most famous CEO, serving from 1981 through 1997.

A legendary businessman and Wall Street darling, Goizueta returned to basics, focusing on the Coke brand and rejuvenating Coca-Cola's traditional corporate culture of product leadership and cost management. During his tenure, Goizueta led the company to widen profit margins from 14 to 20 percent, boosted sales from $6 billion to $18 billion, drove profits from less than $1 billion to nearly $4 billion, and pushed returns on equity from 20 to 30 percent.[21] These measures were propelled by expanding Coke's global network and the successful 1982 launch of Diet Coke.

There were, of course, a few errors along the way. One, the lamentable 1985 birth and death of New Coke after it flopped with consumers, simply revealed the power of the core brand. Another was Coca-Cola's 1982 acquisition and 1987 divestiture of Columbia Pictures after it had become disillusioned with the inscrutable ways of Hollywood. But this diversion simply proved the durability of Coke's corporate culture—and was also lucrative, as the company paid $750 million for Columbia and sold it for $3.4 billion.

In 1988 and 1989, Buffett heralded Goizueta's achievements when Berkshire bought the large block of Coca-Cola shares it still owns today and Buffett joined the board (on which he served until 2006). After

Goizueta's sixteen years, however, the company's CEOs came and went more like temps, four in thirteen years. But despite mistakes, none could fail so spectacularly as to ruin the Coke brand or Coca-Cola's corporate culture. Douglas Ivester (1997–2000) swapped the contour-shaped Coke bottle for a larger unfamiliar variant, compromising a valued trademark. Douglas N. Daft (2000–2004) fired large numbers of people, a slap in the face to the employee-centric culture that prided itself on lifetime employment.[22]

Yet as Durk Jager's stint at P&G taught, changing strong corporate cultures is not easy, and at Coca-Cola, successors quickly reversed course. E. Neville Isdell, who returned from retirement to right the ship, and Muhtar A. Kent, who took over in 2009, revived a decentralized structure and the professional style that Goizueta favored. They also understood the importance of international markets, especially in southeast Asia, where growth prospects remain strong. Kent celebrates Coca-Cola's greatest tradition, epitomized by its history of using hundreds of bottling partners: being simultaneously global and local.[23]

Coca-Cola has been a profitable investment for Berkshire—worth today twelve times what Berkshire paid for it. And Buffett's son Howard has been on its board since 2010. The company appears to be prospering, and the Buffetts are bullish on it. Buffett and Munger continue to give the brand free advertising by sipping it on the podium at Berkshire's annual meetings. But skeptics wonder about the durability of its economic characteristics in a health-conscious world turning away from carbonated beverages.[24]

∾

In 2006 and again in 2009, Berkshire accumulated a substantial stake in Walmart, the massive retailer that sold McLane to Berkshire in 2003. Walmart is a young corporation for its size, begun in 1962, by brothers Samuel Moore and J. L. ("Bud") Walton in Arkansas.[25] Their first store grew to a chain of eighteen within a decade, and the brothers took the company public in 1970, listing on the New York Stock Exchange two years later. In a business sprint, Walmart's revenues hit $1 billion by 1979.

Amplifying models established by such Berkshire mainstays as Nebraska Furniture Mart, Walmart perfected the budget approach to merchandising, cutting costs to give shoppers deep discounts on a wide inventory. Competitors that ran periodic sales had to advertise them, whereas Walmart's "everyday low prices" required no such promotional expense, reducing Walmart's ad budget. Another entrepreneurial innovation, reminiscent of how McLane grew: Walmart built its own warehouses to stock large volumes bought at discounts and then opened its stores within a few hundred miles. A third Walmart practice paralleled that of Jordan's Furniture: Walmart built large stores (called Hypermarts or supercenters) and added entertainment for children. A further connection: from 1966, the Marmon Group's L.A. Darling division supplied Walmart's store display systems.[26]

Intense expansion through the 1980s made Walmart the largest retailer in the United States by 1990, when it began propagating its budget-minded and entrepreneurial model worldwide, including the acquisition of F. W. Woolworth stores in Canada in 1994. In 1997, Walmart joined the Dow Jones Industrial Average of thirty bellwether companies—replacing Woolworth, a former Berkshire investee. Geometric results followed, as Walmart's 1997 revenues blew past $100 billion, and the company acquired peers worldwide to cement its global leadership among retailers, spanning Mexico (1997), Germany (1997), the United Kingdom (1999), and Japan (2002). Revenues climbed to $244 billion in 2003.

Sam Walton died in 1992, but the Walton family continues to own nearly half of Walmart's stock. Walton's son became chairman, and the chief spot went to David Glass until 2000, when he bought the Kansas City Royals baseball team and handed leadership to H. Lee Scott Jr., a senior Walmart executive for two decades. Many wondered how Walmart would survive without Sam Walton, but despite some sluggishness, Glass and Scott both proved it was possible.[27] While frenetic growth subsided, the company has continued a steady pace of expansion under successive chiefs Mike Duke (2009–2014) and Doug McMillon (since). Revenues in 2013: $473 billion.

A company that gains so much wealth and power so quickly attracts critics. Vendors complained that Walmart abused its buying power, insisting on cut-throat pricing, dictating terms, bypassing sales representatives, and shunning independent manufacturers. Competitors objected that the massive suburban sprawls the company created disrupted small towns, emptied downtown shopping districts, and hurt local retailers, mom-and-pop shops, and other small businesses that had been the heart of America (including the distributors of Berkshire's Benjamin Moore).

Workers fought low wages and high turnover. Social critics questioned Walmart's share of the U.S. gross domestic product—nearly 3 percent, or as great as historical Goliaths like U.S. Steel Corporation in 1917 and General Motors in 1955. The most devastating critique shook the company in 1993.

It was discovered that Walmart merchandise was being produced in factories with child laborers in Bangladesh. Items stamped "Made in the U.S.A." as part of a Walmart promotion were in fact made overseas.

Walmart responded with improved monitoring along its supply chain and supervisor oversight of worker conditions, community giving programs, and other good corporate citizenship efforts. While remaining the budget-conscious retailer extraordinaire, Walmart regained consumer trust, positioning the company to defend its turf against onslaughts from newcomers like Amazon, whose online retailing prowess may threaten to do to Walmart what Walmart has done to others. All in all, Walmart is better suited to be a Berkshire investee than a subsidiary, although the presence of a large family ownership block would make a negotiated acquisition involving an exchange of values tempting.

∾

Berkshire's intangible values vividly prove their economic value when the company's common stock investments begin opportunistically, in options, warrants, convertible preferred, or debt of imperiled companies. Historic examples stretch back to the late 1980s when Berkshire invested in companies like Gillette and Salomon Brothers. Economic terms—high dividends and attractive conversion rates—were favorable to Berkshire because managers of the investees valued its intangible commitments of autonomy and permanence that deterred hostile takeover bids.

The financial crisis of 2008 showcased the long-term value of Berkshire's reputation for offering patient hands-off capital. Berkshire provided capital in varying amounts to companies as diverse as Bank of America, General Electric, Goldman Sachs, Harley-Davidson, Swiss Re, and Tiffany & Co.[28] Amid frozen credit markets, all faced temporary liquidity crises of varying degrees of severity. For Goldman, to illustrate one of the larger deals, Berkshire staked $5 billion for preferred stock, paying a 10-percent dividend redeemable for a 10-percent premium. Berkshire also received an option to buy a similar amount of Goldman common stock at $115 per share, below the prevailing market price of $125, making the option "in the money."

In early 2011, with credit markets working and the financial sector stabilized, Goldman redeemed the preferred. Berkshire earned a few years of dividends plus the buyback premium, adding up to $1.8 billion. In early 2013, Berkshire exercised its option to buy Goldman common. Rather than pay the

$5 billion cash price for it (then worth $6.4 billion), Goldman let Berkshire take stock valued at the difference of $1.4 billion. Berkshire's total gain on its $5 billion investment was $3.2 billion, 64 percent in a few years—along with ownership of 3 percent of Goldman's common stock. Berkshire's other investments during the period fared proportionally.[29]

From an ownership viewpoint, the most consequential of Berkshire's interventions during the crisis of 2008 was a near-doubling of its long-standing stake in USG Corporation. USG is the world's largest manufacturer of gypsum wallboard and strives to be the low-cost producer—both essential to its moat given that its industry is competitive, price sensitive, and easy to enter.[30]

Gypsum is a white mineral, often called alabaster, found throughout North America. Heating it removes water and crystallizes it into material commonly known as plaster of Paris. The plaster is malleable and, after adding water, can be twisted into any shape. It can also be strengthened for use in the construction industry by adding retardants to form wallboard (often called drywall or sheetrock, the latter a brand name USG minted).

In the late nineteenth century, scores of gypsum companies emerged, with thirty-five of them consolidating in 1901 to form the United States Gypsum Company, as it was originally named. The company was run through 1951 by Sewell L. Avery, a large USG stockholder. Avery, who later served on the board of U.S. Steel Corporation at the request of J. P. Morgan, defined USG's culture as budget conscious, research driven, and acquisitive—traits that endure today.[31]

An early acquisition in 1909 picked up Sackett Plaster Board Company, named for Augustine Sackett, who had invented gypsum wallboard. The product, which provides insulation and fireproofing, consists of layers of gypsum plaster held between sheets of paper. USG improved on Sackett's wallboard by reducing the number of layers and sealing the edges to avoid crumbling. Throughout the twentieth century, USG's market share ranged from one-third to one-half. USG's size and culture proved to be durable competitive advantages, as it expanded internationally in the 1950s and pioneered the home renovation industry of the 1960s.

Like Johns Manville, but on a smaller scale, USG had used asbestos in some specialty products through 1977, making it a defendant in the litigation that erupted in the 1980s. Like Gillette during the same period, USG twice fought off hostile takeover bids. The takeover defenses were costly, including recapitalizations that added substantial debt.[32] Weakened by such adversity, when the U.S. housing industry took a downturn in the late 1980s, USG was imperiled.

USG tried to restructure its debt but defaulted in 1991, struggling for a year, then filing for bankruptcy in 1993. In a negotiated resolution (prepackaged bankruptcy), USG cut its debt and preserved the value of its equity.[33] The housing market soon improved, and USG returned to profitability by 1996. The company reinvested in its core business, building new plants, which generated organic growth. It managed asbestos litigation by pressing its insurers to provide coverage, which kept the liabilities from crushing the company.

In 2000, Berkshire bought a 15 percent stake in USG when its market price was $15.[34] During the first half of 2001, the company fought to maintain the edge in asbestos battles, but reversals, including adverse jury verdicts, induced surrender. So it opted for another trip through bankruptcy.[35] USG's second bankruptcy spanned five years before the company emerged afresh in 2006. Thanks to the skill of its chairman, William C. Foote, USG again discharged all debt while preserving value for its common stock. Buffett called it "the most successful managerial performance in bankruptcy that I've ever seen."[36]

In 2006, a frothy U.S. housing market spelled a business boom. But the construction industry's cyclical nature was magnified when the financial crisis of 2008 struck and the housing market dove. USG's stock price spiked to $100 in 2006 and then plunged to $6 by late 2008.[37] At that point, amid the depths of the financial crisis, Berkshire invested $300 million in USG debt, yielding 10 percent annually and convertible into USG common stock at $11.40 a share.[38]

In 2009 and 2010, USG incurred significant losses and laid off five thousand employees—reducing its workforce to nine thousand.[39] During economic recessions, many companies skimp on research and development, but USG doubled down after 2008.[40] Responding to customer demand, USG researchers created sheetrock one-third lighter than historical offerings. It is easier to lift and maneuver, saving costs and meeting customer preferences.

USG returned to profitable growth in 2013. Once the U.S. economy and USG recovered, USG's stock price rose to $29. Berkshire then converted its debt into common equity. Besides earning 10 percent for five years, the conversion doubled the value of Berkshire's investment at a fraction of the cost, boosting its equity ownership of USG to one-fourth; and given its fit with Berkshire culture, USG is a prime candidate for full acquisition.

∼

In 2013, in an unusual move, Berkshire co-invested with 3G Capital, a Brazilian private equity firm run by billionaire Jorge Paulo Lemann, to acquire H. J. Heinz Company. Each staked $12 billion, with 3G funding part of its interest using debt and Berkshire receiving part of its investment in preferred stock. At the 50 percent ownership level, for Berkshire, Heinz is neither a typical controlled subsidiary nor a conventional investee position, but something in between—a new deal structure for Berkshire that Buffett says could become a model for its future.[41]

The company was formed in 1869 by Henry J. Heinz and L. C. Noble as Heinz, Noble & Company to sell bottled horseradish.[42] After failing amid the panic of 1875, Henry reorganized it with a focus on ketchup. In 1888, taking control of the company, he renamed it H. J. Heinz Company. The marketing slogan "57 varieties" first appeared in 1892; by 1900, though the company already had some 200 products—including pickles, mustard, vinegar, and olives—the slogan graced New York City's earliest electronic billboards, including a forty-foot long pickle at Fifth Avenue and 23rd Street.

Pioneers in global trade, the company opened its first facility abroad, in England, in 1905. Heinz's factories were considered models for their safety and considerate treatment of employees. Breaking ranks with his industry, Heinz supported the Pure Food and Drug Act of 1905, the progressive federal legislation intended to promote purity in processed foods; he supported it because he believed it would help to promote consumer confidence.

Henry died in 1919, handing leadership to his son Howard until 1941, when Howard's son, H. J. ("Jack") Heinz II succeeded him. During Jack's lengthy tenure (he was chief executive until 1966 and chairman until his death two decades later), the company expanded at home and abroad. It went public in 1946 and then pursued an impressive acquisition program that included StarKist tuna (1963), Ore-Ida Foods, Inc. (1965), and Weight Watchers, International (1978). Heinz participated in the era's industry shifts, as supermarket chains developed and new distribution systems emerged (including those pioneered by Berkshire's McLane).

In 1979, a non-family member became chief executive, Anthony J. F. O'Reilly, a workaholic taskmaster who drove the business in even bolder directions. Heinz made an additional twenty acquisitions during the 1980s. The company met the competition from generic products head-on, employing creative cost-cutting measures such as using thinner glass bottles to reduce expenses of both packaging and shipping, shrinking the size of some products, and minimizing labeling. Sales doubled during the 1980s: from $3 billion in 1980 to $6 billion in 1990.

Amid the globalization of the 1990s, the company engaged in a major reorganization, akin to what P&G had done in the same period, along product lines worldwide rather than the traditional geographic approach. The program included a combination of downsizing (facility closures and layoffs) and selected divestitures (including Weight Watchers, though it maintained a co-marketing relationship). In 1994–1995, Heinz acquired Budget Gourmet (frozen meals) and the pet food businesses of Quaker Oats Company (Kibbles 'n Bits, Gravy Train, and Ken-L Ration).

In 1998, William R. Johnson succeeded O'Reilly as chief executive while annual sales approached $10 billion. Sales remained steady for years, however, as Johnson maintained scale rather than expand it. In 2006, concerned about modest results, Nelson Peltz, a corporate raider turned shareholder activist, targeted Heinz in a proxy contest, winning seats on the board. Yet the business continued its steady rather than rapid growth, becoming a company with more promise than performance. Sales in 2012 were $12 billion, as the company remained best known for ketchup, while selling thousands of food products in every nook of the globe.

In January 2013, Berkshire and 3G offered $70 per share in an unsolicited bid, a 20-percent premium over the prevailing per-share price. The Heinz board responded by requesting more money and stressing that no deal could be made without assurances that the buyers would maintain Heinz's presence and heritage in Pittsburgh. Berkshire and 3G upped their bid to $72.50 and made the Pittsburgh commitment.

Among unusual features of this transaction for Berkshire were the making of an unsolicited offer, which Berkshire had always shunned, and the presence of a co-investor, which it had disfavored. On the other hand, Lemann, whom Buffett has known and admired since the two served together on Gillette's board, brought the idea to Buffett, and the two agreed that 3G rather than Berkshire would call the shots at Heinz. This decision explained another twist: Lemann quickly appointed a new CEO, the former head of Burger King, and a series of management changes ensued.[43]

As a prototype for future Berkshire acquisitions, the Heinz deal is savvy. The private equity partner likely will wish to sell within five to ten years, and assuming the improvements it makes at the company are effective, Berkshire will then acquire the rest. In this model, private equity firms become another potential source of Berkshire acquisitions, teeing up opportunities in which the shorter-term needs of private equity can be married to Berkshire's patient capital. The prospects are good that Berkshire will acquire the rest of Heinz, which is a Berkshire kind of company, while replicating the structure in other acquisitions.

∼

Aside from shedding indirect light on Berkshire culture, profiles of corporate icons in its portfolio show the power of culture to transcend individuals. Formidable figures—whether Kay Graham at the *Washington Post*, Sam Walton at Walmart, or Sewell Avery at USG—put indelible stamps on their companies. However, chief executives come and go, whereas corporate cultures endure: P&G had twelve chiefs in twelve decades amid a consistent button-down brand-centric culture that at least one, Durk Jager, found resisted change. Coca-Cola had four chiefs in thirteen years yet preserves moorings that its early leaders would recognize—despite the mark left by the intervening stewardship of the legendary Roberto Goizeuta. He and successive chiefs at companies from Gillette to Heinz, as well as Graham's successors at the *Post* and Walton's at Walmart, remind us that few business leaders are indispensable to their companies.

Berkshire's stock portfolio can be seen as a business unit akin in magnitude to Berkshire Hathaway Energy, BNSF, GEICO, Gen Re, Lubrizol, the Marmon Group, or McLane, with corresponding importance for who makes investment decisions. Historically this has been Buffett, along with Lou Simpson for GEICO's portfolio until 2010. That year, Berkshire added sub-portfolio managers, Todd Combs and Ted Weschler, whose investees include DaVita HealthCare Partners Inc., the medical equipment manufacturer, and DirecTV. Buffett heralds the duo as "models of integrity, helpful to Berkshire in many ways beyond portfolio management, and a perfect cultural fit."[44] To date, the unit's operation both reaffirms the distinctiveness of Berkshire culture and suggests the promise of its durability, which will be discussed in the next part of this book.

14

Succession

In January 2012, clients of Larson-Juhl, a custom picture frame maker that Berkshire Hathaway acquired a decade earlier, received a letter from Drew Van Pelt. The young executive, new to the industry, announced he had become chief executive of the company and reported the departure of his predecessor, Steve McKenzie, after two decades at Larson-Juhl.[1] The move came as a complete surprise to many.

Larson-Juhl's roots date to 1893, with the formation of Pacific Picture Frame in Seattle. Pacific grew as the industry did, booming with the invention of frame clamps and improved machinery to cut mats. In 1968, Pacific merged with Juhl, Inc., another major frame manufacturer that had been founded ten years earlier, and Juhl-Pacific became the dominant frame maker in the western United States. In 1988, Juhl-Pacific merged with Larson Picture Frame to form the industry leader, with sixty-seven manufacturing facilities in seventeen countries serving thousands of framing shops catering to a high-end clientele.

Larson-Juhl president, Craig Ponzio, who had overseen the 1988 merger, proposed in 2001 that Berkshire acquire the company. Buffett had never heard of it, but within two weeks made a deal for the business, then generating annual sales of $314 million. Ponzio retired while McKenzie stayed on as chief executive. Through the mid-2000s, the company prospered, expanding into sales of artwork. Yet profits slipped amid challenging industry economics. Consumers objected to the cost of custom framing—routine jobs run hundreds of dollars—while retailers insisted on high margins to enable offering a wide choice of styles.

Back at Berkshire headquarters, Buffett had asked Tracy Britt Cool, another young manager, to help oversee some of Berkshire's smaller companies or those needing help from headquarters—and Larson-Juhl fell into both categories. For Cool at Larson-Juhl that winter of 2012, one task was to seek a replacement for McKenzie, and Van Pelt got the job. Since then, Van Pelt has been toiling to vindicate the vote of confidence, heralding a "strong culture" at Larson-Juhl and trying to navigate the squeeze between frame shop demand for high margins and consumer aversion to high prices.[2]

Buffett's 2009 hiring of Cool unloaded some responsibilities and expanded institutional memory as Berkshire's growth exploded and Buffett continued to plan ahead. Steps like these help clarify Berkshire's future beyond Buffett and are the start of an answer to the perennial question: "What happens to Berkshire if Buffett gets hit by a truck?"[3]

This question has nagged the company's constituents for two decades. The concern was that the fate of the man and the company he built were one. With Buffett's demise went Berkshire. But after years of intensive definition, by words, deeds, and training, Buffett has institutionalized Berkshire's attitudes and practices so that it is poised to endure long after his departure. (He is also in very good health, so using the example of a truck in the perennial question remains apt.)

~

Since 1993, Buffett has written about what will happen after he's gone, and he and the Berkshire board have formalized the plan. As updated in 2006, the succession plan prescribes splitting Buffett's job in two: management (a chief executive officer) and investment (one or more investment officers). On the investment side, Buffett wrote:

> At one time, Charlie was my potential replacement for investing, and more recently Lou Simpson has filled that slot. Lou is a top-notch investor with an outstanding long-term record of managing GEICO's equity portfolio. But he is only six years younger than I. If I were to die soon, he would fill in magnificently for a short period. For the long term, though, we need a different answer.[4]

So Berkshire recruited younger investment managers Todd Combs and Ted Weschler. They, and maybe one more officer to assist them, should be able to handle the investment line of Buffett's job. They possess the necessary skills to manage the securities investments and have proven track records—surpassing Buffett in some years.[5]

In many ways, it will be more difficult than in the past, however. Combs and Weschler run only a portion of Berkshire's portfolio, $7 billion each out of $115 billion total at year-end 2013. Without Buffett, the portfolio they are eventually to run will be far larger than what they have managed in the past. All else being equal, it is harder to outperform the market with a large portfolio than with a small one.

The number of holdings in Berkshire's portfolio will also grow. Today, Berkshire's portfolio is concentrated. Its largest four positions—American Express, Coca-Cola, IBM, and Wells Fargo—are worth $60 billion, more than half the portfolio; its largest eight (adding ExxonMobil, Munich Re, P&G, and Walmart) represent more than 70 percent. One duty will be to monitor these positions and, if economic characteristics deteriorate, to sell. There will be scant opportunities to reinvest such large blocs—averaging $10 billion—in single companies. That means adding diverse stocks, making it harder to outperform.

On the other hand, Berkshire's unmatched capital resources and culture make it an investor of choice for those seeking financing. Whether for corporations needing liquidity amid distress, such as Goldman Sachs or USG in 2008, or private equity firms like 3G seeking partners to co-invest in large companies like Heinz in 2013, Berkshire is uniquely positioned to attract investment opportunities. Its chief investment officers—Combs and Weschler or others—will field them.

The job of chief executive officer—overseeing the subsidiaries, allocating corporate capital, and making new acquisitions—will be demanding. Oversight will be harder for a successor than for Buffett. It is one thing for the founder who was there at every acquisition to support and review the managers and distribute capital among them; for any other person, the task is daunting. Still, Berkshire subsidiary executives constitute a deep bench on the managerial side.

The most important general trait for Buffett's successor as chief executive is a knowledgeable commitment to Berkshire culture, including permanence, autonomy, and acquisitiveness. Therefore, the best candidates are insiders, those now managing Berkshire subsidiaries, as Berkshire's succession plan contemplates. Among these candidates, especially promising are individuals with strengths like lengthy service history at Berkshire; proficiency leading its largest, most sprawling operations; and experience running subsidiaries bearing most of the specific traits that constitute Berkshire culture. Experience leading a large public company would also be a plus.

Such factors explain why for many years observers correctly perceived that Buffett considered Sokol to be a top candidate, and many viewed Santulli that way, too. Santulli displayed earnestness and entrepreneurship in founding NetJets, taking it public, and selling it to and running it within Berkshire for a decade. But ultimately he seemed to show insufficient budget consciousness. Sokol built MidAmerican Energy into a sizable public company, made shrewd acquisitions for it as a Berkshire subsidiary for thirteen years, identified Lubrizol as a Berkshire acquisition candidate, was ruthlessly budget conscious at NetJets, and simultaneously participated in oversight at Johns Manville. But, in the end, Sokol was short on sensitivity to reputation.

There are a number of promising candidates. In my research for this book, including interviews and surveys of Berkshire insiders and shareholders, I was able to identify at least ten who are capable of executing acquisitions and allocating capital, cheerleading, advising, and occasional intervention. Ajit Jain of NICO is among the longest-serving Berkshire senior executives.[6] He runs a powerful engine of Berkshire's capital generation and is the executive Buffett showers with heaviest praise, although he has not run a public company. The CEOs of Berkshire's largest subsidiaries are often identified as candidates: Greg Abel of Berkshire Hathaway Energy is among the most acquisitive Berkshire managers, and Matthew Rose of BNSF Railway is the one with the most extensive public company service, having served in executive positions at BNSF since 1997.

Perhaps the executive with the most germane experience is Frank Ptak of the Marmon Group, a genuine mini-Berkshire, who also offers an impressive acquisition record; experience as co-head of Illinois Tool Works, a public company; and investment knowledge as a director of Morningstar. Among many other exemplary managers mentioned: Tad Montross of Gen Re, who runs a large and prosperous company; James Hambrick, who led Lubrizol as a public company and has a strong acquisition record; Grady Rosier of McLane, who shoots the lights out year in and year out at a massive decentralized enterprise; Kevin Clayton of Clayton Homes, who plays all the positions; and Bruce Whitman of FlightSafety, who is among the longest-serving heads of a classic, prosperous, and once-public Berkshire subsidiary. This list could go on but these examples suffice to suggest the abundant talent available to fill outsized shoes.

In filling those shoes, Buffett's successors could benefit from the example of what John Nichols did at the Marmon Group after succeeding Bob Pritzker: organize the company into sectors supervised by divisional presidents. Nichols' reasoning applies equally to the challenge Buffett's successor will face at Berkshire:

> There's a difference between a founder who has personally built an organization, acquiring entities and being intimately involved, and someone like me who comes in with a similar management style but not the intimate knowledge. Bob maintained very horizontal operations at the Marmon Group; at Illinois Tool Works, I believed in structuring operations into business sectors. So when I came [to Marmon], we built ten different sectors with a president for each. It gave me the ability to have a number of managers who day to day could create and implement strategy. With about 150 companies in a diverse set of ten specialized niches, there's no way I could be there to make everything happen myself.[7]

And it worked:

> While [Bob Pritzker and I] use many of the same management techniques, the [Marmon] organization was changed to build on the fundamental culture Bob had established. As a testament to our success, we have had virtually no management turnover.[8]

Berkshire could be organized along the lines suggested by the approach used in Buffett's shareholders' letters: insurance (especially GEICO, Gen Re, and NICO); regulated/capital-intensive companies (primarily Berkshire Hathaway Energy and BNSF Railway); finance (Clayton Homes, CORT, and XTRA); and the final sector, which could be subdivided into any of several different ways, including apparel (Brooks, Fruit of the Loom, Garan, H. H. Brown, Justin Brands); building materials (Acme, Benjamin Moore, Johns Manville, MiTek); and retail (Ben Bridge Jeweler, Helzberg Diamonds, Nebraska Furniture Mart, Star Furniture).

Each group would have a president reporting to the CEO. Such a structure simplifies management while minimizing bureaucracy and maintaining autonomy. The result would resemble not only the Marmon model but those at McLane, MiTek, and Scott Fetzer. Scores of candidates stand out to head these business sectors and would assure a smooth transition for the successor CEO of Berkshire.

∼

While most corporate succession plans address personnel, Berkshire's also addresses ownership, as Buffett has been Berkshire's controlling share-holder since 1965. Buffett most recently held 34 percent of Berkshire's voting power and 21 percent of its economic interest, always represent-ing 99 percent of his net worth.* He has been slowly reducing his stake by planned annual transfers to charitable foundations, a process that will continue for many years after his death.

Since 2006, for example, Buffett has been annually transferring Class B shares to the Bill and Melinda Gates Foundation in a pledge that will accu-mulate through 2026 to 500 million shares (about 45 percent of that class today), with the proviso that the Foundation's giving increase in tandem. In effect, the Foundation is entitled to yearly share transfers only so long as it sells them and makes grants in roughly the same amount it receives. Buffett has been making similar but smaller transfers of Class B shares to founda-tions of his children and late wife, aggregating 102,500 million (about 9 percent), and those foundations likewise liquidate shares to make grants, though not as a condition of Buffett's pledge.[9]

Buffett's estate will succeed him as Berkshire's controlling shareholder, while his executors gradually distribute his shares. During that time, which experts estimate could take up to twelve years, the executors will control a large, declining, block of Berkshire shares. As fiduciaries, the executors will act in accordance with Buffett's instructions, which will address choosing and electing directors, overseeing managers, and voting as shareholders in accordance with prevailing Berkshire principles.

So for a decade or more after Buffett's passing, his Berkshire shares will have a variety of owners he designates, some with sizable positions. He will no longer be Berkshire's controlling shareholder, but rather than an abrupt

---

*Berkshire has two classes of stock, A and B, with different voting and economic rights. Class A shares have one vote per share and the equivalent claim to the economic inter-est such as dividends, while the Class B shares have 1/10,000 of that voting power and 1/1,500 of that economic interest.

switch to the absence of a controlling shareholder, there will be a lengthy transition.

Berkshire's durability is reinforced by a shareholder body that generally agrees with the principles that Buffett injected into the company. Despite being a massive public corporation, Berkshire's shareholder character is that of partnership. Buffett forged this conception by stating it repeatedly in his annual letters and acting like the managing partner of a partnership. He explains business decisions candidly, admits mistakes, and catalogues the events that have defined Berkshire culture.

Reciprocally, the owners of the company's equity act more like partners in a private firm than shareholders of a public company. Many Berkshire shares are owned by people for whom Berkshire is among their largest holdings.[10] In the past decade, share turnover has been less than 1 percent compared to 3, 4, or 5 percent for other conglomerates, large insurance companies, or Berkshire's formerly public subsidiaries.[11]

Berkshire's low share turnover ties in to another unusual feature: most Berkshire shares are owned by individuals and families, not firms and funds. Typically, large public companies see 70 to 80 percent of their shares controlled by institutional investors.[12] Decisions are often made by committee and based on financial models and forecasts that can lead to trading the stock for reasons unrelated to the company. In contrast, at Berkshire a large portion of the voting power and economic interest are controlled by individuals and families, who focus on its specific economic and cultural characteristics.

Berkshire shareholders flock to its annual meetings. Attendance has risen from 7,500 in 1997 to 21,000 in 2004; 35,000 in 2008; and 40,000 in 2013.[13] They study Berkshire's annual report, Buffett's shareholder letters, and other reference materials. At most large public companies, individual shareholders are rationally apathetic. They skip reading the reports and rarely attend meetings, which verge on formal ritual. In contrast, substantive business discussion takes place at Berkshire's annual meeting, where the passion for the company is palpable.

Berkshire is not a family company in the same way that Ben Bridge Jeweler or RC Willey Home Furnishings are, but many families treat Berkshire shares as prized parts of their financial picture to be preserved by successive generations.[14] They are led by the examples at the top. Howard Buffett's Berkshire shares give him 0.12 percent of the voting power and 0.07 percent of the economic interest. (For perspective, each 0.01 percent of Berkshire's economic interest, one "basis point", is worth about $30 million.) Charlie

Munger's brood—eight children and dozens of grandchildren—owns more than 1.00 percent of the voting power and nearly 1.00 percent of the economic interest, with public instructions from the curmudgeonly patriarch "not to be so stupid as to sell."[15]

Certain owners of substantial amounts of Berkshire stock also manage institutions whose clients, wealthy individuals and families, are large Berkshire holders. Berkshire director Sandy Gottesman, for example, personally owns shares yielding 2.02 percent of Berkshire's voting power and 1.29 percent of its economic interest. Clients of First Manhattan, the firm Gottesman formed in 1964 and where his son Robert W. Gottesman is a senior manager, command another 1.91 percent of the voting power and 1.22 percent of the economic interest.

Berkshire director Bill Gates personally owns Class A shares with 0.45 percent of the voting power and 0.26 percent of the economic power, whereas the Bill and Melinda Gates Foundation receives and distributes the millions of Class B shares Buffett pledged to it (counting which would boost Gates' voting power to 1.32 percent and economic interest to 3.70 percent).[16] Meryl Witmer bought seven Class A shares shortly after being elected a director in 2013 and is part-owner of Eagle Capital, whose holdings include Class B shares with 0.16 percent of Berkshire's voting power and 0.53 percent of its economic interest.

Among other Berkshire directors with meaningful stock ownership, Thomas S. Murphy commands 0.14 percent of the voting power and 0.08 percent of the economic interest (see table 14.1). Managers of Berkshire's subsidiaries also own considerable Berkshire stock. Most are independently wealthy, and many own greater stakes in Berkshire than all but the most invested directors do. Like those directors, they believe in Berkshire culture and eat their own cooking.

Few investors will continue to own a stock for sentimental reasons, but many Berkshire stockholders are friends of Buffett's, revere Berkshire culture, and, of course, are making a great deal of money from the investment. For example, Shelby Davis, who founded Davis Select Advisers in 1969 (now run by his son Christopher C. Davis), owns an undisclosed personal stake in Berkshire, and the firm's clients own shares commanding 1.19 percent of Berkshire's voting power and 0.79 percent of the economic interest. Other long-time shareholders own sizable blocks through firms with reputations in sync with Berkshire's culture, including the sense of permanence: Ruane Cunniff & Goldfarb (1.15 percent and 0.85 percent, respectively); Gardner Russo & Gardner (0.53 percent and 0.40 percent);

Table 14.1
Berkshire Directors

	Birth Year	Election Year	Class A Shares	Class B Shares	Voting Power (%)	Economic Interest (%)
Warren E. Buffett	1930	1965	336,000	1,469,357	34.41	20.50
David S. Gottesman	1926	2003	19,538	2,393,398	2.02	1.29
Charles T. Munger	1924	1978	5,324	750	0.53	0.32
William H. Gates III	1955	2004	4,350	0	0.45	0.26
Thomas S. Murphy	1925	2003	1,376	26,976	0.14	0.08
Howard G. Buffett	1954	1993	1,200	2,450	0.12	0.07
Ronald L. Olson	1941	1997	306	17,500	0.03	0.02
Charlotte Guyman	1956	2003	100	600	*	*
Donald R. Keough	1927	2003	100	60	*	*
Walter Scott, Jr.	1931	1988	100	0	*	*
Stephen B. Burke	1958	2009	22	0	*	*
Meryl B. Witmer	1962	2013	7	0	*	*
Susan L. Decker	1962	2007	0	3,125	*	*
					37.70%	22.54%

*Each is de minimis but together total 0.03% of the voting power and 0.02% of the economic interest.

Note: Class A shares have one vote per share and the equivalent right to dividends and other economic distributions; Class B shares have 1/10,000 the voting power of the Class A shares and 1/1,500 the economic interest. So any given director's or shareholder's voting power is the portion of Class A shares owned plus 1/10,000 of the portion of Class B shares owned, whereas the economic interest is the portion of Class A shares owned plus 1/1,500 of the portion of Class B shares owned. Data in the accompanying tables are as of year-end 2013. At that time, with Berkshire's aggregate market value of about $300 billion, one basis point (0.01%) of economic interest represented $30 million.

Source: Berkshire Hathaway Annual Proxy Statement (2014); Bloomberg (year-end 2013).

Brown Brothers Harriman (0.49 percent and 0.47 percent); Markel Corporation (0.21 percent and 0.21 percent); and Tweedy Browne (0.13 percent and 0.09 percent). (See table 14.2.)

Sophisticated investors generally follow conventional wisdom to avoid concentrating portfolios in the stock of one company. Among holders who publicly disclose stakes, for instance, few of the largest hundred shareholders of blue chip companies like Apple, ExxonMobil, and General Electric allocate more than 5 percent of their portfolios to that company's stock.[17] In contrast, many Berkshire shareholders concentrate in its stock, following the

Table 14.2

Most Influential Publicly Disclosed Non-Director Owners

	Class A Shares	Class B Shares	Voting Power (%)	Economic Interest (%)
FMR (Fidelity)	29,493	10,006,024	3.12	2.20
First Manhattan	18,419	2,438,265	1.91	1.22
Davis Selected Advisers	11,367	2,424,072	1.19	0.79
Ruane Cunniff & Goldfarb	10,710	4,773,987	1.15	0.85
Vanguard Group	3,593	76,265,844	1.15	3.31
Capital Group	9,332	3,067,498	0.99	0.69
Blackrock	1,350	79,992,047	0.96	3.33
State Street	830	78,145,827	0.89	3.22
Norges Bank	6,233	*	0.64	0.38
Gardner Russo & Gardner	4,953	2,317,684	0.53	0.40
Brown Brothers Harriman	4,309	5,130,657	0.49	0.47
Bank of New York Mellon	2,772	18,467,142	0.47	0.92
First Eagle	3,815	*	0.39	0.23
LourdMurray Capital	2,838	472,377	0.30	0.19
Legal & General	2,203	4,700,001	0.27	0.32
Northern Trust Corp.	307	21,215,675	0.25	0.88
Water Street Capital	1,909	3,295,776	0.23	0.25
Intl. Value Advisers	2,068	161,530	0.21	0.13
Markel Corporation	1,752	2,553,764	0.21	0.21
Bank of America	1,307	5,434,334	0.19	0.30
CalPERS	1,427	3,327,100	0.18	0.22
Wells Fargo	1.099	5,363,611	0.17	0.28
Eagle Capital	320	12,625,866	0.16	0.53
Everett Harris	1,480	814,362	0.16	0.12
PNC	1,418	1,237,468	0.16	0.14
Geode Capital	*	13,629,477	0.14	0.55
Stewart West Indies	1,335	*	0.14	0.08
INVESCO	1,099	2,057,949	0.13	0.15
Mackenzie Financial	1,249	*	0.13	0.08
Tweedy Browne	1,184	412,914	0.13	0.09
Goldman Sachs	384	5,624,318	0.10	0.25
Morgan Stanley	208	7,497,457	0.10	0.32
American Century	313	1,912,350	0.05	0.10
TOTAL			17.28 %	21.00 %

*Unreported or zero.

Source: Bloomberg (year-end 2013).

example of Berkshire's own portfolio concentration. To illustrate, forty-four of the hundred largest publicly disclosed Class A owners hold more than 5 percent of their portfolio in the stock, starting with Buffett.[18] Seventeen of the largest one hundred holders of the Class B are so concentrated, counting Buffett and seven others who also concentrate their wealth in Class A (see tables 14.3 and 14.4).

America's blue chip companies tend to have the same largest shareholders, chiefly big banks, investment advisors, and money managers. For example, institutions like Blackrock, Fidelity, State Street, and Vanguard own 2 to 5 percent of the stock of such companies, dominating their shareholder lists. While many also own Berkshire, they are not Berkshire's dominant shareholders.

Berkshire's unusual shareholder body thus includes an affiliation of readily coordinated shareholders with a meaningful percentage of the voting power and economic interest that is rare in corporate America. Its sizable group of stalwart shareholders bears a partnership conviction about Berkshire and faith in the owner orientation of the company and its subsidiaries.[19] True, their fondness for Buffett overflows, and they believe that no one can replace him, yet they appreciate what he built and believe in its durability beyond him. The voting power they wield will help shape Berkshire's future.

Successors will therefore find it desirable to adhere to Berkshire's business model. The pledges of managerial freedom and Berkshire's continued ownership of acquired businesses create a unique asset. If anyone at Berkshire proposed to preempt managerial authority or sell a subsidiary as if it were mere merchandise, they would be rebuked by a chorus of purists willing to use their voting power accordingly, especially in the election and removal of directors. Berkshire's subsidiary managers would also object and, in addition to voting their shares, threaten to resign or quit, causing disruption that no successor to Buffett and no Berkshire director would want.

So it is unlikely that Berkshire would soon lose what is distinctive about it and revert to being just another conglomerate or takeover boutique. You can take Buffett out of Berkshire, but you can't take Berkshire out of the subsidiaries.

∼

For many purposes, the views of the vast majority of Berkshire shareholders will align, particularly amid strong profitability and performance. As a public company, however, Berkshire will face external pressure endangering its

Table 14.3
100 Largest Publicly Disclosed Class A Owners

	Number of Shares	Percentage of Class		Number of Shares	Percentage of Class
Warren E. Buffett	336,000	39.11	Bank of America	1,307	0.15
FMR (Fidelity)	29,493	3.43	Mackenzie Financial	1,249	0.14
David S. Gottesman	19,538	2.27	Howard G. Buffett	1,200	0.14
First Manhattan	18,419	2.14	State Farm Mutual Auto	1,186	0.14
Davis Selected Advisers	11,367	1.32	Tweedy Browne Co.	1,184	0.14
Ruane Cunniff & Goldfarb	10,710	1.24	Boulder Inv. Advisers	1,156	0.13
Capital Group	9,332	1.08	INVESCO Ltd.	1,099	0.13
Norges Bank	6,233	0.72	Wells Fargo & Co.	1,099	0.13
Charles T. Munger	5,324	0.62	Wellcome Trust	1,000	0.12
Gardner Russo & Gardner	4,953	0.57	Clearbridge Investments	933	0.11
William H. Gates III	4,350	0.50	Hikari Tsushin Inc.	887	0.10
Brown Brothers Harriman	4,309	0.50	State Street Corp.	830	0.10
First Eagle Investment	3,815	0.44	Legg Mason, Inc.	778	0.09
Vanguard Group	3,593	0.42	Pacific Financial (Clipper)	709	0.08
LourdMurray Capital	2,838	0.33	Baldwin Investment Mgmt	.707	0.08
Bank of New York Mellon	2,772	0.32	Sleep, Zakaria & Co.	666	0.08
Legal & General Group	2,203	0.25	US Bancorp	636	0.07
Intl. Value Advisers	2,068	0.24	IG Investment Mgmt.	552	0.06
Water Street Capital	1,909	0.22	Eaton Vance Mgmt.	526	0.06
Markel Corporation	1,752	0.20	Eagle Capital Mgmt.	520	0.06
Everett Harris & Co.	1,480	0.17	Investment Taktiengesell	511	0.06
CalPERS	1,427	0.17	Troy Asset Mgmt.	500	0.06
PNC Financial Services	1,418	0.16	Allen Holding Inc.	500	0.06
Thomas S. Murphy	1,376	0.16	Universal Investment Co.	471	0.05
Blackrock	1,350	0.16	Henry H. Armstrong Assoc.	469	0.05
Stewart W. Indies Trading	1,335	0.15	UBS	400	0.05

Table 14.3
(*Continued*)

	Number of Shares	Percentage of Class		Number of Shares	Percentage of Class
Timucuan Asset Mgmt.	392	0.05	Brown Advisory Inc.	269	0.03
Goldman Sachs	384	0.04	Hartline Investment Corp.	263	0.03
Virtu Financial	384	0.04	JPMorgan Chase	232	0.03
Falcon Edge Capital	377	0.04	KCG Holdings	221	0.03
Punch Card Capital	373	0.04	RBF LLC	220	0.03
Union Investment	371	0.04	Aviva PLC	218	0.03
Gamco	360	0.04	Kovitz Inv. Group	213	0.02
Whalerock Point	359	0.04	Morgan Stanley	208	0.02
Vontobel Holding AG	347	0.04	Fenimore Asset Mgmt.	207	0.02
HSBC Holdings	342	0.04	Budros Ruhin & Roe	201	0.02
Auto Owners Group	333	0.04	Stearns Financial	200	0.02
Royal Bank of Canada	322	0.04	Shelter Ins. Group	199	0.02
Bridges Inv. Mgmt.	314	0.04	Matthew 25 Mgmt. Corp.	197	0.02
American Century Cos.	313	0.04	State Farm Ins. Cos.	197	0.02
Ronald L. Olson	306	0.04	Great Lakes Advisors	196	0.02
Northern Trust Corp. Cos.	307	0.04	Irish Life Inv. Mgrs.	171	0.02
Chou Associates	300	0.03	Suntrust Banks	171	0.02
Fayez Sarofim	300	0.03	TDAM USA Inc.	163	0.02
Credit Agricole	290	0.03	CMT Asset Mgmt.	159	0.02
Franklin Resources	289	0.03	Ballentine Finn	154	0.02
Amundi SA	289	0.03	Insight 2811	153	0.02
Degroof Gestion Inst.	288	0.03	Toronto Dominion Bank	145	0.02
Deutsche Bank	286	0.03	Forum Inv. Advisors	144	0.02
Burgundy Asset Mgmt.	277	0.03	Arlington Value Capital	140	0.02

Note: Shaded entries indicate portfolio concentration; portfolio concentration refers to an investor with more than 5 percent of its portfolio invested in Berkshire (whether Class A or Class B); entities that have multiple funds are so counted if at least one fund is so concentrated.
Source: Bloomberg (year-end 2013).

Table 14.4
100 Largest Publicly Disclosed Class B Owners

	Number of Shares	Percentage of Class		Number of Shares	Percentage of Class
Gates Foundation	81,384,404	6.91	Legal & General	4,700,001	0.49
Blackrock	79,992,047	6.79	Deutsche Bank	4,462,645	0.38
State Street	78,145,827	6.63	Neuberger Berman	4,393,807	0.38
Vanguard	76,265,844	6.47	Canada Pension Plan	4,272,687	0.37
Northern Trust Corp.	21,215,675	1.80	SE Asset Mgmt. (Longleaf)	4,240,058	0.36
BONY Mellon	18,467,142	1.57	Caisse de Depot	4,131,100	0.35
Geode Capital	13,629,477	1.15	T. Rowe Price Group	3,962,531	0.34
Eagle Capital	12,625,866	1.07	Charles Schwab Inv.	3,909,676	0.33
FMR (Fidelity)	10,006,024	0.85	Primecap Mgmt.	3,853,924	0.33
D. E. Shaw & Co.	8,297,240	0.70	N.Y. State Teachers Ret.	3,733,504	0.32
TIAA-CREF	8,071,048	0.69	Columbia Mgmt.	3,625,473	0.31
Robeco Group NV	7,775,857	0.66	Sumitomo Mitsui Trust	3,447,571	0.29
Morgan Stanley	7,497,457	0.64	CalPERS	3,327,100	0.28
UBS	6,848,650	0.59	Water Street Capital	3,295,776	0.28
Fiduciary Mgmt.	6,809,912	0.58	Cal. State Teachers	3,258,400	0.28
Alliance Bernstein	6,508,151	0.56	Prudential Financial	3,146,939	0.27
JPMorgan Chase	5,854,663	0.50	Credit Suisse	3,091,442	0.26
Goldman Sachs	5,624,318	0.48	Capital Group	3,067,498	0.26
Bank of America	5,434,334	0.46	Rhumbline Advisers	3,020,881	0.26
Wells Fargo	5,363,611	0.46	Mitsubishi UFJ	2,984,453	0.26
Fisher Investments	5,190,077	0.44	Florida State Board	2,982,011	0.25
Norges Bank	5,157,763	0.44	Adage Capital	2,775,977	0.24
Brown Bros. Harriman	5,130,657	0.44	Wedgewood Partners	2,698,966	0.23
New York State C.R.	5,126,517	0.44	Acadian Asset Mgmt.	2,672,776	0.23
Manulife Financial	5,067,856	0.43	Susquehanna Intl.	2,606,017	0.22
Ruane Cunniff	4,773,987	0.41	Markel Corp.	2,553,764	0.22

Table 14.4
(*Continued*)

	Number of Shares	Percentage of Class		Number of Shares	Percentage of Class
First Manhattan	2,438,265	0.21	Sprucegrove Inv. Mgmt.	1,574,265	0.13
Davis Select Advisers	2,424,072	0.21	Great West Life Assur.	1,558,404	0.13
David S. Gottesman	2,393,398	0.20	Wisconsin Inv. Bd.	1,552,376	0.13
Janus Capital	2,372,483	0.20	Mizuho Financial	1,540,497	0.13
Gardner Russo & Gardner	2,317,684	0.20	Ohio Public Emp. Ret.	1,518,038	0.13
Principal Financial Group	2,305,645	0.20	State of Tennessee	1,490,061	0.13
Teachers Advisors Inc.	2,267,430	0.19	Citigroup	1,474,054	0.13
Royal Bank of Canada	2,251,053	0.19	Warren E. Buffett	1,469,357	0.13
Allianz	2,240,609	0.19	Baillie Gifford & Co.	1,463,455	0.13
Clearbridge Investments	2,236,151	0.19	STRS	1,353,327	0.12
INVESCO	2,057,949	0.18	BNP Paribas	1,311,726	0.11
Cortland Advisers	2,000,000	0.17	HSBC	1,266,295	0.11
BMO Financial	1,961,063	0.17	Eaton Vance Mgmt.	1,244,371	0.11
American Century	1,912,350	0.16	PNC	1,237,468	0.11
ING Inv. Mgmt.	1,890,652	0.16	Wintergreen Advisers	1,222,090	0.10
Parametric Portfolio	1,841,284	0.16	Klingenstein Fields	1,179,926	0.10
Check Capital Mgmt.	1,782,399	0.16	AXA	1,161,424	0.10
Dimensional Fund	1,768,096	0.16	Gateway Inv. Advisors	1,132,067	0.10
SQ Advisors	1,754,366	0.16	Prudential	1,125,510	0.10
Frank Russell Trust Co.	1,751,443	0.16	Weitz Wallace	1,118,981	0.10
APG All Pensions Group	1,698,381	0.15	Met Life	1,115,353	0.10
Barclays	1,658,413	0.14	Toronto Dominion Bank	1,101,182	0.09
Chevy Chase Trust	1,646,451	0.14	Creative Planning	1,074,700	0.09
Legg Mason	1,586,376	0.14	Brown Advisory	1,051,916	0.09

Note: Shaded entries indicate portfolio concentration.

Source: Bloomberg (year-end 2013).

commitment to permanence. Large public companies are closely watched by activist shareholders and widely followed by analysts who fixate on quarterly and year-to-year results. Buffett's presence assures Berkshire's adherence to its values, including its elongated time horizon; in his absence, a tug-of-war could emerge between owners who share these convictions and more activist investors who prefer short-term gain to long-term value.

Berkshire's traditionalist owners and activist shareholders might have sharply different preferences in a number of scenarios. One concerns Berkshire's dividend policy, which is to retain each dollar of earnings if it increases market value by at least one dollar, and otherwise to pay dividends. Under that policy, Berkshire has not paid a dividend since 1967. As Berkshire grows, the likelihood of paying dividends under this test increases—and shareholders of all stripes could endorse this possibility. But activist shareholders unaligned with Berkshire tradition may agitate to change its dividend policy to make large and frequent cash distributions.

Another scenario is dealing with poor performance. Amid serious or prolonged stagnation, whether at particular subsidiaries or Berkshire-wide, activists may seek radical change, not only divesting targeted businesses but stripping Berkshire down, splitting it up, or selling off its parts. They may be more impatient than Berkshire's traditionalist shareholders. Some might even prescribe both asset divestitures and dividends of the proceeds.

To fight such battles, imagine that Berkshire stalwarts consider taking the company private. A giant undertaking, going-private transactions are never easy. At Berkshire, it would invite competing bids from groups prepared to break the company up for short-term gain as well as lawsuits challenging the fairness of the process and price. But the threat of a going-private transaction may be enough to get ambivalent shareholders to favor traditional Berkshire values and defeat rivals.

To go private, stalwarts would need to corral a group of up to three hundred holders to continue owning Berkshire as a closely held firm (that figure is the legal cutoff distinguishing public from private companies). Depending on the exact distribution of shares among stalwarts, including Buffett and/or his estate and legatees, a group of three hundred would command a large portion of the voting power, at least two-thirds and as much as three-fourths. To acquire the remainder would therefore require some $75–100 billion, much larger than any buyout in history but within reach given the resources such a group commands.

The real test would be persuading other shareholders to agree. Short-term holders will surely tender for a small premium to the market price; long-term devotees of Berkshire culture will hold out as they always have.[20]

If the latter represent a meaningful portion of the shareholder body, a going-private offer would fail, and the traditionalists would be vindicated. Such a result would be the ultimate validation of the durability of Berkshire culture.

But suppose that proved incorrect: suppose opponents of traditional Berkshire values prevailed, and enough shares were tendered to take Berkshire private. That might do Berkshire a favor as an institution, because it may be better off as a private company owned by its traditional stalwarts than a public one exposed to short-term pressures from analysts and activists. For Berkshire, there are few advantages to being a public company and numerous disadvantages.

While Berkshire may have gained net advantages from its status as a public company in earlier decades, it is not clear that being public remains beneficial.[21] Berkshire does not need the public capital markets, as it is a net *supplier* of capital, generating vast amounts of it from operations and investing it across wide sectors of the economy. If Berkshire desired external capital, its decentralized structure would pinpoint the particular subsidiary of interest. The subsidiary could go directly to the debt market to supply it, as Berkshire Hathaway Energy and BNSF do.

Likewise, Berkshire does not need the currency of a publicly traded stock to pay managers or use in acquisitions as many companies do. Berkshire avoids using its stock to compensate anyone—even its directors; Buffett has signaled willingness to do so only in narrow circumstances, such as to compensate his successor as chief executive or when acquiring a company whose managers own stock options in it. (Berkshire's acquisition of Burlington Northern Santa Fe is an example.) Berkshire rarely uses its stock in acquisitions.

Benefits of being public are for shareholders rather than Berkshire as an institution, the biggest being the presence of a liquid market for transferring shares cheaply; this matters less to a small group of very rich owners than a going-private transaction would yield. It also matters to foundations needing to liquidate the Berkshire shares Buffett pledges to them, but private placements can be arranged, which some buyers may prefer. If the costs of short-term pressures prove too great, going private would be a small price to pay to avoid them.

On the other hand, inimitable as it is, Berkshire's vaunted values are a beacon worthy of emulation. They are a role model for corporate America and offer an aspiration for others. Were Berkshire private, these values would be hidden from public view. In the end, therefore, staying public may be part of Berkshire's commitment—as well as its identity. Given the long-term nature of Buffett's estate, the presence of so many stalwarts, and the melded quality of Berkshire culture, the logical prediction is that Berkshire will indefinitely remain a public company conglomerate after Buffett.

∾

As a public company, Berkshire's board will play a role in its future beyond Buffett, particularly in setting dividend policy and resolving strategic disagreements among shareholders. While Berkshire shareholders will continue to elect the board and choose directors according to their fidelity to Berkshire culture, the succession plan contemplates one action entrusted to the board itself: designating a chairman. Buffett, who has served this role as well as being chief executive, recommends that a member of the Buffett family serve as non-executive chairman of the board.[22]

Berkshire would thus join the growing number of large corporations that have different people in the two top roles of chairman and chief executive. To fill the outsized shoes at Berkshire after Buffett, splitting the roles may be desirable to share the burden.

While one could imagine promoting other directors to the chairmanship, particularly one with the gravitas of Bill Gates, it is logical to ask Howard Buffett to serve in that role. Half of Berkshire's other directors are in their seventies or older, and among those of his generation, Howard is the longest-serving Berkshire director (see table 14.1). As a Buffett family member and loyal son, he has a unique perspective on Buffett's values and sense of Berkshire culture. For a succession plan, it is hard to see a better choice. As Howard Buffett expressed it in correspondence for this book, "Berkshire has been my father's lifetime work, and it means a lot to me to preserve it."[23]

∾

Berkshire's succession plan is intended to secure the company's permanence. By installing exceptional managers in a variety of roles historically handled by a single person, succession is calculated to succeed. Buffett's estate planning envisions a lengthy transition in which his influence as Berkshire's controlling shareholder gradually abates. During and after that extended process, a stalwart group of Berkshire owners who share the partnership attitude at Berkshire will contribute to its longevity. Berkshire is Buffett's lifetime achievement, and one destined to have a lifetime of its own. But there will be additional challenges, as anticipated in the next chapter.

15

Challenges

In 2001, Julian Robertson, founder of the pre-eminent Tiger Fund, signaled to Buffett his willingness to sell a large stake in XTRA Corporation, the truck leasing company.[1] Upping the ante, Berkshire proposed to XTRA's board a tender offer to the public company's shareholders, which it endorsed, and Berkshire soon closed.

XTRA is the industry leader in renting and leasing trailers for trucks to commercial organizations. Founded in 1957, it went public in 1961, listing on the New York Stock Exchange and joining the Dow Jones index of twenty transportation stocks. Today it manages vast fleets for large corporate customers such as FedEx and UPS in package shipping; Home Depot, Kroger, and Walmart in retailing; Kraft and Pepsi in merchandising; and J.B. Hunt, Penske, and YRC in freight hauling.[2] The company's fleet of 80,000 trailers includes chassis, flatbeds, dry vans, refrigerated vans, storage vans, and specialty equipment.

XTRA was among the first U.S. leasing companies to lease trailers on flat cars, an early form of intermodal transport nicknamed "piggybacking."[3] With piggybacking, a truck trailer can be readily lifted onto a railcar. Historically, transportation systems were segmented, with each mode (pallets, tractors, trailers, railcars, barges, ocean vessels, storage facilities) vying with the others rather than coordinating. In recent decades, XTRA has participated in the global integration of these modes, producing intermodal elements ultimately suitable for universal container shipping.

When Berkshire acquired XTRA, its chief executive was Lewis Rubin, headquarters were in Westport, Connecticut, and the company was engaged in both trailer leasing and intermodal container operations. But overhead was high, return on assets low, and earnings modest. Within three years after Berkshire's acquisition, Rubin was replaced by William H. Franz, a long-time company executive; headquarters were relocated from Westport to St. Louis; and XTRA divested its container and intermodal business to focus on leasing tractor trailers. The goal was to reduce overhead, improve asset utilization, and boost profits. It is rare for any one of these reforms to follow a Berkshire acquisition, let alone all three. XTRA is a reminder that Berkshire is a business and its culture without fairy tales, despite lofty aspirations and a solid record of achieving them.

Remembering that the Berkshire model has limits, and that mistakes are inevitable, helps sustain the company by avoiding nostalgia traps. Read Buffett's annual letters and you will find him acknowledging mistakes, including several referenced in this book. For example, Buffett miscalculated in Berkshire's acquisition of Dexter, the shoe subsidiary acquired in 1993, and folded it into H.H. Brown when it couldn't survive. Berkshire's 1998 acquisition of Gen Re ultimately proved valuable, but not before several years of cost to shareholders and angst for managers. Buffett learned this lesson early on, as the original acquisition of Berkshire Hathaway was a doozie.

Autonomy is sacrosanct at Berkshire. The hands-off approach, however, is not intended to be an abdication, though it can come close. When it does, the consequences are significant even if the net benefits are positive. Autonomy in the case of NetJets resulted in balance sheet management and cost structures Buffett ultimately disliked, prompting him in 2009 to ask Richard Santulli to withdraw and David Sokol to step in. The trust implicit in the notion of autonomy was a cause of the crisis in 2011 when Sokol bought Lubrizol shares ahead of pitching the company as a Berkshire acquisition.

Buffett has a gift for choosing outstanding managers, and Berkshire prides itself on the long tenure of its executives, making the exceptions stand out. In the 1990s, Fechheimer had a series of presidents, including Richard Bentley, who had been promoted from a divisional head within Scott Fetzer; in 1998, he resigned from Fechheimer without comment by him or Berkshire, succeeded by Patrick Byrne, who stayed just two years.[4] In 2002, Sheila O'Connell Cooper, chief executive of the Pampered Chef, left after five months on the job without a trace.[5] In 2006, Barry Tatelman withdrew from management of Jordan's Furniture to embark on a career in the arts, leaving his brother Eliot in charge.[6] While these departures do not usually lead to revelations of any particular difficulties, they can cause upheaval at the subsidiaries. Buffett's successors must vet managers carefully.

Buffett has a unique approach to acquisitions, which has served Berkshire well but is difficult to emulate. Most corporations, including conglomerates, adopt a formal plan charting desired sectors in which to expand, sometimes even naming acquisition targets. In contrast, when describing given transactions in his annual letters, Buffett calls Berkshire's acquisition strategy "haphazard"[7] and "serendipitous,"[8] neither "carefully crafted" nor "sophisticated."[9] He considers Berkshire's lack of a plan a strong plus. Plans constrain judgment and discretion, both of which are vital in making acquisitions prudently.

In the acquisitions market, companies commonly hire investment banks and other intermediaries to broker deals. Buffett prefers to avoid these.[10] In fact, Berkshire does not usually initiate the process but rather responds to proposals from sellers. Here are the sources of the thirty-five deals for which information appears in Berkshire disclosure.[11] *Eleven* involved sellers contacting Berkshire;[12] *nine* arose when existing business relationships contacted Buffett;[13] *seven* involved friends or relatives reaching out to Buffett;[14] *four* involved Berkshire contacting the seller directly;[15] *three* were teed up by strangers or acquaintances;[16] and only *one* came from a broker Berkshire retained, the anomalous case of Sokol hiring Citi in the hunt that led to Lubrizol.

In typical acquisitions, accountants test a company's internal controls and financial statement figures, and lawyers probe contracts, compliance, and litigation. Such examinations are usually done at corporate headquarters, along with meetings during which principals get acquainted with each other and tour facilities. The process can take weeks or months. Berkshire—proudly—does none of this.[17] Buffett sizes people up in short order, often in less than a minute.[18] Deals are reached without delay, sometimes in an initial phone call;[19] often in meetings of less than two hours;[20] invariably "quickly"[21] or "promptly;"[22] and in any event "soon"[23] or "before long"[24] after getting started; a week might be typical.[25]

Formal contracts follow swiftly, within a week, ten days, or a month.[26] Deals—including big ones involving billions of dollars—can close within a month of contact.[27] Even for public company acquisitions, a Berkshire transaction moves faster than average. A few examples: the MidAmerican

Energy deal was concluded in two short meetings; Shaw Industries was broached in June and signed in August; Benjamin Moore began in July and closed in December.

People commonly haggle over price. Tactics include sellers naming an asking price they don't expect to get and buyers making a lowball bid. Some people enjoy the give and take, and many believe it is the most economical way to produce value in exchange. Buffett considers such exercises a waste of time. He wants a single price at which each side can say yes—or walk away. His bid is his bid; when he gives you a bid, you have what most people classify as the "best price," "final offer," or "highest bid." Buffett names a price at which Berkshire will buy and sticks with it. In several cases, the seller came back to Buffett and asked for a higher price. In all such cases, he said no.[28]

Berkshire's subsidiaries have an extensive acquisition practice, and the experienced executives who succeed Buffett will bring their own style and skills to this part of the job. But departures in style or procedure will not undermine Berkshire culture. Some, like executives at Marmon, clearly follow much of Buffett's practice, especially in terms of acting opportunistically and letting sellers make the first move; others, like those at Lubrizol and MiTek, define a strategic objective and scout for targets. Successors may benefit from an approach that is closer to Buffett's than to that of rivals in the acquisitions market. But, whatever they do, the greater challenge may be resisting any temptation to try to emulate Buffett.

In the early 2000s, before Fruit of the Loom acquired it, Russell Corporation signed major licensing agreements to produce sportswear adorned with popular logos. It made contracts with scores of U.S. universities and signed a large deal with the National Basketball Association. The trouble was, the goods affixed with licensed Russell logos were made in factories in China and Honduras that engaged in objectionable conduct. In China, the company's products were manufactured in sweatshops that violated principles of international human rights; in Honduras, company officials boarded up the plant and ousted the workforce in retaliation for attempts to unionize.

Such misbehavior drew the attention of activists across the United States, including a group of college students who demanded that universities terminate the licensing agreements. In 2009, a former employee of the

Honduras facility took the floor at the Berkshire annual meeting to report on the conditions and demand a response. Russell's operating activities contrasted with Berkshire's tenets of integrity and repute; promptly upon learning of the problems, Fruit of the Loom corrected them.

This case highlights the challenges Buffett's successor will face in over-seeing the sprawling array of operations. It illustrates the downside of cor-porate decentralization. When it comes to potential subsidiary violations of company policy or law, information must reach Berkshire headquarters immediately. But the existing framework is informal. It is based heavily on the mandate of subsidiary managers: report bad news early. In the distinc-tive context of Berkshire culture, steeped in integrity, such an approach may be satisfactory. In the spirit of autonomy, it is essential.

But many give Berkshire a pass on certain matters because of Buffett's presence. His eventual absence will remove this benefit of the doubt. Suc-cessors will need to assure both continuity and reliability. Surprises could result in government authorities imposing more radical, less desirable changes if Berkshire has to contain a controversy, rather than be in front of it. The Russell episode is both an exception to Berkshire's norm and a reason to consider formal oversight of its subsidiaries.

While Berkshire has won plaudits for good corporate citizenship,[29] critics complain about the absence of conglomerate-wide reporting on items such as social responsibility and sustainability.[30] Many Berkshire subsidiaries—including Brooks, Johns Manville, Lubrizol, and Shaw—are in the vanguard of such corporate stewardship. They join elite global com-panies in the practice of issuing formal responsibility and sustainability statements and audited reports on the corporate treatment of stakeholders, especially employees at home and abroad, and of the environment.

Berkshire is unusual in that its structure does not lend itself to issuing a formal corporate report at the parent level. And the number and size of Berkshire's subsidiaries can obscure some of their internal measurement and reporting efforts. Critics urge consolidated policies, including a con-glomerate statement of responsibility or charter of sustainability. It may unduly interfere with subsidiary autonomy to set corporate-level policy, but a consolidated report will prove valuable in order to highlight the vary-ing ways that Berkshire subsidiaries embrace stewardship—and assure con-tinued adherence.

Shaw Industries, for example, led the carpet industry to newfound appreciation for its responsibility concerning environmental protection and sustainable development.[31] During the 1990s, people began to realize the environmental costs of using non-biodegradable artificial fibers to make carpets; disposing of them presented a significant waste management problem. Shaw then started to promote carpet recycling programs. It began to produce synthetic yarn sourced from recycled plastics such as soda bottles and developed a polyolefin backing material that cut raw material use in half.

McLane embraces a "green advantage initiative" to manage its fleet of trucks that stock America's supermarkets.[32] The initiative stresses reducing environmental impact and increasing operational efficiency. Efforts include improving gas mileage by lowering truck highway speeds and recycling thousands of gallons of water used to wash produce. McLane installed $7 million of efficient lighting in its distribution centers and invested $100 million in automation scheduling technologies to plan truck shipments, reducing the cost and impact of its fleet.[33]

Acme Brick makes an ecological product: bricks of earthen clay.[34] The bricks provide efficient insulation, thereby reducing energy usage and costs. Since its founding in 1891, Acme has built plants near distribution destinations—an idea codified in today's environment design protocols that define a five-hundred-mile radius.[35] Recycling incorporates scrap clay and sawdust into the brick. Reclamation programs create wetlands for wildlife and plant whole forests on former production sites. Acme Brick has won numerous industry awards for its environmental stewardship.[36]

Concerning employees, finally, Brooks, like many apparel, footwear, and sporting equipment makers, remembers the furor that engulfed Nike, Inc. in the late 1990s and early 2000s when customers learned of abusive labor practices in its Asian factories. They boycotted Nike products in protest, and the company reformed. Many factors contributed to Nike's transgressions, including relentless cost pressures in its competitive markets. The price of athletic footwear declined rapidly in the late 1990s and early 2000s, and Nike competed by finding the cheapest ways to make shoes, which included inhumane labor practices.[37]

Brooks avoided this vise thanks to a business model focused on a premium brand at premium prices, a piece of equipment for the serious runner, selling higher-priced shoes in specialty stores. Brooks is not the low-cost producer in its industry, and its overseas factories are not the low-cost factories. As chief executive officer Jim Weber explained in an interview for this book, his customers value the company's investment in such responsible behavior.[38]

Retaining subsidiary autonomy at Berkshire is important, both as a cultural matter and because the needs of the businesses vary so greatly. For example, jewelry companies focus on the ethical mining of minerals; home furnishing companies on preserving forests; transportation companies on reducing fuel usage and emissions; and energy companies on targeting renewable sources. For some companies, priority rivets on internal operations, whereas others look to the supply chain; for some the concern is employee safety while others attend to a particular customer type. At the same time, it may be valuable for Berkshire as a group to collect and publicize results.

The need for internal control systems and consolidated reporting will likely increase as Berkshire expands into the international arena. A few subsidiaries boast major global operations, especially ISCAR/IMC, as well as Gen Re, Lubrizol, and MiTek. Others have important overseas operations, including Berkshire Hathaway Energy, CTB, Dairy Queen, Flight-Safety, Justin, and Larson-Juhl. A majority of the companies have at least some operations in Canada and Mexico (e.g., Benjamin Moore, Fruit of the Loom, Johns Manville, and the Marmon Group), and many manufacturing companies own or operate facilities in Asia (e.g., Brooks and TTI). Yet until its acquisition of ISCAR/IMC, begun in 2006 and completed in 2013, Berkshire had acquired only American companies.

Given globalization, it will be inviting to enlarge Berkshire's acquisition universe. The timing may be propitious, as the accumulation and flow of intergenerational family wealth that occurred in the United States during Berkshire's early decades is recurring across Asia and Latin America. But when going global, the need for centralized internal control and conglomerate reporting will intensify.

～

A final managerial challenge is recognizing that, even if all of Berkshire's traits are desirable, the values will inevitably conflict. Fechheimer once closed its Cincinnati plant—where it had operated for more than a century—and moved to lower-cost San Antonio and ultimately shuttered that facility. How should managers balance cost savings with community impacts? Should the decision be for managers at Berkshire or Fechheimer?

How should managers at Clayton Homes or MiTek evaluate an acquisition that will automatically result in plant closings or layoffs? Berkshire shuns hostile takeovers yet gives autonomy to its subsidiaries. So what should happen if a subsidiary proposes a hostile bid, as the Pritzkers occasionally did at the Marmon Group and David Sokol did several times when building MidAmerican Energy before Berkshire acquired it?

Or suppose a conflict arises between entrepreneurial expansion and a modest financial structure. For instance, what is the prudent level of debt to fund expansion of the core fleet at NetJets? What is the right number of flight simulators to build market share at FlightSafety? Or, for Shaw Industries, what's more important, the value of autonomy in a decentralized organization or the cost savings that accrue through vertical integration and more centralized oversight?

Berkshire culture offers guidance on the trade-offs within its own value system. Managers have authority over all decisions except those affecting Berkshire's reputation or capital allocation. Managers have free rein, but it is based on informed consent and earned trust; breaches warrant revocation, including replacing CEOs. Berkshire is ruthless on ethics.

Bottom line: all of the foregoing questions belong to the managers in the first instance subject to overruling by Berkshire at its prerogative. And this reveals the ultimate meaning of "owner orientation" at Berkshire. As Lubrizol chief executive James Hambrick explained in an interview for this book, neither he nor his colleagues have employment contracts; they all serve at the pleasure of Berkshire, and they are all answerable to it.[39]

~

Skeptics of the durability of Berkshire point to Teledyne, Inc., a conglomerate begun in 1960 by Dr. Henry E. Singleton.[40] Singleton built Teledyne by acquiring scores of diverse companies, initially concentrated in the sciences but ultimately including consumer products, finance, and insurance.[41] Singleton and his co-executives were hands-on managers, active in setting business strategy and deploying tactics for its subsidiaries. Their acumen proved valuable in producing impressive periodic results.

Ironically, they were so valuable that they became indispensable to the organization. In the years after Singleton's 1989 retirement, the company was vastly reconfigured. It was first stripped down by spin-offs and divestments and the remainder merged into Allegheny Ludlum Corporation in 1996.[42] Then in 1999, Allegheny Ludlum spun off two businesses, one in consumer products, the other primarily in electronics and aerospace. The latter, today's Teledyne Technologies Inc., has grown through acquisitions under the leadership of Robert Mehrabian, former President of Carnegie Mellon University. It runs science and technology businesses not unlike those of the original Teledyne but is an entirely different company.[43]

Berkshire culture is so different from that of the old Teledyne that such a fate is unlikely. Berkshire is thoroughly decentralized, with managers commanding vast autonomy. All operating decisions—concerning employees, warehouses, manufacturing, sourcing, marketing, distribution, pricing, and so on—are made by the managers of the respective subsidiaries. There are no meetings at headquarters and no budgeting or planning exercises. There is no corporate bureaucracy.

Berkshire managers, entrepreneurial by nature, are empowered to tend and widen their corporate moat as they see fit. Berkshire's decentralized culture and elongated time horizon are not the idiosyncrasies of its current chairman but features fused into its operations. With Singleton's centralization at Teledyne, he was essential; with Berkshire's decentralization, Buffett is not.

Another comparison can be made with General Electric Company, a great conglomerate on about the same scale as Berkshire. Thomas A. Edison co-founded General Electric in 1892 by merging his fourteen-year-old electric company with two others. The culture at today's GE still owes much to Edison's values and leadership, especially his spirit of invention. Today's GE also reflects the stamp of John F. ("Jack") Welch, GE's celebrated chairman from 1981 to 2001, who announced that GE would stay in businesses only when they were first or second. He said all other businesses would be closed or sold. This imperative transmitted a survival-of-the-fittest objective, contributing to a highly competitive corporate culture. Dog ate dog, and the fittest survived. Those who did not measure up were driven into the dustbins of GE history.

Buffett has instilled in Berkshire a different culture but one likely to last longer. The Berkshire way is to make acquisition decisions only once, when deciding whether to buy or not. It seeks businesses of proven profitability, with excellent management, and good returns on unleveraged equity. Once an acquisition is made, however, the idea of closing or selling a business is anathema. Berkshire's owner's manual explains:

> Regardless of price, we have no interest at all in selling any good businesses that Berkshire owns. We are also very reluctant to sell sub-par businesses as long as we expect them to generate at least some cash and as long as we feel good about their managers and labor relations. We hope not to repeat the capital-allocation mistakes that led us into such sub-par businesses. And we react with great caution to suggestions that our poor businesses can be restored to satisfactory profitability by major capital expenditures. Nevertheless, gin rummy

managerial behavior (discard your least promising business at each turn) is not our style. We would rather have our overall results penalized a bit than engage in that kind of behavior.[44]

At Berkshire, problems will arise from the acquisition model, hands-off management, and a sprawling decentralized structure that eludes tight control and consolidated non-financial reporting. It will help Berkshire's durability to remember these challenges, living with them when warranted, amending them when prudent. People outside Berkshire who are attracted to its model should likewise adapt it to their needs rather than blindly imitate it, as the final chapter will explore.

16
B.E.R.K.S.H.I.R.E.

Annually from 2000 through 2009, among the largest donors listed in the *Chronicle of Philanthropy* was Lorry I. Lokey.[1] Lokey founded Business Wire, which Berkshire acquired in 2005 for $600 million. A native of Portland, Oregon, and a graduate of Stanford University, Lokey's donations target universities, including Portland State, Stanford, and the University of Oregon. Lokey's total giving as of the time of Berkshire's acquisition was $160 million; since then, the total has surpassed $400 million.[2]

After service in the Army in World War II, Lokey was as an editor of the *Pacific Stars & Stripes.* He majored in journalism at Stanford and edited the school paper. He went on to work for United Press, now United Press International, and various papers and public relations firms.

In 1961, Lokey began Business Wire as a sole proprietor in a nine-by-twelve foot leased office in San Francisco with seven clients.[3] The business concentrated on distributing press releases for corporations to news organizations. Lokey boosted the number of clients to twenty-two within four months. In those days, the primary task of the staff was typing information received from customers over the telephone. Within a few years, Lokey added bureaus in Boston and Seattle.

In 1979, Lokey ran a classified ad in a San Francisco paper. He interviewed and hired Cathy Baron Tamraz, a twenty-five-year-old English major. She took dictation over the phone and then edited press releases submitted by clients and formatted them for distribution. In 1980, Lokey opened a New York City office. Tamraz, a native Long Islander who once spent a summer as a taxi driver there, spearheaded the effort.

Over the next thirty years, Lokey, Tamraz, and a staff of several hundred grew Business Wire to thirty global offices generating worldwide revenue exceeding $100 million. In the Internet era, Business Wire quickly adapted to exploit all available technologies; amid globalization, it was equally agile in spreading its franchise worldwide, starting in Europe and following across Asia. Today it has more than 25,000 clients for which it disseminates news releases in 150 countries.

In November 2005, Tamraz wrote Buffett a letter explaining why she believed Business Wire and Berkshire would be a good mutual fit. The following passage stood out:

> We run a tight ship and keep unnecessary spending under wraps. No secretaries or management layers here. Yet we'll invest big dollars to gain a technological advantage and move the business forward.[4]

In December 2005, Lokey named Tamraz as president and chief executive. In January 2006, Berkshire agreed to buy Business Wire. As Buffett put it when describing the acquisition:

> Lokey's story, like those of many entrepreneurs who have selected Berkshire as a home for their life's work, is an example of what can happen when a good idea, a talented individual, and hard work converge.[5]

Many stories of successful, thrifty, earnest, reputable, self-starters fill the pages of this book. What lessons can others take away from Berkshire and its subsidiaries?

Berkshire's distinctive features are tailor-made for its special circumstances. Berkshire boasts an atypical shareholder body that relishes the company's distinctiveness. One universal trait of the Berkshire managers and subsidiary personnel portrayed in this book is their belief that corporate culture matters. From Berkshire's example, one can adapt specific values profitably. Berkshire offers lessons to be learned in a number of areas.

~

Berkshire's secret to managing a large complex organization is to manage parsimoniously—as little as possible. Berkshire appears well managed based on an exceptionally successful performance record and might therefore be a model of business management, worthy of study. But the results of such a study might surprise. You will not find tutorials on organizational charts, budgeting reviews, presentations, client meetings, deal pitches, human resources management, present value analysis, or other business school staples. Berkshire uses none of these tools.

Rather than typical textbook lessons, the stories of Berkshire subsidiaries animate a few fundamentals. First among these is to be budget conscious, especially by cost minimization that underlies the business model at GEICO and the furniture and jewelry stores, where low prices multiply volume and profits. A related implication: avoid costly debt. Ben Bridge experienced the perils of leverage during the Great Depression, and his sage aversion to it lives on at his fifth-generation jewelry store chain. Other Berkshire subsidiaries learned this lesson later in their corporate histories, for example when Bill Child inherited RC Willey from his spendthrift father-in-law, after the excesses of leveraged buyouts bankrupted Fruit of the Loom in the 1980s, and both Forest River and Oriental Trading more recently.

Reinvest profits in promising businesses; this is the central bastion of Berkshire culture driving its acquisitions. Do this to stimulate a complacent workforce as James Hambrick did at Lubrizol; to build a company through steady bolting-on and tucking-in the way MiTek does; or to become an industry force like Berkshire Hathaway Energy. But avoid adding capital to businesses that do not generate high returns, such as the *Buffalo News* and See's Candies. A residual point: commit to permanence but know when to walk away, as Buffett shuttered the mills of Berkshire Hathaway in the 1980s and the manufacturing plants of Dexter two decades later.

Nurture entrepreneurship, where rewards can be great, as illustrated by the multiple revenue streams Clayton Homes built around the manufactured housing business; the successful branding of cowboy boots and bricks by the tenacious John Justin Jr. or the Garanimals line at Garan; and the creation of whole new industries to fill a void in the marketplace, whether training of aviators at FlightSafety or fractional aircraft ownership at NetJets. Encourage small businesses to grow and expand one step at a time, even if haphazardly, as the accumulation of individual achievement can add up to huge enterprises, like the many success stories in building Dairy Queen. Let entrepreneurial energy fuel growth through geographic expansion of existing products, done so well at McLane as it blanketed the country with grocery distribution centers.

But also stick to your knitting, as BNSF Railway has done for a century and a half, and as other Berkshire subsidiaries teach by their mistaken diversions: GEICO offering credit cards to insurance customers or Shaw Industries futilely attempting to brand commodity carpets and compete with its retail customers. Learn from these and other mistakes, whether perilous underwriting at Gen Re or life-threatening myopia to the hazards of asbestos at Johns Manville.

Offer autonomy to business teammates, as they are likely to thrive on it, as proven by distributors of Benjamin Moore paints, divisional managers at Clayton Homes, franchisees at Dairy Queen, dealers in Scott Fetzer's products, or consultants of the Pampered Chef. And have their backs, as Berkshire stood behind the Pampered Chef consultants to avoid boycotts of their products and supports Benjamin Moore distributors despite economic challenges. But do not allow anyone to damage business reputation, being ruthless with managers skating close to the edge of thin ice.

For family businesses, address the inherent vexing challenges by promoting the values of family identity and legacy. Family businesses sold to Berkshire—See's, Fechheimer, Jordan's, Nebraska Furniture Mart, Star Furniture, RC Willey, Helzberg Diamonds, Ben Bridge—all boast strong cultures that likely would have sustained the companies absent of Berkshire. But the sale both fortified this longevity and added flexibility as families grew and interests became complicated.

Make money, lots of money, but without losing sight of the long term. Compare what happened to Brooks, the running shoe company: it struggled for decades under short-term serial ownership then prospered when able to adopt a fifty-year time horizon. Manage knowing that people value intangibles, especially permanence, as seen in numerous Berkshire acquisitions made at discounts to business value: most of the family companies; all those acquired out of bankruptcy, such as Fruit of the Loom and Johns Manville; and several others, including Dairy Queen and NetJets.

Above all, stress integrity, central to so many Berkshire stories, including how Clayton Homes watches out for its customers; how NICO provides ironclad insurance promises; and how people like the Pritzkers from the Marmon Group—and Warren Buffett—have made their word their bond.

Many people are interested in replicating Berkshire. They dream of creating conglomerates in its image in much the way proverbial literary types want to write the next great novel. It is unlikely to be done on the same scale or with the same results, but rewards are available from establishing mini-Berkshires. There are quite a few of these, including several Berkshire subsidiaries: Berkshire Hathaway Energy, MiTek, the Marmon Group, and Scott Fetzer. There are also companies that have consciously adapted the Berkshire model.

A prominent example is Markel Corporation, a third-generation Richmond, Virginia, business with deep and enduring roots in the insurance field. In addition to being a sizable investor in Berkshire since 1990, the multi-billion-dollar public company manages an impressive securities investment portfolio and, since 2005, has acquired a dozen operating companies. These subsidiaries engage in an array of activities—manufacturing, consumer, healthcare, business services, and financial services—and were acquired under a value system that closely resembles that of Berkshire.[6] Chief among these is its commitment to provide "permanent capital."

Adapting the Berkshire model, Markel and others create a competitive advantage over rivals in the acquisition market such as private equity firms and leveraged buyout operators. The advantage arises because these firms use their own corporate capital to invest, whereas rivals deploy money staked by others expecting payback over short periods of time. For example, private equity firms are short term by design, as they create funds with ten-year lives (five to sow then five to reap), and investors start looking for their payback in year six. Proponents have explained the virtues of such business models, which arise from features such as discipline and expertise.[7] Berkshire and its progeny compete by offering autonomy, permanence, and other valuable non-monetary benefits.

For public companies, the most important value to import from Berkshire is its long-term outlook. Under the constant surveillance of analysts and activist shareholders hounding them on the latest quarter, public company managers face intense pressure to deliver short-term results. Yet the long-term gains of overlooking short-term hiccups compound over time. Investing in a reputation for serious long-term focus—and delivering the results over rolling periods of five and ten years—can be a valuable achievement for a public company.

≈

Buffett famously jokes that his job is so wonderful that he tap dances to work; he quotes Ronald Reagan's quip: "They say hard work never killed anyone, but I figure, why take the chance." Yet whatever conditions might be at the helm of Berkshire, those prevailing in the corner offices of its subsidiaries are often taxing. Building and sustaining the kinds of businesses we have reviewed puts heavy demands on a company's founders and leaders, often at some cost to the personal side of living. We've seen several leaders emphasize the importance of balance, explicitly when Doris Christopher created the Pampered Chef to enable squaring career with family life and when Barnett Helzberg Jr. cut his workload after his seven-year-old son innocently criticized his workaholic tendencies.

Rose Blumkin was a workaholic. Aside from her family, her life consisted entirely of running Nebraska Furniture Mart, and as a family business in which many members also worked, there was scant separation between family and business. Her store was her existence, and she spent most waking hours in it. Late in life, she acknowledged: "I live alone now, and so that's why I work. I hate to go home. I work to avoid the grave."[8] Many marvel at such stamina, and some consider it worthy of emulation. But most would say there is more to life than work, no matter how rewarding toil might be.

Jim Clayton, in his memoirs, celebrates a vaunted career but also makes note of his three marriages.[9] Scions inherit both the advantages and the woes of family businesses, the latter often meaning complicated personal relationships and confusing expectations that can lead to alcohol abuse, addictive gambling, or other negative coping mechanisms. This reportedly occurred to Terry Watanabe, the second generation owner-manager of Oriental Trading, who in 2007 accumulated losses of $127 million in Las Vegas casinos, eroding his personal fortune.[10] Harry See took the opposite approach, staying out of the family chocolate business altogether, in favor of tending his vineyard.

Randy Watson, chief executive of Justin Brands, offers sage advice: "Working hard is good. But please, if you have children, attend all their events. You can have thirty or even fifty years with a company, but your kids only go through first grade once."[11] Marla Gottschalk, the Pampered Chef's former chief executive, who embraces the "work hard, play hard" motto, echoed Watson's advice, noting that it holds throughout children's lives: "After work, I go support my daughters at their swimming practice."[12]

∼

With Lorry Lokey as the catalytic philanthropist, other Berkshire constituents have become generous benefactors, too. Another extraordinary example concerns the program begun by FlightSafety founder, the late Al Ueltshci. Ending blindness was his quest. He created a flying eye hospital called ORBIS International to provide sight-saving surgery and training for surgeons worldwide. With his son James, he sought to eradicate cataract blindness in the developing world. To do this, he adapted the knowledge he gained at FlightSafety to create simulation devices to train eye surgeons to be able to serve local communities.

A third exemplar of philanthropy's spirit was Jeffrey Comment, longtime chief executive of Helzberg Diamonds. For many years at Christmas, Comment visited numerous children's hospitals across the U.S. dressed as Santa Claus. His purpose was to share some joy with seriously ill children. In his tear-jerking memoir about this outreach, Comment said that his inspiration was the marvelous sense of innocent hope he saw in these children.[13]

Customers, employees, and other constituents chip in to philanthropic efforts at some Berkshire subsidiaries. The thousands of franchisees of Dairy Queen, for example, support the Children's Miracle Network (CMN) Hospitals.[14] Since 1984, they have generated more than $100 million, making Dairy Queen among the small group of corporations in its "Founders Circle."[15] Funds are drawn from customers' spare change, events at the shops, and sales of "Miracle Balloons." Since 1986, employees of McLane have raised more than $65 million for CMN Hospitals, putting it in an elite group of corporations called "Partners" of the effort.[16]

The philanthropic interests of Berkshire subsidiary executives are as varied as the group is diverse. John Justin Jr. was passionate about western U.S. heritage and the rodeo. In 1988, he contributed $3.4 million to help build the $17.4 million Will Rogers Equestrian Center in Fort Worth, Texas.[17] Justin Jr. supported the creation of a sports medicine program for the National Finals Rodeo. One component is the Justin Cowboy Crisis Fund. It gives financial aid to injured rodeo performers and their families.[18]

Fellow Texan, Drayton McLane Jr., third-generation manager of his family's grocery wholesaler and distributor, is a generous benefactor of Baylor University.[19] Donations include forty-eight cast bronze bells hoisted in the tower of the school's central administrative building.

Utah-based Bill Child, who built RC Willey with his family, was drawn to donate millions to American Indian Services and funding scholarships for Native Americans. Like McLane and other Berkshire builders, Child also supported higher education, making large gifts to the University of

Utah, as well Brigham Young, Dixie State, and Weber State Universities. In 2003, the Childs gave $3 million to support the William H. and Patricia W. Child Emergency Center at the University of Utah Hospital.

New Englander Harold Alfond, founder of Dexter, contributed much of his $3 billion in net worth to support colleges, scholarships, and community centers in Maine and Massachusetts. Gifts funded construction projects at Boston College, the University of Maine, and the University of Massachusetts, often requiring that facilities be shared with surrounding communities.[20]

Philanthropy means giving in both money and time. Ed Bridge, for one, is a board member and past chairman of Jewelers for Children, an industry non-profit formed in 1999. Through 2013, it raised more than $43 million for child victims of catastrophic illness, abuse, and neglect.[21] For another, Stan Lipsey, long-time head of the *Buffalo News*, raised $14 million to restore Buffalo's 1907 Darwin Martin House complex, designed by Frank Lloyd Wright.

In the arts, Shirley and Barnett Helzberg Jr. donated millions to Kansas City's Kaufman Center for the Performing Arts, naming Helzberg Hall there, as well as to the Kansas City Zoo. Jim Clayton, a Tennessee native and art lover, donated $5 million to the Knoxville Museum of Art for a new building, then the largest gift to the arts in the state's history. Clayton also donated $1 million to build a birthing center at the hospital where his children were born.[22]

The Pritzker family is exceptional for both its wealth and its philanthropy. A dozen family members have net worth exceeding $1 billion, ranking high on the Forbes 400 list; members have endowed numerous academies, centers, galleries, institutes, prizes, and schools in their native Chicago to as far away as Cambodia. Among these are galleries at the Art Institute of Chicago, the medical school of the University of Chicago, a legal research program at Northwestern University, and an engineering center within the Illinois Institute of Technology.

Charlie Munger has donated hundreds of millions of dollars to a variety of causes, often in the form of Berkshire stock. Beneficiaries are family alma maters, the University of Michigan (including a single gift of $110 million), Stanford University ($43 million), and Harvard University. Endowments include a named professorship in business at Stanford University Law School; the Munger Research Center wing of the Huntington Library in San Marino, California; and the Munger Science Center at Harvard-Westlake School, a Los Angeles preparatory school where many Munger offspring have been educated.

Buffett is giving all his wealth to charity, including through the Bill and Melinda Gates Foundation and foundations organized by Buffett's children. This is an uncommon move in corporate-philanthropic history. Other magnates have left a legacy graced by their name in perpetuity, whether via foundations or schools—besides Munger and Pritzker, think of Carnegie, Ford, Kellogg, or Rockefeller. Buffett's route is characteristically unusual, even as it speaks to an aspiration widely held. Most of us wish to leave a mark, something lasting. Buffett's legacy is not ultimately measured in money but in Berkshire, its values, its people, and its businesses.

～

In poker, Buffett has often noted, they say that if you have joined a game but do not know who the patsy is, then you are the patsy. Traits that characterize Berkshire culture form the foundation of trustworthiness: it is reasonable to trust companies and managers who are budget-conscious, earnest, reputable, kin-like, self-starters. Being hands-off and granting autonomy, then, is an act of faith, based on trust. It is not an act of blind faith, however, so long as the trusting soul knows something about the matters entrusted. This, in turn, implicates the rudimentary trait, referring to a business that is basic and easy to understand.

Neutralize the risk of being the patsy by sticking with simple, basic businesses both sides would be happy to live with forever, and then collect group members who value those other traits. This is a promising recipe for success. It works for Berkshire—in the past as it should in the future—and can work for other organizations. The values underlying the model can be readily adapted. And, ultimately, always remember that there is value in values.

Epilogue

Warren Buffett is sui generis, and there is no other company like Berkshire Hathaway. The company cannot be replicated, and the man cannot be replaced. But having infused the business with a set of transcendent values, the company promises to survive the man. As usual, Warren's words are apt: "The special Berkshire culture is deeply ingrained throughout our subsidiaries, and these operations won't miss a beat when I die."[1] We all hope the proverbial truck is another decade or more off and will lament its arrival whenever it comes. Yet, as Buffett quipped at the 1997 conference where we introduced *The Essays*, it won't be as bad for the rest of us as it will be for him.

I've examined Berkshire and its subsidiaries to generate a picture of Berkshire's corporate culture. Businesses are imbued with venerable values: thrift at GEICO car insurance, integrity at Clayton trailer homes, and honor at Benjamin Moore paint. We've met family businesses, belonging to the Blumkins, Bridges, and Childs. We've encountered entrepreneurs: Al Ueltschi at FlightSafety, Richard Santulli at NetJets, John Justin Jr. at his family boot business, and the many entrepreneurs who shaped Dairy Queen. We've considered companies offering tremendous autonomy, such as the Pampered Chef and divisions of Scott Fetzer. We've identified savvy investors who grow businesses by reinvesting in expansion or acquisition, especially Berkshire Hathaway Energy, Lubrizol, McLane, and MiTek. We've seen businesses focused on basics, sticking to their knitting, like Burlington Northern Santa Fe, Fruit of the Loom, and Shaw Industries.

What we've seen in all these subsidiaries—despite their number and diversity—are shared values. Ultimately, we witnessed a common outlook of permanency among all such companies, many of which had faced the travails of serial ownership by corporate parents, leveraged buyout operators, or private equity firms. We saw that there is good precedent for believing that even such a vast and decentralized enterprise can endure well beyond its founders, as the Marmon Group endures without the iconic Pritzker brothers.

Buffett has a knack for selecting outstanding managers. His track record is imperfect, but the batting average inducts him into the Hall of Fame. Buffett's instinct for discerning intangible human qualities is rare, a sense that may leave Berkshire with him. Buffett once noted that no top executive had left Berkshire to join a competitor, despite offers of richer compensation packages. Buffett motivates and retains managers, making them want to make him proud, another trait that might die with him. Buffett's refusal to imitate and his decisiveness on acquisitions, which are made with no review by anyone else, are informed by gargantuan daily reading and a prodigious memory, the incalculable value of which may not endure beyond him either.

At Berkshire after Buffett, expect slippage. Deals may not come Berkshire's way. Offers Berkshire makes may not be on terms as agreeable as they have been. Negotiations may be less favorable. Getting through the screen may be a few more subpar businesses or disappointing managers. If the big deals do not come or the great managers do not follow, returns will be lower. But absent some extraordinary disruption, returns will not be so disappointing as to warrant dismembering Berkshire or some other radical change. Its design for sustainability is more powerful than that.

Buffett's folksy demeanor, Midwest sensibilities, negotiating techniques, and writing style are inimitable. Berkshire's deals will be handled differently, shareholder letters will strike a different tone, and the annual meetings will feel odd. But Berkshire will always acquire new businesses, readers will continue to study Berkshire's annual shareholder letters, and shareholders will still flock to the annual meetings.

As a new guard leads the evolution of Berkshire beyond Buffett, they will set its course and the company will never be the same. Yet the core values that define it have proven to offer unique sustaining value. It is hard to imagine Berkshire without Buffett. But it seems wiser to believe in Berkshire beyond Buffett, an institution that transcends the man and will be his legacy.

Appendix

Berkshire Hathaway is structurally complex and highly decentralized. The parent owns at least fifty significant direct operating subsidiaries; these direct subsidiaries in turn own an aggregate of at least 225 subsidiaries, divisions, or branches. The latter group in turn owns a total of at least another two hundred business units. These, in yet another turn, own sixty-five units, and another twelve are owned by that lot.

In total, the Berkshire family includes at least 425 operating subsidiaries, along with seventy-five divisions, twenty-five branches, and twenty-five units. Beyond these entities, there are at least another fifty shell subsidiaries, as well as numerous affiliates, joint ventures, and plants. This aggregates to nearly six hundred business units. (For comparison, measured the same way, General Electric has approximately three hundred business units.)

The following list, adapted primarily from data collated by LexisNexis, is compiled from public rather than corporate records. It is unlikely to be complete, as business units may be created internally without a public record, and internal operations follow different structures. Even so, the list closely approximates Berkshire's breadth.

Numerals below designate levels in the corporate hierarchy, with (1) designating a direct Berkshire subsidiary, (2) direct ownership by that subsidiary, and so on through (3), (4), and (5). The following notes are used: (S) for subsidiary, (B) for branch, (D) for division, and (U) for unit. The list is organized in three parts, larger insurance companies first, then smaller ones, followed by non-insurance operations. Bold is used to highlight the companies discussed in this book.

LARGER INSURANCE OPERATIONS

(1) **GEICO** Corporation (S), Washington, DC

(2) GEICO Casualty Company (S), Washington, DC

(2) GEICO General Insurance Company (S), Chevy Chase, MD

(2) GEICO Indemnity Company (S), Washington, DC

(2) Resolute Reinsurance Company (S), Stamford, CT

(3) Resolute Management Corp. (S), Stamford, CT

(1) **General Reinsurance** Corporation (S), Stamford, CT

(2) General Reinsurance Corporation (16 U.S. branches)

(2) General Re Corporation (S), Stamford, CT

(3) Berkshire Hathaway Homestate Insurance Company (S), Omaha, NE

(3) Continental Divide Insurance Company (S), Greenwood Village, CO

(3) Gen Re Intermediaries Corporation (S), Stamford, CT

(3) Gen Re Securities Holdings LLC (S), New York, NY

(4) General Re Financial Products (Japan) Inc. (S), Tokyo, Japan

(3) General Star Indemnity Company (S), Stamford, CT

(3) General Star National Insurance Company (S), Stamford, CT

(4) General Cologne Re (S), Stamford, CT

(4) Genesis Underwriting Management Company (S), Stamford, CT

(3) Genesis Indemnity Insurance Company (S), Stamford, CT

(3) Genesis Insurance Company (S), Stamford, CT

(3) Faraday Holdings Limited (S), London, UK

(4) Faraday Reinsurance Company Ltd. (S), London, UK

(4) Faraday Underwriting Limited (S), London, UK

(2) United States Aircraft Insurance Group (S), New York, NY

(2) General Reinsurance AG (D), Cologne, Germany

(3) General Re Riga SIA (S), Riga, Latvia

(3) General Reinsurance Scandinavia A/S (S), Copenhagen, Denmark

(3) General Cologne Re Iberica Corresdores de Reaseguros (S), Madrid, Spain

(3) General Cologne Re Ruckversicherungs-AG (S), Vienna, Austria

(2) Gen Re Corporation (S), Dublin, Ireland

(2) Gen Re Mexico (S), Mexico, Mexico

(2) Gen Re New England Asset Management (S), Farmington, CT

(2) General & Cologne RE (Sur) Compania de Reaseguros (S), Buenos Aires, Argentina

(2) General Life Re UK Limited (S), London, UK

(2) General Re Beirut (S), Beirut, Lebanon

(2) General Re UK Limited (S), London, UK

(2) General Reinsurance Africa Ltd. (S), Cape Town, South Africa

(3) General Reinsurance Africa Ltd. (B), Johannesburg, South Africa

(2) General Reinsurance Australia Ltd. (S), Sydney, Australia

(3) General Re Australia Ltd. (B), Perth, ACN, Australia

(3) General Re Australia Ltd. (B), Melbourne, ACN, Australia

(3) General Re Australia Ltd. (B), Auckland, New Zealand

(2) General Reinsurance Corporation (S), Toronto, ON, Canada

(2) General Reinsurance Life Australia Ltd. (S), Sydney, NSW, Australia

(2) General Reinsurance UK Limited (S), London, UK

(1) **National Indemnity Company** (S), Omaha, NE

(2) BH Specialty Insurance (D), Boston, MA

(2) Clal U.S. Holdings Inc. (S), Wilkes Barre, PA

(2) Columbia Insurance Co. (S), Omaha, NE

(3) Hartford Life International, Ltd. (S), Weatogue, CT

(2) GUARD Insurance Group, Inc. (S), Wilkes Barre, PA

(3) InterGUARD, Ltd. (S), Wilkes Barre, PA

(3) NorGUARD Insurance Company (S), Wilkes Barre, PA

(2) National Fire & Marine Insurance Company (S), Omaha, NE

(3) NFM of Kansas Inc. (S), Kansas City, KS

(3) Redwood Fire & Casualty Insurance Company Inc. (S), Omaha, NE

(2) National Indemnity Company of Mid-America (S), Omaha, NE

(2) National Indemnity Company of the South (S), Omaha, NE

(2) National Liability and Fire Insurance Company (S), Omaha, NE

SMALLER INSURANCE OPERATIONS

(1) Applied Underwriters, Inc. (S), Omaha, NE
(1) Boat America Corporation (S), Alexandria, VA
(1) California Insurance Company (S), Foster City, CA
(1) Central States Indemnity Co. of Omaha (S), Omaha, NE
(1) Cypress Insurance Company (S), San Francisco, CA
(1) Kansas Bankers Surety Company (S), Topeka, KS
(1) Medical Protective Corporation (S), Fort Wayne, IN
(1) Oak River Insurance Company (S), Omaha, NE

NON-INSURANCE OPERATIONS

(1) **Acme Brick** Company (S), Fort Worth, TX
(2) Acme-Ochs Brick and Stone, Inc. (S), Edina, MN
(2) Featherlite Building Products (S), Round Rock, TX
(2) Jenkins Brick Company, Inc. (S), Montgomery, AL
(3) Jenkins Brick Company, Inc. -Attalla (B), Attalla, AL
(1) The **Ben Bridge** Corporation (S), Seattle, WA
(2) Ben Bridge Jeweler, Inc. (S), Seattle, WA
(1) **Benjamin Moore** & Co. (S), Montvale, NJ
(2) Insl-X Products Corp. (S), Montvale, NJ
(3) Lenmar Corporation (S), Baltimore, MD
(2) Janovic-Plaza Inc. (S), Long Island City, NY
(2) Benjamin Moore & Co. (U), Pell City, AL
(2) Benjamin Moore & Co., Limited (S), Concord, ON, Canada
(1) **Berkshire Hathaway Energy Co.** (please see the entry for MidAmerican Energy Holdings Company)
(1) **BH Media** Group Inc. (S), Omaha, NE
      (comprised of at least 69 newspapers, including the following)
(2) Bristol Herald Courier (U), Bristol, VA
(2) Culpeper Star-Exponent (U), Culpeper, VA
(2) The Daily Nonpareil, Council Bluffs, IA
(2) The Daily Progress (U), Charlottesville, VA
(2) Danville Register (U), Danville, VA
(2) The Dothan Eagle (U), Dothan, AL
(2) Eden Daily News (U), Reidsville, NC
(2) Enterprise Ledger (U), Enterprise, AL
(2) Greensboro News & Record, Greensboro, NC

(2) Hickory Daily Record (U), Hickory, NC

(2) Morning News (U), Florence, SC

(2) The News & Advance (U), Lynchburg, VA

(2) The News Virginian (U), Waynesboro, VA

(2) Omaha World-Herald (U), Omaha, NE

(2) Opelika-Auburn News (U), Opelika, AL

(2) The Press of Atlantic City (U), Atlantic City, NJ

(2) The Reidsville Review (U), Reidsville, NC

(2) Richmond Times-Dispatch (U), Richmond, VA

(2) Roanoke (U), Roanoke, VA

(2) Tribune Herald (U), Waco, TX

(2) Tulsa World (U), Tulsa, OK

(2) Virginia Business Magazine (U), Richmond, VA

(2) Winston-Salem Journal (U), Winston Salem, NC

(1) **Borsheim** Jewelry Company, Inc. (S), Omaha, NE

(1) **Brooks** Sports Inc. (S), Bothell, WA

(1) The **Buffalo News** (S), Buffalo, NY

(1) **Burlington Northern Santa Fe**, LLC (S), Fort Worth, TX

(2) BNSF Railway Company (S), Fort Worth, TX

(3) The Belt Railway Company of Chicago (S), Bedford Park, IL

(3) Los Angeles Junction Railway Company (S), Vernon, CA

(3) SFP Pipeline Holdings, Inc. (S), Fort Worth, TX

(3) Central California Traction Company (Affiliate), Stockton, CA

(3) Burlington Northern (Manitoba) Limited (S), Winnipeg, MB, Canada

(2) FreightWise, Inc. (S), Fort Worth, TX

(3) BNSF Logistics, LLC (S), Springdale, AR

(4) BNSF Logistics International (D), Grapevine, TX

(4) BNSF Logistics, LLC (D), Versailles, OH

(2) Meteor Communications Corporation, Inc. (S), Kent, WA

(1) **Business Wire**, Inc. (S), San Francisco, CA

(1) **Clayton Homes**, Inc. (S), Maryville, TN

(2) CMH Homes, Inc. (S), Maryville, TN

(2) CMH Manufacturing, Inc. (S), Maryville, TN

(2) CMH Parks, Inc. (S), Maryville, TN

(2) Southern Energy Homes, Inc. (S), Addison, AL

(3) Cavalier Homes, Inc. (S), Addison, AL

(4) Cavalier Home Builders, LLC (S), Addison, AL

(4) Cavalier Homes (S), Addison, AL

(3) Classic Panel Design, Inc. (S), Hartselle, AL

(2) Vanderbilt Mortgage & Finance, Inc. (S), Maryville, TN

(3) Schult Homes Corp. (S), Middlebury, IN

(4) Crest Homes Corporation (S), Middlebury, IN

(5) Crest Homes Corporation (Plant), Milton, PA

(4) Marlette Homes, Inc. (S), Lewistown, PA

(1) **CTB** International Corp. (S), Milford, IN

(2) Chore-Time/Brock International (D), Milford, IN

(2) Chore-Time Cage Systems (D), Milford, IN

(2) Chore-Time Equipment (D), Milford, IN

(2) CTB, Inc. (S), Milford, IN

(3) Ironwood Plastics, Inc. (S), Ironwood, MI

(3) Shore Sales of Illinois Inc. (S), Rantoul, IL

(3) Meyn Food Processing Technology B.V. (S), Oostzaan, Netherlands

(4) Meyn America, LLC (S), Ball Ground, GA

(2) Fancom B.V. (S), Panningen, Netherlands

(3) Fancom E.u.r.l. (S), Vitre, France

(1) The **Fechheimer** Brothers Company (S), Cincinnati, OH

(2) All-Bilt Uniform Corp. (S), Cincinnati, OH

(1) **FlightSafety** International, Inc. (S), Flushing, NY

(2) FlightSafety International Courseware Support (D), Hurst, TX

(2) FlightSafety International Simulation Systems (D), Broken Arrow, OK

(2) FlightSafety Services Corporation (S), Englewood, CO

(2) FlightSafety International (U), Hazelwood, MO

(1) **Forest River,** Inc. (S), Elkhart, IN

(2) Coachmen Recreational Vehicle Company (D), Middlebury, IN

(3) Coachmen Recreational Vehicle Company of Georgia (S), Fitzgerald, GA

(3) Pro Designs (S), Elkhart, IN

(3) Viking Recreational Vehicles LLC (S), Centreville, MI

(2) Forest River Inc. (D), Goshen, IN

(1) **Fruit of the Loom**, Inc. (S), Bowling Green, KY

(2) Fruit of the Loom Sports & Licensing (D), Bowling Green, KY

(2) Russell Corporation (S), Bowling Green, KY

(3) Russell Corp. Alexander City (B), Alexander City, AL

(3) Jerzees (D), Atlanta, GA

(3) Russell Athletic (D), Atlanta, GA

(3) Spalding (D), Springfield, MA

(3) American Athletic Inc. (S), Jefferson, IA

(3) DeSoto Mills, Inc. (S), Bowling Green, KY

(3) Russell Europe Limited (S), Livingston, W Lothian, UK

(2) Union Underwear Company, Inc. (S), Bowling Green, KY

(2) Vanity Fair Brands, Inc. (S), Alpharetta, GA

(3) Vanity Fair Brands-Knitting Plant (Plant), Jackson, AL

(3) Vanity Fair Brands (Plant), McAllen, TX

(3) VF Intimates (Plant), Monroeville, AL

(2) Fruit of the Loom de Mexico S.A. de C.V. (S), Mexico, DF, Mexico

(2) Fruit of the Loom Limited (S), Telford, Shropshire, UK

(1) **Garan**, Incorporated (S), New York, NY

(2) Garan Manufacturing Corp. (S), Starkville, MS

(1) **Helzberg** Diamond Shops, Inc. (S), Kansas City, MO

(1) **H.H. Brown Shoe** Company, Inc. (S), Greenwich, CT

(2) Cove Shoe Company (S), Martinsburg, PA

(2) Dexter Shoe Company (S), Hanover, MA

(3) Dexter Shoe Company (S), Dexter, ME

(2) Double H Boot Company (S), Martinsburg, PA

(2) Sofft Shoe Company, Inc. (S), Andover, MA

(1) **H. J. Heinz** Company (50% owned; accounted for using the equity method), Pittsburgh, PA

(2) H. J. Heinz Company, L.P. (S), Pittsburgh, PA

(3) Heinz North America (Division), Pittsburgh, PA

(4) Alden Merrell Fine Desserts (S), Newburyport, MA

(4) Escalon Premier Brands (S), Escalon, CA

(4) Lea & Perrins Inc. (S), Fair Lawn, NJ

(4) Portion Pac (S), Mason, OH

(4) Quality Chef Foods Inc. (S), Cedar Rapids, IA

(4) Todds (S), Irvine, CA

(4) Truesoups LLC (S), Kent, WA

(3) Alimentos Heinz C.A. (S), Caracas, Venezuela

(3) Cairo Foods Industries SAE (S), Cairo, Egypt

(3) Heinz European Holding B.V. (S), Zeist, Utrecht, Netherlands

(4) H. J. Heinz B.V. (S), Zeist, Netherlands

(4) Heinz Iberica, S.A. (S), Madrid, Spain

(4) Heinz Italia S.p.A. (S), Milan, Italy

(4) Heinz Polska Sp. (S), Dzialdowo, Poland

(4) H. J. Heinz Belgium S.A. (S), Turnhout, Belgium

(4) H. J. Heinz Company (Ireland) (S), Blackrock, Dublin, Ireland

(4) H. J. Heinz Company Limited (S), Hayes, Mddx, UK

(4) H. J. Heinz Company, Limited (S), Hayes, Middlesex, UK

(5) H. J. Heinz Foodservice (S), Hayes, Middlesex, UK

(5) H. J. Heinz Frozen & Chilled Foods Limited (S), Grimsby, North East Lincolnshire, UK

(4) H. J. Heinz France S.A.S. (S), Paris, France

(4) H. J. Heinz GmbH (S), Dusseldorf, Germany

(4) Kgalagadi Soap Industries (Pty) Ltd. (S), Gaborone, Botswana

(4) Refined Oil Products (Pty.) Ltd. (S), Gaborone, Botswana

(3) Heinz-UFE Ltd. (S), Guangzhou, Guangdong, China

(3) Heinz Win Chance Ltd. (S), Samut Prakan, Thailand

(3) H. J. Heinz Company Australia Ltd. (S), South Melbourne, VIC, Australia

(4) Heinz-Wattie's Australasia (Unit), Parnell, Hawksby, New Zealand

(3) H. J. Heinz Co. of Canada Ltd. (S), North York, ON, Canada

(4) Renee's Gourmet Foods, Inc. (S), North York, ON, Canada

(3) Sugalidal-Industrias de Alimentacao, SA. (S), Lisbon, Portugal

(2) H. J. Heinz Finance Company (S), Pittsburgh, PA

(1) **HomeServices of America**, Inc. (S), Minneapolis, MN (comprised of more than 20,000 agents through scores of entities, increasingly using "Berkshire Hathaway" in the brand name, including the following)

(2) Berkshire Hathaway HomeServices Carolinas Reality (S), Charlotte, NC

(2) Berkshire Hathaway HomeServices California Properties (S), San Diego, CA (formerly Prudential California Realty)

(2) Berkshire Hathaway HomeServices First Realty (S), West Des Moines, IA (formerly First Realty/GMAC)

(2) Berkshire Hathaway HomeServices Fox & Roach, Inc. (S), Devon, PA (formerly Prudential Fox & Roach)

(2) Berkshire Hathaway HomeServices Georgia Properties (S), Atlanta, GA

(2) Berkshire Hathaway HomeServices New England Properties (S), Wallingford, CT) (formerly Prudential Connecticut Realty LLC)

(2) Berkshire Hathaway HomeServices Northwest Real Estate (S), Portland, OR

(2) CBSHOME Real Estate (S), Omaha, NE

(2) Champion Realty Inc. (S), Severna Park, MD

(2) Dauphin Realty Corporation (S), Mobile, AL

(3) Dauphin Realty of Mobile, Inc. (S), Mobile, AL

(2) Edina Realty, Inc. (S), Minneapolis, MN

(3) Edina Realty Title (S), Edina, MN

(3) Edina Realty (S), Baxter, MN

(2) Esslinger-Wooten-Maxwell Realtors, Inc. (S), Coral Gables, FL

(2) Harry Norman Realtors (S), Atlanta, GA

(2) Home Real Estate Inc. (S), Lincoln, NE

(2) Iowa Realty Co., Inc. (S), West Des Moines, IA

(2) Koenig & Strey GMAC Real Estate (S), Skokie, IL

(2) Long Realty Company (S), Tucson, AZ

(2) RealtySouth (S), Birmingham, AL

(2) Rector-Hayden Realtors (S), Lexington, KY

(2) Reece & Nichols Realtors (S), Shawnee Mission, KS

(2) Semonin Realtors (S), Louisville, KY

(2) Woods Bros Realty, Inc. (S), Lincoln, NE

(1) **International Dairy Queen, Inc.** (S), Minneapolis, MN

(2) American Dairy Queen Corporation (S), Minneapolis, MN

(2) Dairy Queen Corporate Store (S), Minneapolis, MN

(2) Orange Julius of America (S), Minneapolis, MN

(2) Dairy Queen Canada, Inc. (S), Burlington, ON, Canada

(2) I.D.Q. Canada, Inc. (S), Burlington, ON, Canada

(2) Orange Julius Canada, Ltd. (S), Burlington, ON, Canada

(1) **IMC** International Metalworking Companies B.V. (S), Gouda, Netherlands

(2) IMC Group USA Holdings, Inc. (S), Arlington, TX

(3) Ingersoll Cutting Tool Company (S), Rockford, IL

(4) Ingersoll Werkzeuge GmbH (S), Haiger, Germany

(2) IMC Holdings GmbH (S), Vaihingen, Baden-Wurttemberg, Germany

(2) Iscar Ltd. (S), Nahariyya, Israel

(3) Iscar Metals, Inc. (S), Bartonsville, PA

(3) ISCAR alati d.o.o (S), Samobor, Croatia

(3) ISCAR Austria GmbH (S), Steyr, Austria

(3) ISCAR Benelux s.a. (S), Dilbeek, Belgium

(3) ISCAR Bulgaria Ltd (S), Kazanlak, Bulgaria

(3) ISCAR CR s.r.o. (S), Plzen, Czech Republic

(3) ISCAR FINLAND OY (S), Espoo, Finland
(3) ISCAR FRANCE SAS (S), Guyancourt, France
(3) ISCAR Germany GmbH (S), Ettlingen, Germany
(3) ISCAR HARTMETALL AG (S), Frauenfeld, Switzerland
(3) ISCAR Hungary Kft. (S), Budapest, Nagytarcsa, Hungary
(3) ISCAR Iberica AS (S), Barcelona, Spain
(3) ISCAR Italia SRL (S), Arese, Italy
(3) ISCAR Netherlands BV (S), Gouda, Netherlands
(3) ISCAR Poland Sp. z o.o. (S), Katowice, Poland
(3) ISCAR Portugal SA (S), Porto, Portugal
(3) ISCAR RUSSIA LLC (S), Moscow, Russia
(3) ISCAR Slovenija d.o.o. (S), Trzin, Slovenia
(3) ISCAR SR, s.r.o. (S), Zilina, Slovakia
(3) ISCAR SVERIGE AB (S), Uppsala, Sweden
(3) ISCAR Tools Ltd. (S), Birmingham, UK
(3) ISCAR Tools SRL (S), Otopeni, Romania
(3) Serbia ISCAR TOOLS d.o.o. (S), Zemun, Serbia
(2) TaeguTec Ltd (S), Taegu, Korea (South)
(2) Tungaloy Corp. (S), Kawasaki, Japan
(1) **Johns Manville** Corporation (S), Denver, CO
(2) Johns Manville (S), Denver, CO
(2) Industrial Insulation Group, LLC (Affiliate), Brunswick, GA
(2) Johns Manville Corp.—Engineered Products, Waterville (Plant), Waterville, OH
(2) Johns Manville Canada Inc.—Innisfail (S), Innisfail, AB, Canada
(2) Johns Manville Canada Inc. (S), Cornwall, ON, Canada
(2) Johns Manville Slovakia (S), Trnava, Slovakia
(2) Schuller GmbH (Holding), Wertheim, Germany
(1) **Jordan's** Furniture, Inc. (S), Avon, MA
(1) **Justin** Brands, Inc. (S), Fort Worth, TX
(2) Chippewa Boot Co., Fort Worth, TX
(2) Highland Shoe Co., Bangor, ME
(2) Justin Boot Company (Plant), Cassville, MO
(2) Nocona Boot Co., Fort Worth, TX
(2) Tony Lama Boot Co., Fort Worth, TX
(1) **Larson-Juhl** (trade name of Albecca Inc. (S), Norcross, GA)
(1) The **Lubrizol** Corporation (S), Wickliffe, OH
(2) Chemtool, Inc. (S), Rockton, IL
(2) Lubrizol Advanced Materials, Inc. (S), Cleveland, OH

(3) Active Organics, Inc. (S), Lewisville, TX

(3) Noveon Hilton Davis Inc. (S), Cincinnati, OH

(3) Lubrizol Advanced Materials, Inc.—Paso Robles (Plant), Paso Robles, CA

(3) Lubrizol Advanced Materials Asia Pacific Limited (S), Wanchai, China (Hong Kong)

(3) Lubrizol Advanced Materials Europe BVBA (S), Brussels, Belgium

(2) Lubrizol Australia (B), Silverwater, NSW, Australia

(2) Lubrizol Canada Ltd. (S), Vaughan, ON, Canada

(2) Lubrizol Deutschland GmbH (S), Hamburg, Germany

(2) Lubrizol do Brasil Aditivos Ltda. (S), Rio de Janeiro, Brazil

(2) Lubrizol Espanola, S.A. (S), Madrid, Spain

(3) Merquinsa (S), Montmelo, Spain

(2) Lubrizol France SAS (S), Paris, France

(2) Lubrizol GmbH (S), Vienna, Austria

(2) Lubrizol Italiana, S.p.A. (S), Milan, Italy

(2) Lubrizol Japan Limited (S), Tokyo, Japan

(2) Lubrizol Limited (S), Chertsey, Surrey, UK

(2) Lubrizol Southeast Asia (Pte.) Ltd. (S), Singapore, Singapore

(2) Terminal Industrial Apodaca S.A. de C.V. (Affiliate), Monterrey, NL, Mexico

(2) Lubrizol India Pvt. Ltd. (Joint Venture), Mumbai, India

(1) **Marmon** Holdings, Inc. (S), Chicago, IL

(2) The Marmon Group LLC (S), Chicago, IL

(3) Marmon Building Wire (D), Chicago, IL

(4) Cerro Wire LLC (S), Hartselle, AL

(3) Marmon Crane Services (D), Chicago, IL

(4) Sterling Crane (S), Edmonton, AB, Canada

(5) Procrane Engineering (D), Edmonton, AB, Canada

(5) Procrane Sales Inc. (D), Edmonton, AB, Canada

(5) Sterling Crane—Contract Lifting Division (D), Edmonton, AB, Canada

(5) Sterling Crane—Rentals Division (D), Edmonton, AB, Canada

(3) Marmon Distribution Services (D), Chicago, IL

(4) Bushwick Metals Inc. (S), Bridgeport, CT

(5) AZCO Steel Company (D), South Plainfield, NJ

(5) Bushwick-Koons Steel (D), Parker Ford, PA

(5) Tarco Steel, Inc. (D), Binghamton, NY

(4) Future Metals, Inc. (S), Tamarac, FL

(4) M/K Express Company Inc. (S), East Butler, PA

(4) Marmon/Keystone LLC (S), Butler, PA

(5) Marmon/Keystone Corporation (S), Butler, PA

(3) Marmon Engineered Wire & Cable (D), Chicago, IL

(4) Cable USA, Inc. (S), Naples, FL

(4) Dekoron Unitherm, Inc. (S), Cape Coral, FL

(4) Dekoron Wire & Cable, Inc. (S), Mount Pleasant, TX

(5) Dekoron Wire & Cable Asia Pte Ltd (S), Singapore, Singapore

(4) Harbour Industries, Inc. (S), Shelburne, VT

(5) Harbour Industries Canada Ltd. (S), Farnham, QC, Canada

(4) Hendrix Marmon Utility LLC (S), Milford, NH

(4) The Kerite Company (S), Seymour, CT

(4) Owl Wire & Cable, Inc. (S), Canastota, NY

(4) RSCC Wire & Cable LLC (S), East Granby, CT

(5) Rockbestos-Surprenant Cable Corp. (S), East Granby, CT

(3) Marmon Flow Products (D), Chicago, IL

(4) Cerro Flow Products, Inc. (S), Sauget, IL

(5) Cerro Flow Products, Inc. (Plant), Shelbina, MO

(3) Marmon Food Service Equipment (D), Chicago, IL

(4) Prince Castle, Inc. (S), Carol Stream, IL

(4) Silver King Refrigeration, Inc (S), Minneapolis, MN

(4) Unarco Industries LLC (S), Wagoner, OK

(4) Catequip S.A. (S), Bouilly, France

(3) Marmon Highway Technologies (D), Birmingham, AL

(4) Fleetline Products (S), Springfield, TN

(4) Fontaine International Inc. (S), Trussville, AL

(4) Fontaine Modification Company (S), Charlotte, NC

(4) Fontaine Trailer Company (S), Haleyville, AL

(4) Hogebuilt, Inc. (S), Springfield, TN

(4) Marmon-Herrington (S), Louisville, KY

(4) Perfection Clutch (S), Timmonsville, SC

(4) Triangle Suspension Systems, Inc. (S), Du Bois, PA

(3) Marmon Industrial Products (D), Chicago, IL

(4) Atlas Bolt & Screw Company (S), Ashland, OH

(4) Cerro Fabricated Products, Inc. (S), Weyers Cave, VA

(4) Deerwood Fasteners International (S), Conover, NC

(4) IMPulse NC, Inc. (S), Mount Olive, NC

(5) EMC Traction, S.r.l. (S), Vimodrone, Italy

(4) Koehler-Bright Star, Inc. (S), Wilkes Barre, PA

(5) Bright Star, Inc. (Unit), Wilkes Barre, PA

(5) Koehler Lighting Products (Unit), Wilkes Barre, PA

(4) Penn Aluminum International, Inc. (S), Murphysboro, IL

(4) Robertson Inc. (S), Milton, ON, Canada

(5) Specialty Bolt & Stud Inc. (S), Milton, ON, Canada

(3) Marmon Retail Store Fixtures (D), Chicago, IL

(4) L.A. Darling Company LLC (S), Paragould, AR

(4) Store Opening Solutions, Inc. (S), Murfreesboro, TN

(4) Streater, Inc. (S), Albert Lea, MN

(4) Thorco Industries, Inc. (S), Lamar, MO

(4) Ecodyne Limited (S), Burlington, ON, Canada

(4) Eden Industries (UK) Limited (S), Wellingborough, Northants, UK

(4) Leader Metal Industry Co., Ltd. (S), Zhongshan, Guangdong, China

(4) The Sloane Group (S), Wellingborough, Northamptonshire, UK

(3) Marmon Transportation Services & Engineered Products (D), Chicago, IL

(4) EXSIF Worldwide, Inc. (S), Purchase, NY

(4) Penn Machine Company (S), Johnstown, PA

(5) Penn Locomotive Gear (D), Blairsville, PA

(5) Midwest Gear (S), Twinsburg, OH

(4) Railserve Inc. (S), Atlanta, GA

(4) Trackmobile, Inc. (S), Lagrange, GA

(4) Uni-Form Components Co. (S), Houston, TX

(4) Union Tank Car Company (S), Chicago, IL

(4) Enersul Inc. (S), Calgary, AB, Canada

(5) Enersul Operations (D), Calgary, AB, Canada

(5) Enersul Technologies (D), Calgary, AB, Canada

(4) Procor Limited (S), Oakville, ON, Canada

(3) Marmon Water Treatment (D), Chicago, IL

(4) Amarillo Gear Company Inc. (S), Amarillo, TX

(5) Amarillo Wind Machine Company Inc. (S), Exeter, CA

(5) Reductores de Mexico S.A. (S), Santa Catarina, Nuevo Leon, Mexico

(4) Ecodyne Heat Exchangers, Inc. (S), Houston, TX

(4) Ecodyne Water Treatment LLC (S), Naperville, IL

(4) EcoWater Systems LLC (S), Woodbury, MN

(5) Ecowater Canada Ltd. (S), Mississauga, ON, Canada

(4) Graver Technologies LLC (S), Glasgow, DE

(4) Graver Water Systems LLC (S), New Providence, NJ

(3) 3Wire Group Inc. (S), Osseo, MN

(3) Display Technologies, LLC (S), Lake Success, NY

(3) IMI Cornelius Inc. (S), Osseo, MN

(4) IMI Cornelius Inc.—Garner (Branch), Garner, IA

(4) IMI Cornelius Inc.—Glendale Heights (Branch), Glendale Heights, IL

(4) IMI Cornelius Australia Pty Ltd (S), Milperra, NSW, Australia

(4) IMI Cornelius de Mexico SA de CV (S), Mexico, Mexico

(4) IMI Cornelius Deutschland GmbH (S), Langenfeld, Germany

(4) IMI Cornelius Espana SA (S), Gava, Spain

(4) IMI Cornelius Europe SA (S), Kapellen, Belgium

(4) IMI Cornelius Hellas SA (S), Athens, Greece

(4) IMI Cornelius Italia srl (S), Merate, Lecco, Italy

(4) IMI Cornelius Osterreich GesmbH (S), Vienna, Austria

(4) IMI Cornelius (Pacific) Ltd (S), Tsuen Wan, China (Hong Kong)

(4) IMI Cornelius (Singapore) Pte Ltd (S), Singapore, Singapore

(4) IMI Cornelius (Tianjin) Co Ltd (S), Tianjin, China

(4) IMI Cornelius Ukraine LLC (S), Kharkiv, UkraineUK

(4) IMI Cornelius (UK) Ltd (S), Brighouse, West Yorkshire, UK

(3) Wells Lamont LLC (S), Niles, IL

(4) Wells Lamont Industry Group LLC (S), Niles, IL

(4) Wells Lamont Retail Group (Unit), Niles, IL

(4) Jomac Canada (D), Stanstead, QC, Canada

(1) **McLane** Company, Inc. (S), Temple, TX[1]

(2) Empire Distributors, Inc. (S), Atlanta, GA

(3) Empire Distributors Inc. (B), Charlotte, NC

(3) Empire Distributors of North Carolina Inc. (S), Durham, NC

(3) Horizon Wine & Spirits, Inc. (S), Nashville, TN

(2) Foodservice/Temple (D), Temple, TX

(2) McLane/America (D), Salt Lake City, UT

(2) McLane Foodservice, Inc. (S), Carrollton, TX

(2) McLane/High Plains (D), Lubbock, TX

(2) McLane/Mid Atlantic (D), Fredericksburg, VA

(2) McLane/Midwest (D), Danville, IL

(2) McLane/Northeast (D), Baldwinville, NY

(2) McLane/Northwest (D), Tacoma, WA

(2) McLane/Pacific (D), Merced, CA

(2) McLane/Southeast (D), Athens, GA
(2) McLane/Southern (D), Brookhaven, MS
(2) McLane/Southern California (D), Sam Bernardino, CA
(2) McLane/Southwest, (D), Temple, TX
(2) McLane/Suneast (D), Kissimmee, FL
(2) McLane/Sunwest (D), Goodyear, AZ
(2) McLane/Western (D), Denver CO
(2) Meadowbrook Meat Co. Inc. (S), Rocky Mount, NC
(2) Professional Datasolutions Inc. (S), Temple, TX
(1) **MidAmerican Energy** Holdings Company (S), Des Moines, IA
     (renamed Berkshire Hathaway Energy Co. in 2014)
(2) Kern River Gas Transmission Company (S), Salt Lake City, UT
(2) MidAmerican Energy Funding, LLC (S), Des Moines, IA
(3) MidAmerican Energy Company (S), Des Moines, IA
(3) Midwest Capital Group, Inc. (S), Des Moines, IA
(2) Northern Natural Gas Company (S), Omaha, NE
(2) NV Energy, Inc. (S), Las Vegas, NV
(3) Nevada Power Company (S), Las Vegas, NV
(3) Sierra Pacific Power Company (S), Reno, NV
(2) PacifiCorp (S), Portland, OR
(3) Pacific Power & Light Company (S), Portland, OR
(3) Rocky Mountain Power (S), Salt Lake City, UT
(2) CE Electric UK (S), Newcastle upon Tyne, UK
(1) **MiTek**, Inc. (S), Chesterfield, MO[2]
(2) Aegis Metal Framing (S), Chesterfield, MO
(2) Benson Industries, Inc. (S), Portland, OR
(3) Benson Ltd. (S), Ulsan, Korea (South)
(2) Blok-Lok, Ltd. (S), Woodbridge, ON, Canada
(2) Buildsoft Pty Ltd. (S), Cambbelltown, NSW, Australia
(2) Cubic Designs, Inc. (S), New Berlin, WI
(2) Gang Nail Brazil (S), Itaquaquecetuba, SP, Brazil
(2) Hardy Frames, Inc. (S), Ventura, CA
(2) Heat Pipe Technology, Inc. (S), Tampa, FL
(2) Hohmann & Barnard Inc. (S), Hauppauge, NY
(3) Dur-O-Wal (S), Hauppauge, NY
(3) Foamtastic Products, Inc. (S), Downingtown, PA
(3) RKL Building Specialties Co., Inc. (S), Astoria, NY
(3) Sandell Industries, Inc. (S), Schenectady, NY
(2) Kova Solutions LLC (S), Woburn, MA

(2) MiTek Australia, Ltd.

(2) MiTek Canada (S), Bradford, ON, Canada

(2) MiTek South Africa Ltd. (S), Blackheath, South Africa

(2) MiTek UK (S), Dudley, West Midlands, UK

(2) MiTek USA, Inc. (S), Chesterfield, MO

(2) Mi-Tek Industries, Inc. (S), Chesterfield, MO

(2) Robbins Engineering (S), Tampa, FL

(2) TMI Climate Solutions (S), Holly, MI

(2) SidePlate Systems Inc. (S), Laguna Hills, CA

(2) United Steel Products Co., Inc. (S), Burnsville, MN

(2) TBS Engineering Ltd. (S), Cheltenham, Gloucestershire, UK

(2) Truss Industry Production Systems, Inc. (S), Britton, SD

(1) **Nebraska Furniture Mart**, Inc. (S), Omaha, NE

(2) Homemakers Plaza, Inc. (S), Irwindale, IA

(1) **NetJets** Inc. (S), Columbus, OH

(2) Marquis Jet Partners Inc. (S), New York, NY

(1) **Omaha World Herald** Company (S), Omaha, NE
     (see also BH Media Group)

(1) **Oriental Trading** Company, Inc. (S), Omaha, NE

(2) MindWare Holdings, Inc. (S), Minneapolis, MN

(1) **The Pampered Chef**, Ltd. (S), Addison, IL

(1) **RC Willey** Home Furnishings (S), Salt Lake City, UT

(1) **Richline** Group, Inc. (S), Tamarac, FL

(2) Aurafin LLC (D), Tamarac, FL

(3) Aurafin OroAmerica (S), Burbank, CA

(2) Bel-Oro International, Inc. (D), Mount Vernon, NY

(3) Michael Anthony Jewelers, Inc. (S), Mount Vernon, NY

(2) HONORA, Inc. (S), New York, NY

(2) Inverness Corporation (D), Attleboro, MA

(3) Inverness France (B), Montereau, France

(3) Inverness UK (B), Bidford-on-Avon, UK

(2) LeachGarner (D), Attleboro, MA

(3) Excell Manufacturing Company (S), Attleboro, MA

(3) Findings Inc. (S), Keene, NH

(3) Stern Metals, Inc. (S), Attleboro, MA

(1) The **Scott Fetzer** Company (S), Westlake, OH

(2) Adalet (D), Cleveland, OH

(2) Altaquip (D), Fort Lauderdale, FL

(2) Arbortech (D), Wooster, OH

(2) Campbell Hausfeld (D), Harrison, OH

(2) Carefree of Colorado (D), Broomfield, CO

(2) Douglas/Quikut (D), Walnut Ridge, AR

(2) France (D), Fairview, TN

(2) Halex (D), Cleveland, OH

(2) Kirby World Headquarters (D), Cleveland, OH

(2) Meriam Instrument (D), Cleveland, OH

(2) Northland Motor Technologies (D), Watertown, NY

(2) Scot Laboratories (D), Chagrin Falls, OH

(2) The ScottCare Corporation (D), Cleveland, OH

(3) Rozinn Electronics, Inc. (S), Woodbury, NY

(2) Stahl (D), Wooster, OH

(2) Wayne Water Systems (D), Harrison, OH

(2) Western Enterprises Division (D), Westlake, OH

(2) Western Plastics (D), Portland, TN

(2) United Consumer Financial Services Company (S), Westlake, OH

(2) World Book/Scott Fetzer Company, Inc. (S), Chicago, IL

(1) **See's Candies**, Inc. (S), South San Francisco, CA

(1) **Shaw Industries** Group, Inc. (S), Dalton, GA

(2) Shaw Industries Inc. (S), Franklin, NC

(2) Shaw Industries Group (Plant), Calhoun, GA

(1) **Star Furniture** Company (S), Houston, TX

(1) **TTI**, Inc. (S), Fort Worth, TX

(2) Mouser Electronics Inc. (S), Mansfield, TX

(3) Mouser Electronics Pte. Ltd. (S), Singapore, Singapore

(2) Sager Electrical Supply Co (S), Middleboro, MA

(1) **Wesco** Financial, LLC (S), Pasadena, CA

(2) **CORT** Business Services Corporation (S), Fairfax, VA

(3) CORT Furniture Rentals (S), West Chester, OH

(3) CORT Furniture Rentals (S), Tampa, FL

(3) Relocation Central, Inc. (S), Santa Clara, CA

(4) Relocation Central, Inc. (S), Oak Brook, IL

(4) Relocation Central, Inc. (S), Rolling Meadows, IL

(2) The Kansas Bankers Surety Company (S), Topeka, KS

(2) Precision Steel Warehouse, Inc. (S), Franklin Park, IL

(1) **XTRA** Corporation (S), Saint Louis, MO

(2) XTRA LLC (S), Saint Louis, MO

(3) XTRA Lease LLC (D), Saint Louis, MO

Notes

Preface

1. For example, Steven M. Davidoff, "With His Magic Touch, Buffett May Be Irreplaceable for Berkshire," *New York Times,* May 22, 2013.

2. The exact number of Berkshire's "direct subsidiaries" depends on how the concept is defined, such as in legal, operational, or functional terms. The appendix presents a list compiled from public records, showing direct and indirect subsidiaries.

3. Among Berkshire subsidiaries possessing all of the conglomerate's cultural traits are Clayton Homes, The Marmon Group, and McLane.

Introduction

1. Many Berkshire shareholders became billionaires or near-billionaires as a result, including: Warren E. Buffett, David S. ("Sandy") Gottesman, Homer and Norton Dodge (early investors), Stewart Horejsi (acquired 4,300 shares in 1980), Charles T. Munger, Bernard Sarnat (cousin in law of Benjamin Graham); and Walter Scott, Jr.; others became billionaires by other routes, including William H. Gates III. See Richard Teitelbaum, "Berkshire Billionaire Found With More Shares Than Gates," *Bloomberg News,* Sept. 17, 2013.

2. Many founders or executives of Berkshire subsidiaries became independently wealthy by building those businesses, including several ranked as Forbes 400 multi-billionaires. Billionaires or near-billionaires include the following: the late Harold Alfond of Dexter Shoe; Jim Clayton of Clayton Homes; William Child of R. C. Willey; Doris Christopher of The Pampered Chef; Barnett Helzberg Jr. of Helzberg's Diamond Shops; Lorry I. Lokey of Business Wire; Drayton McLane of McLane Co. Inc.; the late Jay and Robert Pritzker of The Marmon Group; Richard Santulli of NetJets; the late Al Ueltshci of FlightSafety; and Stef Wertheimer of ISCAR/IMC.

3. See Jim Clayton & Bill Retherford, *First A Dream* (FSB Press, 2002), 260.

4. John W. Mooty, telephone interview by the author, October 2, 2013.

5. See Doris Christopher, *The Pampered Chef* (New York: Doubleday, 2005), 123 ("our salespeople can earn six-figure incomes . . . with almost no capital at risk").

6. See Michael E. Porter, *Competitive Advantage: Creating and Sustaining Business Performance* (New York: Free Press 1998).

7. See "Fitch Downgrades Berkshire Hathaway," *CPI Financial* (March 16, 2009).

8. Craig E. Aronoff & John L. Ward, *Family Business Values* (Basingstoke, UK: Palgrave MacMillan 2001, 2011), 14.

9. Lawrence H Kaufman, "Leaders Count: The Story of BNSF Railway" (*Texas Monthly* / Texas A&M University Press 2005), 20–21.

10. These figures are widely quoted. See, e.g., Keanon J. Alderson, *Understanding The Family Business* (2011), 57.

11. Lawrence H Kaufman, "Leaders Count," 340 (quoting Grinstein).

12. See Berkshire Hathaway Annual Report, Financial Statements (2013), 28–29 (balance sheet lists market value of equity securities at $115 billion with total assets, mostly at book value, of $485 billion; income statement indicates total revenue of $182 billion with $15 billion from investments).

13. Jeff Benedict, *How to Build a Business Warren Buffett Would Buy: The R. C. Willey Story* (Salt Lake City, Utah: Shadow Mountain 2009), 1.

14. Ibid.

15. Berkshire-BNSF Joint Prospectus and Proxy Statement (December 23, 2009), 35–39.

16. I found an analogy in my own life to the various transactions discussed throughout this book. I began my career as a high-paid corporate lawyer at the prosperous New York law firm of Cravath, Swaine & Moore. There I had at least some prospect of making partner and an excellent chance of becoming partner at some other firm upon leaving Cravath. Then a different future appeared: a professorship, first at Yeshiva University's Cardozo Law School and later at Boston College and George Washington University.

Partner draws at Cravath and other private firms dwarf the pay at GW, BC, or Cardozo. But there are compensating values of the professorial position, including tenure and academic freedom. I traded the higher pay in part for those commitments of permanence and autonomy. Sellers of companies to Berkshire make a similar calculation: taking less in cash or stock while being compensated for that in the commitments of permanence and autonomy—as well as the other values that Berkshire culture offers.

Scolds will tell you that comparing cash (salary) payments to such intangibles is to compare apples and oranges. They will say the values are incommensurate, one measured in money and the other in a different index altogether. It is not possible, in this view, simply to assign to the intangibles money value inferred from how much more or less someone charges or takes when the other values are also being exchanged.

The "price" of autonomy or permanence cannot be easily reduced to monetary terms. (The difficulty recalls the classic credit card commercials showing a series of goods and their prices—a movie cost ten dollars, popcorn costs five dollars—with the punch line, time with family, "priceless.") Certainly translating such intangibles into a money value is not the same as calculating the present value of an annuity or a cash flow pattern. But it increases the chances that two sides discussing a business acquisition will be able to reach agreement.

17. See Dale A. Oesterle, *The Law of Mergers & Acquisitions* (Eagan, MN: West Group, 3d ed. 2010) (discussing such an example and related research).

18. See Warren E. Buffett, "The Superinvestors of Graham-and-Doddsville," *Hermes, The Columbia Business School Magazine* (1984). Graham's books include *Security Analysis* (with David Dodd), *The Intelligent Investor*, and *The Interpretation of Financial Statements*. See Lawrence A. Cunningham, *How to Think Like Benjamin Graham and Invest Like Warren Buffett* (New York: McGraw Hill, 2001).

1. Origins

1. Among these businesses, which remain active, were Columbia Insurance Company, Cornhusker Casualty Company, Continental Divide Insurance Company, Cypress Insurance Company, National Fire & Marine (NFM) Insurance Company of Kansas, and Redwood Fire & Casualty Insurance Company.

2. Berkshire sold this business in 1981 to Bruce Sagan; this is before the 1985 closing of the Berkshire textile business that cemented a policy of never selling subsidiaries.

3. Alice Schroeder, *The Snowball: Warren Buffett and the Business of Life* (New York: Bantam, 2008), 359 (quoting $209 million).

4. Ibid., 377.

5. Katharine Graham, *Personal History* (New York: Vintage, 1998), 511–5, 530–7; Deborah A. DeMott, "Agency Principles and Large Block Shareholders," *Carlozo Law Review* 19 (1997): 321–40.

6. The firm's name evolved as partnership membership changed, roughly as follows: Munger, Tolles & Hills (1962–1966); Munger, Tolles, Hills & Rickershauser (1966–1975); Munger, Tolles & Rickershauser (1975–1986); and Munger, Tolles & Olson (since 1986).

7. Janet Lowe, *Damn Right! Behind the Scenes with Berkshire Hathaway Billionaire Charlie Munger* (Hoboken, N.J.: Wiley, 2000), 112–13.

8. Schroeder, *The Snowball*, 331.

9. Ibid., 318, 319.

10. Ibid., 344–45.

11. Ibid., 345; Lowe, *Damn Right!*, 126–27.

12. The historical facts concerning See's may be found in *International Directory of Company Histories*, vol. 30 (Detroit, Mich.: St. James, 2000) (hereafter cited as *IDCH, See's*); the See's company website, www.sees.com; and Margaret Moos Pick, *See's Old Time Candies* (San Francisco: Chronicle, 2005).

13. Schroeder, *The Snowball*, 345.

14. William N. Thorndike Jr., *The Outsiders: Eight Unconventional CEOs and Their Radically Rational Blueprint for Success* (Boston: Harvard Business Review, 2012), 174.

15. Berkshire Hathaway, Inc., *1991 Annual Report*, February 28, 1992, chairman's letter:

> The nominal price that the sellers were asking—calculated on the 100 percent ownership we ultimately attained—was $40 million. But the company had $10 million of excess cash, and therefore the true offering price was $30 million. Charlie and I, not yet fully appreciative of the value of an economic franchise, looked at the company's mere $7 million of tangible net worth and said $25 million was as high as we would go (and we meant it). Fortunately, the sellers accepted our offer.

16. *IDCH*, See's.

17. David Kass, comment on Warren Buffett, "Warren Buffett's Meeting with University of Maryland MBA Students—November 15, 2013," *Dr. David Kass: Commentary on Warren Buffett and Berkshire Hathaway*, December 8, 2013, http://blogs.rhsmith. umd.edu/davidkass/2013/12.

18. In the Matter of Blue Chip Stamps et al., SEC File No. HO-784.

19. Schroeder, *The Snowball*, 408, note 23.

20. Ibid., 410.

21. Complaint, Securities and Exchange Commission v. Blue Chip Stamps, No. 76–1009 (DC Cir. June 9, 1976).

22. Blue Chip acquired 80 percent of Wesco, with the remainder being publicly listed and the company chaired by Munger; Berkshire took over that holding in 1983. In 2011, Wesco merged into Berkshire; Berkshire paid about $550 million in a combination of cash and Berkshire stock for the remaining shares. Berkshire Hathaway press release, "Berkshire Hathaway Inc. to Acquire Outstanding Common Stock of Wesco Financial Corporation Not Presently Owned," February 7, 2011.

23. Obituary of Edward H. Butler Sr., *New York Times*, March 10, 1914.

24. Michael Dillon, *The Life and Times of Edward H. Butler, Founder of* The Buffalo News *(1850–1914): A Crusading Journalist Navigates the Gilded Age*, Mellen Studies in Journalism, Series 5 (Lewiston, N.Y.: Edwin Mellen, 2003).

25. Murray B. Light, *From Butler to Buffett: The Story Behind* The Buffalo News (Amherst, N.Y.: Prometheus, 2004), 105, 133.

26. Ibid., 195.

27. Ibid., 196–97.

28. Ibid., 197.

29. Buffalo Courier-Express, Inc. v. Buffalo Evening News, Inc., 441 F. Supp. 628 (W.D.N.Y. 1977).

30. Buffalo Courier-Express, Inc. v. Buffalo Evening News, Inc., 601 F.2d 48 (2d Cir. 1979) (Friendly, J.).

31. Berkshire Hathaway Inc., *2012 Annual Report*, chairman's letter, 3.

32. Minorco stood for Mineral and Resources Corporation, a Luxembourg-based investment arm of Harry Oppenheimer's Anglo American Corporation of South Africa and De Beers Consolidated Mines Ltd.

33. For details on the Salomon preferred stock, see Schroeder, *The Snowball*, 541, 901–2nn73,81.

34. Warren E. Buffett, Before the Subcommittee on Telecommunications and Finance of the Energy and Commerce Committee of the U.S. House of Representatives (1991), reprinted in the *Wall Street Journal*, May 1, 2010. Buffett writes in a biennial missive to Berkshire's chief executives:

> Let's be sure that everything we do in business can be reported on the front page of a national newspaper in an article written by an unfriendly but intelligent reporter.

Quoted in Robert Miles, *The Warren Buffett CEO: Secrets from the Berkshire Hathaway Managers* (Hoboken, N.J.: Wiley, 2003), 357–58.

35. Anthony Bianco, "The Warren Buffett You Don't Know," *BusinessWeek*, July 5, 1999, p. 54.

2. Diversity

1. See James B. Stewart, *Den of Thieves* (New York: Touchstone, 1992).

2. Most of the historical facts concerning Scott and Fetzer can be found in *International Directory of Company Histories*, vol. 12 (Detroit, Mich.: St. James, 1996).

3. The exact amount of Berkshire's acquisition of Scott Fetzer has been reported at different levels, presumably because it was paid in a combination of cash and the assumption of certain liabilities. E.g., Schroeder, *The Snowball*, 900n52 (mentioning $320 million or $230 million) and 531 ($410 million); Berkshire Hathaway, Inc., *1986 Annual Report*, chairman's letter (listing $315 million).

4. See, for example, the Buy American Act of 1933, 41 U.S.C. 10a–10d, as amended by the Barry Amendment addressing military uniforms.

5. Berkshire Hathaway, Inc., *2013 Annual Report*, 64.

6. Berkshire Hathaway, Inc., *2010 Annual Report*, chairman's letter.

7. The real cost was greater than the $443 million purchase price, moreover, since it was paid in Berkshire stock. The stock paid represented 1.6 percent of Berkshire, which in 2007 would have been worth $3.5 billion.

8. Berkshire Hathaway, Inc., *1991 Annual Report*, chairman's letter.

9. Ibid.

10. Legend has it that before Rooney married Frances Heffernan the old man told him he would not be welcomed working at H.H. Brown. Berkshire Hathaway, Inc., *1991 Annual Report*, chairman's letter.

11. Ibid.

12. Instances are: Applied Underwriters (bought 81 percent); Central States (bought 82 percent; the Kizer family kept 18 percent); Nebraska Furniture Mart (bought 90 percent; the Blumkins kept 10 percent for themselves and for compensation to other managers); Fechheimer (bought 84 percent; the Heldman family kept 16 percent).

13. Instances are: Shaw Industries (80 percent initially); ISCAR/IMC (80 percent initially); and the Marmon Group (60 percent initially).

14. For profiles of the company and selected personnel, see Guy Rolnik, "Who on Earth Is Jacob Harpaz?," *Haaretz*, July 15, 2009; and Tali Heruti-Sover, "Their Hearts Belong to Iscar," *Haaretz*, September 29, 2012.

15. Berkshire Hathaway, Inc., *2006 Annual Report*, chairman's letter.

3. Culture

1. E.g., Berkshire Hathaway, Inc., *2010 Annual Report*, chairman's letter.

2. See, e.g., Eric Van den Steen, "On the Origin of Shared Beliefs (and Corporate Culture)," *Rand Journal of Economics* 41 (2010): 617.

3. See Terrence E. Deal and Allan A. Kennedy, *Corporate Cultures: The Rites and Rituals of Corporate Life* (Reading, Mass.: Addison-Wesley, 1982).

4. Some of Berkshire's owner-related business principles apply to the parent level but not so much to the subsidiaries. For example, many address topics relevant only to public companies—linking dividend policy to stock price, aspiring to have one's stock trade at a fair price, or relating stock price to intrinsic value—and others only to the Berkshire level but not the subsidiary level—being reluctant to use Berkshire stock to pay for acquisitions, because it dilutes the interests of current owners.

5. See chap. 14, including tables 14.1 through 14.4.

6. Ibid.

7. Ibid., combining data from tables 14.1 and 14.2.

8. Anthony Bianco, "The Warren Buffett You Don't Know," *BusinessWeek*, July 4, 1999.

9. See Ronald Chan, *Behind the Berkshire Hathaway Curtain: Lessons from Warren Buffett's Top Business Leaders* (Hoboken, N.J.: Wiley, 2010), 100.

10. See L. J. Rittenhouse, *Investing Between the Lines* (New York: McGraw-Hill, 2013).

11. See, e.g., Moody's October 8, 2013, report on Berkshire Hathaway.

12. Craig E. Aronoff and John L. Ward, *Family Business Values* (New York: Palgrave Macmillan 2001, 2011), 16: "A stable, trustworthy . . . firm with a long-term orientation has a distinct competitive advantage."

13. See John Kotter and James Heskett, *Corporate Culture and Performance* (New York: Free Press, 1992).

14. See Deal and Kennedy, *Corporate Cultures*.

15. See John Mackey and Rajendra Sisodia, *Conscious Capitalism: Liberating the Heroic Spirit of Business* (Boston: Harvard Business Review Press, 2013); and James Collins and Jerry Porras, *Built to Last* (New York: Harper Business 1994).

16. See Robert Mondavi and Paul Chutkow, *Harvests of Joy: How the Good Life Became Great Business* (Boston: Houghton Mifflin Harcourt, 1998).

17. Aronoff and Ward, *Family Business Values*, 8–10.

4. Budget-conscious and Earnest

1. The historical facts concerning GEICO can be found in William K. Klingaman, *GEICO: The First Forty Years* (Washington, D.C.: GEICO, 1994); in *International Directory of Company Histories*, vol. 40 (Detroit, Mich.: St. James, 2001) (hereafter cited as *IDCH*, GEICO); and on the company's website (www.geico.com).

2. GEICO website. Buffett has put the initial investment at $200,000. Berkshire Hathaway, Inc., *2004 Annual Report*, chairman's letter.

3. Klingaman, *GEICO*, 15.

4. *IDCH*, GEICO.

5. Klingaman, *GEICO*, 12.

6. Ibid., 31.

7. This was the principal means of train transport between New York and Washington in this period. Bruce F. Smith (president, Pennsylvania Railroad Technical and Historical Society), e-mail to author, February 13, 2014.

8. This was the sixth floor of GEICO's building; GEICO moved offices on numerous occasions over ensuing decades. *IDCH*, GEICO.

9. Berkshire Hathaway, Inc., *1995 Annual Report*, chairman's letter.

10. The article is reproduced at p. 24 of the chairman's letter in Berkshire Hathaway, Inc., *2005 Annual Report*.

11. Klingaman, *GEICO*, 65 (1960 figures).

12. GEICO website.

13. Klingaman, *GEICO*, 100.

14. Ibid., 96.

15. Berkshire Hathaway, Inc., *1986 Annual Report*, chairman's letter. For additional detail about this multifaceted crisis, see Klingaman, *GEICO*, 104–22.

16. Byrne left GEICO in 1985 to run Fireman's Fund. He later led the formation of White Mountain Insurance, in which Berkshire made a substantial investment.

17. Berkshire Hathaway, Inc., *1986 Annual Report*, chairman's letter.

18. Ibid.

19. Berkshire Hathaway, Inc., *1990 Annual Report*, chairman's letter.

20. Berkshire Hathaway, Inc., *1996 Annual Report*, chairman's letter.

21. Berkshire Hathaway, Inc., *2010 Annual Report*, chairman's letter.

22. Berkshire Hathaway, Inc., *2006 Annual Report*, chairman's letter.

23. See Geraldine Fabrikant, "A Maestro of Investments in the Style of Buffett," *New York Times*, April 23, 2007.

24. Berkshire Hathaway, Inc., *2004 Annual Report*, chairman's letter.

25. Berkshire Hathaway, Inc., *1997 Annual Report*, chairman's letter; and Berkshire Hathaway, Inc., *1998 Annual Report*, chairman's letter.

26. Berkshire Hathaway, Inc., *1999 Annual Report*, chairman's letter.

27. Berkshire Hathaway, Inc., *1997 Annual Report*, chairman's letter; and Berkshire Hathaway, Inc., *1998 Annual Report*, chairman's letter.

28. See Phil Gusman, "Nomura Auto Insurance All About Price; Independent Agent Role Diminishing," *Property Casualty 360°*, October 16, 2013 (noting 9.9 percent market share as of mid-2013); Berkshire Hathaway, Inc., *2006 Annual Report*, chairman's letter; and Berkshire Hathaway, Inc., *2009 Annual Report*, chairman's letter (noting 8.1 percent).

29. Berkshire Hathaway, Inc., *2010 Annual Report*, chairman's letter.

30. Berkshire Hathaway, Inc., *1998 Annual Report*, chairman's letter.

31. See Andrew Kilpatrick, *Warren Buffett: The Good Guy of Wall Street* (New York: Primus/Donald I. Fine, 1992), 73.

32. Robert Dorr, " 'Unusual Risk' Ringwalt Specialty," *Omaha World Herald*, March 12, 1967.

33. National Indemnity website (www.nationalindemnity.com).

34. Jack Ringwalt in *Tales of National Indemnity Company and Its Founder*, as quoted in Roger Lowenstein, *Buffett: The Making of an American Capitalist* (New York: Random House, 1995), describing the memoir as "a hilarious romp past the characters, not always savory, in the back alleys of the insurance business" (133).

35. Lowenstein, *Buffett*, 134.

36. Ibid.; Berkshire Hathaway, Inc., *1992 Annual Report*, chairman's letter.

37. E.g., Dean Starkman, "AIG's Other Reputation: Some Say the Insurance Giant is Too Reluctant to Pay Up," *Washington Post*, August 21, 2005.

38. See "Insurance Regulators Scrutinize New Owners," *Des Moines Register*, August 11, 2013.

39. National Indemnity website.

40. Berkshire Hathaway, Inc., *2000 Annual Report*, chairman's letter; Berkshire Hathaway, Inc., *2003 Annual Report*, chairman's letter.

41. See Chris Chase, "What Are the Odds of a Perfect NCAA Bracket?" *USA Today*, March 19, 2013, crediting DePaul University math professor Jay Bergen with the figure.

42. Berkshire Hathaway, Inc., *1992 Annual Report*, chairman's letter.

43. Berkshire Hathaway, Inc., *1997 Annual Report*, chairman's letter.

44. Berkshire Hathaway, Inc., *1999 Annual Report*, chairman's letter.

45. See Steve Jordon, "National Indemnity Has Been a Foundation of Berkshire Hathaway's Strategy," *Omaha World-Herald*, April 24, 2005.

46. See Berkshire Hathaway, Inc., *2008 Annual Report*, chairman's letter.

47. *International Directory of Company Histories*, vol. 24 (Detroit, Mich.: St. James, 1999).

48. Cologne Re is formally called Kölnische Rückversicherungs-Gesellschaft AG.

49. Judy Greenwald, "General Re Consolidates Its Lead: Acquisition of National Re Seen as Strategic Move and a Good Fit for Reinsurer," *Business Insurance*, July 8, 1996; Leslie Scism, "General Re Agrees to Buy National Re in Deal Valued at About $940 Million," *Wall Street Journal*, July 2, 1996.

50. See Andrew Kilpatrick, *Of Permanent Value: The Story of Warren Buffett* (Birmingham, Ala.: Andy Kilpatrick Publishing Empire, 2011), 283–84.

51. See Berkshire Hathaway, Inc., *1998 Annual Report*, chairman's letter.

52. Klingaman, *GEICO*, 137.

53. Mark A. Hoffman, "Warren Buffett Accepts Blame for General Re's Poor Results," *Business Insurance*, March 18, 2002; Steve Jordon, "General Re Is the Key to Berkshire's Ignition, Underwriting Losses," *Omaha World-Herald*, April 28, 2002.

54. Berkshire Hathaway, Inc., *2002 Annual Report*, chairman's letter.

55. Ibid.

56. See Berkshire Hathaway, Inc., *2007 Annual Report*, chairman's letter.

57. See Maurice R. Greenberg and Lawrence A. Cunningham, *The AIG Story* (Hoboken, N.J.: Wiley, 2013), 171–202.

58. Ibid., 178–79.

59. Steve Jordon, "Buffett Urged to Dump Boss at Gen Re: A Report Says Prosecutors Are Asking for the CEO's Removal," *Omaha World-Herald*, April 7, 2008.

60. See Noah A. Gold, "Corporate Criminal Liability: Cooperate and You Won't Be Indicted," *Georgetown Journal of Law and Public Policy* 8, 147-165 (2010).

61. United States v. Stein, 541 F.3d 130 (2d Cir. 2008).

62. "Brandon Leaves Gen Re Under a Cloud," *Reactions*, May 1, 2008, quoting Justin Fuller, analyst at Morningstar.

63. Ibid., noting continued high ratings and positive commentary from AM Best and Standard & Poor's.

64. Berkshire Hathaway, Inc., *2005 Annual Report*, chairman's letter. Among other smaller Berkshire insurers are three that are exceptionally entrepreneurial: Boat America Corporation (or Boat Owners Association of the United States) is akin to AAA automobile clubs for boat owners, offering boat insurance and other services; Applied Underwriters couples payroll services with workers' compensation insurance; and Kansas Bankers Surety was built by creating direct relationships with hundreds of bankers in a dozen states. Another pair—Berkshire Hathaway Homestate and Guard Insurance—cater to smaller businesses, while two others are family businesses, one which pays monthly credit card bills of the disabled or unemployed (Central States Indemnity) and another covering unusual risks (U.S. Liability), known as "excess and surplus lines" in insurance argot.

5. Reputation

1. See Jim Clayton and Bill Retherford, *First a Dream* (Knoxville, Tenn.: FSB, 2002). Some of the historical facts concerning Clayton Homes can be found in *International Directory of Company Histories*, vol. 54 (Detroit, Mich.: St. James, 2003) (hereafter cited as *ICDH*, Clayton).

2. They were not Kirby vacuums, however.

3. The facts in this paragraph appear in Clayton and Retherford, *First a Dream*, p. 236.

4. Ibid.

5. See *ICDH*, Clayton; Clayton Homes corporate personnel, e-mail to author, February 18, 2013.

6. Clayton and Retherford, *First a Dream*, 193.

7. Ibid., 256.

8. Berkshire Hathaway, Inc., *2003 Annual Report*, chairman's letter.

9. See Denver Area Meat Cutters v. Clayton, 209 S.W.3d 584 (Tenn. Ct. App. 2006); Denver Area Meat Cutters v. Clayton, 120 S.W.3d 841 (Tenn. Ct. App. 2003).

10. Clayton and Retherford, *First a Dream*, 93–94.

11. Berkshire Hathaway, Inc., *2009 Annual Report*, chairman's letter.

12. Ibid.

13. See John Mackey and Rajendra Sisodia, *Conscious Capitalism: Liberating the Heroic Spirit of Business* (Boston: Harvard Business Review Press, 2013), 285; Andrew Kilpatrick, *Of Permanent Value* (Birmingham, Ala.: Andy Kilpatrick Publishing Empire, 2011), 483: "An average furniture store turns over inventory one or two times a year."

14. Why Samuel called his store Jordan's remains a business mystery.

15. Michael Roberto, Bryant University, "Jordan's Furniture: Shoppertainment," *Professor Michael Roberto's Blog*, October 27, 2009, http://michael-roberto.blogspot.com/2009/10/jordans-furniture-shoppertainment.html.

16. Berkshire Hathaway, Inc., *1997 Annual Report*, chairman's letter; Berkshire Hathaway, Inc., *1999 Annual Report*, chairman's letter.

17. Berkshire Hathaway/Jordan's Furniture, press release, October 11, 1999.

18. The historical highlights concerning Benjamin Moore may be found in *International Directory of Company Histories*, vol. 38 (Detroit, Mich.: St. James, 2001) (hereafter cited as *IDCH*, Benjamin Moore).

19. Federal efforts to reduce the use of lead-containing paint began in the 1970s and lasted through the early 1990s.

20. *IDCH*, Benjamin Moore.

21. Jane Applegate, "Moore's Program Lays the Base Coat for Minority-Owned Paint Stores," *Los Angeles Times*, August 31, 1993; Jane Applegate, "Minority Businesses Get a Head Start on Ownership," *Washington Post*, September 20, 1993.

22. Robert H. Mundheim, "Deals Without Bankers: Salomon and Benjamin Moore," *Concurring Opinions* (blog), May 21, 2013, www.concurringopinions.com/archives/author/robert-mundheim.

23. Robert Mundheim, author telephone interview (January 21, 2014).

24. Berkshire Hathaway, Inc., *2000 Annual Report*, chairman's letter.

25. Denis Abrams (Benjamin Moore) interview on *Nightly Business Report*, May 2, 2007.

26. Ibid. Berkshire set no targets for sales or profits, Abrams said.

27. James Covert, "Margaritaville Memo: Execs May Walk Plank," *New York Post*, June 26, 2012.

28. James Covert, "Brooklyn Paint Dealers Say Buffett Rolled All Over Them," *New York Post*, October 14, 2013.

29. See Steve Jordon, "Warren Buffett Says He Replaced Benjamin Moore's CEO to Keep a Promise," *Omaha World-Herald*, October 16, 2013 (reporting that Buffett said Benjamin Moore generated $1.5 billion in profit during the previous decade).

30. James Covert, "Warren Buffett Fired Benjamin Moore CEO After Bermuda Cruise," *New York Post*, June 15, 2012.

31. James Covert, "Warren Buffett Cans Benjamin Moore CEO," *New York Post*, September 27, 2013.

32. Warren Buffett letter to Denis Abrams, June 16, 2013.

33. James Covert, "Boxed in by Lowe's," *New York Post*, June 29, 2012.

34. Covert, "Warren Buffett Fired Benjamin Moore CEO After Bermuda Cruise."

35. Covert, "Warren Buffett Cans Benjamin Moore CEO."

36. Benjamin Moore, press release.

37. Kim Freeman, who wrote in response to my blog post of this story, at concurringopinions.com.

38. Michael Searles, author interview at Berkshire Hathaway annual meeting, Omaha (May 4, 2014).

39. Historical facts concerning Johns Manville can be found in *International Directory of Company Histories*, vol. 64 (Detroit, Mich.: St. James, 2004) (hereafter cited as *IDCH*, Johns Manville).

40. See Sloan Wilson, *The Man in the Gray Flannel Suit* (Simon & Schuster, 1955).

41. See Paul Brodeur, *Outrageous Misconduct: The Asbestos Industry on Trial* (New York: Pantheon, 1985).

42. *IDCH*, Johns Manville.

43. Ibid.

44. Borel v. Fibreboard Paper Products, 493 F.2d 1076 (5th Cir. 1973).

45. Stephen Solomon, "The Asbestos Fallout at Johns-Manville," *Fortune* (May 7, 1979).

46. *IDCH*, Johns Manville.

47. Berkshire Hathaway, Inc., *2000 Annual Report*, chairman's letter.

48. Ibid.

49. Peter Lattman & Geraldine Fabrikant, "Buffett's Favor for Now-Fallen Deputy Perplexed People Working for Him," *New York Times* (April 28, 2011).

50. An autobiographical feature on Mr. Raba appeared in Vanessa Small, "New at the Top: To Meet Warren Buffett, This Outdoorsman Didn't Stay Lost in the Woods,"

Washington Post, October 27, 2013, www.washingtonpost.com/business/economy/new-at-the-top-to-meet-warren-buffett-this-outdoorsman-didnt-stay-lost-in-the-woods/20 13/10/27/924ffe10-3d83-11e3-b6a9-da62c264f40e_story.html.

51. See Johns Manville, *We Build Environments: 2012 Sustainability Report* (Denver, Colo.: Johns Manville, 2013).

52. David Vogel, *The Market for Virtue: The Potential and Limits of Corporate Social Responsibility* (Washington, D.C.: Brookings Institute, 2005), 48–54.

6. Kinship

1. Barnaby J. Feder, "Rose Blumkin, Retail Queen, Dies at 104," *New York Times*, August 13, 1998.

2. Ibid.

3. Berkshire Hathaway, Inc., *1989 Annual Report*, chairman's letter.

4. See Alice Schroeder, *The Snowball: Warren Buffett and the Business of Life* (New York: Bantam Dell, 2008), 493–94, naming Mohawk as the supplier.

5. Berkshire Hathaway, Inc., *1983 Annual Report*, chairman's letter.

6. Schroeder, *The Snowball*, 501.

7. See Jeff Benedict, *How to Build a Business Warren Buffett Would Buy: The R. C. Willey Story* (Salt Lake City: Shadow Mountain, 2009), 1.

8. Stephen W. Gibson, "R.C. Willey Got Its Humble Start Selling Refrigerators to Farmers," *Deseret News* (Salt Lake City), April 11, 1999.

9. *International Directory of Company Histories*, vol. 72 (Detroit, Mich.: St. James, 2005).

10. Benedict, *The R. C. Willey Story*, 25.

11. Ibid., 158.

12. Ibid., 49, 54.

13. Ibid., 79.

14. Lynn Arave, "R.C. Willey Has Hot Dog of a Slogan," *Deseret News* (Salt Lake City), January 15, 2002; Benedict, *The R. C. Willey Story*, 85–86.

15. Benedict, *The R. C. Willey Story*, 87–89.

16. Ibid.

17. Ibid., 91–93.

18. Berkshire Hathaway, Inc., *1995 Annual Report*, chairman's letter; Berkshire Hathaway, Inc., *1999 Annual Report*, chairman's letter.

19. Benedict, *The R. C. Willey Story*, 110–12.

20. Ibid., 115.

21. Berkshire Hathaway, Inc., *1999 Annual Report*, chairman's letter.

22. Benedict, *The R. C. Willey Story*, 134,

23. Berkshire Hathaway, Inc., *1999 Annual Report*, chairman's letter.

24. William H. Child, email to author, May 20, 2014.

25. Facts in the discussion of Star Furniture may be found in a lecture by Melvyn Wolff (Distinguished Leaders Series, Bauer College of Business, University of Houston, March 8, 2005).

26. Ibid.

27. Background concerning Helzberg may be found in *International Directory of Company Histories*, vol. 40 (Detroit, Mich.: St. James, 2001); Ann F. Schulte, *So Far: The Story of Helzberg Diamonds* (Kansas City, Mo.: Helzberg's Diamond Shops, 1990); Barnett C. Helzberg, *What I Learned Before I Sold to Warren Buffett: An Entrepreneur's Guide to Developing a Highly Successful Company* (Hoboken, N.J.: Wiley, 2003).

28. Kevin Coleman, "Rough Start Taught Helzberg Lessons: Perseverance Key to Success," *Columbia Daily Tribune* (Missouri), November 3, 2006.

29. Helzberg, *What I Learned*, xv; Jennifer Mann Fuller, "Warren Buffett to Buy Helzberg Shops; No Plans to Change Location of Headquarters, Management," *Kansas City Star* (Missouri), March 11, 1995.

30. Helzberg, *What I Learned*, xvii; Don Dodson, "Jewelry Firm Sold to Berkshire Hathaway; Dream Comes True," *The News-Gazette* (Champaign-Urbana, Ill.), May 3, 2004.

31. Details in this and ensuing paragraphs draw on Berkshire Hathaway, Inc., *1995 Annual Report*, chairman's letter; Helzberg, *What I Learned*, xv; and Joyce Smith, "Multifaceted Advice: Jeweler Barnett Helzberg Shares Some Secrets Behind His Success," *Kansas City Star* (Missouri), April 9, 2003, reviewing Helzberg's autobiography.

32. See Nick Wreden, "Key to Elevator Pitch: Get Their Attention," *South Florida Sun-Sentinel*, February 11, 2002 (adapted from a Harvard Business School Publishing newsletter).

33. Berkshire Hathaway, Inc., *1995 Annual Report*, chairman's letter: "It took us awhile to get together on price."

34. Helzberg, *What I Learned*, xviii; Dodson, "Jewelry Firm Sold to Berkshire Hathaway", reporting on Helzberg's remarks in a lecture at the University of Illinois College of Business.

35. Exact figures have not been publicly disclosed, but Barnett Jr. has written that his ask was twice what Berkshire ultimately paid, which regulatory filings show were 7,510 Berkshire shares; those closed at $22,200 per share on March 10, 1995, the day the Berkshire-Helzberg deal was announced.

36. Helzberg, *What I Learned*, xvii; Smith, "Multifaceted Advice," reviewing Helzberg's autobiography.

37. Fuller, "Warren Buffett to Buy Helzberg Shops."

38. Historical facts concerning Ben Bridge may be found in *International Directory of Company Histories*, vol. 60 (Detroit, Mich.: St. James, 2004) (hereafter cited as *IDCH*, Bridge).

39. Victoria Gomelsky, "Ed Bridge: Best in the West," *National Jeweler*, August 1, 2003, 58, interview with Ed Bridge, grandson of Ben Bridge.

40. *IDCH*, Bridge.

41. *IDCH*, Bridge; David Volk, "Building a 'Bridge' That Lasts," *Puget Sound Business Journal*, July 17, 1992, 18, interview with Ed Bridge, grandson of Ben Bridge.

42. Ibid.

43. Ibid.

44. Berkshire Hathaway, Inc., *2000 Annual Report*, chairman's letter.

45. Berkshire subsidiaries are encouraged to make acquisitions that help their businesses grow, and subsidiary CEOs to report any other acquisition opportunities to Berkshire. Acting on that policy, an ingrained trait, is especially prevalent among Berkshire's family businesses. For instance, Rose Blumkin of Nebraska Furniture Mart had a sister, Rebecca Friedman, who escaped Russia along with her husband, Louis, just after Mrs. B had. The Blumkins introduced Rebecca's family, which owned Borsheim, an Omaha jewelry store, to Buffett. Berkshire soon acquired it—for the same reasons and following the same pattern as the other family business acquisitions.

46. Berkshire Hathaway, Inc., *1997 Annual Report*, chairman's letter.

47. Berkshire Hathaway, Inc., *1995 Annual Report*, chairman's letter.

7. Self-starters

1. Several managers of Berkshire subsidiaries have received the Horatio Alger Award, including Jim Clayton, Doris Christopher (the Pampered Chef), and Al Ueltschi (FlightSafety). Walter Scott, Berkshire board member and co-owner of Berkshire Hathaway Energy, served as president of the Horatio Alger Society.

2. A. L. Ueltschi, *The History and Future of FlightSafety International* (New York: FlightSafety International, 1999), 26–29. For additional background on FlightSafety, see *International Directory of Company Histories*, vol. 29 (Detroit, Mich.: St. James, 1999).

3. Ueltschi, *The History and Future of FlightSafety International*, 34.

4. Ibid., 44.

5. Bruce N. Whitman, telephone interview by the author, February 10, 2014.

6. Ueltschi, *The History and Future of FlightSafety International*, 56.

7. Bruce N. Whitman, interview by the author at FlightSafety offices, New York, January 14, 2014.

8. Ueltschi, *The History and Future of FlightSafety International*, 68; Whitman, interview, January 14, 2014.

9. Whitman, interview, January 14, 2014.

10. Ueltschi, *The History and Future of FlightSafety International*, 70.

11. Berkshire Hathaway, Inc., *1996 Annual Report*, chairman's letter.

12. Whitman, interview, February 10, 2014.

13. Ibid.

14. Ibid.

15. Historical facts about NetJets may be found in *International Directory of Company Histories*, vol. 36 (Detroit, Mich.: St. James, 2001) (hereafter cited as *IDCH*, NetJets).

16. Anthony Bianco, "What's Better Than a Private Plane? A Semiprivate Plane," *BusinessWeek*, July 21, 1997, 52.

17. Richard T. Santulli, telephone interview by the author, January 24, 2014; see also Warren Berger, "Hey, You're Worth It (Even Now)," *Wired*, June 2001.

18. *IDCH*, NetJets.

19. William Garvey, "Viewpoint: A Head for Business," *Business & Commercial Aviation*, February 1, 2011.

20. *IDCH*, NetJets.

21. New entrants included JetCo, a service of Air London International, and the Business Jet Solutions program offered jointly by Bombardier Aerospace Group and AMR Combs, Inc., the charter affiliate of American Airlines. See *IDCH*, NetJets.

22. *IDCH*, NetJets.

23. Bianco, "What's Better Than a Private Plane?," 52.

24. *IDCH*, NetJets.

25. Santulli, interview.

26. Berkshire Hathaway, Inc., *1998 Annual Report*, chairman's letter.

27. Santulli, interview.

28. Ibid.

29. Ibid.

30. E.g., Berkshire Hathaway, Inc., *2004 Annual Report*, chairman's letter; and Berkshire Hathaway, Inc., *2007 Annual Report*, chairman's letter.

31. Santulli, interview.

32. Santulli, interview; Ravi Nagarajan, Berkshire Hathaway: In Search of the "Buffett Premium," *The Rational Walk*, 2011, 70, 116–17.

33. E.g., Berkshire Hathaway, Inc., *2009 Annual Report*, chairman's letter.

34. Nagarajan, "Buffett Premium," 117, notes 19–20 (containing references).

35. The facts concerning Garan, Inc., can be found in *International Directory of Company Histories*, vol. 64 (Detroit, Mich.: St. James, 2004).

36. See Garan company website: www.garanimals.com/history.htm; and Nina S. Hyde, Fashion Notes, *Washington Post*, November 4, 1979.

37. Ramon F. Adams, *Western Words: A Dictionary of the Range, Cow Camp and Trail* (Norman: University of Oklahoma Press, 1944).

38. Irvin Farman, *Standard of the West: The Justin Story* (Fort Worth: Texas Christian University Press 1996), 127. Good background about Justin Industries may be found in *International Directory of Company Histories*, vol. 19 (Detroit, Mich.: St. James,1998) (hereafter cited as *IDCH*, Justin).

39. Farman, *Standard of the West*, 133.

40. Ibid., 138.

41. Ibid., 136–37.

42. Ibid., 153–54.

43. Ibid., 155.

44. Farman, *Standard of the West*, 157–58.

45. *IDCH*, Justin.

46. Farman, *Standard of the West*, 172–73.

47. Ibid., 177–83.

48. See Peppercorn Learning, "Selling a Commodity? Baloney!," Pepper Group, www.peppergroup.com/images/PepLearning_CommodityBaloney.pdf.

49. See Ronald Chan, *Behind the Berkshire Hathaway Curtain: Lessons from Warren Buffett's Top Business Leaders* (Hoboken, N.J.: Wiley, 2010), 27–28, recounting an interview with Watson.

50. Berkshire Hathaway, Inc., *2000 Annual Report*, chairman's letter.

51. Chan, *Behind the Berkshire Hathaway Curtain*, 30.

52. Ibid.

53. See Martha Deller, "Top CEO, Strategic Management, Randy Watson of Justin Books," *Fort Worth Business Press*, August 23, 2013.

54. Ibid.

55. Edwin E. Lehr, *Colossus in Clay: Acme Brick Company* (Marceline, Mo.: Walsworth, 1998), 237.

56. Good background about Dairy Queen may be found in *International Directory of Company Histories*, vol. 39 (Detroit, Mich.: St. James, 2001); Caroline Hall Otis, *The Cone with the Curl on Top: The Dairy Queen Story, 1940–1980* (Minneapolis: International Dairy Queen, 1990); and Bob Miglani, *Treat Your Customers: Thirty Lessons on Service and Sales That I Learned at My Family's Dairy Queen Store* (New York: Hyperion, 2006).

57. Otis, *The Cone with the Curl on Top*, 11.

58. Ibid., 34, quoting Sam Temperato.

59. Ibid., 56–57.

60. See William L. Killion, "The Modern Myth of the Vulnerable Franchisee: The Case for a More Balanced View of the Franchisor-Franchise Relationship," *Franchise Law Journal* 23 (2008): 28.

61. Business franchising offered a model that appealed simultaneously to two paradoxical beliefs of many Americans: a veneration of small business and sense that big business is necessary for success. Franchises offered both the personal payoffs of proprietorship along with the competence of corporate America. Thomas S. Dicke, *Franchising in America: The Development of a Business Method, 1840–1980* (Chapel Hill: University of North Carolina Press, 1992). Franchises also have hallmarks of the American dream. For a relatively low initial investment, an entrepreneur of modest means can own and operate a business. Today, this is a standard business model, drawing millions to the excitement of building a business supported by a coordinating organization.

Around 1970, Dairy Queen and numerous other franchisors nationwide faced difficulties. A franchising boom had developed in the 1960s, sprouting 670,000 franchises under 1,000 brands. See Harry Kursh, *The Franchise Boom* (Englewood Cliffs, N.J.: Prentice Hall, 1968). The boom turned to bust, however. A chorus of critics aired tales of unscrupulous franchisors preying on naïve aspirants. These were the "mom-and-pop" proprietors who dreamed of running a business but lacked experience or sophistication. But the reality was not as bad as the salient negative stories suggested. In fact, the U.S. Federal Trade Commission identified occasional rather than pervasive problems. Killion, "The Modern Myth," 26–27nn56–57, quoting FTC's general counsel. Researchers at the University of Wisconsin concluded that the net economic effects of franchising were positive, especially in providing the opportunity of owning a business—the American dream for self-starters. Urban B. Ozanne and Shelby D. Hunt, *The Economic Effects of Franchising* (Washington, D.C.: Government Printing Office, 1971).

62. Killion, "The Modern Myth," 25

63. John W. Mooty, telephone interview by the author, October 3, 2013.

64. Otis, *The Cone with the Curl on Top*, 81–82.

65. Ibid., 82.

66. Ibid., 94; Mooty, interview.

67. Otis, *The Cone with the Curl on Top*, 121.

68. Susan Feyder, "Auto Dealer's Death Influenced IDQ's Decision to Sell," *Star-Tribune*, November 22, 1997.

69. Mooty, interview.

70. Ibid.

71. Stephanie Steinberg, "Around the Water Cooler with Dairy Queen's CEO," *U.S. News & World Report*, July 23, 2013.

72. Michael Webster, "GE Capital Provides $26.5 Million to Dairy Queen Franchisee," *Franchise-Info*, April 27, 2011.

73. Otis, *The Cone with the Curl on Top*, 67, quoting Sam Temperato.

8. Hands Off

1. See, e.g., the classic work of Douglas McGregor, *The Human Side of Enterprise* (1960; annotated ed., New York: McGraw-Hill, 2005).

2. Doris Christopher, *The Pampered Chef: The Story of One of America's Most Beloved Companies* (New York: Currency Doubleday 2005). Additional resources concerning the Pampered Chef include Karen Linder, *The Women of Berkshire Hathaway: Lessons from Warren Buffett's Female CEOs and Directors* (Hoboken, N.J.: Wiley, 2012), chap. 3; Doris Christopher, *Come to the Table* (New York: Hachette, 2008); and *International Directory of Company Histories*, vol. 18 (Detroit, Mich.: St. James, 1997).

3. Michele L. Fitzpatrick, "Recipe for Success," *Chicago Tribune*, April 14, 1996.

4. Linder, *The Women of Berkshire Hathaway*, 76–77.

5. Robert A. Mamis, "Master of Bootstrapping Administration," *Inc.*, August 1, 1995.

6. Christopher, *The Pampered Chef*, 111, 198.

7. Ibid., 148.

8. Ibid., 124, 126.

9. Ibid., 173.

10. Ibid., 173.

11. Ibid., 162–67.

12. Ibid., 166–67. Other Berkshire subsidiaries have resolved the dilemma in the same way. Bill Child of RC Willey said:

> If you grow too fast, the infrastructure and systems of a company aren't able to handle it. Those must grow at the same level that sales grow. Otherwise a company becomes inefficient in the delivery of its product. The result is higher costs and decreased customer satisfaction.

Quoted in Jeff Benedict, *How to Build a Business Warren Buffett Would Buy: The R. C. Willey Story* (Salt Lake City: Shadow Mountain, 2009), 108–9. Before becoming Berkshire subsidiaries, some companies failed to observe such principles. See chap. 11 for the example of Brooks Sports, Inc.

13. Berkshire Hathaway, Inc., *2002 Annual Report*, chairman's letter.

14. Christopher, *The Pampered Chef*, 243–44.

15. Ibid., 196, 242.

16. Berkshire Hathaway, Inc., *1981 Annual Report*, chairman's letter.

17. See Ronald Chan, *Behind the Berkshire Hathaway Curtain: Lessons from Warren Buffett's Top Business Leaders* (Hoboken, N.J.: Wiley, 2010), 116.

18. Ibid., 118.

19. Doris Christopher, author interview at Berkshire Hathaway annual meeting, May 3, 2014.

20. See Jordan v. Scott Fetzer Co., No. 4:07-CV-80, 2009 WL 1885063 (M.D. Ga. June 30, 2009).

21. See Joseph Cahill, "Here's the Pitch: How Kirby Persuades Customers to Shell Out $1,500 for Vacuum," *Wall Street Journal*, October 4, 1999; Greg Dawson, "Kirby Always Cleaning Up After Others," *Orlando Sentinel*, August 27, 2004.

22. See Lee Howard, "Ex-Kirby Employees Can Join Suit," *The Day* (New London, Conn.), March 28, 2012.

23. See Cahill, "Here's the Pitch"; Dawson, "Kirby Always Cleaning Up After Others."

24. See Jordan v. Scott Fetzer Co., No. 4:07-CV-80, 2009 WL 1885063 (M.D. Ga. June 30, 2009); Howard, "Ex-Kirby Employees Can Join Suit."

25. See Robert P. Miles, *The Warren Buffett CEO: Secrets from the Berkshire Hathaway Managers* (Hoboken, N.J.: Wiley, 2003), 357–58, quoting Buffett's written instructions.

26. Alice Schroeder, *The Snowball: Warren Buffett and the Business of Life* (New York: Bantam Dell, 2008), 482.

27. Berkshire Hathaway, Inc., *2009 Annual Report*, chairman's letter.

28. Ibid.

29. In late 2010, Sokol was serving as chairman, CEO, and president of NetJets as well as chairman of both MidAmerican Energy and Johns Manville.

30. Berkshire Hathaway, Inc., 2011 annual meeting, transcript (on file with the author), Buffett's opening comments.

31. Ibid.

32. Ibid., Buffett responding to shareholder questions.

33. See Steve Schaefer, "Buffett Breaks Out Elephant Gun for $9B Lubrizol Buy," *Forbes*, March 14, 2011.

34. See Katya Wachtell, "Meet John Freund: Warren Buffett's Broker of 30 Years and the City Banker Who Alerted Him to Sokol's Deception," *Business Insider*, May 2, 2011.

35. See also, "David Sokol Defends His Controversial Lubrizol Stock Purchases," CNBC transcript, April 1, 2011, www.cnbc.com/id/42365586.

36. Ruling of the Court on Defendants' Motion to Dismiss, In re Berkshire Hathaway Inc. Deriv. Litig., No. 6392-VCL, 2012 WL 978867 (Del. Ch. Mar. 19, 2012).

37. Berkshire Hathaway, Inc., 2011 annual meeting, transcript, Buffett responding to shareholder questions.

38. Ibid., Munger responding to shareholder questions.

39. The Salomon incident is noted in chap. 1.

40. Ben Berkowitz, "Sokol Affair Tarnishes Buffett Style," *Globe & Mail*, March 31, 2011, quoting Charles Elson of the University of Delaware: "The fact that this could happen does raise questions as to the effectiveness of the company's controls to prevent something like this from happening."

41. Berkshire Hathaway, Inc., *2010 Annual Report*, chairman's letter.

42. Jenny Strasburg, "Buffett Is Seen as Too Trusting," *Wall Street Journal*, March 31, 2011.

43. Berkowitz, "Sokol Affair Tarnishes Buffett Style," quoting John C. Coffee of Columbia University Law School: "It's the kind of behaviour that, as a matter of corporate governance, sophisticated companies try to avoid."

44. There was little reason to believe that a more elaborate control system would have made Sokol do anything differently. Suppose Berkshire had a large compliance department with detailed commands and controls, including a specific procedure for clearing personal investments through a compliance committee. If long-standing general policies Berkshire censured Sokol for violating did not dissuade Sokol's trade, it is not obvious that an additional layer of bureaucracy would. On the contrary, it is possible that command and control would displace the value of the autonomy-and-trust culture and stimulate more behavior that veered close to the edge.

To illustrate, many companies, including Berkshire, have a specific rule barring employee trades in a list of restricted securities. Berkshire's restricted list consists of securities of companies in which it owns positions. But Berkshire's policies are broader, also including a general standard barring trades in securities that Berkshire may acquire. It is easy to compile a complete list of securities a company owns; it is impossible to ensure the completeness of a list of securities it may acquire. A rule-bound command-and-control culture can restrict the former but not the latter; some degree of autonomy and trust is required for that.

45. Berkshire Hathaway 2011 annual meeting, transcript, Munger responding to shareholder questions.

46. See Buffett's testimony before the Subcommittee on Telecommunications and Finance of the Energy and Commerce Committee of the U.S. House of Representatives (1991), reported in "Buffett's 1991 Salomon Testimony," *Wall Street Journal*, May 1, 2010. Buffett's admonition began with the following:

> The spirit about compliance is as important or more so than words about compliance. I want the right words and I want the full range of internal controls. But I also have asked every Salomon employee to be his or her own compliance officer. After they first obey all rules, I then want employees to ask themselves whether they are willing to have any contemplated act appear

the next day on the front page of their local paper, to be read by their spouses, children, and friends, with the reporting done by an informed and critical reporter. If they follow this test, they need not fear my other message to them: Lose money for the firm, and I will be understanding; lose a shred of reputation for the firm, and I will be ruthless.

47. Berkshire Hathaway 2011 annual meeting transcript, Buffett responding to shareholder questions. By blasting Sokol, the audit committee sent an express warning to all Berkshire personnel. In authorizing Buffett to release the report publicly, it stressed:

> Such a public statement will demonstrate to all who work for Berkshire, as well as the other constituencies Berkshire serves, that the Company takes its policies very seriously, and that its instruction to all its representatives to play in the middle of the court is Company policy, not public relations. We expect this report to send a loud message that those policies are designed to be read broadly, and to deter anyone who may be contemplating a violation of the spirit or letter of those policies in the future.

48. The Sokol affair prompted some Berkshire shareholders to sue the board in Delaware, Berkshire's state of incorporation. They argued that the board had failed to maintain an adequate system of internal control. The complaint echoed the public criticism of Berkshire's autonomy-and-trust culture and urged that the board botched its oversight role by abjuring a command-and-control structure. The court dismissed the assertion as "profoundly weak." Ruling of the Court on Defendants' Motion to Dismiss, In re Berkshire Hathaway Inc. Deriv. Litig., No. 6392-VCL, 2012 WL 978867 (Del. Ch. Mar. 19, 2012).

These shareholders also tried to sue Sokol to recover $3 million in profits for Berkshire, which the board had declined to do. Boards have the say over whether a corporation should sue someone unless shareholders can show that a board is unable to act impartially. The shareholders could not show that the Berkshire board's independence was compromised concerning whether to sue Sokol. The Delaware court acknowledged that Buffett's press release colored the matter, suggesting coziness between Sokol and Buffett that could have biased the board. But that was mere "smoke," the court said, not enough to infect the board's judgment. Ibid.

49. The Sokol affair also reflects Berkshire's sensitivity to public perceptions, which undergirds Buffett's admonition to test employee behavior according to how it would look if reported on the front page of a newspaper. Suppose Sokol, when he first called Buffett, had said, "Warren, I think Lubrizol is an attractive company—so attractive that I just bought $10 million for myself, and I think you ought to look at it for Berkshire." That disclosure would have negated the story. Moreover, Sokol might have gone an extra step to eliminate any doubt about propriety and said, "If Berkshire would like to buy my shares at cost, I'm happy to sell." Buffett's probable response would have been something like, "No, that's fine. If we end up buying it, you're entitled."

50. Dickstein Shapiro, "Statement of Dickstein Shapiro Partner Barry Wm. Levine, Attorney for David Sokol," press release, April 27, 2011.

51. Benedict, *How to Build a Business Warren Buffett Would Buy*, 55–56.

52. Ibid., 56. In some businesses, autonomy can offer integrity to the brand. For example, among Berkshire's scores of newspapers—headlined by the *Buffalo News*—Berkshire management avoids involvement in decisions concerning content or opinion. Managerial oversight is supplied by senior managers at one of the larger papers, the *Omaha World-Herald*. Employees value the autonomy and appreciate the confidence as they respond by respecting journalistic ethics and newspaper editorial policy.

53. Kevin T. Clayton, author's survey of Berkshire executives, October 3, 2013.

54. Jim Clayton and Bill Retherford, *First a Dream* (Knoxville, Tenn.: FSB, 2002), 99.

55. James L. Hambrick, telephone interview by the author, December 20, 2013.

9. Investor Savvy

1. Berkshire Hathaway, Inc., *2013 Annual Report*, 64; W. Grady Rosier (CEO, McLane Company), letter to the author, September 23, 2013.

2. Historical facts concerning McLane may be found in Martha Kahler and Jeff Hampton, *McLane Company, Inc.: The First One Hundred Years* (Temple, Tex.: McLane Company, 1994); see also *International Directory of Company Histories*, vol. 13 (Detroit, Mich.: St. James, 1996).

3. Actually $3.8 million to be more precise. Kahler and Hampton, *McLane*, 63.

4. Ibid., 63.

5. Ibid., 58–59, 62.

6. Ibid., 63.

7. Ibid., 63.

8. See "Berkshire Unit Invests in Missouri Beverage," *St. Louis Post-Dispatch*, April 26, 2013.

9. The strategy to grow by geography is obvious at some Berkshire subsidiaries, such as BH Media, which acquires local newspapers that cater to specific regions, and HomeServices of America, which acquires local residential real estate brokerages that practice in given locales. On the international stage, ISCAR/ICM has grown through serial acquisition of operations in country after country across Europe. In all three cases, tremendous growth opportunities are ahead.

10. See Lawrence A. Cunningham, *Outsmarting the Smart Money* (New York: McGraw-Hill, 2002).

11. The others: Ben Bridge Jewelers, BNSF, Dexter Shoe, FlightSafety, and Gen Re.

12. For example, during its first two decades with Berkshire, See's generated profit of nearly $400 million, yet only required $18 million to reinvest in its business—Berkshire allocated the rest. Berkshire Hathaway, Inc., *1991 Annual Report*, chairman's letter. See's grew sales from $29 million in 1972 to $196 million in 1991; profits grew from $4.2 million pre-tax in 1972 to $42.4 million in 1991. See's delivered its 1991 results on the strength of only $25 million in net worth, the $7 million it boasted in 1971 plus a grand total of $18 million that Berkshire had See's retain. The rest of the earnings See's

generated during that period, a cumulative $410 million, were used by Berkshire for other purposes. By 2013, See's was generating $80 million in annual earnings. David Kass, "Remarks of Warren Buffett at University of Maryland on November 15, 2013," *Robert H. Smith School of Business Blog*, December 8, 2013, http://blogs.rhsmith.umd. edu/davidkass/2013/12.

13. See Prem C. Jain, *Buffett Beyond Value* (Hoboken, N.J.: Wiley, 2010), 139: "From 1986 to 1994, Scott Fetzer's total earnings were $555.4 million, but most were not plowed back into Scott Fetzer."

14. Michael D. Sorkin, "Paul Cornelsen Dies, Former Ralston Exec Won Battlefield Command from Gen. George Patton," *St. Louis Post Dispatch*, January 1, 2012.

15. See Hunter v. MiTek Industries, 721 F.Supp. 1102 (E.D. Mo. 1989).

16. Thomas J. Manenti, telephone interview by the author, October 2, 2013.

17. Jim Healey, *MiTek: A Global Success Story: 1981–2011* (St. Louis, Mo.: MiTek, 2012), 66.

18. Manenti, interview, October 2, 2013.

19. Berkshire Hathaway, Inc., *2001 Annual Report*, chairman's letter.

20. Rexam proved a tough negotiator, responding to Berkshire's initial offer with a counteroffer that it attributed to a recent MiTek acquisition Rexam believed Berkshire's offer had neglected. Berkshire accepted the counteroffer. Healey, *MiTek*, 72–73.

21. Thomas J. Manenti, telephone interview by the author, February 12, 2014.

22. Gibraltar Steel Corporation, press release.

23. As another example, in 2000, Nebraska Furniture Mart acquired Iowa-based Homemakers Plaza, Inc., and in 2005 sold its nonretail manufacturing division. Andrew Kilpatrick, *Of Permanent Value: The Story of Warren Buffett* (Birmingham, Ala.: Andy Kilpatrick Publishing Empire, 2011), 533.

24. Manenti, interview, October 2, 2013.

25. Historical facts concerning Lubrizol may be found in *International Directory of Company Histories*, vol. 30 (Detroit, Mich.: St. James, 2000).

26. Lubrizol-Noveon, press release, April 2004.

27. James L. Hambrick, telephone interview by the author, December 20, 2013.

28. Ibid.

29. Jefferies Research Analyst Report, December 2006, noting that Noveon's private equity sponsors had made deep cuts in its R&D.

30. Jefferies Research Analyst Report, December 2006.

31. See Ian Austen and Nathaniel Popper, "Paper or Plastic: Britain Joining Currency Trend," *The New York Times*, December 20, 2013.

32. Robert Westervelt, "Lubrizol: Maintaining Margins and Adding Growth to the Mix," *Chemical Week*, September 20, 2010.

33. Peter Rea (former Baldwin Wallace University professor and expert on corporate ethical culture who had researched Lubrizol), email to author, January 8, 2014; see also Alan Kolp and Peter Rea, *Integrity Is a Growth Market* (Mason, Ohio: Atomic Dog, 2005).

34. Jefferies Research Analyst Report, December 2006.

35. Some reports indicated that the sellers could not accept Lubrizol's higher bid because they had made an exclusivity commitment to BASF, while others attributed the decision to a belief that BASF's offer was more likely to close and its funding more secure. Compare "BASF Will Purchase Cognis for $3.9 Billion," *Star-Ledger* (Newark, N.J.), June 23, 2010, with "BASF Close to Cognis Deal as Owners Reject Lubrizol's Offer," *Chemical Week Business Daily*, June 21, 2010.

36. Westervelt, "Lubrizol: Maintaining Margins."

37. Hambrick, interview, December 20, 2013.

38. Berkshire Hathaway, Inc., *2011 Annual Report*, chairman's letter.

39. Jefferies Research Analyst Report, October 2010.

40. See Ronald Chan, *Behind the Berkshire Hathaway Curtain: Lessons from Warren Buffett's Top Business Leaders* (Hoboken, N.J.: Wiley, 2010), 134, calling it a "distressed company" as of 1991.

41. See Jeffrey L. Rodengen, *Kiewit: An Uncommon Company* (Ft. Lauderdale, Fla.: Write Stuff Enterprises, 2009), 155.

42. Ibid., 80, 95, 98.

43. Ibid., 98.

44. Jeff Pelline, "California Energy Relocating to Omaha," *San Francisco Chronicle*, June 20, 1991.

45. Ibid.

46. Judy Schriener, "No Grand Plan but Plenty of Cash," *Engineering News*, March 22, 1993.

47. California Energy Co., Inc., press release, January 10, 1995.

48. See Edward B. Flowers, *U.S. Utility Mergers and the Restructuring of the New Global Power Industry* (Westport, Conn.: Quorum, 1998).

49. James Miller, "CalEnergy Ends $1.92 Billion Bid," *Wall Street Journal*, August 18, 1997.

50. "Cal Energy Board Okays $1.16 Billion Buyout of Kiewit's 30% Stock Holding," *Global Power Report*, September 19, 1997.

51. Chan, *Behind the Berkshire Hathaway Curtain*, 136

52. Ron Insana, Street Signs interview, CNBC, October 25, 1999.

53. Ibid.

54. Ibid.

55. Northern Natural was originally an Omaha-based business, begun in the 1930s. Berkshire Hathaway, Inc., *2002 Annual Report*, chairman's letter. In 1985, Northern Natural, then called Inter North (after a 1980 name change), merged with Houston Natural Gas. The deal called for maintaining headquarters in Omaha, having Inter North's CEO stay in office, and keeping the Inter North name. Within a year, however, Houston Natural Gas breached all three promises: headquarters were moved to Houston, Kenneth R. Lay became CEO, and the name was changed to Enron. Over the next fifteen years, Enron developed exciting energy-based financial projects that were intermingled with elaborate accounting tricks. See Bethany McLean and Peter Elkind, *The Smartest*

Guys in the Room: The Amazing Rise and Scandalous Fall of Enron (New York: Portfolio, 2003).

In late 2001, just before Enron's fraud was uncovered, it obtained financing from Dynegy, a high-flying crosstown rival. As collateral for that loan, Enron staked the old Northern Natural pipeline. When Enron soon defaulted, Dynegy seized it. Shortly thereafter, Dynegy faced financial problems of its own. Seeking liquid funds on a Friday in late July 2001, Dynegy executives called MidAmerican Energy offering to sell Northern Natural. They signed a contract the following Monday. Berkshire Hathaway, Inc., *2002 Annual Report*, chairman's letter.

56. Berkshire Hathaway, Inc., *2008 Annual Report*, 71; Ravi Nagarajan, "Berkshire Hathaway: In Search of the 'Buffett Premium,' " *The Rational Walk*, March 1, 2011, 115.

57. See Richard H. Thaler, *The Winner's Curse: Paradoxes and Anomalies of Economic Life* (Princeton, N.J.: Princeton University Press, 1994).

58. Berkshire Hathaway, Inc., *2013 Annual Report*, chairman's letter.

59. Another example of this more capital-oriented view of acquisitions is Richline Group, a jewelry supplier. Its origins were more the dream of a capitalist entrepreneur than a typical business manager. In May 2006, Buffett gave a lunch talk at Ben Bridge, Berkshire's Seattle-based jewelry chain. The audience included company vendors, among them Dennis Ulrich, owner of a small manufacturer of gold jewelry. In January 2007, Ulrich made Buffett a pitch. With Berkshire capital at his disposal, he could establish a force in the jewelry supply business by acquisitions, he ventured. Buffett bit.

On day one, to form Richline, Berkshire acquired both Aurafin and Bel-Oro International, Inc., each a small jewelry maker, one owned by Ulrich, the other a direct competitor owned by Dave Meleski. Not long after, Bel-Oro made three further acquisitions: Michael Anthony Jewelers, Inverness Corporation, and Leach Garner. In turn, Leach Garner soon made three more acquisitions: Excell Manufacturing, Findings, Inc., and Stern Metals. Presto: at least eight small jewelry makers were combined to forge a much more powerful whole—and there is no doubt more to come. In 2013, Richline acquired HONORA, Inc., a specialist in pearls. Growth has been both geographic and product oriented, but the ultimate motivation? Pooling capital of small operators in order to secure the power of scale.

60. Berkshire Hathaway, Inc., *2012 Annual Report*, chairman's letter; and Berkshire Hathaway, Inc., *2013 Annual Report*, chairman's letter.

10. Rudimentary

1. Anthony B. Hatch, "Railway Industry Update," presented at Railway Interchange 2011, Minneapolis, Minn., September 18–21, 2011, www.arema.org/files/library/2011_ Conference_Proceedings/Hatch-Rail_Renaissance_Final-2011.pdf.

2. Lawrence H. Kaufman, *Leaders Count: The Story of BNSF Railway* (Austin: Monthly Custom Publishing/Texas A&M University Press, 2005), 198–99. Kaufman's book offers an excellent and comprehensive treatment, on which this section draws heavily. The section is supplemented by notes from interviews of rail industry analysts

and investors developed by Steven Keating of the George Washington University Investment Office (hereafter cited as Keating, Interview Notes).

3. See Frank N. Wilner, *Railroad Mergers: History, Analysis, Insight* (New York: Simmons-Boardman, 1997).

4. In 1980, Burlington Northern acquired the St. Louis–San Francisco Railway (Frisco), which was also created in 1849, whose main lines linked Chicago and Seattle with branches off to Alabama, Texas, and Wyoming. By 1994, Burlington Northern was the largest of the dozen American railways in its class.

5. Kaufman, *Leaders Count*, 266.

6. Ibid., 266, 268.

7. Ibid., 230.

8. Ibid., 227.

9. Ibid., 225.

10. Keating, Interview Notes.

11. Kaufman, *Leaders Count*, 171.

12. Ibid., 268–69.

13. Ibid., 274.

14. Ibid., 282–83.

15. Ibid., 320.

16. Ibid.

17. Ibid., 323.

18. Ibid., 328.

19. Berkshire Hathaway, Inc., *2013 Annual Report*, 64–65.

20. Keating, Interview Notes.

21. Ibid.

22. Berkshire-BNSF Joint Prospectus and Proxy Statement, December 23, 2009, 35–39.

23. Kaufman, *Leaders Count*, 344, 371 (Rose).

24. In late 2013, BNSF announced a managerial transition, in which Rose, who had been CEO and chairman, relinquished those roles and became executive chairman, while Ice, who had been president, retained that role and added the role of CEO. BNSF, "BNSF Railway Announces CEO, Executive Chairman Transition," press release, December 11, 2013.

25. For a rich and fascinating history of Shaw Industries, on which this section draws, see Randall L. Patton, *Shaw Industries: A History* (Athens: University of Georgia Press, 2002).

26. Ibid., 85.

27. Ibid., 152.

28. Ibid.

29. Berkshire Hathaway, Inc., *2000 Annual Report*, chairman's letter.

30. Ibid.

31. Berkshire Hathaway, Inc., *2004 Annual Report*, chairman's letter, noting that Shaw's costs "remain under pressure today" but "earned an outstanding 25.6 percent on

tangible equity in 2004," being a "powerhouse." The downturn in the housing sector that began in 2008 posed challenges, of course.

32. Historical facts concerning Fruit of the Loom may be found in *International Directory of Company Histories*, vol. 25 (Detroit, Mich.: St. James, 1999) (hereafter cited as *IDCH*, Fruit of the Loom).

33. Psalm 127:3.

34. Historians debate the meaning of the term *union suit*. Some believe it described the outfit, a combination of underpants and undershirt, joined together about the waist. Others say the name referenced those who famously wore them, namely the troops of the Union Army during the Civil War. Either way, Goldfarb adapted the label as the moniker for his fledgling company, the Union Underwear Company. *IDCH*, Fruit of the Loom.

35. Ibid.

36. David Greising, "Bill Farley in on Pins and Needles," *BusinessWeek*, September 18, 1989, 58; Jonathan R. Laing, "Love that Leverage!" *Barron's*, May 1, 1989, 6.

37. Michael Oneal, "Fruit of the Loom Escalates the Underwars," *BusinessWeek*, February 22, 1988, 114.

38. "Profit Surges 38 Percent on Moves to Reduce Labor Expenses," *Wall Street Journal*, April 16, 1998.

39. Buffett summarized the deal. *Buyer*: Philadelphia and Reading Coal and Iron (P&R), an anthracite producer with a declining business but lots of cash and tax credits. *Seller*: Union Underwear had $5 million in cash with annual pre-tax earnings of $3 million. *Terms*: purchase price of $15 million, paid for as follows: $9 million of non–interest bearing notes payable from 50 percent of Union earnings in excess of $1 million; $2.5 million from Union's existing cash balances; and the rest ($3.5 million) apparently paid by P&R in cash. Buffett wrote of the deal in his 2001 letter to Berkshire shareholders: "Those were the days; I get goose bumps just thinking about such deals." Berkshire Hathaway, Inc., *2001 Annual Report*, chairman's letter.

40. There had been several other final bidders in an active process during which the administrators identified as many as twenty-nine prospective buyers. Fruit of the Loom Bankruptcy Disclosure Statement (Dec. 28, 2001) (filed on Form 8-K with the Securities and Exchange Commission).

11. Eternal

1. Jim Weber, telephone interview by the author, October 11, 2013.

2. Historical facts about Brooks may be found in *International Directory of Company Histories*, vol. 32 (Detroit, Mich.: St. James, 2000) and Liz Murtaugh Gillespie, *Running Through the First 100 Years* (Seattle, Wash.: Brooks Sports, Inc., 2014) .

3. Jeanne Sather, "Shoemaker Brooks Takes Its First Steps on Comeback Trail," *Puget Sound Business Journal*, July 1, 1994, 6.

4. Helen Jung, "Brooks Shoe Chief Wants to Run Up Profits, Reputation," *Knight-Ridder/Tribune Business News*, January 31, 1994.

5. Leigh Gallagher, "Runner's World," *Forbes*, February 22, 1999, 96.

6. Weber, interview; see Catherine New, "Brooks' CEO Jim Weber Explains How He Turned Around a Near-Bankrupt Business," *Huffington Post*, April 24, 2013.

7. The anecdote is from the telephone interview with Jim Weber.

8. Weber, interview.

9. Ibid.

10. Joel Silvey, email to author (April 3, 2014). Some of the historical facts concerning Forest River may be found at Joel Silvey's website *Pop-up Camper History*, www.popupcamperhistory.com/rockwood.php.

11. Sherman Goldenberg, "RVB Announces '05 Newsmaker of the Year," *RV Business*, November 17, 2005.

12. Berkshire Hathaway, Inc., *2005 Annual Report*, chairman's letter.

13. Ibid.

14. Ibid. Here is Buffett's succinct version of this tale from his 2005 chairman's letter:

> Pete is a remarkable entrepreneur. Some years back, he sold his business, then far smaller than today, to an LBO operator who promptly began telling him how to run the place. Before long, Pete left, and the business soon sunk into bankruptcy. Pete then repurchased it. You can be sure that I won't be telling Pete how to manage his operation.

15. Berkshire Hathaway, Inc., *2005 Annual Report*, chairman's letter.

16. Ibid.

17. Berkshire Hathaway, Inc., *2010 Annual Report*, chairman's letter.

18. Berkshire Hathaway, Inc., *2005 Annual Report*, chairman's letter.

19. Berkshire Hathaway, Inc., *2012 Annual Report*, inside back cover.

20. Berkshire Hathaway, Inc., *2013 Annual Report*, inside back cover.

21. Berkshire Hathaway, Inc., *2013 Annual Report*, chairman's letter.

22. Sherman Goldenberg, "Berkshire Hathaway to Purchase Forest River," *RV Business*, July 20, 2005.

23. Michael J. De La Merced, "Berkshire to Buy Oriental Trading Co.," *New York Times*, November 2, 2012.

24. Dawn McCarty, "Oriental Trading Co. Files for Bankruptcy in Delaware," *Bloomberg*, August 25, 2010.

25. Berkshire Hathaway-Oriental Trading, "Berkshire Hathaway to Acquire Oriental Trading," press release, November 2, 2012.

26. "CTB Inc. Founder Howard S. Brembeck Dies at 100," *Grain News*, December 7, 2010.

27. www.legacy.com/obituaries/onlineathens/obituary.aspx?page=lifestory&pid=145385602#fbLoggedOut

28. CTB, "CTB International Corp. Announces Agreement to Be Acquired by Berkshire Hathaway," press release (August 19, 2002).

29. *International Directory of Company Histories*, vol. 26 (Detroit, Mich.: St. James, 1999).

30. Technically, the buyer was Wesco Financial Corporation, then an 80 percent–owned Berkshire subsidiary subsequently merged into Berkshire. Wesco, which had been overseen for many years by Berkshire vice chairman Charlie Munger, owned a few subsidiaries.

31. Berkshire Hathaway, Inc., *2000 Annual Report*, chairman's letter.

32. Units Magazine, National Apartment Association, August 1, 2012, vol. 36, issue 8.

33. Berkshire Hathaway, Inc., *2013 Annual Report*, chairman's letter.

34. Andrew Kilpatrick, *Of Permanent Value: The Story of Warren Buffett* (Birmingham, Ala.: Andy Kilpatrick Publishing Empire, 2011), 585.

35. Berkshire Hathaway, Inc., *2006 Annual Report*, chairman's letter.

36. Berkshire Hathaway, Inc., *2010 Annual Report*, chairman's letter.

37. Berkshire Hathaway, Inc., *2006 Annual Report*, chairman's letter.

38. Ibid.

39. Ibid.

40. Berkshire Hathaway, Inc., *2010 Annual Report*, chairman's letter; and Berkshire Hathaway, Inc., *2013 Annual Report*, chairman's letter.

41. Berkshire Hathaway, Inc., *1985 Annual Report*, chairman's letter.

12. All One

1. Berkshire acquired 60 percent of the Marmon Group in 2008, with planned incremental additions over ensuing years through 2014 to reach 100 percent.

2. Jeffrey L. Rodengen, *The Marmon Group: The First Fifty Years* (Ft. Lauderdale, Fla.: Write Stuff Syndicate, 2002). Historical facts concerning the Marmon Group may also be found in *International Directory of Company Histories*, vol. 70 (Detroit, Mich.: St. James, 2005) (hereafter cited as *IDCH*, Marmon); and in Cynthia Hutton, "The Pritzkers: Unveiling a Private Family," *Fortune*, April 25, 1988.

3. Another brother, A.N.'s youngest son Donald, shared such genes, building the Hyatt Hotel chain before dying at age 39 in 1972.

4. Berkshire has the same policy. But given that it generally does not do turnarounds, it has seldom been applied. To the extent that Berkshire might engage in something like a turnaround, it would tend to involve a financial rather than an operational turnaround, i.e., improving a weak balance sheet rather than retooling manufacturing, distribution, and other business infrastructure.

5. Some aspects of the saga are recorded in one of the resulting lawsuits, Schulwolf v. Cerro Corp., 380 N.Y.S.2d 957 (Sup. Ct. N.Y. 1976), which also references the proxy statement and other transaction documents.

6. Frederick C. Klein, "Family Business: The Pritzkers Are an Acquisitive Bunch Which Pays Off Well," *Wall Street Journal*, March 27, 1975.

7. Wells Lamont has been an exhibitor at Berkshire Hathaway annual meetings.

8. Rodengen, *The Marmon Group*, 11, 58.

9. *IDCH*, Marmon.

10. Smith v. Von Gorkom, 488 A.2d 858 (Del. 1985).

11. Ibid.

12. Rodengen, *The Marmon Group*, 73.

13. *IDCH*, Marmon: "During the late 1980s, The Marmon Group had grown to such an extent that some observers had begun to question the ability of its corporate structure to handle its holdings, which were becoming increasingly diverse, both technically and geographically."

14. See Taina Rosa, "Sentinel Capital Takes Colson Group," *Daily Deal*, April 17, 2012; "Contify, Advent, Goldman Sachs to Acquire Trans Union," February 18, 2012.

15. For details of ITW's corporate history, see *ITW: Forging the Tools of Excellence*, ITW, www.itw.com/100Years/Book.

16. Ross Foti, "John Nichols Takes Charge," *Forward Online*, May/June 2005, http://forward.msci.org/articles/?id=50. By 2012, ITW had 800 businesses, which signaled its maximum, as two successive CEOs embarked on a divestiture program to scale back the number by 25 percent. See Meribah Knight, "Retooling: ITW's New CEO Plots Change While Preserving Culture," *Crain's Chicago Business*, March 25, 2013.

17. Foti, "John Nichols Takes Charge."

18. The purchase price was in part a function of earnings variables that would not be known until the end of the purchase period in 2014.

19. Berkshire Hathaway, Inc., *1988 Annual Report*, chairman's letter; and Berkshire Hathaway, Inc., *2008 Annual Report*, chairman's letter.

20. The Marmon Group LLC, *2012 Annual Brochure*.

21. James E. Schrager, "Pritzker Deliberate and Clear," *Chicago Tribune*, November 6, 2011.

22. See David Roeder, "In a Town That Beckons the Dealmaker, Jay Pritzker Was the Biggest," *Chicago Sun Times*, January 29, 1999.

23. Klein, "Family Business." As the investment banker J. Ira Harris explained during this period, that collegiality "gives them the kind of flexibility that doesn't exist elsewhere at their level of operations. They've closed a lot of important deals because they were able to move faster than the competition."

24. Marylin Bender, "Another Gamble for the Pritzkers," *New York Times*, February 26, 1984.

25. Ibid.

26. William Gruber, "The Marmon Group Catalogs 39 Percent Drop in Profits," *Chicago Tribune*, May 13, 1991.

27. Bender, "Another Gamble for the Pritzkers."

28. Rodengen, *The Marmon Group*, 69, quoting Robert C. Gluth, executive vice president and treasurer.

29. Tony Kaye, "The Marmon Group Keen to Expand Atlas to Asia," *The Age* (Australia), September 2, 1995.

13. Berkshire's Portfolio

1. Berkshire-BNSF Joint Prospectus and Proxy Statement, December 23, 2009, 35–39; Scott A. Barshay (Cravath, Swaine & Moore, counsel for BNSF), e-mail to the author, February 22, 2014.

2. See Prem C. Jain, *Buffett Beyond Value* (Hoboken, N.J.: Wiley, 2010), 173.

3. See Berkshire Hathaway, Inc., *2013 Annual Report*, note 4 to "Consolidated Financial Statements." This is Berkshire's actual purchase price and tax basis, not adjusted for inflation.

4. Berkshire's total assets were then reported at $485 billion—understated because reported mostly at historical cost, less depreciation, rather than at market value.

5. Andrea Frazzini, David Kabiller, and Lasse H. Pedersen, "Buffett's Alpha," National Bureau of Economic Research Working Paper No. 19681 (Cambridge, Mass.: National Bureau of Economic Research, 2013).

6. In 2008, Berkshire invested in $4.4 billion of 11.45 percent notes of Wrigley when Mars, Inc. acquired it, and the debt was extinguished in 2013. Berkshire Hathaway, Inc., *2013 Annual Report*, note 3 to "Consolidated Financial Statements."

7. Graham Holdings, "Graham Holdings and Berkshire Hathaway Reach Agreement in Principle for Berkshire Hathaway to Acquire WPLG-TV," press release, March 12, 2014.

8. The historical facts concerning the Washington Post Company may be found in the *International Directory of Company Histories*, vol. 20 (Detroit, Mich.: St. James, 1998), on which this section draws heavily.

9. New York Times Co. v. United States, 403 U.S. 713 (1971).

10. Katharine Graham, *Personal History* (New York: Vintage, 1998), 441–42.

11. Donald E. Graham, "Mr. Buffett Joins a Board," *Concurring Opinions* (blog), May 20, 2013, www.concurringopinions.com/archives/author/donald-graham.

12. Graham, *Personal History*, 534.

13. Historical facts about brand development and acquisitions by P&G in this section can be found in *International Directory of Company Histories*, vol. 67 (Detroit, Mich.: St. James, 2005); see also Davis Dyer, Frederick Dalzell, and Rowena Olegario, *Rising Tide: Lessons from 165 Years of Brand Building at Procter & Gamble* (Boston: Harvard Business School Press, 2004).

14. E.g., Michael Barnett, "Ten Brands that Gain the Most Admiration from Marketers," *Marketing Week*, August 2, 2012.

15. I have been a shareholder of P&G since 1997 (and of Gillette from 1998 through its merger with P&G) and report stock price figures from my year-end account

statements. As it happens, I added a significant number of shares in P&G in March 2000 at a price of $61.625 per share.

16. "12 CEOs in 12 Decades," P&G, www.pg.com/en_US/downloads/media/Fact_Sheets_Leadership.pdf. See Dyer, Dalzell, and Rowena, *Rising Tide*, 301–30, referring to the period as a crisis and pointing to problems arising from Jager's reorganization effort, including impaired morale, disempowerment, lack of collaboration, insufficient attention to supporting management systems, and other cultural problems.

17. See Ellen Byron, "P&G and Gillette Find Creating Synergy Can Be Harder Than It Looks," *Wall Street Journal*, April 24, 2007.

18. Ray Fisman, "Culture Clash: Even a Merger Made in Heaven Can Get Off to a Rocky Start," *Slate*, December 3, 2013.

19. Robert J. Hagstrom, *The Warren Buffett Way*, 3d ed. (Hoboken, N.J.: Wiley, 2013), 103.

20. Obituary, *New York Times*, December 27, 1985.

21. Glenn Collins, "Shift in Focus Is Expected at Coca-Cola," *New York Times*, October 20, 1997; Hagstrom, *The Warren Buffett Way*, 105.

22. Tammy Joyner, "Impact on Morale, Corporate Culture at Firm to Suffer [as] Coke Slims," *Atlanta Journal and Constitution*, January 27, 2000; Amanda Andrews, "Fizz Falls Flat for Drink That was the Tops," *Express on Sunday* (U.K.), February 20, 2005.

23. Wang Zhuoqiong, "The Endless Quest to Quench Palates," *China Daily*, June 14, 2013.

24. See James B. Stewart, "For Coke, Challenge Is Staying Relevant," *New York Times*, February 28, 2014.

25. This profile of Walmart draws on *International Directory of Company Histories*, vol. 63 (Detroit, Mich.: St. James, 2004).

26. Jeffrey L. Rodengen, *The Marmon Group: The First Fifty Years* (Write Stuff Syndicate, 2002), 47.

27. See Patricia Sellers and Suzanne Barlyn, "Can Wal-Mart Get Back the Magic?," *Fortune*, April 29, 1996; Carol J. Loomis, "Sam Would Be Proud," *Fortune*, April 17, 2000.

28. See Andrew Kilpatrick, *Of Permanent Value: The Story of Warren Buffett* (Birmingham, Ala.: Andy Kilpatrick Publishing Empire, 2011), 613.

29. Berkshire Hathaway, Inc., *2013 Annual Report*, note 4 to "Consolidated Financial Statements."

30. Historical facts about USG Corporation may be found in *International Directory of Company Histories*, vol. 26 (Detroit, Mich.: St. James, 1999); and Thomas W. Foley, *United States Gypsum: A Company History (1902–1994)* (Chicago: USG Corporation, 1995).

31. Foley, *United States Gypsum*, 49.

32. Christina Duff, "Costly Recapitalization Drives USG Corp. to the Wall," *Wall Street Journal*, June 3, 1992.

33. James P. Miller, "USG Modifies 'Prepackaged' Chapter 11 Plan," *Wall Street Journal*, January 25, 1993.

34. "Berkshire Hathaway Reports Big Stake in USG," *New York Times*, November 28, 2000.

35. Jonathan D. Glanter, "Asbestos Bankruptcies Face Setbacks on Two Fronts," *New York Times*, June 4, 2004.

36. Sandra Guy, "USG Chairman Foote to Retire; CEO to Take Over," *Chicago Sun-Times*, September 27, 2011.

37. H. Lee Murphy, "Focus: Corporate Boards," *Crain's Chicago Business*, October 4, 2010.

38. Holly LaFon, "Warren Buffett Owns 30% of USG After Converting Crisis-Era Notes," *GuruFocus*, January 3, 2014, www.gurufocus.com/news/241558/warren-buffett-owns-30-of-usg-in-fruition-of-crisisera-deal.

39. Guy, "USG Chairman Foote to Retire."

40. Jim Metcalf, interview by Sara Eisen, *Bloomberg Surveillance*, Bloomberg TV, November 7, 2013.

41. Berkshire Hathaway, Inc., *2013 Annual Report*, chairman's letter.

42. Historical highlights about Heinz in this section can be found in *International Directory of Company Histories*, vol. 36 (Detroit, Mich.: St. James, 2001); see also Robert C. Alberts, *The Good Provider: H.J. Heinz and His 57 Varieties* (Boston: Houghton Mifflin, 1973); and Eleanor Foa Dienstag, *In Good Company: 125 Years at the Heinz Table, 1869–1994* (New York: Warner, 1994).

43. Annie Gasparo, "Three More Longtime Executives Leaving Heinz," *Dow Jones*, January 13, 2014.

44. Berkshire Hathaway, Inc., *2012 Annual Report*, chairman's letter.

14. Succession

1. See Van Pelt's letter at www.larsonjuhl.com/docs/Customer%20Communication.pdf. The letter continued:

> This change may come as a surprise and you may have questions or concerns. I can assure you that the company remains committed to serving your framing needs in the future. Further, I've personally received a commitment from Warren Buffett that Berkshire Hathaway has no intention of selling Larson-Juhl and that he continues to believe strongly in the prospects for the company and the industry. Over the next 30 days, I will be in "learning mode." . . . I ask for your patience as I learn more about your businesses and the custom framing industry.

2. Noah Buyayar and Laura Colby, "Buffett Leans on 29-Year-Old to Oversee Problems," *Bloomberg BusinessWeek*, January 21, 2014.

3. I published a different version of this overview as "Buffett's Ultimate Achievement: Berkshire Is Bigger than Him," *Beyond Proxy* (blog), April 14, 2013, www.beyondproxy.com/lawrence-cunningham-the-essays-of-warren-buffett.

4. Berkshire Hathaway, Inc., *2006 Annual Report*, chairman's letter.

5. E.g., Berkshire Hathaway, Inc., *2012 Annual Report*, chairman's letter; and Berkshire Hathaway, Inc., *2013 Annual Report*, chairman's letter.

6. Other long-serving Berkshire subsidiary executives are Tony Nicely of GEICO (employee since 1961, CEO since 1993); Irv and Ron Blumkin of Nebraska Furniture Mart (employees since their youth at the company Berkshire acquired in 1983); and Brad Kintsler of See's (began at Berkshire in 1987).

7. Ross Foti, "John Nichols Takes Charge," *Forward Online*, May/June 2005, http://forward.msci.org/articles/?id=50.

8. Ibid.

9. Buffett's letters describing these pledges are posted on the Berkshire Hathaway website.

10. In shareholder surveys for this book, a substantial majority indicated that Berkshire is among their largest holdings.

11. For example, from 2001 through 2012, share turnover in Berkshire stock was never greater than 0.34 percent for Class A or 0.615 percent for Class B, except that Class B in the later years increased after Berkshire split that class of stock and used it to pay for the BNSF acquisition. (See table 14.5.)

For comparison, consider Berkshire's two most recently acquired public companies. From 2001 through its acquisition by Berkshire, BNSF stock turned over as much as 3.00 percent; in six of those years greater than 1 percent; and always higher than Berkshire. Lubrizol turnover was as high as 3.6 percent; nine of those years greater than 1 percent; and always higher than Berkshire.

Turnover is low compared with other insurance companies: ACE is always at least 0.966 percent and as high as 2.873 percent; Allstate is always higher than 0.886 percent and as high as 2.785 percent. Finally, compare Berkshire to various conglomerates, such as General Electric, United Technologies, Danaher, Robert Half, Fluor, or Level 3 Communications, which turned over during that period as much as 6 percent, always greater than 1 percent, and often around 4 or 5 percent.

12. In table 14.5, for example, all companies but Berkshire and General Electric are held 80 to 90 percent by institutions, with General Electric's institutional holders around 60 percent.

13. Debbie Bosanek (assistant to Warren Buffett), e-mail exchange with author, March 7–8, 2014. I reference the historical figures and the sources in *The Essays of Warren Buffett: Lessons for Corporate America* (New York: Cunningham Group, 1997, 2001, 2008, 2013).

14. See Andrew Kilpatrick, *Of Permanent Value: The Story of Warren Buffett* (Birmingham, Ala.: Andy Kilpatrick Publishing Empire, 2011), chap. 170.

15. See Andrew Ross Sorkin, "For Buffett, the Past Isn't Always Prologue," *New York Times*, May 6, 2013, quoting Munger's admonition to "the many Mungers in the audience" at Berkshire's 2013 annual meeting. Munger has in recent years transferred a substantial portion of his Berkshire shares to charitable organizations and family members. See Steve Jordan, "Donations Bring the Value of Charlie Munger's Berkshire Stock Below \$1 Billion," *Omaha World-Herald*, June 13, 2013.

Table 14.5
Stock Turnover in Related Companies

	Class A	Class B	BNSF	Lubrizol	GE	UT	DHR	R. Half	LLL	Fluror	ACE	Allstate
2001	0.060	0.538	0.857	1.056	0.549	1.332	1.777	0.911	4.337	1.689	1.795	0.934
2002	0.064	0.449	0.867	0.846	0.691	1.437	1.926	1.145	4.824	1.532	2.124	0.857
2003	0.072	0.457	0.822	0.969	0.504	1.220	1.628	1.173	3.035	1.797	1.472	0.886
2004	0.057	0.398	1.017	1.741	0.524	1.066	1.114	1.412	2.067	1.898	1.152	0.909
2005	0.078	0.430	1.442	1.420	0.477	0.895	1.234	1.329	1.874	2.012	1.230	1.062
2006	0.082	0.369	1.747	1.129	0.605	0.901	1.076	1.663	2.095	2.877	0.966	1.033
2007	0.103	0.304	2.243	1.940	0.921	1.159	1.346	1.827	1.743	3.644	1.338	1.576
2008	0.240	0.564	3.033	2.662	1.982	1.800	2.024	2.876	2.186	6.172	2.873	2.373
2009	0.239	0.615	2.692	3.183	2.798	1.583	1.841	2.987	2.324	5.272	1.822	2.785
2010	0.346	2.085	0.585	2.797	1.706	1.286	1.393	2.570	2.052	3.698	2.146	2.205
2011	0.151	1.324		3.605	1.522	1.290	1.465	2.994	2.255	3.211	1.641	2.373
2012	0.157	0.981			1.085	1.138	1.131	2.371	1.700	2.583	1.186	2.124

GE, General Electric; UT, United Technologies; DHR, Danaher; R. Half, Robert Half; LLL, Level 3 Communications.

16. Gates owns a large portion of Berkshire Class A shares through a company he owns called Cascade Investment LLC.

17. Shareholder portfolio concentration is also rare in most companies in which Berkshire has concentrated holdings, such as a Coca-Cola, IBM, and P&G. It is more common at American Express and Wells Fargo due to the presence of a number of Berkshire shareholders who likewise hold concentrated positions in those companies.

18. Berkshire's shareholder demographic more closely resembles that of other conglomerates with influential founding shareholders, such as Danaher (founded and controlled by Mitchell and Steven Rales) and Level 3 Communications (founded and controlled by Berkshire board member Walter Scott).

19. In shareholder surveys for this book, nearly 100 percent of respondents agreed with the assertions that Berkshire is best conceived of as a partnership and boasts an owner orientation.

20. In shareholder surveys for this book, no one indicated willingness to accept a premium of less than 30 percent, a majority indicated unwillingness to sell except for a minimum premium of 50 percent, and a sizable portion said they would hold out for at least a 100 percent premium.

21. I published a different version of this overview as "Should Berkshire Hathaway Go Private?," *Beyond Proxy* (blog), April 15, 2013, www.beyondproxy.com/berkshire-hathaway-go-private.

22. E.g., Warren E. Buffett, "An Owner's Manual," Berkshire Hathaway, first published in June 1996, updated March 1, 2014, www.berkshirehathaway.com/ownman.pdf.

23. Howard G. Buffett, e-mail to the author, March 6, 2014.

15. Challenges

1. Berkshire Hathaway, Inc., *2001 Annual Report*, chairman's letter.

2. Yellow Freight and Roadway Express merged in 2003 and in 2009 renamed the resulting company YRC for Yellow Roadway Corporation.

3. See Jean-Paul Rodrigue and Brian Slack, "Intermodal Transportation and Containerization," in *The Geography of Transport Systems* (New York: Routledge, 2013), chap. 3, concept 6, http://people.hofstra.edu/geotrans/eng/ch3en/conc3en/ch3c6en.html.

4. Geert De Lombaerde, "Fechheimer President Exits," *Cincinnati Business Courier*, May 16, 1998; Andrew Kilpatrick, *Of Permanent Value: The Story of Warren Buffett* (Birmingham, Ala.: Andy Kilpatrick Publishing Empire, 2011), 438.

5. See Karen Linder, *The Women of Berkshire Hathaway: Lessons from Warren Buffett's Female CEOs and Directors* (Hoboken, N.J.: Wiley, 2012), 93.

6. "Barry Tatelman Leaves Jordan's Furniture," *Boston Globe*, December 21, 2006.

7. Berkshire Hathaway, Inc., *1985 Annual Report*, chairman's letter (discussing Scott Fetzer: "Haphazard approach to acquisitions . . . no master strategy, no corporate planners.").

8. Berkshire Hathaway, Inc., *2000 Annual Report*, chairman's letter (regarding Justin: "Here again, our acquisition involved serendipity").

9. Berkshire Hathaway, Inc., *1996 Annual Report*, chairman's letter (regarding Kansas Bankers Surety: "Carefully crafted and sophisticated acquisition strategy").

10. See Deborah DeMott, "The Skeptical Principal," *Concurring Opinions* (blog), May 21, 2013, www.concurringopinions.com/archives/2013/05/the-skeptical-principal.html.

11. References to companies in the notes accompanying this discussion are to Buffett's descriptions of the acquisitions in related shareholder letters found in the Berkshire Hathaway annual reports. A few acquisitions involved interesting stories that make the source harder to classify. Examples include BNSF and GEICO, gradual acquisitions of control, the latter dating back many decades to Ben Graham; Nebraska Furniture Mart (through Omaha connections); and Clayton Homes (suggested by University of Tennessee students of Prof. Al Auxier; Berkshire followed up with owner directly).

12. Seller overture (in a pure sense; if it was the owner's idea but prompted by other links, the deal is listed under those other links): Fechheimer Bros.; Helzberg Diamonds (walking down the street in New York City); Ben Bridge (Ed Bridge called, after talking with Barnett Helzberg); MiTek (subsidiary CEO sent package in mail with parent's permission); Larson-Juhl; Forest River; Business Wire (actually from CEO, suggesting owner would approve); ISCAR; Richline (owner heard Buffett speak at a Ben Bridge lunch); Star Furniture (through an intermediary; endorsed by Blumkins and Child; contacted Robert Denham); Willey (through an intermediary; Child asked Irv Blumkin).

13. Business relationship: Gen Re (Ronald Ferguson); U.S. Liability (Ferguson); Applied Underwriters (Ajit Jain did a deal with owners); Dairy Queen (banker introduced a year before Rudy Luther died, then done quickly); Benjamin Moore (Robert Mundheim); NetJets (customer; Richard Santulli called); Shaw Industries (after discussing aborted insurance deal); McLane (Byron Trott, Goldman Sachs); the Marmon Group (seeds date to 1954 when Buffett met Jay Pritzker).

14. Friend/relative: NICO (Jack Ringwalt); Central States (Bill Kizer); Kansas Bankers Surety (at niece's birthday party); H.H. Brown (John Loomis golfing with Frank Rooney); XTRA (Julian Robertson); TTI (John Roach, friendship seemed to arise with Justin); MidAmerican (Walter Scott Jr.).

15. Berkshire overture: Scott Fetzer (wrote CEO amid waning takeover contest); Jordan's Furniture (implicitly, asking Blumkins, Bill Child, and Melvyn Wolff); Johns Manville (announced deal broke off; Berkshire stepped up); Fruit of the Loom (made offer in bankruptcy).

16. Stranger: CORT (acquaintance sent fax); FlightSafety (shareholder of both wrote to Robert Denham); Justin (someone faxed about co-investing proposal).

17. The Marmon Group ("Done in the way Jay would have liked . . . price using only Marmon's financial statements, no advisors, no nit-picking."); Fechheimer (no visit to Cincinnati headquarters); Borsheim (no due diligence).

18. The Pampered Chef ("Took me about ten seconds to decide"); FlightSafety ("In about 60 seconds I knew"); MiTek ("It took me only a minute to realize").

19. Ben Bridge (Ed Bridge called Buffett).

20. Larson-Juhl ("In ninety minutes we reached an agreement"); Star Furniture (we "made a deal in a single, two-hour session"); McLane ("single meeting of about two hours"); TTI (met in the morning "and made a deal before lunch").

21. NetJets ("We quickly made a $725 million deal"); CORT ("quickly purchased").

22. The Pampered Chef ("We promptly made a deal").

23. Jordan's Furniture ("We soon signed an agreement"); Justin ("Soon after [meeting], we bought Justin for $570 million in cash"); Clayton ("soon thereafter"); Richline ("soon made a deal . . . ").

24. MiTek ("We made a cash offer . . . and before long had a deal"); Kansas Bankers Surety ("Before long we had a deal"); Business Wire (reached agreement "before long").

25. Forest River (offer made on June 22; handshake agreement reached on June 28).

26. Johns Manville ("A week later we signed a contract"); Larson-Juhl ("In ten days we had signed a contract"); FlightSafety ("A month later, we had a contract").

27. McLane ("Twenty-nine days later Walmart had its money").

28. The following summaries are based on SEC filings for the respective transactions. Benjamin Moore (Berkshire offered price; no counter); BNSF (Berkshire offered price; seller asked for more; Berkshire said no); Clayton Homes (Berkshire offered price; board had CEO ask for more; Berkshire said no); CTB (Berkshire offered price, actually went down a quarter for adviser fees; Berkshire said that is it); Dairy Queen (Berkshire offered price; no further discussion); Fruit of the Loom (Berkshire offered single bid in bankruptcy at end of auction process and won); Garan (seller sought price above $60; Berkshire offered $60 and that was that); Gen Re (Buffett proposed the exchange ratio and Gen Re went along); Johns Manville (Berkshire offered price; board tried to get more; Berkshire said no); Justin (Berkshire offered price; there was another bidder in the picture who left; no further discussion); Lubrizol (Berkshire offered price; seller tried to get more; Berkshire said no); Shaw Industries (Berkshire offered price; board/banker asked for more; Berkshire said that is our best price); XTRA (Berkshire offered $59; seller asked is that your best offer; Berkshire said it was).

In the case of public company acquisitions, there were only two exceptions to this dynamic, when a seller replied to a bid seeking more and extracted a higher bid. But in each of these two deals, Buffett and Berkshire had investment partners in the transaction and it was they, the disclosure suggests, who were willing to play the dickering game. One involved Heinz, an acquisition in which Berkshire is a 50 percent partner with 3G Capital. The buyers bid $70 per share; Heinz asked for more, and the buyers upped and closed at $72.50. The other involved MidAmerican Energy (later renamed Berkshire Hathaway Energy). In that deal, Berkshire was joined by co-investors Walter Scott and David Sokol. The bid was $34.60; the sellers got the buyers to move first to $35 and finally to $35.05. Had Buffett/Berkshire been negotiating that deal alone, the record suggests they would not have budged.

29. E.g., the Boston College Center for Corporate Citizenship's Corporate Reputation and Social Responsibility Rankings of the Most Respected U.S. Companies 2008 ranked Berkshire ninth out of 203 companies analyzed based on survey data of 20,000 people.

30. Elaine Cohen, "Warren Buffett on Sustainability: Not," *CSR-Reporting*, June 12, 2010, http://csr-reporting.blogspot.com/2010/06/warren-buffett-on-sustainability-not.html.

31. Randall L. Patton, *Shaw Industries: A History* (Athens: University of Georgia Press, 2002), 180.

32. See McLane company website: www.mclaneco.com/content/mclane/en/about-us/green-advantage.html.

33. See "Top Green Providers," *Food Logistics*, June 1, 2013.

34. See Acme Brick company website: www.brick.com/homebuyer/sustainability.htm.

35. E.g., U.S. Green Building Council, Leadership in Energy and Environmental Design (LEED) Rating Systems, www.usgbc.org/leed/rating-systems.

36. See "Lean and Green," *Ceramic Industry*, August 1, 2009.

37. David Vogel, *The Market for Virtue: The Potential and Limits of Corporate Social Responsibility* (Washington, D.C.: Brookings Institute, 2005), 77–78, 93–94.

38. Jim Weber, telephone interview by the author, October 11, 2013.

39. James L. Hambrick, telephone interview by the author, December 20, 2013.

40. Douglas A. Kass, a noted investor and Berkshire skeptic, raised the example in questions to Buffett at the 2013 Berkshire Hathaway annual meeting. See Andrew Ross Sorkin, "For Buffett, the Past Isn't Always Prologue," *New York Times*, May 6, 2013.

41. For an account of Teledyne and Singleton by the latter's second-in-command, see George A. Roberts (with Robert J. McVicker), *Distant Force: A Memoir of the Teledyne Corporation and the Man Who Created It* (Thousand Oaks, Calif.: Teledyne Corporation, 2007).

42. Ibid., 249–50.

43. Simon M. Lorne (Teledyne director), e-mail to author, January 3, 2014.

44. Warren E. Buffett, "An Owner's Manual," Berkshire Hathaway, first published in June 1996, updated March 1, 2014, ¶11, www.berkshirehathaway.com/ownman.pdf.

16. B.E.R.K.S.H.I.R.E.

1. See "Notice, Online Discussion Next Week: What Motivates Top Donors," *Chronicle of Philanthropy*, January 23, 2009.

2. See "Lokey Gives UO Largest Gift: $74.5M," *Portland Business Journal*, October 15, 2007.

3. Karen Linder, *The Women of Berkshire Hathaway: Lessons from Warren Buffett's Female CEOs and Directors* (Hoboken, N.J.: Wiley, 2012), 97–101.

4. Ibid., 112; Berkshire Hathaway, Inc., *2005 Annual Report*, chairman's letter.

5. Ibid.

6. Thomas S. Gayner (Markel Corporation), telephone interview by the author, February 13, 2014.

7. See, e.g., David Carey and John E. Morris, *King of Capital: The Remarkable Rise, Fall, and Rise Again of Steve Schwarman and Blackstone* (New York: Crown Business, 2010). For a critical view, see Eileen Appelbaum and Rosemary Batt, *Private Equity at Work* (New York: Russell Sage Foundation, 2014).

8. Andrew Kilpatrick, *Of Permanent Value: The Story of Warren Buffett* (Birmingham, Ala.: Andy Kilpatrick Publishing Empire, 2011), 423.

9. Jim Clayton and Bill Retherford, *First a Dream* (Knoxville, Tenn.: FSB, 2002), 76, 211–12, 228, 285.

10. See Alexandra Berzon, "The Gambler Who Blew $127 Million," *Wall Street Journal*, December 5, 2009.

11. Ronald Chan, *Behind the Berkshire Hathaway Curtain: Lessons from Warren Buffett's Top Business Leaders* (Hoboken, N.J.: Wiley, 2010), 35–36.

12. Ibid., 119.

13. Jeffrey W. Comment, *Santa's Gift: True Stories of Courage, Humor, Hope & Love* (Hoboken, N.J.: Wiley, 2002).

14. Caroline Hall Otis, *The Cone with the Curl on Top: The Dairy Queen Story, 1940–1980* (Minneapolis: International Dairy Queen, 1990), 129, 152.

15. Children's Miracle Network Hospitals, corporate partners page, http://child rensmiraclenetworkhospitals.org/Partners/Sponsors.

16. Ibid.; Martha Kahler and Jeff Hampton, *McLane Company, Inc.: The First One Hundred Years* (Temple, Tex.: McLane Company, 1994), 35, 49.

17. Irvin Farman, *Standard of the West: The Justin Story* (Fort Worth: Texas Christian University Press, 1996), 190, 216–21.

18. Ibid., 227.

19. Kahler and Hampton, *McLane*, 35.

20. See Richard Pérez-Peña, "Harold Alfond, Donor and Shoe Factory Owner, Dies at 93," *New York Times*, November 17, 2007.

21. Jewelers for Children, board listing, www.jewelersforchildren.org/our-board.htm.

22. Clayton and Retherford, *First a Dream*, 263–67.

Epilogue

1. Warren E. Buffett, "An Owner's Manual," Berkshire Hathaway, first published in June 1996, updated March 1, 2014, ¶11, www.berkshirehathaway.com/ownman.pdf.

Appendix

1. Information concerning McLane draws in part on Martha Kahler and Jeff Hampton, *McLane Company, Inc.: The First One Hundred Years* (Temple, Tex.: McLane Company, 1994), 58, 90.

2. Information concerning MiTek draws in part on Jim Healey, *MiTek: A Global Success Story, 1981–2011* (St. Louis, Mo.: MiTek, 2012), 145.

Selected Bibliography

Research for this project benefited from the following books, which address Berkshire or given subsidiaries; the research benefited from books addressing other topics as well, but these and other materials are referenced in the notes as warranted.

Benedict, Jeff. *How to Build a Business Warren Buffett Would Buy: The R. C. Willey Story*. Salt Lake City: Shadow Mountain, 2009.

Chan, Ronald. *Behind the Berkshire Hathaway Curtain: Lessons from Warren Buffett's Top Business Leaders*. Hoboken, N.J.: Wiley, 2010.

Christopher, Doris. *The Pampered Chef*, New York: Doubleday Currency, 2005.

Clayton, Jim, and Bill Retherford. *First a Dream*. Knoxville, Tenn.: FSB, 2002.

Cunningham, Lawrence A. *The Essays of Warren Buffett: Lessons for Corporate America*. New York: Cunningham Group, 1997, 2001, 2008, 2013.

Farman, Irvin. *Standard of the West: The Justin Story*. Fort Worth: Texas Christian University Press, 1996.

Gillespie, Liz Murtaugh. *Running Through the First 100 Years*. Seattle, Wash: Brooks Sports, Inc., 2014.

Graham, Katharine. *Personal History*. New York: Vintage, 1998.

Hagstrom, Robert J. *The Warren Buffett Way*, 3d ed. Hoboken, N.J.: Wiley, 2013.

Healey, Jim. *MiTek: A Global Success Story, 1981–2011*. St. Louis, Mo.: MiTek, 2012.

Helzberg, Barnett C., Jr. *What I Learned Before I Sold to Warren Buffett: An Entrepreneur's Guide to Developing a Highly Successful Company*. Hoboken, N.J.: Wiley, 2003.

International Directory of Company Histories, vols. 12–75. Detroit, Mich.: St. James, 1996–2005.

Jain, Prem C. *Buffett Beyond Value: Why Warren Buffett Looks to Growth and Management when Investing*. Hoboken, N.J.: Wiley, 2010.

Kahler, Martha, and Jeff Hampton. *McLane Company, Inc.: The First One Hundred Years*. Temple, Tex.: McLane Company, 1994.

Kaufman, Laurence H. *Leaders Count: The Story of BNSF Railway*. Austin: Monthly Custom Publishing/Texas A&M University Press, 2005.

Kilpatrick, Andrew. *Of Permanent Value: The Story of Warren Buffett*. Birmingham, Ala.: Andy Kilpatrick Publishing Empire, 2011.

——. *Warren Buffett: The Good Guy of Wall Street*. New York: Primus/Donald I. Fine, 1992.

Klingaman, William K. *GEICO: The First Forty Years*. Washington, D.C.: GEICO, 1994.

Lehr, Edwin E. *Colossus in Clay: Acme Brick Company*. Marceline, Mo.: Walsworth, 1998.

Light, Murray B. *From Butler to Buffett: The Story Behind* The Buffalo News. Amherst, N.Y.: Prometheus, 2004.

Linder, Karen. *The Women of Berkshire Hathaway: Lessons from Warren Buffett's Female CEOs and Directors*. Hoboken, N.J.: Wiley, 2012.

Loomis, Carol J. *Tap Dancing to Work: Warren Buffett on Practically Everything, 1966–2012*. New York: Portfolio, 2012.

Lowe, Janet. *Damn Right! Behind the Scenes with Berkshire Hathaway Billionaire Charlie Munger*. Hoboken, N.J.: Wiley, 2000.

Lowenstein, Roger. *Buffett: The Making of an American Capitalist*. New York: Random House, 1995.

Miglani, Bob. *Treat Your Customers: Thirty Lessons on Service and Sales That I Learned at My Family's Dairy Queen Store*. New York: Hyperion, 2006.

Miles, Robert P. *The Warren Buffett CEO: Secrets from the Berkshire Hathaway Managers*. Hoboken, N.J.: Wiley, 2003.

Moos Pick, Margaret. *See's Old Time Candies*. San Francisco: Chronicle, 2005.

Otis, Caroline Hall. *The Cone with the Curl on Top: The Dairy Queen Story, 1940–1990*. Minneapolis: International Dairy Queen, 1990.

Patton, Randall L. *Shaw Industries: A History*. Athens: University of Georgia Press, 2002.

Rodengen, Jeffrey L. *The Marmon Group: The First Fifty Years*. Ft. Lauderdale, Fla.: Write Stuff Syndicate, 2002.

Schroeder, Alice. *The Snowball: Warren Buffett and the Business of Life*. New York: Bantam Dell, 2008.

Schulte, Ann F. *So Far: The Story of Helzberg Diamonds*. Kansas City, Mo.: Helzberg's Diamond Shops, 1990.

Sokol, David L. *Pleased but Not Satisfied*. Self-published, 2007.

Thorndike, William N., Jr. *The Outsiders: Eight Unconventional CEOs and Their Radically Rational Blueprint for Success*. Boston: Harvard Business Review Press, 2012.

Ueltschi, A. L. *The History and Future of FlightSafety International*. New York: FlightSafety International, 1999.

Index

Abel, Gregory E., 131, 133, 134, 196

Abrams, Denis, 66–67

accident, Berkshire as, 1

Acme Brick Company, 97, 98–99, 216

acquisitions, business or corporate:
aviation industry, 89, 91–92; Berkshire
compared to typical, 213–14; Berkshire
corporate culture in, 36–37, 103,
122–23, 126, 170–71, 189, 219–20;
Berkshire future, 189–90; in Berkshire
origins, 9, 10–18, 254n15, 254n22;
"bolt-on" and "tuck-in," 125–26;
borrowing and debt in, 123, 133, 145;
Buffett, Warren's, approach to, 10–11,
213–14, 286nn11–22, 287nn23–28;
building, housing, and furniture
industry, 61–62, 64, 65–66, 70, 74,
76, 77–78, 80, 124–27, 147, 148–49,
187, 193; chemical industry, 114, 127,;
clothing industry, 29–30, 95, 98,
151, 154–55, 276n40; competitive
advantage of corporate culture in, 225;
of conglomerates, 163, 167; corporate
culture offering value to, 5; criteria
for, 36–37, 138, 161, 170–71, 189, 213;
dispersed and family ownership in,
30, 31; diversity of, 22–23, 25–26,
26, 27, 29–30; employees sharing
in proceeds in, 64, 85, 108; energy
sector, 131–34, 273n55, 274n59; in
food industry, 13–15, 103, 108, 121–22,
188–90, 254n15; full stock ownership
in, 30, 32, 256nn12–13; globalization
spurring, 217; industry leadership,
management, and profitability in, 23;
insurance company, 31, 48, 49, 51, 53,
54, 58; by investees, 180–81, 182, 184,
188; of investees, 179, 180, 182–83, 187,
188, 189–90; investigations into, 16,
115–17, 269n40, 269nn43–44; involving
U.S. manufacturing, 29–30; jewelry
industry, 82, 83–85, 263n35; Marmon
Group and, 163, 164–66, 167, 170–71,
173, 278n1, 279n13, 279n18; mistakes

earnestness, 50–51, 53–54, 168
80/20 principle, 166–67
employees: acquisitions and shared
    proceeds with, 64, 85, 108; health and
    safety, 69, 140–41; profit sharing, 50,
    124, 179
employment numbers, subsidiary, 28
energy sector, 24, 131–34, 273n55, 274n59
entrepreneurs and entrepreneurship:
    Berkshire culture and spirit of, 104,
    219; commodity businesses requiring,
    146; Horatio Alger Award winners
    of, 86, 264n1; Marmon Group as,
    169; subsidiaries and nurturing,
    223–24; values conflict involving,
    218. See also FlightSafety; Garan,
    Inc.; International Dairy Queen,
    Inc.; Justin cowboy boots or Justin
    Industries; NetJets
environmental consciousness, 65, 69–70,
    215–16, 260n19
estate and estate planning, 121, 160,
    198–99

family business or ownership:
    acquisitions involving, 30, 31;
    advantages and challenges of, 72,
    75–76, 80; Berkshire culture for,
    75–76, 78, 80–81, 85; estate planning
    in, 121, 160; leadership succession
    in, 79, 80, 81, 83–84, 96–97; long-
    term future in, 84; sale of, 75–76;
    sustainability of, 85; values in, 72, 85,
    224. See also specific families
FCSB. See Financial Corporation of Santa
    Barbara
Fechheimer Brothers Company: debt,
    22–23; innovation at, 22; LBO of,
    22–23; leadership succession in, 22,
    23; nature and makeup of, 23; in
    organizational structure, 24; price of,
    25
Ferguson, Ronald E., 54, 55, 56

finance sector, 24
financial: characteristics, unique, 27, 28,
    29; crisis, 2008, 59, 62, 66, 185–86
Financial Corporation of Santa Barbara
    (FCSB), 15–16
financial distress: in Berkshire origins,
    9–10; Fruit of the Loom, 151; Gen Re,
    55; International Dairy Queen, 101;
    NetJets, 91, 92
FlightSafety, 86; aviation pilot training
    at, 87–89; business model, 89;
    commercial airline and military work
    with, 88; flight simulators from, 88;
    insurance industry credit for, 88–89;
    leadership succession at, 87, 89;
    manufacturers using, 88; as regulated
    or capital-intensive industry, 24
flight simulators, 88
food industry, acquisitions in, 13–15, 103,
    108, 121–22, 188–90, 254n15
Forest River, Inc., 155–57, 277n14
founding, of subsidiaries, 32, 32
franchises and franchising, 100–103,
    266n61
Frauenshuh, Matthew, 103
Friedman, Rebecca, 264n45
Friendly, Henry, 17
Fruit of the Loom: acquisition of,
    151, 276n40; advertising, 149, 150;
    bankruptcy and financial distress, 151;
    Brooks integration with, 153, 154–55;
    history, 149–50, 276n34, 276n39;
    LBO, 150; Russell's objectionable
    manufacturing and, 214–15
fuel costs, 143
furniture industry. See building, housing,
    and furniture industry

Gainor, John, 103
Garan, Inc., 93–95
Garanimals, 93–94
Gates, Bill, 38, 198, 200, 229, 283n16
GE. See General Electric Company